2020 release

Adobe Photoshop & Dreamweaver

Web Design Portfolio

AGAINST THE CLOCK

mastering graphic technology

Managing Editor: Ellenn Behoriam
Cover & Interior Design: Erika Kendra

The fonts utilized in these training materials are the property of Against The Clock, Inc. and are supplied to the legitimate buyers of the Against The Clock training materials solely for use with the exercises and projects provided in the body of the materials. They may not be used for any other purpose, and under no circumstances may they be transferred to another individual, nor copied or distributed by any means whatsoever.

Against The Clock and the Against The Clock logo are trademarks of Against The Clock, Inc., registered in the United States and elsewhere. References to and instructional materials provided for any particular application program, operating system, hardware platform, or other commercially available product or products do not represent an endorsement of such product or products by Against The Clock, Inc.

Photoshop, Acrobat, Illustrator, InDesign, Flash, Dreamweaver, and PostScript are trademarks of Adobe Systems Incorporated. Macintosh is a trademark of Apple Computer, Inc. Word, Excel, Office, Microsoft, and Windows are either registered trademarks or trademarks of Microsoft Corporation.

Other product and company names mentioned herein may be the trademarks of their respective owners.

Cover image by StockSnap from Pixabay .

10 9 8 7 6 5 4 3 2 1

Print ISBN: 978-1-946396-44-0
Ebook ISBN: 978-1-946396-45-7

AGAINST THE CLOCK
mastering graphic technology

4710 28th Street North, Saint Petersburg, FL 33714
800-256-4ATC • www.againsttheclock.com

About Against The Clock

Against The Clock, long recognized as one of the nation's leaders in courseware development, has been publishing educational materials for the graphic and computer arts industries since 1990. The company has developed a solid and widely respected approach to teaching people how to effectively use graphics applications while maintaining a disciplined approach to real-world problems.

Having developed the *Against The Clock* and the *Essentials for Design* series with Prentice Hall/Pearson Education, ATC drew from years of professional experience and instructor feedback to develop *The Professional Portfolio Series*, focusing on the Adobe Creative Suite. These books feature step-by-step explanations, detailed foundational information, and advice and tips from professionals that offer practical solutions to technical issues.

About the Author

Erika Kendra holds a BA in History and a BA in English Literature from the University of Pittsburgh. She began her career in the graphic communications industry as an editor at Graphic Arts Technical Foundation, and has been a full-time professional graphic designer since 1999.

Erika is the author or co-author of more than forty books about Adobe graphic design software. She has also written several books about graphic design concepts such as color reproduction and preflighting and dozens of articles for graphics and print industry journals. Working with Against The Clock for almost twenty years, Erika was a key partner in developing *The Professional Portfolio Series* of software training books.

Contributing Editors and Artists

A big thank you to the people whose comments and expertise contributed to the success of these books:

- **Tony Cowdrey,** technical editor
- **Roger Morrissey,** technical editor
- **Gary Poyssick**, technical editor
- **Andrew Clark,** copy editor
- **Grace Veach**, copy editor

Images used in the projects throughout this book are in the public domain unless otherwise noted. Individual artists' credit follow:

Project 1:
Images used in this project are copyright Against The Clock, Inc.

Project 2:
Images in this project are from PublicDomainPictures.net.

Project 3:
Images used in this project are copyright Against The Clock, Inc. Roshambo.jpg photo by Charlie Essers.

Project 4:
culture1.jpg by Pixabay.com
culture2.jpg by Liam Penjur on Pexels.com
culture3.jpg by skeeze on Pixabay.com
culture4.jpg by Miguel Bruna on Unsplash.com
fantasy1.jpg by Anthony Tran on Unsplash.com
fantasy2.jpg by Ambar Simpang on Unsplash.com
fantasy3.jpg by Darcy Delia on Pexels.com
fantasy4.jpg by Couleur on Pixabay.com
feature1.jpg by Joy Anne Pura on Pexels.com
feature2.jpg by Vinicius Vilela on Pexels.com
feature3.jpg by Kathleen Sullivan on Pexels.com
theater1.jpg by Sasint on Pixabay.com
theater2.jpg by Cesira Alvarado on Unsplash.com
theater3.jpg by A. Zuhri on Unsplash.com

Project 5:
Images copyright Erika Kendra.

Project 6:
Background image by Marcus dePaula on Unsplash.com.

Project 7:
adults.jpg by Alex Jones on Unsplash.com.
chalk.jpg photo by Tina Floersch on Unsplash.com.
pencils background image by Stefan Schweihofer on Pixabay.com.

Project 8:
All images used in this project are courtesy of the Getty's Open Content Program: getty.edu/about/whatwedo/opencontentfaq.html

Project Goals

Each project begins with a clear description of the overall concepts that are explained in the project; these goals closely match the different stages of the project workflow.

The Project Meeting

Each project includes the client's initial comments, which provide valuable information about the job. The Project Art Director, a vital part of any design workflow, also provides fundamental advice and production requirements.

Project Objectives

Each Project Meeting includes a summary of the specific skills required to complete the project.

Real-World Workflow

Projects are broken into logical lessons, or "stages," of the workflow. Brief introductions at the beginning of each stage provide vital foundational material required to complete the task.

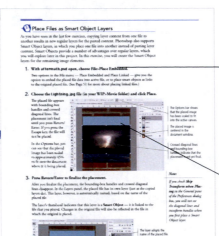

Step-By-Step Exercises

Every stage of the workflow is broken into multiple hands-on, step-by-step exercises.

Visual Explanations

Wherever possible, screen captures are annotated so students can quickly identify important information.

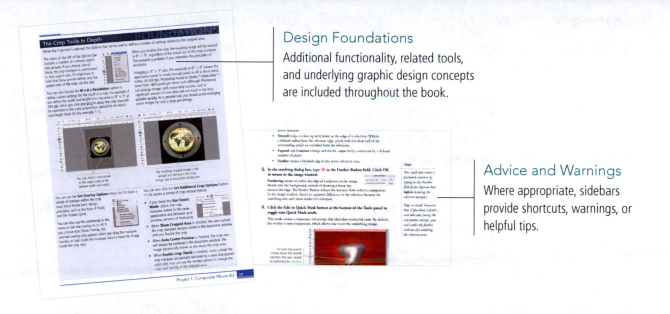

Design Foundations
Additional functionality, related tools, and underlying graphic design concepts are included throughout the book.

Advice and Warnings
Where appropriate, sidebars provide shortcuts, warnings, or helpful tips.

Project Review
After completing each project, students can complete these fill-in-the-blank and short-answer questions to test their understanding of the concepts in the project.

Portfolio Builder Projects
Each step-by-step project is accompanied by a freeform project, allowing students to practice skills and creativity, resulting in an extensive and diverse portfolio of work.

Visual Summary
Using an annotated version of the finished project, students can quickly identify the skills used to complete different aspects of the job.

PROJECTS AT A GLANCE

project 1 — Composite Movie Ad

- ❏ Compositing Images and Artwork
- ❏ Managing Layers
- ❏ Creating Complex Selections
- ❏ Saving Files for Multiple Media

project 3 — City Promotion Cards

- ❏ Creating New Files
- ❏ Manipulating Pixels
- ❏ Working with Type
- ❏ Creating Style with Layers
- ❏ Working in 3D

project 2 — Car Magazine Cover

- ❏ Enlarging Source Files
- ❏ Working with Vector Tools
- ❏ Applying Styles and Filters

project 4 — Web Page Design

- ❏ Automating Repetitive Tasks
- ❏ Editing Layers for Visual Effect
- ❏ Generating Web-Ready Assets

the portfolio series

Against The Clock's *The Professional Portfolio Series* teaches graphic design software tools and techniques entirely within the framework of real-world projects; we introduce and explain skills where they would naturally fall into a real project workflow.

The project-based approach in *The Professional Portfolio Series* allows you to get in depth with the software beginning in Project 1 — you don't have to read several chapters of introductory material before you can start creating finished artwork.

Our approach also prevents "topic tedium" — in other words, we don't require you to read pages and pages of information about text (for example); instead, we explain text tools and options as part of a larger project (in this case, as part of a set of promotional ads).

Clear, easy-to-read, step-by-step instructions walk you through every phase of each job, from creating a new file to saving the finished piece. Wherever logical, we also offer practical advice and tips about underlying concepts and graphic design practices that will benefit students as they enter the job market.

The projects in this book reflect a range of different types of design jobs, from designing a composite layout to building a Web page with CSS. When you finish the projects in this book (and the accompanying Portfolio Builder exercises), you will have a substantial body of work that should impress any potential employer.

The eight projects are described briefly here; more detail is provided in the full table of contents (beginning on Page viii).

CONTENTS

CONTENTS

Project 7
Arts Council Website 361

Project 8
Museum CSS Layout 413

GETTING STARTED

Prerequisites

The Professional Portfolio Series is based on the assumption that you have a basic understanding of how to use your computer. You should know how to use your mouse to point and click, as well as how to drag items around the screen. You should be able to resize and arrange windows on your desktop to maximize your available space. You should know how to access drop-down menus, and understand how check boxes and radio buttons work. It also doesn't hurt to understand how your operating system organizes files and folders, and how to navigate your way around them. If you're familiar with these fundamental skills, then you know all that's necessary to use the Portfolio Series.

Resource Files

All the files you need to complete the projects in this book — except, of course, the Adobe application files — are on the Student Files Web page at againsttheclock.com. See the inside back cover of this book for access information.

Each archive (ZIP) file is named according to the related project (e.g., **Silk_Web20_RF.zip**). At the beginning of each project, you must download the archive file for that project and expand that archive to access the resource files that you need to complete the exercises. Detailed instructions for this process are included in the Interface chapter.

Files required for the related Portfolio Builder exercises at the end of each project are also available on the Student Files Web page; these archives are also named by project (e.g., **Covers_Web20_PB.zip**).

ATC Fonts

You must download and install the ATC fonts from the Student Files Web page to ensure that your exercises and projects will work as described in the book. Specific instructions for installing fonts are provided in the documentation that came with your computer. You should replace older (pre-2013) ATC fonts with the ones on the Student Files Web page.

System Requirements

The Professional Portfolio Series was designed to work on both Macintosh or Windows computers; where differences exist from one platform to another, we include specific instructions relative to each platform.

One issue that remains different from Macintosh to Windows is the use of different modifier keys (Control, Shift, etc.) to accomplish the same task. When we present key commands, we always follow the same Macintosh/Windows format — Macintosh keys are listed first, then a slash, followed by the Windows key commands.

Software Versions

This book was written and tested using the 2020 release of the Adobe Creative Cloud (CC) software:

- Adobe Photoshop — v 21.0
- Adobe Dreamweaver — Version 20.0

(You can find the specific version number of your applications in the Splash Screen that appears while an application is launching.)

Because Adobe has announced periodic upgrades rather than releasing new full versions, some features and functionality might have changed since publication. Please check the Errata section of the Against The Clock Web site for any significant issues that might have arisen from these periodic upgrades.

Adobe Photoshop is the industry-standard application for working with pixels — both manipulating existing ones and creating new ones. Photo retouching, artistic painting, image compositing, and color correction are only a few of the types of work you can create with Photoshop. Our goal in this book is to teach you how to use the available tools to succeed with different types of jobs you might encounter in your professional career.

The simple exercises in this introduction are designed to let you explore the Photoshop user interface. Whether you are new to the application or upgrading from a previous version, we highly recommend following these steps to click around and become familiar with the basic workspace.

Note:

Although not intended as a layout-design application, many people create advertisements, book covers, and other projects entirely in Photoshop. We do not advocate doing all or even most layout composite work in Photoshop, but because many people use the application to create these designs, we feel the projects in this book portray a realistic workflow.

Explore the Photoshop Interface

The first time you launch Photoshop, you will see the default user interface (UI) settings as defined by Adobe. When you relaunch after you or another user has quit, the workspace defaults to the last-used settings — including open panels and the position of those panels on your screen. We designed the following exercises so you can explore different ways of controlling panels in the Photoshop user interface.

1. **Create a new empty folder named WIP (Work in Progress) on any writable disk (where you plan to save your work).**

2. **Download the InterfacePS_Web20_RF.zip archive from the Student Files web page.**

3. **Macintosh users: Place the ZIP archive in your WIP folder, then double-click the file icon to expand it.**

   Windows users: Double-click the ZIP archive file to open it. Click the folder inside the archive and drag it into your primary WIP folder.

   The resulting **InterfacePS** folder contains all the files you need to complete the exercises in this introduction.

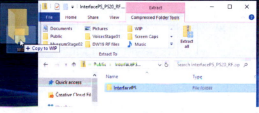

Macintosh: Double-click the archive file icon to expand it.

Windows: Open the archive file, then drag the InterfacePS folder from the archive to your WIP folder.

4. **Macintosh users: While pressing Command-Option-Shift, launch Photoshop. Click Yes when asked if you want to delete Settings files.**

   Windows users: Launch Photoshop, and then immediately press Control-Alt-Shift. Click Yes when asked if you want to delete the Settings files.

5. **Macintosh users: Open the Window menu and make sure the Application Frame option is toggled on.**

This option should be checked.

   Many menu commands and options in Photoshop are **toggles**, which means they are either on or off. When an option is already checked, that option is toggled on (visible or active). You can toggle an active option off by choosing the checked menu command, or toggle an inactive option on by choosing the unchecked menu command.

Note:

On Windows, the Application Frame menu command is not available; you can't turn off the Application Frame on the Windows OS.

6. **Review the options in the Home screen.**

   The default user interface shows a stored "Home" workspace. No panels are visible in this workspace. Instead, you have buttons to create a new file or open an existing one; links to tutorial videos about new features; and one-click access to recently opened files (if any).

Macintosh

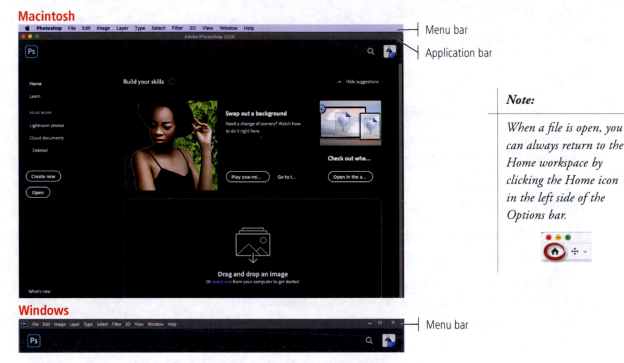

Menu bar

Application bar

Note:

When a file is open, you can always return to the Home workspace by clicking the Home icon in the left side of the Options bar.

Windows

Menu bar

The Home workspace appears whenever Photoshop is running, but no file is open. As soon as you open or create a file, the interface reverts to show the last-used workspace arrangement.

The Macintosh and Windows workspaces are virtually identical, with a few primary exceptions:

- On Macintosh, the Close, Minimize, and Restore buttons appear on the left side of the application bar, and the Menu bar is not part of the Application frame.

- On Windows, the Close, Minimize, and Restore buttons appear at the right end of the Menu bar, which is part of the overall Application frame.

- On Macintosh, the Apple menu provides access to system-specific commands. The Photoshop menu follows the Macintosh system-standard format for all applications; this menu controls basic application operations such as About, Hide, Preferences, and Quit.

7. **In Photoshop with no file open, click the Photoshop icon in the top-left corner of the Home screen.**

Click this icon to enter the Photoshop workspace.

   Clicking this icon enters into the Photoshop workspace so you can access the various panels, even when no file is open.

Understanding the Application Frame

On Windows, each running application is contained within its own frame; all elements of the application — including the Menu bar, panels, tools, and open documents — are contained within the Application frame.

Adobe also offers the Application frame to Macintosh users as an option for controlling the workspace. When the Application frame is active, the entire workspace exists in a self-contained area that can be moved around the screen. All elements of

the workspace (excluding the Menu bar) move when you move the Application frame.

The Application frame is active by default, but you can toggle it off by choosing Window>Application Frame. If the menu option is checked, the Application frame is active; if the menu option is not checked, it is inactive. On Windows, the Application Frame menu command is not available. You can't turn off the Application Frame on the Windows OS.

When the Application frame is not active, the desktop is visible behind the workspace elements.

8. **Choose Window>Workspace>Essentials (Default).**

    The software includes a number of built-in saved workspaces, which provide one-click access to a defined group of panels, designed to meet common workflow needs.

9. **Choose Window>Workspace>Reset Essentials.**

    This step might or might not do anything, depending on what was done in Photoshop before you started this project. If you or someone else changed anything, and then quit the application, those changes are remembered when Photoshop is relaunched. You are resetting the user interface in this step so what you see will match our screen captures.

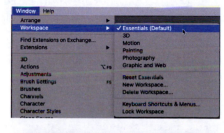

10. **Macintosh users: Choose Photoshop>Preferences>Interface.**
   Windows users: Choose Edit>Preferences>Interface.

Remember that on Macintosh systems, the Preferences dialog box is accessed in the Photoshop menu. Windows users access the Preferences dialog box in the Edit menu.

Preferences customize the way many of the program's tools and options function. When you open the Preferences dialog box, the active pane is the one you choose in the Preferences submenu. Once open, however, you can access any of the categories by clicking a different option in the left pane. The right side of the dialog box displays options related to the active category.

Macintosh   Windows

In the User Interface preferences, you control the overall appearance of the workspace:

- **Color Theme.** You might have noticed the rather dark appearance of the interface background. Photoshop uses the medium-dark "theme" as the default.

- **Color and Border.** You can use the four options below Color Theme — Standard Screen Mode, Full Screen with Menus, Full Screen, and Artboards — to change the color of the area around an open file (sometimes called the pasteboard), as well as the border that appears around the canvas (the actual file area) for each screen mode. (The various screen modes are explained beginning on Page 23.)

- **UI Language.** If you have more than one localized version of the software, you can use this menu to change the language used throughout the interface.

- **UI Font Size.** You can use this option to increase the size of type that appears in Photoshop's user interface elements (panels, and so on).

- **Scale UI To Font.** If you check this option, all UI elements — tabs, tools, etc. — will be enlarged to match the font size if you choose a different UI Font Size than the default Small.

- **Show Channels in Color.** If this option is checked, individual color channels appear in shades of the representative color instead of the default grayscale. (Color channels are explained in Project 1: Composite Movie Ad.)

- **Show Menu Colors.** Some built-in workspaces include colored menu items. You can also edit application menus to define custom highlight colors to appear behind specific menu commands. When this option is checked, any defined colors appear behind the related items in the application menus. If you uncheck this option, all menu items appear in the application's default color theme, regardless of the defined color.

- **Dynamic Color Sliders.** If the Color panel appears in a mode that includes sliders for the various color components (CMYK, RGB, etc.), the sliders default to show the composite color that results from the values in all available sliders. If you uncheck this option, each slider shows only the color of that slider (for example, the cyan slider shows only a gradient of cyan.)

Note:

*As you work your way through this book, you will learn not only what you can do with these different collections of Preferences, but also **why** and **when** you might want to adjust them.*

Note:

If you change the Language or UI Font Size, you have to restart the application for your changes to take effect.

11. **In the Color Theme section, choose any option you prefer.**

We use the Light color theme option throughout this book because text in the interface elements is easier to read in printed screen captures.

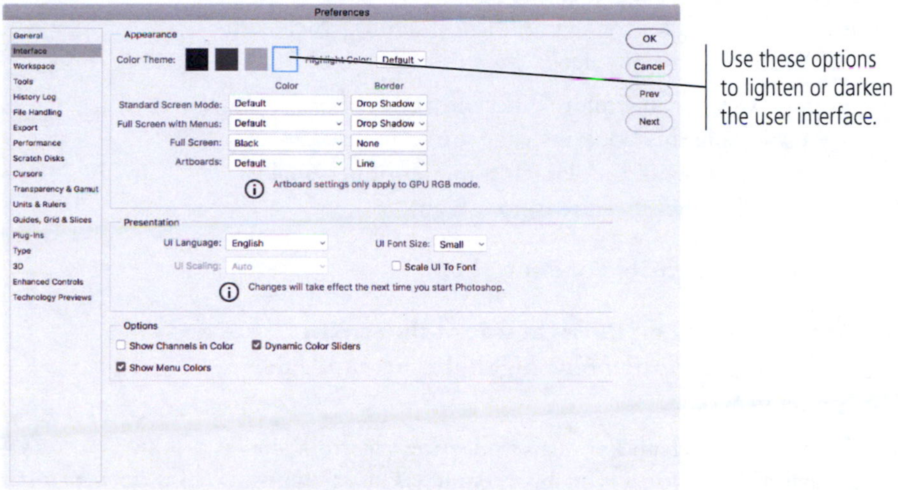

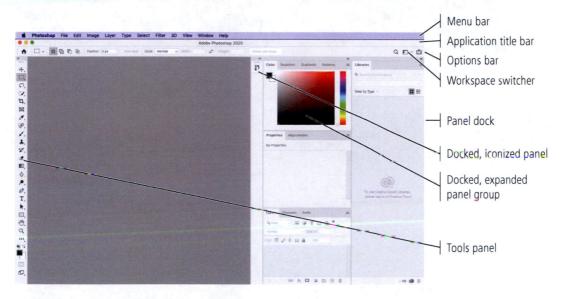

Use these options to lighten or darken the user interface.

12. **Click OK to close the Preferences dialog box.**

13. **With Photoshop open, review the options in the user interface.**

The default Essentials workspace includes the Tools panel on the left side of the screen, the Options bar at the top of the screen, and a set of panels attached to the right side of the screen. The area where the panels are stored is called the **panel dock**.

Menu bar

Application title bar

Options bar

Workspace switcher

Panel dock

Docked, iconized panel

Docked, expanded panel group

Tools panel

14. **Continue to the next exercise.**

Explore the Arrangement of Photoshop Panels

As you gain familiarity with Photoshop, you will develop personal artistic and working styles. Adobe recognizes this wide range of needs and preferences among users. Photoshop includes a number of options for managing the numerous panels so you can customize the workspace to suit your specific needs.

We designed the following exercise so you can explore different ways of controlling Photoshop panels. The projects in this book instruct you to use certain tools and panels, but because workspace preferences are largely a matter of personal taste, where you place those elements within the interface is up to you.

1. **Make sure the Essentials workspace is visible in Photoshop.**

2. **If you see the Libraries panel expanded on the right side of the screen, click the Libraries panel tab and drag until a blue highlight surrounds the Properties/Adjustments panel group.**

   Depending on your screen resolution, the default Essentials workspaces vary from one machine to another. This step makes the workspaces on most computers match more closely, so the following steps and explanations will make sense to users on either OS.

   If you see different panels in different locations, we still encourage you to follow the steps as written. Your final workspace arrangement might be slightly different than what you see in our screen captures, but the overall processes still work.

Note:

*If you do **not** see the Libraries panel in its own column in the default Essentials workspace, then your Properties panel is docked and iconized below the History panel in the left dock column.*

We cannot explain the discrepancy, but it has no significant effect on the steps in this exercise.

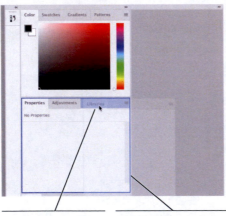

Click a panel tab and drag to move the panel to another location.

The blue highlight shows where the panel will be placed if you release the mouse button.

When you release the mouse button, the Libraries panel becomes part of a Properties/ Adjustment panel group.

3. **Control/right-click the title bar above the right column of docked panels. Choose Auto-Collapse Iconic Panels in the contextual menu to toggle on that option.**

As we explained in the Getting Started section, when commands are different for the Macintosh and Windows operating systems, we include the different commands in the Macintosh/Windows format. In this case, Macintosh users who do not have right-click mouse capability can press the Control key and click to access the contextual menu. You do not have to press Control *and* right-click to access the menus.

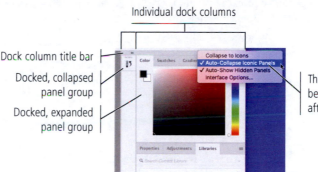

Individual dock columns

Dock column title bar

Docked, collapsed panel group

Docked, expanded panel group

This option should be checked (active) after you select it.

Control/right-clicking a dock title bar opens the dock contextual menu, where you can change the default panel behavior. If you toggle on the Auto-Collapse Iconic Panels option — which is inactive by default — a panel collapses as soon as you click away from it. Auto-Collapse Iconic Panels is also available in the Workspace pane of the Preferences dialog box, which you can open directly from the dock contextual menu.

4. **In the left column of the panel dock, hover your mouse cursor over the top button until you see the name of the related panel ("History") in a tool tip.**

5. **Click the History button to expand that panel group.**

The expanded panel is still referred to as a **panel group**, even though the History panel is the only panel in the group.

If you expand an iconized panel that shares a group with other panels, the entire group expands; the button you clicked is the active panel in the expanded group.

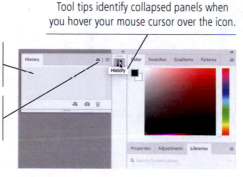

Tool tips identify collapsed panels when you hover your mouse cursor over the icon.

Clicking a panel button expands that panel to the left of the button.

Click here to manually collapse the panel back into the dock.

6. **Click away from the expanded panel, anywhere in the workspace.**

Because the Auto-Collapse Iconic Panels option is toggled on (from Step 3), the History panel collapses as soon as you click away from the panel.

Note:

If you're using a Macintosh and don't have a mouse with right-click capability, we highly recommend you purchase one.

Note:

*Collapsed panels are referred to as **iconized** or **iconic**.*

Note:

Each column of panels, technically considered a separate dock, can be expanded or collapsed independently of other columns.

7. **Click the History panel button to re-expand the panel. Control/right-click the expanded panel tab and choose Close from the contextual menu.**

The panel group's contextual menu is the only way to close a docked panel. You can choose Close to close only the active panel, or close an entire panel group by choosing Close Tab Group from the contextual menu.

Control/right-click a panel tab or icon to access that panel group's contextual menu.

Closing all panels in a column effectively removes that column from the dock.

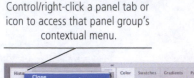
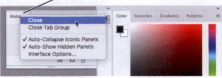

8. **If any other panel remains in the left dock column, repeat the process from Step 7 to close it as well.**

9. **In the remaining dock column, Control/right-click the drop zone of the Libraries/Adjustments/Properties panel group and choose Close Tab Group from the contextual menu.**

When you close a docked group, other panel groups in the same column expand to fill the available space.

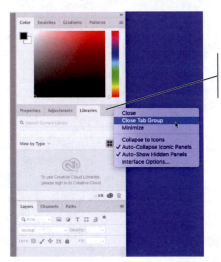

The area behind a panel group's tabs is called the drop zone.

The remaining groups in the dock column expand to fill the available space.

10. **Click the Layers panel tab and drag left, away from the panel dock.**

A panel that is not docked is called a **floating panel**. You can iconize floating panels (or panel groups) by double-clicking the title bar of the floating panel group.

Macintosh **Windows**

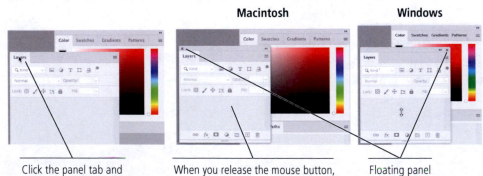

Click the panel tab and drag to move the panel.

When you release the mouse button, the panel floats over the workspace.

Floating panel Close button

Note:

All panels can be toggled on and off using the Window menu.

If you choose a panel that is open but icon-ized, the panel expands to the left of its icon.

If you choose a panel that is open in an expanded group, that panel comes to the front of the group.

If you choose a panel that isn't currently open, it opens in the same position as when it was last closed.

Note:

Many screen captures in this book show floating panels so we can focus on the most important issue in a particular image. In our produc-tion workflow, we make heavy use of docked and iconized panels, and we take full advantage of saved custom work-spaces.

11. **Click the Layers panel tab (in the floating panel group). Drag between the two existing docked panel groups until a blue line appears, then release the mouse button.**

To move a single panel to a new location, click the panel tab and drag. To move an entire panel group, click the panel group drop zone and drag. If you are moving panels to another position in the dock, the blue highlight indicates where the panel (or group) will be placed when you release the mouse button.

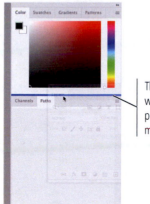

The blue highlight shows where the panel will be placed if you release the mouse button.

When you release the mouse button, the Layers panel becomes part of a separate panel group.

To add a panel to an existing group, drag the panel to the target group's drop zone. A blue highlight will surround the group where the moved panel will be added.

To create a new dock column, drag a panel or panel group until a pop-out "drawer" outlines the edge where the new column will be added.

12. **Control/right-click the drop zone behind the Colors/Swatches/Gradients/Patterns panel group, and choose Minimize from the contextual menu.**

When a group is minimized, only the panel tabs are visible. Clicking a tab in a collapsed panel group expands that group and makes the selected panel active.

You can also double-click a panel tab to minimize the panel group.

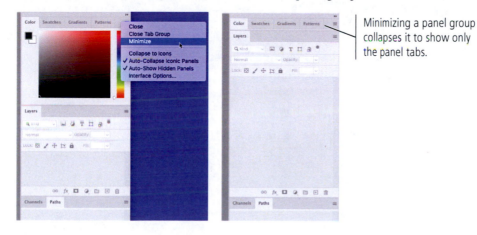

Minimizing a panel group collapses it to show only the panel tabs.

13. Move the cursor over the line between the Layers and Channels/Paths panel groups. When the cursor becomes a double-headed arrow, click and drag up or down until the Layers panel occupies approximately half of the available dock column space.

You can drag the bottom edge of a docked panel group to vertically expand or shrink it. Other panels in the same column expand or contract to fit the available space.

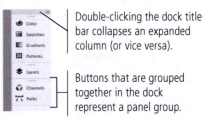

When the cursor becomes a double-headed arrow, click and drag the line between panel groups to change the height of a panel.

Note:

Dragging the left edge of a dock column changes the width of all panels in that dock column. This works for both iconized and expanded columns.

14. Double-click the title bar above the column of docked panels to collapse those panels to icons.

Double-clicking the dock title bar collapses an expanded column (or vice versa).

Buttons that are grouped together in the dock represent a panel group.

15. Move the cursor over the left edge of the dock column. When the cursor becomes a double-headed arrow, click and drag right.

If you only see the icons, you can also drag the dock edge to the left to reveal the panel names. This can be particularly useful until you are more familiar with the application and the icons used to symbolize the different panels.

Click here and drag right to hide the panel names.

16. On the left side of the workspace, double-click the Tools panel title bar.

The Tools panel can't be expanded, but it can be displayed as either one or two columns; double-clicking the Tools panel title bar toggles between the two modes.

The one- or two-column format is a purely personal choice. The one-column layout takes up less horizontal space on the screen, which can be useful if you have a small monitor. The two-column format fits in a smaller vertical space, which can be especially useful if you have a widescreen monitor.

The Tools panel can also be floated by clicking its title bar and dragging away from the edge of the screen. To re-dock the floating Tools panel, simply click the title bar and drag back to the left edge of the screen; when the blue line highlights the edge of the workspace, releasing the mouse button puts the Tools panel back into the dock.

Double-click the Tools panel title bar to toggle between the one- and two-column layouts.

Note:

Throughout this book, our screen captures show the Tools panel in the one-column format. Feel free to work with the panel in two columns if you prefer.

17. Continue to the next exercise.

Customizing the Tools Panel

Near the bottom of the Tools panel, the Edit Toolbar button ···| provides access to a dialog box where you can customize the options that appear in the Tools panel. If you click and hold on this button, you can choose the Edit Toolbar option in the pop-up menu.

In the Customize Toolbar dialog box, you can select and move individual tools or entire groups of tools into the Extra Tools window. Any tools in that window are moved from their regular position in the default Tools panel to a single position, nested under the Edit Toolbar option.

You can toggle the buttons in the bottom-left corner of the dialog box to show or hide several options in the Tools panel. From left to right:

- Edit Toolbar
- Default Foreground and Background Colors
- Edit in Quick Mask Mode
- Change Screen Mode

If you choose to hide the Edit Toolbar option, any tools in the Extra Tools list are simply hidden; you will not be able to access them unless you customize the Tools panel again. (In this case, you can accomplish this task by choosing Edit>Toolbar.)

Clicking the Restore Defaults button in the Customize Toolbar dialog box resets all tools and options in the panel to their original default positions and visibility.

Click and drag tools from the Toolbar list to the Extra Tools list.

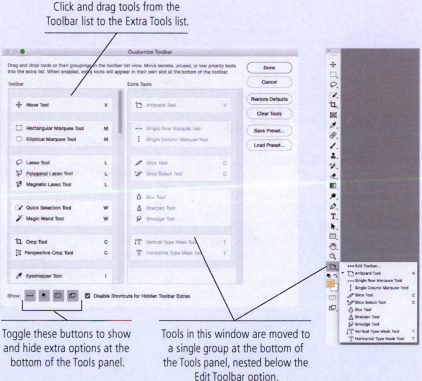

Toggle these buttons to show and hide extra options at the bottom of the Tools panel.

Tools in this window are moved to a single group at the bottom of the Tools panel, nested below the Edit Toolbar option.

In the Tools panel, tools with a small mark in the lower-right corner have **nested tools**.

This arrow means the tool has other nested tools.

Rich tool tip

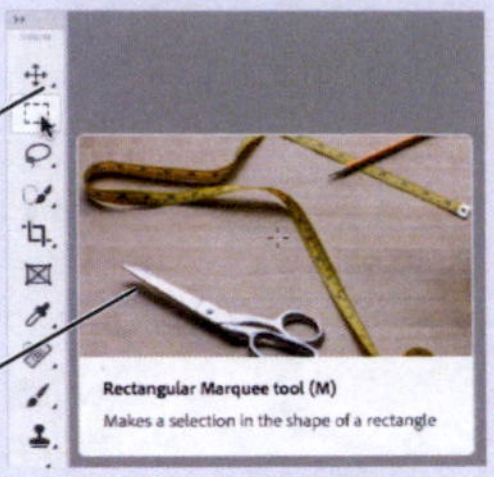

Rectangular Marquee tool (M)
Makes a selection in the shape of a rectangle

If you hover your mouse over a tool, a rich **tool tip** shows the name of the tool, keyboard shortcut (if any), a small animation related to that tool, and a link to video tutorials related to the specific tools.

You can disable overall tool tips or rich tool tips in the Tools pane of the Preferences dialog box. If you disable only rich tool tips, you would see only the tool name and keyboard shortcut when you hover over a tool.

You can access nested tools by clicking the primary tool and holding down the mouse button, or by Control/right-clicking the primary tool to open the menu of nested options.

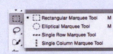

If a tool has a defined shortcut, pressing that key activates the associated tool. Most nested tools have the same shortcut as the default tool. By default, you have to press Shift plus the shortcut key to access the nested variations. You can change this behavior in the Tools pane of the Preferences dialog box by unchecking the Use Shift Key for Tool Switch option; when unchecked, you can simply press the shortcut key multiple times to cycle through variations.

Finally, if you press and hold a tool's keyboard shortcut, you can temporarily call that tool (called **spring-loaded keys**). After releasing the shortcut key, you return to the previous tool. For example, you might switch temporarily from the Brush to the Eraser tool while painting.

The following chart offers a quick reference of nested tools, as well as the shortcut for each (if any). Nested tools are shown indented.

Move tool (V)
- Artboard tool (V)

Rectangular Marquee tool (M)
- Elliptical Marquee tool (M)
- Single Row Marquee tool
- Single Column Marquee tool

Lasso tool (L)
- Polygonal Lasso tool (L)
- Magnetic Lasso tool (L)

Object Selection tool (W)
- Quick Selection tool (W)
- Magic Wand tool (W)

Crop tool (C)
- Perspective Crop tool (C)
- Slice tool (C)
- Slice Select tool (C)

Frame tool (I)

Eyedropper tool (I)
- 3D Material Eyedropper tool (I)
- Color Sampler tool (I)
- Ruler tool (I)
- Note tool (I)
- Count tool (I)

Spot Healing Brush tool (J)
- Healing Brush tool (J)
- Patch tool (J)
- Content Aware Move tool (J)
- Red Eye tool (J)

Brush tool (B)
- Pencil tool (B)
- Color Replacement tool (B)
- Mixer Brush tool (B)

Clone Stamp tool (S)
- Pattern Stamp tool (S)

History Brush tool (Y)
- Art History Brush tool (Y)

Eraser tool (E)
- Background Eraser tool (E)
- Magic Eraser tool (E)

Gradient tool (G)
- Paint Bucket tool (G)
- 3D Material Drop tool (G)

Blur tool
- Sharpen tool
- Smudge tool

Dodge tool (O)
- Burn tool (O)
- Sponge tool (O)

Pen tool (P)
- Freeform Pen tool (P)
- Curvature Pen tool (P)
- Add Anchor Point tool
- Delete Anchor Point tool
- Convert Point tool

Horizontal Type tool (T)
- Vertical Type tool (T)
- Vertical Type Mask tool (T)
- Horizontal Type Mask tool (T)

Path Selection tool (A)
- Direct Selection tool (A)

Rectangle tool (U)
- Rounded Rectangle tool (U)
- Ellipse tool (U)
- Polygon tool (U)
- Line tool (U)
- Custom Shape tool (U)

Hand tool (H)
- Rotate View tool (R)

Zoom tool (Z)

Create a Saved Workspace

You have extensive control over the appearance of your Photoshop workspace. You can choose which panels are visible, where they appear, and even the size of individual panels or panel groups. Over time you will develop personal preferences — the Layers panel always appears at the top, for example — based on your work habits and project needs. Rather than re-establishing every workspace element each time you return to Photoshop, you can save your custom workspace settings so they can be recalled with a single click.

Note:

Because workspace preferences are largely a matter of personal taste, the projects in this book instruct you regarding which panels to use, but not where to place those elements within the interface.

1. **Choose Window>Workspace>New Workspace.**

   Saved workspaces can be accessed in the Window>Workspace submenu, as well as the Workspace switcher on the Options bar.

2. **In the New Workspace dialog box, type Portfolio and then click Save.**

   You didn't define custom keyboard shortcuts, menus, or toolbars, so those options are not relevant in this exercise.

Note:

The Delete Workspace option opens a dialog box where you can choose a specific user-defined workspace to delete. You can't delete the default workspaces that come with the application.

3. **Open the Window menu and choose Workspace>Essentials (Default).**

   Calling a saved workspace restores the last-used state of the workspace. You made a number of changes since calling the Essentials workspace at the beginning of the previous exercise, so calling it now restores the last state of that workspace. In essence, nothing changes from the saved Portfolio workspace.

   Custom workspaces appear at the top of the list.

   Options in this submenu are also available in the Workspace switcher.

   Access saved workspaces in the Workspace Switcher.

4. **Open the Workspace switcher and choose Reset Essentials (or choose Window>Workspace>Reset Essentials).**

   Remember, saved workspaces remember the last-used state. Calling a workspace again restores the panels exactly as they were the last time you used that workspace. For example, if you close a panel that is part of a saved workspace, the closed panel will not be reopened the next time you call the same workspace. To restore the saved state of the workspace — including opening closed panels or repositioning moved ones — you have to use the Reset option.

Note:

If you change anything and quit the application, those changes are remembered, even when Photoshop is relaunched.

5. **Using the Window>Workspace menu or the Workspace switcher, call the saved Portfolio workspace.**

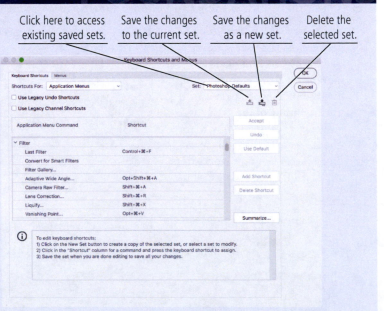

6. **Continue to the next exercise.**

Customizing Keyboard Shortcuts and Menus

People use Photoshop for many different reasons; some use only a limited set of tools to complete specific projects. Photoshop allows you to define the available menu options and the keyboard shortcuts that are associated with menu commands, panel menus, and tools.

At the bottom of the Edit menu, two options (Keyboard Shortcuts and Menus) open different tabs of the same dialog box. If you don't see the Keyboard Shortcuts or Menus options in the Edit menu, choose Show all Menu Items to reveal the hidden commands.

Once you have defined custom menus or shortcuts, you can save your choices as a set so you can access the same custom choices again without having to redo the work.

Click here to access existing saved sets.

Save the changes to the current set.

Save the changes as a new set.

Delete the selected set.

Explore the Photoshop Document Views

There is much more to using Photoshop than arranging the workspace. What you do with those panels — and even which panels you need — depends on the type of work you are doing in a particular file. In this exercise, you open a Photoshop file and explore interface elements that will be important as you create digital artwork.

1. **In Photoshop, choose File>Open. If you see a warning message about insufficient vRAM, click OK.**

   Photoshop's 3D features require a graphics card with at least 512 MB of video RAM (vRAM). The first time you try to create a new file or open an existing one, you will see a warning message if your hardware is not sufficient to run those features.

Note:

If you see this message, you will not be able to complete the final stage of Project 3: City Promotion Cards.

2. **If necessary, click the On Your Computer button in the bottom-left corner of the dialog box to show the system-standard navigation dialog box.**

Cloud documents ⓘ

No cloud documents—yet

All your cloud documents from Photoshop on Mac, Windows, and iPad will be right here.

Click here to access folders and files on your local drives.

On your computer   Cancel

Note:

Press Command/ Control-O to access the Open dialog box.

3. **Navigate to your WIP>InterfacePS folder and select hubble.jpg in the list of available files. Press Shift, and then click supernova.jpg.**

   The Open dialog box is a system-standard navigation dialog. This is one area of significant difference between Macintosh and Windows users.

   On both operating systems, this step selects all files, including those between the two you click. Pressing Shift allows you to select multiple consecutive files in the list. You can also press Command/Control and click to select multiple, non-consecutive files.

Macintosh

Windows

4. **Click Open.**

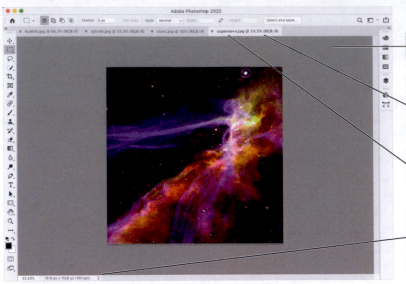

Photoshop files appear in the document window.

Each open file is represented by a document tab, showing the file name, view percentage, color space, and current viewing mode.

The active file tab is lighter than the others.

Use this menu to show different information, such as file size (default), color profile, dimensions, etc.

5. **Click the spirals.jpg tab to make that document active.**

6. **Highlight the current value in the View Percentage field (in the bottom-left corner of the document window). Type 45, then press Return/Enter.**

Different people prefer larger or smaller view percentages, depending on a number of factors (eyesight, monitor size, and so on). As you complete the projects in this book, you will see our screen captures zoom in or out as necessary to show you the most relevant part of a particular file. Unless it is specifically required for the work being done, we do not tell you which view percentage to use for an exercise.

Note:

*Macintosh users:
If you turn off the
Application frame,
opening multiple files
creates a document win-
dow that has a separate
title bar showing the
name of the active file.*

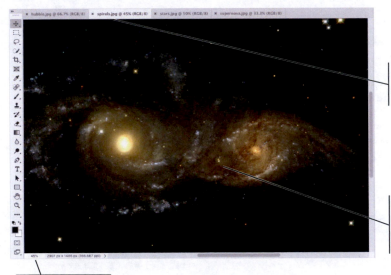

Click the tab to activate a specific file in the document window.

Changing the view percentage of the file does not affect the size of the document window.

View Percentage field

7. **Choose View>100%.**

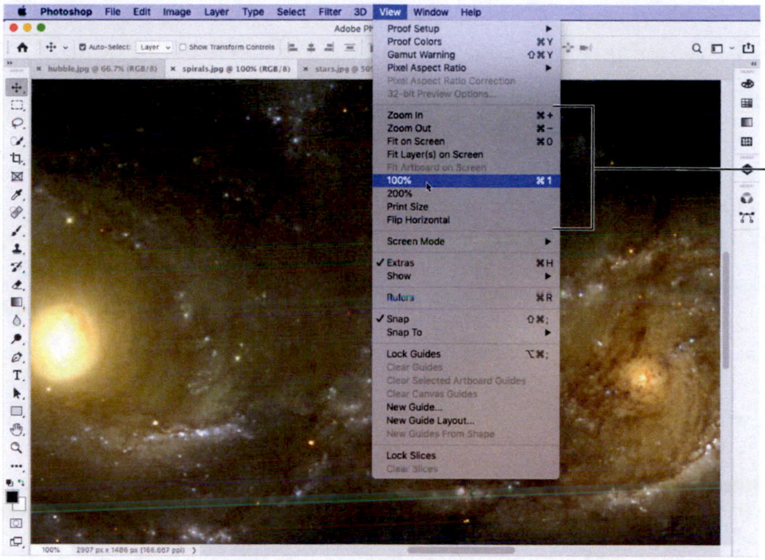

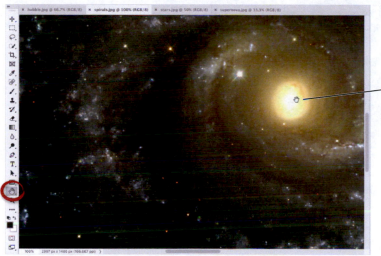

These options affect the file's view percentage.

Note:

If a menu option is grayed out, it is not available for the active selection.

8. **Click the Hand tool (near the bottom of the Tools panel). Click in the document window, hold down the mouse button, and drag around.**

The Hand tool is a very easy and convenient option for changing the area of an image currently visible in the document window.

If the Scroll All Windows option is checked in the Options bar, dragging in one window affects the visible area of all open files.

Hand tool cursor

Note:

You can press the Space-bar to access the Hand tool when another tool (other than the Type tool) is active.

9. Click the Zoom tool in the Tools panel. Press Option/Alt, and then click anywhere in the document window.

Again: we list differing commands in the Macintosh/Windows format.
On Macintosh, you need to press the Option key; on Windows, press the Alt key.
We will not repeat this explanation every time different commands are required for the different operating systems.

Clicking with the Zoom tool enlarges the view percentage in specific, predefined percentage steps. Pressing Option/Alt while clicking with the Zoom tool reduces the view percentage in the reverse sequence of the same percentages.

If Scrubby Zoom is not active in the Options bar, clicking and dragging with the Zoom tool enlarges the selected area to fill the document window. If Scrubby Zoom is active, clicking and dragging dynamically enlarges (if you drag right) or reduces (if you drag left) the image in the document window.

You can zoom a document between approximately 0.098% and 3200%. We say approximately because the actual smallest size is dependent on the original image size. You can zoom out far enough to show the image as a single tiny square, regardless of the percentage of the image that represents.

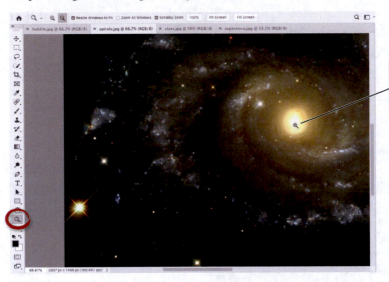

When the Zoom tool is active, pressing Option/Alt changes the cursor to the Zoom Out icon.

10. **In the Options bar, click the Fit Screen button.**

The Options bar appears by default at the top of the workspace below the Menu bar. It is context sensitive, which means it provides different options depending on which tool is active. When the Zoom tool is active:

- If **Resize Windows to Fit** is checked, zooming in a floating window affects the size of the actual document window.

- If **Zoom All Windows** is checked, zooming in one window affects the view percentage of all open files.

- **Scrubby Zoom** enables dynamic image zooming depending on the direction in which you drag in the document window.

- The **100%** button changes the view percentage to 100%.

- The **Fit Screen** option changes the image view to the percentage necessary to show the entire image in the document window. This has the same effect as choosing Window>Fit on Screen.

- The **Fill Screen** button changes the image view to whatever percentage is necessary to fill the available space in the document window.

Note:

You can toggle the Options bar on or off by choosing Window>Options.

Note:

If you check the Enable Narrow Options Bar option in the Workspace pane of the Preferences dialog box, many options in the Options bar will appear as small icons that you can click to toggle on and off. This saves horizontal space on narrow monitors.

The Fit Screen command automatically calculates view percentage based on the size of the document window.

11. **In the Tools panel, choose the Rotate View tool (nested under the Hand tool). Click in the top half of the document window and drag right to turn the document clockwise.**

The Rotate View tool turns an image without permanently altering the orientation of the file; the actual image data remains unchanged. This tool allows you to more easily work on objects or elements that are not oriented horizontally (for example, working with text that appears on an angle in the final image).

In the Options bar, you can type a specific angle in the Rotation Angle field, or click the rotation proxy icon, to dynamically rotate the view. At any time, you can click the Reset View button to restore the original rotation (0°) of the image. If Rotate All Windows is checked, dragging in one window affects the view angle of all open files.

Note:

If you are unable to rotate the image view, your graphics processor does not support OpenGL — a hardware/software combination that makes it possible to work with complex graphics operations. If your computer does not support OpenGL, you will not be able to use a number of Photoshop features (including the Rotate View tool).

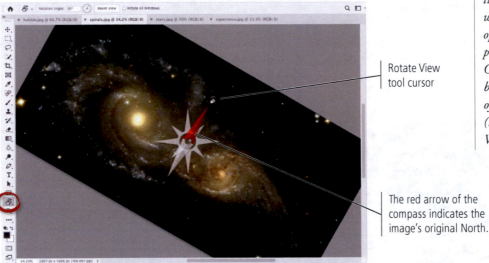

Rotate View tool cursor

The red arrow of the compass indicates the image's original North.

12. **In the Options bar, click the Reset View button.**

As we said, the Rotate View tool is **nondestructive** (i.e., it does not permanently affect the pixels in the image). You can easily use the tool's options to define a specific view angle or to restore an image to its original orientation.

Resetting the view restores the image's original orientation.

13. **Continue to the next exercise.**

Summing Up the Photoshop View Options

Most Photoshop projects require some amount of zooming in and out to various view percentages, as well as navigating around the document within its window. As we show you how to complete different stages of the workflow, we usually won't tell you when to change your view percentage because that's largely a matter of personal preference. However, you should understand the different options for navigating around a Photoshop file so you can easily and efficiently get to what you want, when you want to get there.

View Percentage Field

You can type a specific percentage in the View Percentage field in the bottom-left corner of the document window.

View Menu

The View menu also provides options for changing the view percentage, including the associated keyboard shortcuts. The Zoom In and Zoom Out options step through the same predefined view percentages the Zoom tool uses.

Zoom In	Command/Control-equals (=)
Zoom Out	Command/Control-minus (-)
Fit On Screen	Command/Control-0 (zero)
Actual Pixels (100%)	Command/Control-1

Zoom Tool

You can click with the **Zoom tool** to increase the view percentage in specific, predefined intervals. Pressing Option/Alt with the Zoom tool allows you to zoom out in the same predefined percentages.

If Scrubby Zoom is active in the Options bar, you can click and drag left to reduce the view percentage, or drag right to increase the view percentage. (The Scrubby Zoom option does not follow predefined stepped percentages.) If Scrubby Zoom is not active, clicking and dragging with the Zoom tool enlarges the selected area to fill the document window.

Hand Tool

At any view percentage, you can use the **Hand tool** to drag the file around in the document window. The Hand tool changes only what is visible in the window; it has no effect on the actual pixels in the image.

Mouse Scroll Wheel

If your mouse has a scroll wheel, rolling the scroll wheel up or down moves the image up or down within the document window. If you press Command/Control and scroll the wheel, you can move the image right (scroll up) or left (scroll down) within the document window. You can also press Option/Alt and then scroll the wheel up to zoom in down to zoom out.

In the General pane of the Preferences dialog box, the Zoom with Scroll Wheel option is unchecked by default. If you check this option, scrolling up or down with no modifier key zooms in or out and does not move the image within the document window.

Navigator Panel

The **Navigator panel** is another method of adjusting how close your viewpoint is, and what part of the page you're currently viewing if zoomed in close enough that you're only seeing a portion of the image. The Navigator panel shows a thumbnail of the active file. A red rectangle represents exactly how much of the document shows in the document window.

Drag the red rectangle to change the visible portion of the file.

Use the slider and field at the bottom of the panel to change the view percentage.

Explore the Arrangement of Multiple Documents

You will often need to work with more than one Photoshop file at once. Photoshop incorporates a number of options for arranging multiple documents. We designed the following simple exercise so you can explore these options.

1. **With all four files from the WIP>InterfacePS folder open, click the hubble.jpg document tab to make that the active file.**

2. **Choose Window>Arrange>Float in Window.**

   You can also separate all open files by choosing Window>Arrange>Float All In Windows.

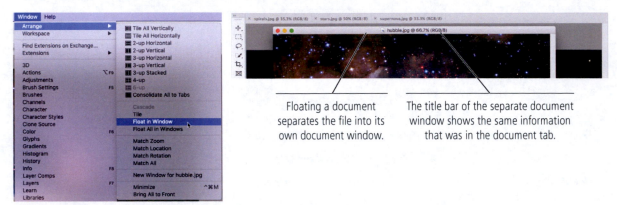

Floating a document separates the file into its own document window.

The title bar of the separate document window shows the same information that was in the document tab.

3. **Choose Window>Arrange>4-up.**

   The defined arrangements provide a number of options for tiling multiple open files within the available workspace. These arrangements manage all open files, including those in floating windows.

   The options' icons suggest the result of each command. The active file remains active; this is indicated by the brighter text in the active document's tab.

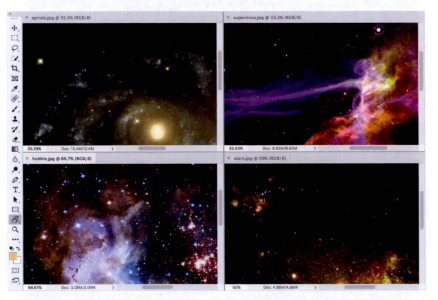

Note:

All open files are listed at the bottom of the Window menu.

Note:

If more files are open than what a specific arrangement indicates, the extra files will be consolidated as tabs into the window with the active file.

4. **Choose Window>Arrange>Consolidate All to Tabs.**

   This command restores all documents — floating or not — into a single tabbed document window.

5. **At the bottom of the Tools panel, click the Change Screen Mode button and hold down the mouse button.**

   Photoshop has three different **screen modes**, which change the way the document window displays on the screen. The default mode, which you saw when you opened these three files, is called Standard Screen mode.

   Note:

   Press F to cycle through the different screen modes.

6. **Choose Full Screen Mode with Menu Bar from the Change Screen Mode menu.**

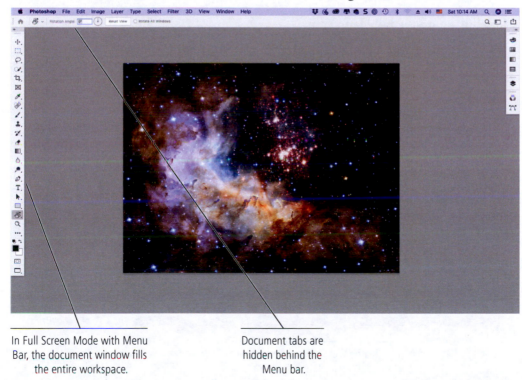

In Full Screen Mode with Menu Bar, the document window fills the entire workspace.

Document tabs are hidden behind the Menu bar.

7. **Click the Change Screen Mode button in the Tools panel and choose Full Screen Mode. Read the resulting warning dialog box, and then click Full Screen.**

In Full Screen Mode, the Menu bar, title bar, and all panels are hidden.

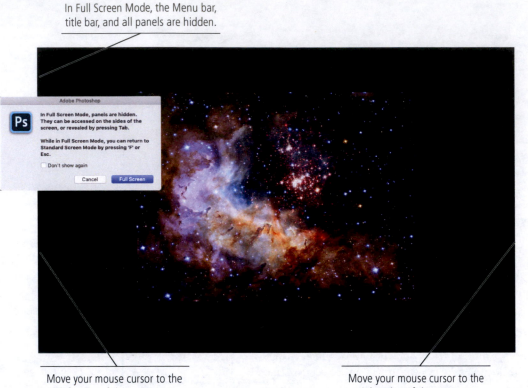

Move your mouse cursor to the left edge of the screen to temporarily show the Tools panel.

Move your mouse cursor to the right edge of the screen to temporarily show docked panels.

8. **Press the Escape key to return to Standard Screen mode.**

9. **Click the Close button on the hubble.jpg tab.**

10. **Macintosh: Click the Close button in the top-left corner of the Application frame.**

Closing the Macintosh Application frame closes all open files, but does *not* quit the application.

Windows: Click the Close button on each document tab to close the files.

Clicking the Close button on the Windows Menu bar closes all open files *and* quits the application. To close open files *without* quitting, you have to manually close each file.

Closing the Application frame closes all open files.

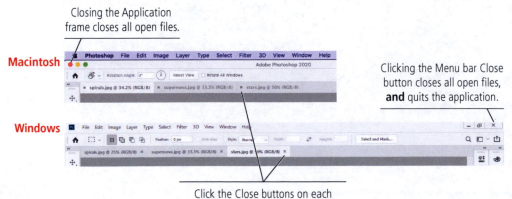

Clicking the Menu bar Close button closes all open files, **and** quits the application.

Click the Close buttons on each document tab to close individual files.

Composite Movie Ad

1

Tantamount Studios, one of the largest film production companies in Hollywood, is developing a new movie called "Aftermath." You have been hired to develop an advertisement that will be used to announce the movie in several trade magazines.

This project incorporates the following skills:

- ❏ Creating a single composite ad from multiple supplied images
- ❏ Compositing multiple photographs, using various techniques to silhouette the focal object in each image
- ❏ Incorporating vector graphics as rasterized and Smart Object layers
- ❏ Scaling and aligning different objects in relation to the page and each other
- ❏ Managing individual layout elements using layers and layer groups
- ❏ Saving multiple versions of a file to meet different output requirements

client comments

Here's a basic synopsis of the movie:

A massive hurricane, unlike anything ever seen on the West Coast of the United States, takes aim at San Francisco. The Category 6 hurricane sparks tidal waves, fires, and floods. The resulting destruction dwarfs even the earthquake and fire of 1906. The movie follows the storm survivors through the process of rebuilding, both personally and politically.

This movie is going to be one of our summer blockbusters, and we're throwing a lot of resources behind it. We'll be putting the same ad in multiple magazines, and they all use different software to create the layouts. We need the ad to work for all of our placements, regardless of the software being used by the publishers.

art director comments

The client loved the initial concept sketch I submitted last week, so we're ready to start building the files. I've had the photographer prepare the images we need, and the client has provided the studio and rating logo files. They also sent me the primary magazine specs:

– Files should be submitted as flattened TIFF files

– Bleed size: 8.75″ × 11.25″

– Trim size: 8.5″ × 11″

– Live area: 8″ × 10.5″

After you have created the final file for printing, I also need you to create a flattened JPEG file for use in digital media.

project objectives

To complete this project, you will:

❏ Resize a raster image to change resolution

❏ Composite multiple images into a single background file

❏ Incorporate both raster and vector elements into the same design

❏ Transform and arrange individual layers to create a cohesive design

❏ Create layer groups to easily manage related layer content

❏ Use selection techniques to isolate images from their backgrounds

❏ Save two types of files for different media requirements

AFTERMATH

STAGE 1 / **Compositing Images and Artwork**

There are two primary types of artwork:

- **Vector graphics** are composed of mathematical descriptions of a series of lines and geometric shapes. These files are commonly created in illustration ("drawing") applications like Adobe Illustrator. Vector graphics are **resolution independent**; they can be freely scaled, and are automatically output at the resolution of the output device.

- **Raster images** are made up of a grid of individual pixels (rasters or bits) in rows and columns, called a **bitmap**. **Line art**, also called a **bitmap image**, is actually a type of raster image that includes only black and white pixels. Raster files are **resolution dependent** — their resolution is determined when you scan, photograph, or create the file.

Photoshop is what some people call a "paint" program — it is primarily used to create and manipulate pixel-based, or raster, images. Raster-image quality depends directly on the resolution. When you create files in Photoshop, you need to understand the resolution requirements from the very beginning of the process.

Pixels per inch (ppi) is the number of pixels in one horizontal or vertical inch of a digital raster file. As a general rule, commercial print jobs require 240–300 pixels per inch at the final output size to achieve good image quality in the printed piece. Some digital media, such as desktop web browsers, typically require much lower resolution, commonly 72 ppi, although monitors and mobile devices with HD display capabilities support higher-resolution images.

It is important to realize that you cannot significantly increase image resolution once a raster image has been created or captured. When you create files that will be used for both print and digital media — as you will for this project — you should start with the higher resolution, and then reduce it after the composition is complete.

The same raster image is reproduced here at 300 ppi (left) and 72 ppi (right). Notice the obvious degradation in quality when the resolution is set to 72 ppi.

Open and Resize an Image

Every raster image has a defined, specific resolution that is established when it is created. If you scan an image to be 3″ high by 3″ wide at 150 ppi, that image has 450 pixels in each vertical column, and 450 pixels in each horizontal row. Simply resizing the image stretches or compresses those pixels into a different physical space, but does not add or remove pixel information. If you resize the 3″ × 3″ image to 6″ × 6″ (200% of the original), the 450 pixels in each column or row are forced to extend across 6″ instead of 3″, causing a marked loss of quality.

The **effective resolution** of an image is the resolution calculated after scaling is taken into account. This number is equally as (and perhaps, more) important as the original image resolution. The effective resolution can be calculated with a fairly simple equation:

$$\text{Original resolution} \div (\%\ \text{magnification} \div 100) = \text{Effective resolution}$$

If a 300-ppi image is magnified 150%, the effective resolution is:

$$300\ \text{ppi} \div 1.5 = 200\ \text{ppi}$$

In other words, the more you enlarge a raster image, the lower its effective resolution becomes. In general, you can make an image 10% or 15% larger without significant adverse effects. The more you enlarge an image, however, the worse the results. Even Photoshop, which offers very sophisticated formulas (called algorithms) for sizing images, cannot guarantee perfect results.

Effective resolution can be a very important consideration when working with client-supplied images, especially those that come from consumer-level digital cameras. Many of those devices capture images with a specific number of pixels, rather than a number of pixels per inch (ppi). In this exercise, you will explore the effective resolution of an image to see if it can be used for a full-page, printed magazine ad.

1. **Download Movie_Web20_RF.zip from the Student Files web page.**

2. **Expand the ZIP archive in your WIP folder (Macintosh) or copy the archive contents into your WIP folder (Windows).**

   This results in a folder named **Movie**, which contains all of the files you need for this project. You should also use this folder to save the files you create in this project.

   If necessary, refer to Page 1 of the Interface chapter for specific information on expanding or accessing the required resource files.

3. **In Photoshop, choose File>Open. If necessary, click the Your Computer button in the bottom-left corner of the dialog box to show the system-standard navigation dialog box.**

   The Open dialog box defaults to show the last-used option, so you might see the Cloud Documents pane, which is used to access any files that have been saved directly into your Creative Cloud (CC) account.

   In this project you are working with files on your local computer (or other local drive), so you might need to click the Your Computer button to access the system-standard navigation dialog box for opening files.

4. **Navigate to your WIP>Movie folder. Select Bricks.jpg and click Open.**

If you see a warning about mismatched profiles at any point in this project, choose the option to use the embedded profile.

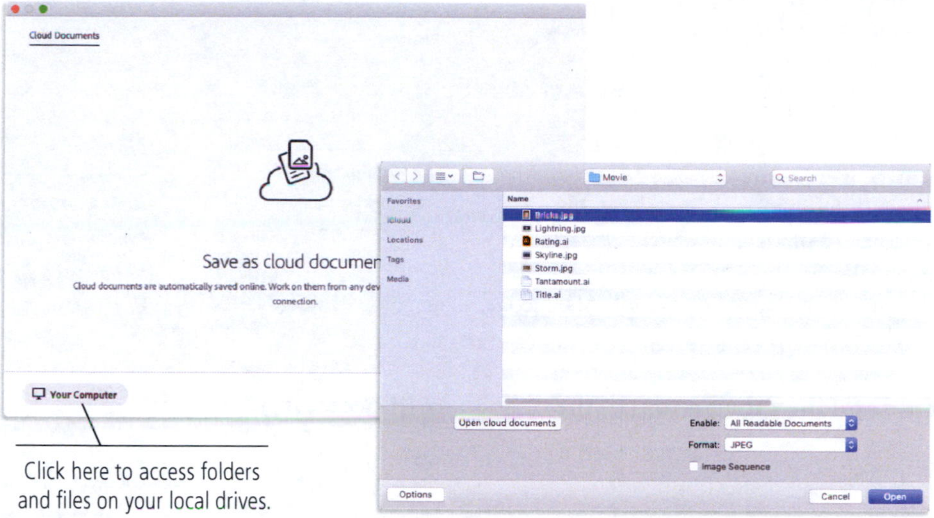

Note:

If you open a Photoshop Cloud file from your account, the document tab shows a cloud icon before the file name.

Click here to access folders and files on your local drives.

5. **If the rulers are not visible on the top and left edges, choose View>Rulers.**

6. **Control/right-click the horizontal ruler and make sure Inches is checked as the default unit of measurement.**

As you can see in the rulers, this image has a very large physical size.

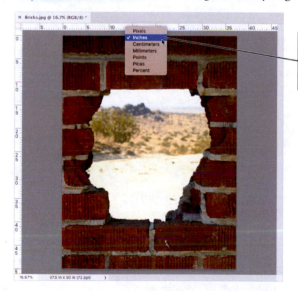

Use the contextual menu to make sure rulers are displayed in Inches.

Note:

Press Command/Control-R to show or hide rulers.

Note:

Although designers trained in traditional (non-digital) methods are sometimes comfortable talking about picas or ciceros, most people use inches as the standard unit of measurement in the U.S.

You can change the default unit of measurement in the Units & Rulers pane of the Preferences dialog box. Double-clicking either ruler opens the appropriate pane of the Preferences dialog box.

7. Choose Image>Image Size.

The Image Size dialog box shows the number of pixels in the image, as well as the image dimensions and current resolution. You can change any value in this dialog box, but you should understand what those changes mean before you do so.

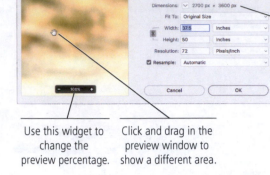

The actual number of pixels in the image is the most important information.

As you can see, this image is currently 37.5 inches wide and 50 inches high, but it was photographed at 72 pixels/inch. For most commercial printing, you need at least 300 ppi. You can use the principle of effective resolution to change the file to a high enough resolution for printing.

Use this widget to change the preview percentage.

Click and drag in the preview window to show a different area.

Note:

Press Command-Option-I/Control-Alt-I to open the Image Size dialog box.

8. Check the Resample option at the bottom of the dialog box (if necessary).

The options in this dialog box remember the last-used choices. The Resample option might already be checked in your dialog box.

Resampling means maintaining the existing resolution in the new image dimensions. In other words, you are either adding or deleting pixels to the existing image. When this option is turned on, you can change the dimensions of an image without affecting the resolution, or you can change the resolution of an image (useful for removing excess resolution or **downsampling**) without affecting the image size.

Note:

When Resample is checked, you can use the attached menu to tell Photoshop how to generate extra pixel data when increasing the image size, or which pixels to discard when reducing the image size.

9. Change the Resolution field to 300 pixels/inch.

When you change the resolution with resampling turned on, you do not change the file's physical size. To achieve 300 ppi resolution at the new size, Photoshop needs to add a huge number of pixels to the image. You can see at the top of the dialog box that this change would increase the total number of pixels from 2700 × 3600 to 11250 × 15000.

When Resample is checked, changing the Resolution value adds or removes pixels.

You can also see that changing the resolution of an image without affecting its physical dimensions would have a significant impact on the file size. Changing the resolution to 300 ppi at the current size would increase the file size to nearly 483 megabytes.

Higher resolution means larger file sizes, which translates to longer processing time for printing, or longer download time over the Internet. When you scale an image to a smaller size, simply resizing can produce files with far greater effective resolution than you need. Resampling allows you to reduce physical size without increasing the resolution, resulting in a smaller file size.

The caveat is that once you delete pixels, they are gone. If you later try to re-enlarge the smaller image, you will not achieve the same quality as the original file before it was reduced. You should save reduced images as copies instead of overwriting the originals.

10. **Press Option/Alt and click the Reset button to restore the original image dimensions in the dialog box.**

In many Photoshop dialog boxes, pressing the Option/Alt key changes the Cancel button to Reset. You can click the Reset button to restore the original values that existed when you opened the dialog box.

Pressing Option/Alt changes the Cancel button to Reset.

11. **Uncheck the Resample option at the bottom of the dialog box.**

12. **Change the Resolution field to 300 pixels/inch.**

Resizing *without* resampling basically means distributing the same number of pixels over a different amount of physical space. When you resize an image without resampling, you do not change the number of pixels in the image. In fact, those fields in the dialog box become simple text; the fields are unavailable and you cannot change the number of pixels in the image.

You can see how changing one of the linked fields (Resolution) directly affects the other linked fields (Width and Height). By resizing the image to be 300 ppi — enough for commercial print quality — you now have an image that is 9″ × 12″.

Note:

Also called "native," the PSD format is the most flexible format to use while building files in Photoshop.

When the Resample option is unchecked, these three fields are all linked.

13. **Click OK to apply the change and return to the document window.**

The rulers change to reflect the new dimensions of the file.

Because you did not resample the image, the screen display does not change.

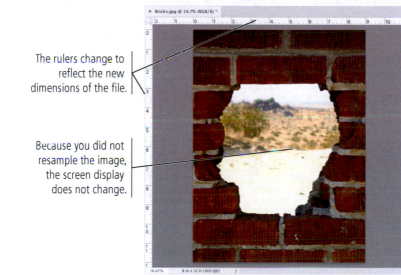

14. **Choose File>Save As. In the resulting dialog box, click the Save on Your Computer button.**

When you save a file in Photoshop, you now have a choice to save the file as a Photoshop Cloud document, or a regular Photoshop file on your desktop. If you choose the Save to Cloud Documents button, the file is saved in your Creative Cloud account with the special extension ".psdc".

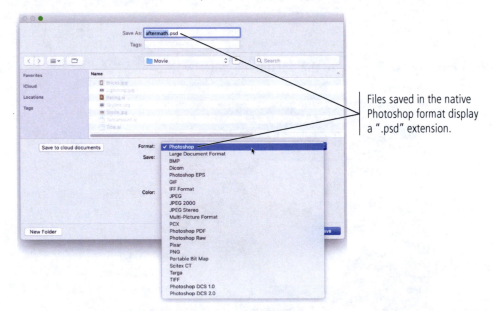

15. **If necessary, navigate to your WIP>Movie folder as the target location. Change the file name (in the Save As/File Name field) to aftermath.**

Since this is a basic image file with only one layer (so far), most of the other options in the Save As dialog box are grayed out (not available).

16. **Choose Photoshop in the Format/Save As Type menu, and then click Save.**

You can save a Photoshop file in a number of different formats, all of which have specific capabilities, limitations, and purposes. While you are still working on a file, it's best to keep it as a native Photoshop (PSD) file. When you choose a different format, the correct extension is automatically added to the file name.

Files saved in the native Photoshop format display a ".psd" extension.

17. **Continue to the next exercise.**

Understanding File Saving Preferences

You can control a number of options related to saving files in the File Handling pane of the Preferences dialog box.

Image Previews. You can use this menu to always or never include image thumbnails in the saved file. If you choose Ask When Saving in this menu, the Save As dialog box includes an option to include the preview/thumbnail.

On Macintosh, you have an additional option to include a thumbnail in the saved file. If checked, the image thumbnail appears in dialog boxes instead of the Photoshop file icon.

Macintosh

Windows

Append File Extension. On Macintosh, you can use this menu to always or never include the file extension in the saved file. If the Ask When Saving option is selected in this menu, the Save As dialog box includes options to append the file extension (in lowercase or not).

On Windows, file extensions are always added to saved files. This preference menu has only two options: Use Upper Case and Use Lower Case.

Save As to Original Folder. When this option is checked, choosing File>Save As automatically defaults to the location where the original file is located.

Save in Background. The Save process occurs by default in the background. In other words, you can continue working even while a file is being saved. Especially when you work with large files, this can be a significant time saver because you don't have to sit and wait the several minutes it might take to save a very large file. The only thing you can't do while a file is being saved is use the Save As command; if you try, you will see a warning advising you to wait until the background save is complete.

When a file is being saved in the background, the completed percentage appears in the document tab.

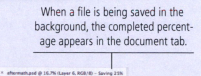

Automatically Save Recovery Information Every... When checked, this option means that your work is saved in a temporary file, every 10 minutes, by default. If something happens — such as a power outage — you will be able to restore your work back to the last autosaved version. In other words, the most you will lose is 10 minutes of work!

✪ Crop the Canvas and Place Ruler Guides

The final step in preparing the workspace is defining the live area of the page. **Trim size** is the actual size of a page once it has been cut out of the press sheet. According to your client, the magazine has a trim size of 8.5″ × 11″.

Any elements that print right to the edge of a page (called **bleeding**) must actually extend beyond the defined trim size. The **bleed allowance** is the amount of extra space that should be included for these bleed objects. Most applications require at least a 1/8″ bleed allowance on any bleed edge.

Because of inherent variation in the mechanical printing and trimming processes, most magazines also define a safe, or **live area**. All important design elements (especially text) should stay within this live area. The live area for this project is 8″ × 10.5″.

1. **With `aftermath.psd` open, choose the Crop tool in the Tools panel.**

   When you choose the Crop tool, a crop marquee appears around the edges of the image. The marquee has eight handles, which you can drag to change the size of the crop area.

Note:

You can press the Escape key to cancel the crop marquee and return to the uncropped image.

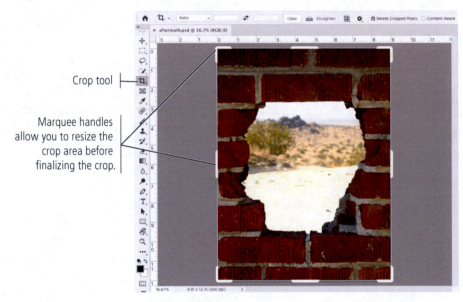

Crop tool

Marquee handles allow you to resize the crop area before finalizing the crop.

Note:

You can rotate a crop marquee by placing the cursor slightly away from a corner handle.

2. **In the Options bar, make sure the Delete Cropped Pixels option is checked.**

   When this option is checked, areas outside the cropped areas are permanently removed from all layers in the file. If this option is not checked, cropped pixels remain in the file, but exist outside the edges of the file canvas. The Background layer, if one exists, is converted to a regular layer (you'll learn more about Background layers later in this project).

   This is an important distinction — by maintaining cropped pixels, you can later transform or reposition layers to reveal different parts of the layer within the newly cropped canvas size.

Note:

It might be helpful to toggle off the Snap feature (View>Snap), which causes certain file elements to act as magnets when you move a marquee or drag a selection.

3. **Click the right-center handle of the crop marquee and drag left until the cursor feedback shows W: 8.750 in.**

When you drag certain elements in the document window, live cursor feedback (also called "heads-up display") shows information about the transformation. When dragging a side crop marquee handle, for example, the feedback shows the new width of the area.

You might need to zoom into at least 50% view percentage to achieve the exact dimensions needed for this project.

Click and drag the marquee handle to resize the crop area.

Use the cursor feedback to find the appropriate measurement.

4. **Repeat Step 3 with the bottom-center handle until feedback shows the area of H: 11.250 in.**

Remember, the defined trim size is 8.5″ × 11″ for this ad. Anything that runs to the page edge has to incorporate a 0.125″ bleed allowance, so the actual canvas size must be large enough to accommodate the bleed allowance on all edges:

[Width]   8.5″ + 0.125″ + 0.125″ = 8.75

[Height]   11″ + 0.125″ + 0.125″ = 11.25

5. **Zoom out until you can see the entire canvas in the document window.**

6. **Click inside the crop area and drag to reposition the image so that it is approximately centered in the crop area.**

When you change the size of the marquee, the area outside the marquee is "shielded" by a darkened overlay so you can get an idea of what will remain after you finalize the crop.

You can drag the image inside the crop area to change the portion that will remain in the cropped image. By default, the crop area remains centered in the document window; instead, the image moves behind the crop area.

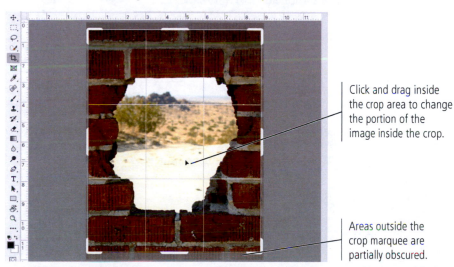

Click and drag inside the crop area to change the portion of the image inside the crop.

Areas outside the crop marquee are partially obscured.

Note:

You should familiarize yourself with the most common fraction-to-decimal equivalents:

1/8 = 0.125

1/4 = 0.25

3/8 = 0.375

1/2 = 0.5

5/8 = 0.625

3/4 = 0.75

7/8 = 0.875

Note:

You can also use the Arrow keys on your keyboard to "nudge" the image in a specific direction.

7. **Press Return/Enter to finalize the crop.**

8. **Choose View>New Guide Layout.**

   This dialog box makes it very easy to
   define a page grid using non-printing
   guides. The dialog box defaults to add
   8 columns with a 20-pixel (0.067 in)
   gutter. In the document window, you
   can see the guides (blue lines) that will
   be created based on the active settings
   in the New Guide Layout dialog box.

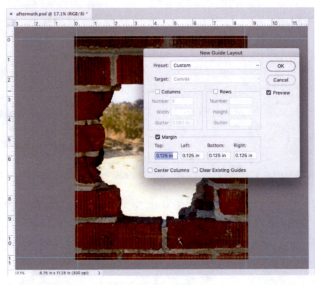

9. **Uncheck the Columns option and check the Margin option. Type 0.125
   in each of the available margin fields.**

   You can use the Margin fields to place
   guides at specific distances from each
   edge of the canvas. You don't need to
   type the unit of measurement because
   the default unit for this file is already
   inches. Photoshop automatically
   assumes the value you type is in the
   default unit of measurement.

10. **Click OK to return to the document and add the required margin guides.**

    At this point you should have four guides — two vertical and two horizontal, each
    1/8″ from the file edges. These mark the trim size of your final 8.5″ × 11″ file.

11. **Choose View>100%.**

    It helps to zoom in to a higher view percentage if you want to precisely place guides. To
    complete the following steps accurately, we found it necessary to use at least 100% view.

12. **Choose the Move tool.**

    For this file, the live area (the area in which important objects should be placed)
    should be 0.25″ inset from the trim edge. This is how we determined that number:

    [Width]   8.5″ − 8.0″ = 0.5 ÷ 2 = 0.25″

    [Height]   11″ − 10.5″ = 0.5″ ÷ 2 = 0.25″

    In the next few steps you will add guides that identify the live area.

13. **In the top-left corner of the document window, click the zero-point crosshairs and drag to the top-left intersection of the guides.**

You can reposition the zero point to the top-left corner of the bleed allowance by double-clicking the zero-point crosshairs.

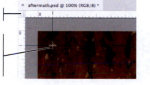

Zero-point crosshairs

Drag to here to change the 0/0 point of the rulers.

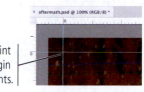

This new zero point will be the origin for measurments.

14. **Click the horizontal page ruler at the top of the page and drag down to create a guide positioned at the 1/4″ (0.25″) mark.**

If you watch the vertical ruler, you can see a marker indicating the position of the cursor. Live cursor feedback also shows the precise numeric position of the guide you are dragging.

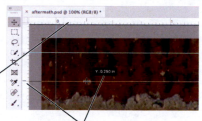

Click and drag from the horizontal ruler to add a horizontal guide.

Watch the ruler or cursor feedback to see the location of the guide you're dragging.

Note:

The X coordinate refers to an object's horizontal position and Y refers to the vertical position.

Note:

Use the Move tool to reposition placed guides. Remove individual guides by dragging them back onto the ruler.

If you try to reposition a guide and can't, choose View>Lock Guides. If this option is checked, guides are locked; you can't move them until you toggle this option off.

15. **Click the vertical ruler at the left and drag right to place a guide at the 0.25″ mark.**

Watch the marker on the horizontal ruler to judge the guide's position.

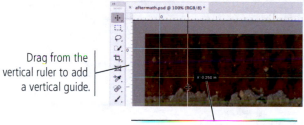

Drag from the vertical ruler to add a vertical guide.

Cursor feedback shows the X location of the guide you're dragging.

16. **Double-click the intersection of the two rulers.**

This resets the file's zero point to the original position (the top-left corner of the canvas).

Double-click the ruler intersection to reset the original zero point.

Note:

Press Option/Alt and click a guide to change it from vertical to horizontal (or vice versa). The guide rotates around the point where you click, which can be useful if you need to find a corner based on the position of an existing guide.

17. **Zoom out so you can see the entire canvas in the document window.**

18. **Choose View>New Guide. In the resulting dialog box, choose the Horizontal option, type 10.875 in the field, and then click OK.**

    This dialog box always measures the position of guides from the canvas's top-left corner, regardless of the zero point as reflected in the rulers.

19. **Choose View>New Guide again. Choose the Vertical option and type 8.375 in the field. Click OK.**

20. **Click the View menu and make sure a check mark appears to the left of Lock Guides. If no check mark is there, choose Lock Guides to toggle on that option.**

    After you carefully position specific guides, it's a good idea to lock them so you don't accidentally move or delete them later. If you need to move a guide at any point, simply choose View>Lock Guides to toggle off the option temporarily.

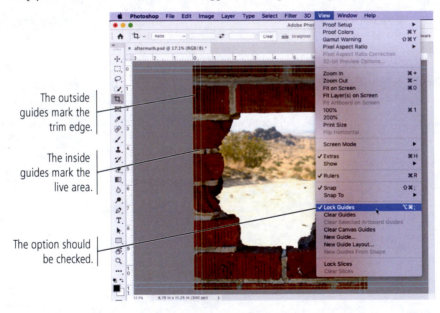

The outside guides mark the trim edge.

The inside guides mark the live area.

The option should be checked.

Note:

Press Command/ Control-; to toggle the visibility of page guides.

21. **Save the file and continue to the next exercise.**

    Because you have already saved this working file with a new name, you can simply choose File>Save, or press Command/Control-S to save without opening a dialog box. If you want to change the file name, you can always choose File>Save As.

When the Crop tool is selected, the Options bar can be used to define a number of settings related to the cropped area.

The menu on the left of the Options bar includes a number of common aspect ratio presets. If you choose one of these, the crop marquee is constrained to that aspect ratio. It's important to note that these presets define only the aspect ratio of the crop, not the size.

You can also choose the **W x H x Resolution** option to define custom settings for the result of a crop. For example, if you define the width and height of a crop area as 9" × 9" at 300 ppi, when you click and drag to draw, the crop area will be restricted to the same proportions defined in the Width and Height fields (in this example, 1:1).

When you finalize the crop, the resulting image will be resized to 9" × 9", regardless of the actual size of the crop marquee. This presents a problem if you remember the principles of resolution.

Enlarging a 3" × 3" area (for example) to 9" × 9" means the application needs to create enough pixels to fill in the 6 extra inches. At 300 ppi, Photoshop needs to create ("interpolate") more than 1800 pixels per linear inch. Although Photoshop can enlarge images with reasonable success, such a significant amount of new data will not result in the best possible quality. As a general rule, you should avoid enlarging raster images by such a large percentage.

The crop area is constrained to the aspect ratio of the defined width and height.

The resulting cropped image is the actual size defined in the Crop Image Size & Resolution dialog box.

You can use the **Set Overlay Options** menu (⌗) to show a variety of overlays within the crop area; these follow basic design principles, such as the Rule of Thirds and the Golden Spiral.

You can also use the commands in this menu to turn the overlay on or off. If you choose Auto Show Overlay, the selected overlay only appears when you drag the marquee handles or click inside the marquee area to move the image inside the crop area.

You can also click the **Set Additional Crop Options** button (⚙.) to access a variety of crop-related choices.

- If you check the **Use Classic Mode** option, the crop marquee reverts to the same appearance and behavior as in previous versions of Photoshop.

- When **Show Cropped Area** is checked, the area outside the crop marquee remains visible in the document window until you finalize the crop.

- When **Auto Center Preview** is checked, the crop area will always be centered in the document window. The image dynamically moves as you resize the crop area.

- When **Enable Crop Shield** is checked, areas outside the crop marquee are partially obscured by a semi-transparent solid color. You can use the related options to change the color and opacity of the shielded area.

When the Crop tool is selected, you can click the **Straighten** button in the Options bar, and then draw a line in the image to define what should be a straight line in the resulting image. The image behind the crop marquee rotates to show what will remain in the cropped canvas. The line you drew is adjusted to be perfectly horizontal or vertical.

Click the Straighten button, then draw a line representing what you want to be "straight" in the cropped image.

The image is rotated behind the crop marquee to be "straight" based on the line you drew.

You can draw a crop area larger than the existing canvas to effectively enlarge the canvas.

Using the default settings, new areas outside the original canvas size become transparent on regular layers, or filled with the background color on the locked Background layer.

If you check the **Content-Aware** option in the Options bar, Photoshop generates new pixels based on the existing image, filling the new pixels with content that better matches the previous image edges.

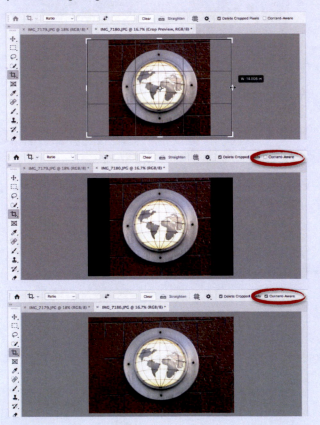

The **Perspective Crop tool** (nested under the Crop tool) can be used to draw a non-rectangular crop area. To define the area you want to keep, simply click to place the four corners of the area, and drag the corners in any direction as necessary. When you finalize the crop, the image inside the crop area is straightened to a front-on viewing angle. You should use this option with care, however, because it can badly distort an image.

In the following example, we used apparent lines in the photograph to draw the perspective crop marquee. After finalizing the crop, the building appears to be straight, rather than the original viewing angle at which it was photographed.

Drag a File to Composite Images

Compositing multiple images in Photoshop is a fairly simple process — or at least, it starts out that way. There are, of course, a number of technical and aesthetic issues that you must resolve when you combine multiple images in a single design.

Note:

When you created the background file for this project, you created a raster image that contains pixels. Digital photographs and scans are also pixel-based, which is why you use Photoshop to edit and manipulate those types of files.

1. **With aftermath.psd open, open the file Storm.jpg from your WIP>Movie folder.**

2. **With Storm.jpg the active file in the document window, open the Image Size dialog box (Image>Image Size).**

   Remember that you can press Command-Option-I/Control-Alt-I to open the dialog box.

   This image is only 180 ppi, but it has a physical size much larger than the defined ad size. As with the original bricks image, the principle of effective resolution might make this image usable in the composite ad.

3. **Click Cancel to close the Image Size dialog box.**

4. **Open the Window>Arrange menu and choose 2-up Vertical to show both open files at once.**

   As you saw in the Interface chapter, these options are useful for arranging and viewing multiple open files within your workspace.

5. **Choose the Move tool in the Tools panel.**

6. **Click in the Storm.jpg image window, drag into the aftermath.psd image window, and then release the mouse button.**

   Basic compositing can be as simple as dragging a selection from one file to another. If no active selection appears in the source document, this action moves the entire active layer from the source document.

Note:

On Windows, the cursor shows a plus sign to indicate that you are adding the image as a new layer in the document to which you dragged it.

Move tool

Click and drag from the Storm.jpg window into the aftermath.psd window.

7. **Click the Close button on the Storm.jpg document tab to close that file.**

   After closing the storm file, the aftermath.psd document window expands to fill the available space.

   If you remember from the Image Size dialog box, the storm image was 17.1″ × 11.4″ at 180 ppi. Photoshop cannot maintain multiple resolutions in a single file. When you move the image content into the aftermath file, it adopts the resolution of the target file (in this case, 300 ppi). The concept of effective resolution transforms the storm image/layer to approximately 10.25″ × 6.825″ at 300 ppi.

8. **Open the Layers panel (Window>Layers).**

   The original aftermath.psd file had only one layer — Background. Before editing, every scan and digital photograph has this characteristic. When you copy or drag content from one file into another, it is automatically placed on a new layer with the default name "Layer *n*," where "n" is a sequential number.

   The document tab shows the name of the active layer.

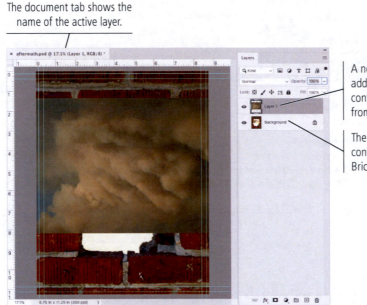

A new layer (Layer 1) is added to contain the contents that you dragged from the Storm.jpg file.

The Background layer contains the original Bricks.jpg file content.

9. **Choose File>Save and read the resulting message.**

   Because this is the first time you have saved the file after adding new layers, you should see the Photoshop Format Options dialog box with the Maximize Compatibility check box already activated. It's a good idea to leave this check box selected so that your files will be compatible with other Adobe applications and other versions of Photoshop.

Note:

If you don't see this warning, check the File Handling pane of the Preferences dialog box. You can set the Maximize PSD and PSB File Compatibility menu to Always, Never, or Ask.

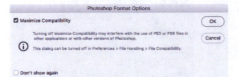

10. **Make sure the Maximize Compatibility check box is selected and click OK.**

11. **Continue to the next exercise.**

Copy and Paste Selected Pixels

In the previous exercise, you used the Move tool to drag an entire layer. You can also use a variety of selection tools to choose only certain areas of a layer that will be moved. In this exercise, you will use the most basic selection tool — the Rectangle Marquee tool.

1. **With aftermath.psd open, choose View>Fit on Screen to show the entire image centered in the document window.**

2. **Open the file Skyline.jpg from your WIP>Movie folder.**

3. **Choose the Rectangular Marquee tool in the Tools panel and review the options in the Options bar.**

   By default, dragging with a marquee tool creates a new selection. The buttons on the left end of the Options bar define what happens if you draw more than one marquee.

   A **New Selection** creates a new selection each time you create a new marquee.

   B **Add to Selection** adds the area of a new marquee to the existing selected area.

   C **Subtract from Selection** removes the new marquee area from the existing selection.

   D **Intersect with Selection** results in a selection only where a new marquee overlaps an existing selection.

   E **Feather** (soften) the edges of a selection by a specified number of pixels.

   F Choose a normal selection, a fixed-ratio selection, or a fixed-size selection.

   G When **Fixed Ratio** or **Fixed Size** is selected, enter the size of the selection in the **Width** and **Height** fields.

   H Click this button to reverse the Width and Height fields.

4. **Choose the New Selection option in the Options bar. Click outside of the top-left corner, drag down past the bottom edge of the image, and drag right to create a selection area that is approximately 8.5″ wide.**

   You can't select an area larger than the current canvas, so the top, left, and bottom edges of the selection snap to the canvas edges. The live cursor feedback, as well as the mark on the horizontal ruler, help to determine the selection area's width.

Note:

The edges of this image will be hidden by the bricks, so you don't need the full 8.75″ width of the overall ad.

Note:

Press Shift while dragging a new marquee to constrain the selection to a square (using the Rectangular Marquee tool) or circle (using the Elliptical Marquee tool).

Selection marquee

Rectangular Marquee tool cursor

5. **Click inside the selection marquee and drag it to the approximate center of the image.**

   When the New Selection option is active, you can move a selection marquee by clicking inside the selected area with the Marquee tool, and dragging to the desired area of the image.

   The live cursor feedback shows how far you have moved the area. The pink horizontal lines that appear as you drag are smart guides, which help you to reposition objects (including selection marquees) relative to other objects or the canvas.

The Marquee tool is still active.

"Marching ants" identify the selected area.

Click inside the marquee and drag to reposition it.

6. **In the Options bar, choose the Subtract from Selection option.**

7. **Click near the waterline at the left edge of the existing selection. Drag down past the bottom edge of the image, and right past the right edge of the existing selection.**

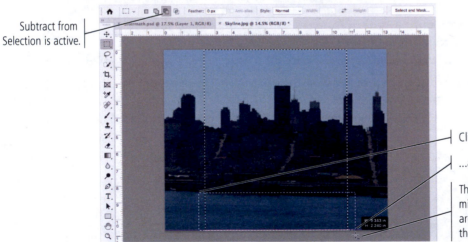

Subtract from Selection is active.

Click here...

...and drag to here.

The cursor shows a minus sign because you are subtracting from the existing selection.

You only want the city to appear in the ad, so you don't need the water area of this image. When you release the mouse button, the selection is the area of the first marquee, minus the area of the second marquee. (This two-step process isn't particularly necessary in this case, but you should know how to add to, and subtract from selections.)

8. **Choose Edit>Copy.**

   The standard Cut, Copy, and Paste options are available in Photoshop, just as they are in most applications. Whatever you have selected will be copied to the Clipboard, and whatever is in the Clipboard will be pasted.

9. **Click the Close button on the Skyline.jpg document tab to close the file. When asked, click Don't Save.**

10. **With the aftermath.psd file active, choose Edit>Paste.**

    The copied selection is pasted in the center of the document window. Because you used the Fit on Screen option at the beginning of this exercise, the pasted image is centered in the document. Another new layer is automatically created to store the pasted content.

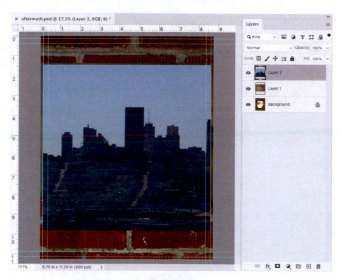

11. **Save the file and continue to the next exercise.**

Understanding Smart Guides

As you dragged the layer in the previous exercise, you might have noticed a series of pink lines appearing in different locations. These lines are a function of Smart Guides, which make it easier to align layer content to other layers or the overall canvas.

Smart Guides are active by default, but you can toggle them on and off in the View>Show submenu.

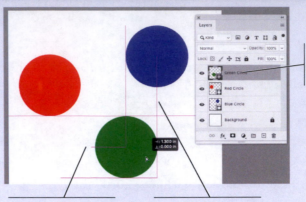

We dragged the Green Circle layer with the Move tool.

Smart Guides identify the center and edges of the overall canvas.

Smart Guides identify the center and edges of content on other layers.

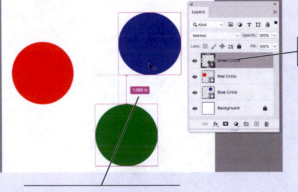

The Green Circle layer is selected.

Press Command/Control and hover over an object to find the distance between it and the selected layer.

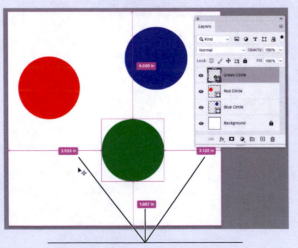

Press Command/Control and hover over the canvas to find the distance between the selected layer content and the canvas edges.

Rasterize a Vector File

Logos and title treatments — such as the ones you will use in this project — are commonly created as vector graphics. Although Photoshop is typically a pixel-based application, you can also open and work with vector graphics created in illustration programs like Adobe Illustrator.

1. **With aftermath.psd open, choose File>Open and navigate to your WIP>Movie folder.**

2. **Select Title.ai in the list of files and then click Open.**

   This is an Adobe Illustrator file of the movie title text treatment. The Format menu defaults to Photoshop PDF because Illustrator uses PDF as its underlying file structure.

3. **If the Width and Height fields show any unit other than Inches, open either menu and choose Inches.**

   When you open a vector file (Illustrator, EPS, or PDF) in Photoshop, it is rasterized (converted to a raster graphic). The resulting Import PDF dialog box allows you to determine exactly what and how to rasterize the file.

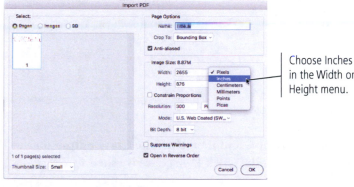

Choose Inches in the Width or Height menu.

   If you're opening a multipage PDF or an Illustrator file with more than one artboard, the preview window on the left side of the dialog box shows thumbnails of each "page" in the file. You can click a specific thumbnail to select anything other than Page 1. Press Shift and click to select multiple consecutive pages, or press Command/Control and click to select multiple, nonconsecutive pages.

   The Crop To options determine the outside dimensions of the opened file. Depending on how the file was created, some of these values might be the same as others:

   - **Bounding Box** is the outermost edges of the artwork in the file.
   - **Media Box** is the size of the paper as defined in the file.
   - **Crop Box** is the size of the page/artboard, including printer's marks.
   - **Bleed Box** is the trim size, plus any defined bleed allowance.
   - **Trim Box** is the trim size as defined in the file.
   - **Art Box** is the area of the page as defined in the file.

4. **Make sure the Constrain Proportions option is checked. Highlight the Width field and type 8, and make sure the Resolution field is set to 300 pixels/inch.**

The Image Size fields default to the settings of the bounding box you select. You can change the size, resolution, color mode, and bit depth by entering new values.

You know the live area of the ad you're building is 8″ wide, so you can import this file at a size small enough to fit into that space. Because the Constrain Proportions option is checked by default, the height changes proportionally to match the new width.

Check this option to maintain the file's original aspect ratio.

5. **Click OK.**

The title treatment file opens in Photoshop. The checkered area behind the text indicates that the background is transparent. If you look at the Layers panel, you see that Layer 1 isn't locked. It is transparent, and it is not considered a background layer.

6. **Choose Select>All.**

This command creates a marquee for the entire canvas.

Using the Select>All command surrounds the entire canvas in a selection marquee.

The gray-and-white checked pattern identifies areas of transparency in the layer content.

7. **Choose Edit>Copy, and then click the Close button on the Title document tab to close that file. Click Don't Save if asked.**

8. **With the aftermath.psd file active, choose Edit>Paste.**

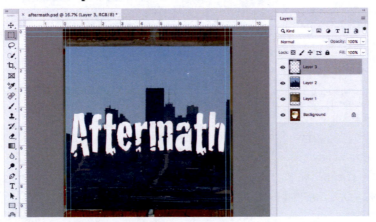

9. **Save aftermath.psd and continue to the next exercise.**

Note:

Command/Control-clicking a layer thumbnail results in a selection around the contents of that layer.

Place Files as Smart Object Layers

As you have seen in the last few exercises, copying layer content from one file to another results in new regular layers for the pasted content. Photoshop also supports Smart Object layers, in which you place one file into another instead of pasting layer content. Smart Objects provide a number of advantages over regular layers, which you will explore later in this project. In this exercise, you will create the Smart Object layers for the remaining image elements.

1. **With aftermath.psd open, choose File>Place Embedded.**

   Two options in the File menu — Place Embedded and Place Linked — give you the option to embed the placed file data into active file, or to place smart objects as links to the original placed file. (See Page 51 for more about placing linked files.)

2. **Choose the Lightning.jpg file (in your WIP>Movie folder) and click Place.**

   The placed file appears with bounding-box handles and crossed diagonal lines. The placement isn't final until you press Return/Enter. If you press the Escape key, the file will not be placed.

   In the Options bar, you can see that the placed image has been scaled to approximately 45% to fit into the document where it is being placed.

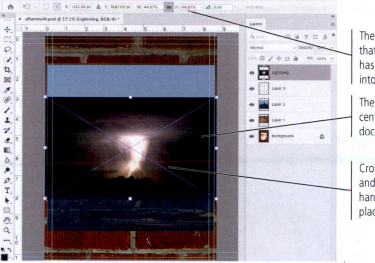

The Options bar shows that the placed image has been scaled to fit into the active canvas.

The placed image is centered in the document window.

Crossed diagonal lines and bounding-box handles indicate that the placement is not yet final.

3. **Press Return/Enter to finalize the placement.**

   After you finalize the placement, the bounding-box handles and crossed diagonal lines disappear. In the Layers panel, the placed file has its own layer (just as the copied layers do). This layer, however, is automatically named, based on the name of the placed file.

   The layer's thumbnail indicates that this layer is a **Smart Object** — it is linked to the file that you placed. Changes in the original file will also be reflected in the file in which the original is placed.

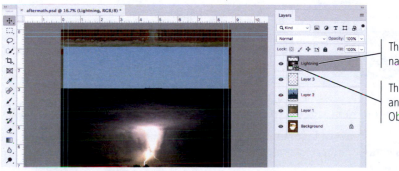

The layer adopts the name of the placed file.

This icon identifies an embedded Smart Object layer.

Note:

If you check **Skip Transform when Placing** *in the General pane of the Preferences dialog box, you will not see the diagonal lines and transform handles when you first place a Smart Object layer.*

4. **Choose File>Place Embedded again. Select Rating.ai and click Place.**

   Vector graphics offer several advantages over raster images, including sharper edges and free scaling without deteriorating image quality. To take advantage of these benefits, you might want to maintain vector files as vector objects instead of rasterizing them. Photoshop gives you the option to do exactly that — maintaining vector information and raster information in the same file.

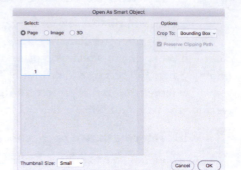

5. **In the resulting Open as Smart Object dialog box, choose Bounding Box in the Crop To menu, and then click OK.**

   Because this is a native Illustrator file (identified by the ".ai" extension), you have the same Crop To options as when you actually open an Illustrator file in Photoshop.

6. **In the Options bar, change the W and H fields to 100%. Press Return/ Enter to finalize the change.**

   Placed files are not always scaled exactly proportionally. It's a good idea to check and (if necessary) restore the original height-to-width aspect ratio.

   Change both fields to 100%.

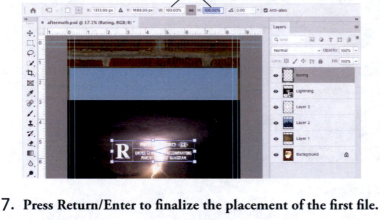

7. **Press Return/Enter to finalize the placement of the first file.**

8. **Repeat Steps 4–7 to place Tantamount.ai as a Smart Object layer.**

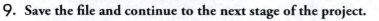

   The three placed files are stored on layers with names based on the placed file names.

   The placed files are Smart Object layers.

9. **Save the file and continue to the next stage of the project.**

   Right now, you have an unorganized mess of four raster images and three embedded Smart Objects all piled on top of one another. You will start to make sense of these files in the next stage of this project.

Note:

Smart Objects provide extremely tight integration between Adobe Photoshop and Adobe Illustrator. You can take advantage of the sophisticated vector-editing features in Adobe Illustrator, and then place those files into Photoshop without losing the ability to edit the vector information.

Note:

Unfortunately, you can only place one file at a time using the Place dialog box.

Working with Embedded and Linked Smart Objects

In this project you used the Place Embedded option to create Smart Object layers containing the placed file data. In this case the embedded file data becomes a part of the parent file.

If you double-click the thumbnail icon of an embedded Smart Object, the embedded file opens in an application that can edit the stored data — AI files open in Illustrator; PSD, TIFF, and JPEG files open in Photoshop.

When you first open a Smart Object file, the application provides advice for working with Smart Objects:

After you make necessary changes, you can save the file and close it, and then return to Photoshop (if necessary). Your changes in the Smart Object file will automatically reflect in the parent file where the Smart Object layer is placed.

Important note: Do not use the Save As option when editing Smart Object layers. The changes will not reflect in the parent file if you save changes with a different file name.

If you choose the Place Linked option in the File menu, Smart Object layer stores a link to the original file data rather than embedding that data inside the parent file.

This icon identifies a linked Smart Object layer.

This provides an opportunity for maintaining consistency because you only need to change one instance of a file to reflect those changes anywhere the file is placed.

Say you place a logo created in Illustrator into a Photoshop file. The same logo is also placed as a link in an InDesign file. If you open the logo in Illustrator and change the main color (for example), when you save the changes in the original logo file, the new color automatically reflects in any file — whether InDesign or Photoshop — that is linked to the edited logo.

If you use the Place Embedded option in Photoshop, the Smart Object layer is not linked to the original, edited logo file; you would have to open the embedded Smart Object and make the same color change a second time.

Linked files also have potential disadvantages. As we mentioned previously, double-clicking a Smart Object layer thumbnail opens the linked or embedded file in an application that can edit the relevant data. If you are working with *linked* Smart Object layers, any changes you make affect the original file data. This means your changes appear not only in the parent Photoshop file where it is linked, but also in any other file that links to the same data.

For a file to output properly, linked Smart Object layers must be present and up to date at the time of output.

If the linked file has been modified while the parent file is open, the changes automatically reflect in the parent file when you return to that document. If the parent file is not open in Photoshop when the linked file is edited, you will see a Modified icon for the linked Smart Object layer.

If the linked file is deleted or moved to another location after it has been placed, the parent file will show a Missing icon for the linked Smart Object layer.

If a linked Smart Object has been moved while the parent file is not open, you will see a warning dialog box when you open the parent Photoshop file. You can use that dialog box to locate the missing link, or close it and use the options in the Layers panel to correct the problem.

Control/right-clicking a linked Smart Object layer name opens a contextual menu with options to update modified content and resolve broken links.

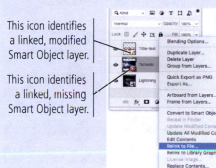

This icon identifies a linked, modified Smart Object layer.

This icon identifies a linked, missing Smart Object layer.

To avoid potential problems with missing linked files, you can use the File>Package command to create a job folder. The parent file is copied to a new folder, along with a Links subfolder containing any files placed as linked Smart Object layers.

STAGE 2 / Managing Layers

When you composite images into a cohesive design, you almost certainly need to manipulate and transform some of the layers to make all of the pieces work together. Photoshop includes a number of options for managing layers: naming layers for easier recognition, creating layer groups so multiple layers can be manipulated at once, moving layers around on the canvas, transforming layers both destructively and nondestructively, controlling individual layer visibility, and arranging the top-to-bottom stacking order of layers to determine exactly what is visible. You will use all of these options in this stage of the project.

Name Layers and Layer Groups

It's always a good idea to name your layers because it makes managing the file much easier — especially when you work with files that include dozens of layers. Even with only four unnamed layers in this file (counting the Background layer), it would be tedious to have to toggle each layer on to find the one you want.

1. **With aftermath.psd open, review the Layers panel.**

2. **Option/Alt-click the Eye icon for Layer 1 to hide all other layers.**

   Toggling layer visibility is an easy way to see only what you want to see at any given stage in a project.

   Clicking the Eye icon for a specific layer hides that layer. Clicking the empty space where the Eye icon should be shows the hidden layer. To show or hide a series of consecutive layers, click the visibility icon (or empty space) for the first layer you want to affect, hold down the mouse button, and drag down to the last layer you want to show or hide.

The checked pattern shows transparent areas of the visible layer(s).

Click an empty space to show a hidden layer.

Click the Eye icons to hide individual layers.

Option/Alt-click an Eye icon to hide all other layers.

3. **Double-click the Layer 1 layer name, and then type Storm. Press Return/Enter to finalize the new layer name.**

   You can rename any layer by simply double-clicking the name and typing.

Double-click the layer name to access it.

Press Return/Enter after typing to finalize the new name.

4. **Click the Eye icon to hide the renamed Storm layer, and then click the empty space to the left of Layer 2 to show only that layer.**

5. **Double-click the Layer 2 name, and then type Skyline. Press Return/Enter to finalize the new layer name.**

6. **Repeat Steps 4–5 to rename Layer 3 as Title.**

7. **Click the spaces on the left side of the Layers panel (where the Eye icons were) to show all hidden layers.**

8. **In the Layers panel, click the Tantamount layer to select it.**

9. **Press Shift and click the Rating layer to select that layer as well.**

   Since the Tantamount layer was already selected, the Rating layer should now be a second selected (highlighted) layer.

Note:

Press Shift and click to select consecutive layers in the Layers panel.

Press Command/Control and click to select non-consecutive layers in the Layers panel.

10. **With the two layers selected, click the Create a New Group button at the bottom of the panel.**

    This button creates a group that automatically contains the selected layers. The new group is automatically named, "Group N" (where N is simply a sequential number). Of course, you can rename a layer group just as easily as you can rename a layer.

Click here to open the panel Options menu.

Two layers are selected.

Create a New Group button

The new group automatically contains the selected layers.

Note:

You can also choose New Group from Layers in the panel Options menu.

To create a new empty layer group, make sure nothing is selected in the Layers panel before clicking the Create a New Group button. Alternatively, choose New Group in the panel Options menu; this option results in an empty layer group even if layers are currently selected.

11. **Double-click the Group 1 name in the Layers panel to highlight it, then type Logos. Press Return/Enter to finalize the new layer group name.**

As with any other layer, you should name groups based on what they contain so you can easily identify them later.

Note:

You can create up to ten levels of nested layer groups, or groups inside of other groups.

12. **Click the arrow to the left of the Logos group name to expand the layer group.**

You have to expand the layer group to be able to access and edit individual layers in the group. If you select the entire layer group, you can move all layers within the group at the same time. Layers in the group maintain their position relative to one another.

Note:

You can click the Eye icon for a layer folder to hide the entire layer group (and all layers inside the folder).

13. **Save the file and continue to the next exercise.**

Move and Transform Smart Object Layers

Photoshop makes scaling, rotating, and other transformations fairly easy to implement, but it is important to realize the potential impact of your transformations.

1. **With aftermath.psd open, click the Tantamount layer (in the Logos folder) in the Layers panel to select only that layer.**

2. **Choose the Move tool in the Tools panel.**

As the name suggests, the Move tool is used to move a selection around on the canvas. You can select a specific area, and then click and drag to move only the selection on the active layer. If there is no active selection area, you can click and drag to move the contents of the entire active layer.

Note:

Deselect all layers by clicking in the empty area at the bottom of the Layers panel.

3. **In the Options bar, make sure the Auto-Select option is not checked.**

When Auto-Select is checked, you can click in the image window and drag to move the contents of the layer containing the pixels where you click; you do not need to first select the layer in the Layers panel before moving the layer content. This is very useful in some cases, as you will see later in this project. However, the Auto-Select option is *not* very useful when the contents of multiple layers are stacked on top of each other (as is the case with your file as it exists now).

4. **Click in the image window and drag until the Tantamount layer content snaps to the bottom-right live-area guides.**

   If you toggled off the Snap feature when you used the Crop tool, you should turn it back on now by choosing View>Snap.

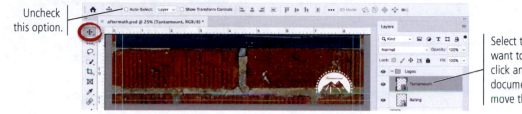

Uncheck this option.

Select the layer you want to move, then click and drag in the document window to move the layer content.

5. **Click the Rating layer in the Layers panel to select it.**

6. **Click in the image window and drag until the Rating layer content snaps to the bottom-left live-area guides.**

7. **With the Rating layer still active, choose Edit>Free Transform.**

   When you use the transform options, bounding-box handles surround the selection in the document window. The Options bar gives you a number of options for controlling the transformations numerically:

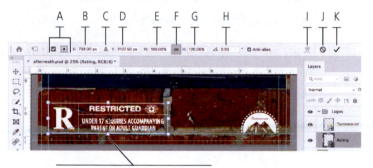

Bounding-box handles surround the content that is being transformed.

   A Reference Point Location. This determines the point around which numeric transformations are made. It defaults to the center point. To choose a different point, you have to check the related box.

   B Set Horizontal Position of Reference Point. This is the X position of the reference point for the content being transformed. If the center reference point is selected, for example, this is the X position of the center point of the active content.

   C Use Relative Positioning for Reference Point. If this option is active, the Set Horizontal Position and Set Vertical Position fields default to 0; changing these values moves the reference point by the value you type. For example, typing "–25" in the Set Horizontal Position field moves the active content 25 pixels to the left.

   D Set Vertical Position of Reference Point. This is the Y position of the reference point for the content being transformed.

   E Set Horizontal Scale. Use this field to change the content's horizontal scale percentage.

   F Maintain Aspect Ratio. When active, the horizontal scale and vertical scale fields are locked to have the same value.

   G Set Vertical Scale. Use this field to change the content's vertical scale percentage.

   H Rotate. Use this field to rotate the transformed content by a specific angle.

   I Switch Between Free Transform and Warp Modes. If available, click this button to apply a built-in warp to the active selection.

   J Cancel Transform. Click this button (or press the Esc key) to exit Free Transform mode without applying any transformation.

   K Commit Transform. Click this button (or press Return/Enter) to finalize the transformation that you applied while in Free Transform mode. You can also simply click away from the area in the bounding box to finalize the transformation.

Note:

You can also use the Edit>Transform sub-menu to apply specific transformations to a layer or selection.

8. **Click the top-right bounding-box handle, and then drag down and left until the layer content is approximately two-thirds the original size.**

The selection (in this case, the entire Rating layer) dynamically changes as you scale the layer.

When you drag the handles to transform a selection, Photoshop automatically constrains the selection's aspect ratio (height-to-width proportions) as you drag. You can press Shift while you drag a handle to transform the selection nonproportionally.

When you release the mouse button, the handles remain in place until you finalize ("commit") the transformation.

Click and drag a handle to scale the content proportionally.

Manual transformations in the document window reflect in the Options bar fields.

While you're manually transforming a layer or selection, the Options bar shows the specifics. You can also type into these fields to apply specific numeric transformations.

9. **Press Return/Enter to finalize the transformation.**

After finalizing the transformation, the bounding-box handles disappear.

10. **With the Rating layer still active, press Command/Control-T to enter Free Transform mode again and look at the Options bar.**

Because the rating layer is a Smart Object layer, the W and H fields still show the scaling percentage based on the original.

11. **On the left side of the Options bar, check the box for the Reference Point option and then choose the bottom-left reference point.**

The reference point, which defaults to the center point, is the point around which numeric transformations are made. To choose a different reference point, you must first activate the check box in the Option bar, and then choose the desired point in the 9-square proxy.

Activate the Reference Point option...

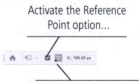

then choose a reference point.

12. **With the Maintain Aspect Ratio option active, highlight the existing Set Horizontal Scale value, and then type 50.**

Because you selected the bottom-left point, the bottom-left corner of the active selection remains in place when you scale the selection. The top-right corner moves based on the scaling you define.

With Maintain Aspect Ratio active, changing one scale value applies the same value to the other scale field.

The bottom-left reference point is selected.

Maintain Aspect Ratio is active.

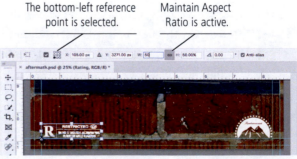

13. **Click the Commit Transform button on the Options bar (or press Return/Enter) to finalize the transformation.**

   If you press Return/Enter, you have to press it twice to finalize the transformation. The first time you press it, you apply the change to the active field; the second time, you finalize the transformation and exit Free Transform mode.

14. **Collapse the layer group by clicking the arrow at the left of the group name.**

15. **Save the file and continue to the next exercise.**

Transform a Regular Layer

Smart Object layers enable nondestructive transformations, which means those transformations can be changed or undone without affecting the quality of the layer content. Transforming a regular layer, on the other hand, is destructive and permanent.

1. **With aftermath.psd open, hide all but the Storm layer. Click the Storm layer in the Layers panel to select it.**

2. **Using the Move tool, drag the layer content so it is centered on the canvas.**

3. **Choose Edit>Transform>Flip Horizontal.**

   The Transform submenu commands affect only the selected layer.

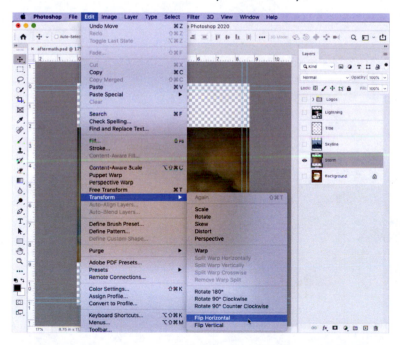

4. **Press Command/Control-T to enter Free Transform mode.**

   Some handles might not be visible within the boundaries of the document window. If necessary, zoom out so you can see all eight handles of the layer content.

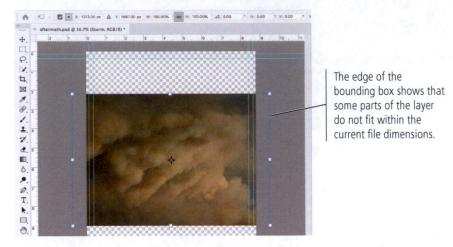

The edge of the bounding box shows that some parts of the layer do not fit within the current file dimensions.

5. **In the Options bar, click the Maintain Aspect Ration button to make that option active.**

6. **Place the cursor over the W field label to access the scrubby slider for that field.**

   When you see the scrubby slider cursor, you can drag right to increase or drag left to decrease the value in the related field.

The center reference point is selected by default.

Maintain Aspect Ratio is active.

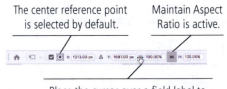

Place the cursor over a field label to access the scrubby slider for that field.

7. **Click and drag left until the W field shows 90%.**

8. **Press Return/Enter to finalize the transformation.**

9. **With the Storm layer still active, press Command/Control-T to re-enter Free Transform mode.**

Once you commit the transformation on a regular layer, the transformation is final. Looking at the Options bar now, you can see that it shows the layer at 100%, instead of the 90% from Step 7.

If you transform a Smart Object layer, the scale percentage is maintained even after you finalize the change, unlike scaling a regular layer, where the layer recalibrates so the new size is considered 100% once you finalize the scaling.

10. **Press Esc to exit Free Transform mode without changing anything.**

11. **Save the file and continue to the next exercise.**

Transform the Background Layer

Your file currently has a number of layers, most of which were created by pasting or placing external files into the original file. Because every photograph and scan (and some images that you create from scratch in Photoshop) begins with a default locked Background layer, it is important to understand the special characteristics of that layer:

- You can't apply layer transformations, styles, or masks to the Background layer.

- You can't move the contents of the Background layer around in the document.

- If you delete pixels from the Background layer, you must determine the color that will be used in place of the deleted pixels.

- The Background layer cannot include transparent pixels, which are necessary for underlying layers to be visible.

- The Background layer is always the bottom layer in the stacking order. You can't add or move layers lower than the Background layer.

In the final composite file for this project, you need to flip the bricks image from top to bottom, and remove the background pixels from inside the hole in the bricks. For either of these options to work properly, you need to convert the default Background layer to a regular layer.

Note:

If you crop an image that includes a Background layer, the Background layer is automatically converted to a regular layer if the Delete Cropped Pixels option is not checked.

1. **With aftermath.psd open, hide the Storm layer and then show the Background layer.**

2. **Click the Background layer to select it and then choose Edit>Transform.**

   The Transform submenu commands are not available for the locked Background layer.

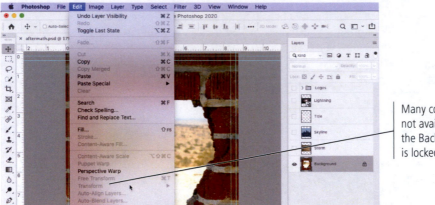

Many commands are not available because the Background layer is locked.

3. **With the Background layer still selected, choose Image>Image Rotation> Flip Canvas Vertical.**

   To affect the locked background layer, you have to flip the actual canvas.

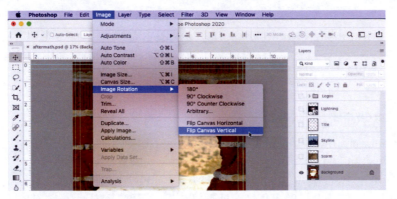

Note:

Although the Background layer exists by default in many files, it is not a required component.

4. **Show the Logos layer group.**

   Because you flipped the canvas, the Tantamount and Ratings layers are also flipped upside-down. Rotating or flipping the entire canvas affects all layers in the file; this is obviously not what you want to do.

Because you flipped the canvas, the logos are now upside-down.

Showing the layer group shows all layers in that group.

5. Choose Edit>Undo Layer Visibility.

The Undo command affects the last action you performed. The actual Undo menu command changes to reflect the action that will be undone.

6. Choose Edit>Undo Flip Canvas Vertical.

Photoshop supports multiple Undo commands. You can use the Undo command to step back through multiple actions.

7. In the Layers panel, click the Lock icon on the Background layer.

Clicking the Lock icon unlocks the layer and immediately converts the previous Background layer to a regular layer named "Layer 0."

Click the Lock icon to unlock the Background layer.

The layer is automatically converted to a regular layer named Layer 0.

8. Double-click the Layer 0 layer name to highlight it, then type Bricks to rename the layer. Press Return/Enter to finalize the new layer name.

9. With the Bricks layer selected in the panel, choose Edit>Transform>Flip Vertical.

Because the layer is no longer locked, you can now access and apply the transform commands that affect only the selected layer.

10. Show all layers in the file.

Because you flipped only the selected layer, the Tantamount and Ratings layers are not flipped; they appear in the correct position and orientation.

11. Choose View>Show>Guides to toggle off the visibility of the page guides.

Page guides are very useful for compositing elements in relation to overall project requirements, but at times they can be distracting. You can always toggle them back on if you need them.

12. Save the file and continue to the next stage of the project.

In addition to using the Undo command to step back through each previous action, you can use the use the History panel (Window>History) to navigate back to earlier stages.

Every action you take is recorded as a state in the History panel. You can click any state to return to that particular point in the document progression. You can also delete specific states, or create a new document from a particular state using the buttons at the bottom of the panel.

By default, the History panel stores the last 50 states; older states are automatically deleted. You can change that setting in the Performance pane of the Preferences dialog box. Keep in mind, however, that storing a larger number of states will increase the memory that is required to work with a specific file.

Keep the following in mind when using the History panel:

- The default snapshot is the image state when it was first opened.

- The oldest state is at the top of the list. The most recent state appears at the bottom.

- You can save any particular state as a snapshot to prevent it from being deleted when that state is no longer within the number of states that can be stored.

- The history is only stored while the file is open. When you close a file, the history and snapshots are not saved.

- When you select a specific state, the states below it are dimmed so you can see which changes will be discarded if you go back to a particular history state.

- Selecting a state, and then changing the image eliminates all states that come after it.

- Deleting a state deletes that state and those after it. If you choose Allow Non-Linear History in the History Options dialog box (accessed in the History panel Options menu), deleting a state deletes only that state.

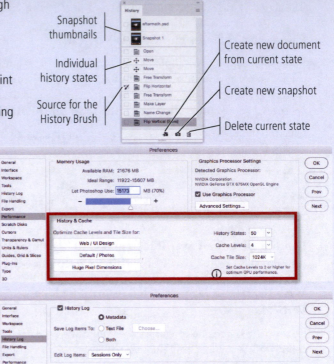

If you need to keep a record of a file's history even after you close the file, you can activate the History Log option in the History Log pane of the Preferences dialog box. When this option is checked, you can save the history log as metadata, in a text file, or both. You can also determine the level of detail that will be recorded in the history log.

- Sessions Only records each time you launch or quit, and each time you open and close individual files.

- Concise adds the text that appears in the History panel to the Sessions information.

- Detailed gives you a complete history of all changes made to files.

STAGE 3 / Creating Complex Selections

At this stage of the project, you still have a few issues to resolve: some of the images are still randomly stacked on top of one another, and some have areas that are hiding other images (the blue sky in the Skyline layer, for example). In this stage, you start fixing these problems.

Virtually any Photoshop project involves making some kind of selection. Making selections is so important, in fact, that there are no fewer than nine tools dedicated specifically to this goal, as well as a whole Select menu, and a few other options for making and refining selections.

In an earlier lesson you learned how to use the Rectangular Marquee tool to draw simple selections. In the next series of exercises, you use several other selection methods to isolate pixels from their backgrounds, called **silhouetting**.

Make a Feathered Selection in a Smart Object

Smart Object layers are actually links to the files that are placed. If you open the linked file and make changes, those changes are automatically reflected in the file in which the Smart Object layer exists. In this exercise, you will explore one of the advantages and disadvantages of Smart Object layers.

1. **With aftermath.psd open, hide all but the Lightning layer.**

2. **Double-click the Lightning layer thumbnail to open the Smart Object file in its own window. If you see a warning message, click OK.**

   This message tells you that you must save the Smart Object with the same name for the changes to reflect in the aftermath file. You can't use the Save As function to save the file with a different name or in a different location.

   Note:

   If you don't see this message, you can open the General pane of the Preferences dialog box and click the Reset All Warning Dialogs button.

Double-click the Smart Object layer thumbnail to open the linked file.

   The Lightning.jpg file opens separately, appearing by default as a separate tab at the top of the document window. This is a JPEG file, which means it is a flat file with only a locked Background layer.

The Lightning image is a flat image, which means it has only a Background layer that is locked.

3. Close the Lightning.jpg file.

Your goal in this exercise is to create a transparent area around the actual lightning bolt.

Flat files (including JPEG) do not support transparency. To save the file with transparency, you should save it as a native Photoshop file with the PSD extension. However, as the warning message indicated, you must save the Smart Object file with the same name — which includes the file extension.

Because you can't save transparency in a JPEG file, you need to break the link to the original JPEG file before you can create that transparency in the composite file.

Note:

If the original placed file was a native Photoshop file, you would not need to rasterize the Smart Object layer to accomplish your goal.

4. With aftermath.psd still open, Control/right-click the Lightning layer name in the Layers panel. Choose Rasterize Layer in the contextual menu.

Rasterizing the Smart Object basically removes the link to any external file, making the Smart Object a part of the file in which it has been placed.

Control/right-click the layer name to open the layer's contextual menu.

After rasterizing, the thumbnail shows that Lightning is now a regular image layer.

5. Select the Lasso tool in the Tools panel.

6. Zoom in so you can clearly see the lightning in the image, and then drag a rough shape around the lightning in the photo.

The Lasso tools allow you to make irregular selections — selections that aren't just rectangular or elliptical. When you release the mouse button, the end point automatically connects to the beginning point of the selection.

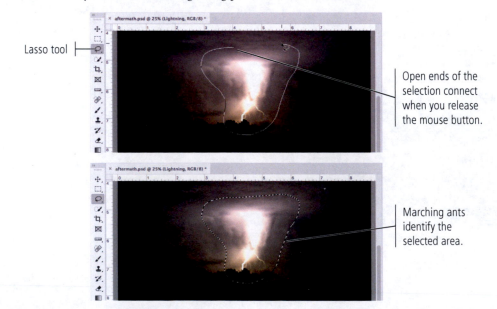

Lasso tool

Open ends of the selection connect when you release the mouse button.

Marching ants identify the selected area.

7. **With the marching ants active, choose Select>Modify>Feather.**

Photoshop offers a number of options for modifying an existing selection marquee.

- **Select>Grow** expands the selection to include all adjacent pixels that fall within the tolerance defined for the Magic Wand tool.

- **Select>Similar** expands the selection to include all pixels throughout the image that fall within the tolerance range, even if they are not adjacent to the active selection.

- **Select>Transform Selection** shows bounding-box handles around the selection marquee, which you can use to transform the selection as you would transform layer content.

In the Select>Modify menu:

- **Border** creates a selection of a defined number of pixels around the edge of the active marquee.

- **Smooth** helps to clean up stray pixels at the edge of a selection. Within a defined radius from the selection edge, pixels with less than half of the surrounding pixels are excluded from the selection.

- **Expand** and **Contract** enlarge and shrink, respectively, a selection by a defined number of pixels.

- **Feather** creates a blended edge to the active selection area.

8. **In the resulting dialog box, type 35 in the Feather Radius field. Click OK to return to the image window.**

Feathering means to soften the edge of a selection so the image blends into the background, instead of showing a sharp line around the edge. The Feather Radius defines the distance from solid to transparent. In the image window, there's no apparent difference in the selection because the marching ants can't show shades of a selection.

9. **Click the Edit in Quick Mask button at the bottom of the Tools panel to toggle into Quick Mask mode.**

This mode creates a temporary red overlay that identifies unselected areas. By default, the overlay is semi-transparent, which allows you to see the underlying image.

The semi-transparent overlay shows the smooth transition that was created by feathering the selection.

Edit in Quick Mask button

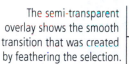

10. **Click the Edit in Standard Mode button at the bottom of the Tools panel to toggle off the Quick Mask.**

When Quick Mask mode is active, the Edit in Quick Mask mode toggles to become the Edit in Standard Mode button.

Note:

*You could also create a feathered selection by typing in the Feather field of the Options bar **before** drawing the selection marquee.*

Keep in mind, however, that if you draw a feathered selection (using the tool option setting), you can't undo the feather without also undoing the selection area.

11. **Choose Select>Inverse.**

    To remove the area around the lightning, you have to select everything *other than* what you originally selected — in other words, the inverse of the previous selection.

Note:

Press Command/Control-Shift-I to invert the active selection.

Marching ants surround the image edge and the original selection.

The area between the two marquees is the current selection.

12. **With the Lightning layer selected in the Layers panel, press Delete/Backspace.**

    Selection marquees are not particular to a specific layer. You have to make sure the correct layer is active before you use the selection to perform some action.

Only the active layer is affected by the deletion.

Pixels in the selection area are permanently removed from the layer.

13. **Choose Select>Deselect to turn off the active selection (marching ants).**

14. **Save the file and continue to the next exercise.**

Understanding the Lasso Tool Variations

The **Polygonal Lasso tool** creates selections with straight lines, anchoring a line each time you click. To close a selection area, click the first point in the selection.

The **Magnetic Lasso tool** snaps to high-contrast edges. You can use the Options bar to control the way Photoshop detects edges:

- **Width** is the distance from the edge the cursor can be and still detect edges; set this higher to move the cursor farther from edges.

- **Contrast** is how different the foreground can be from the background and still be detected; if there is a sharp distinction between the foreground and background, you can set this value higher.

- **Frequency** is the number of points that will be created to make the selection; setting this number higher creates finer selections, while setting it lower creates smoother edges.

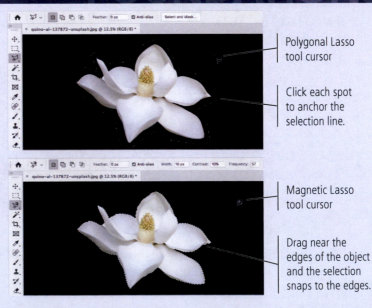

Polygonal Lasso tool cursor

Click each spot to anchor the selection line.

Magnetic Lasso tool cursor

Drag near the edges of the object and the selection snaps to the edges.

Understanding Channels

You need a bit of background about channels to understand what's happening in the Quick Mask you will use in the next exercise. (You will use channels extensively in later projects.)

Every image has one channel for each component color. Each channel contains the information for the amount of that component color in any given pixel. An RGB image has three channels: Red, Green, and Blue (right top). A CMYK image has four channels: Cyan, Magenta, Yellow, and Black (right bottom).

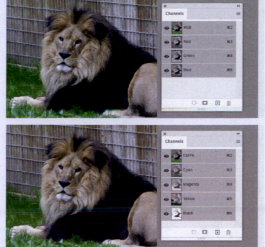

In RGB images, the three additive primaries can have a value of 0 (none of that color) to 255 (full intensity of that color). Combining a value of 255 for each primary results in white. A value of 0 for each primary results in black.

In CMYK images, the three subtractive primaries plus black are combined in percentages from 0 (none of that color) to 100 (full intensity of that color) to create the range of printable colors. Channels in a CMYK image represent the printing plates or separations required to output the job.

Understanding Alpha Channels

An Alpha channel is a special type of channel, in which the value determines the degree of transparency of a pixel. In other words, a 50% value in the Alpha channel means that area of the image will be 50% transparent.

When working in Quick Mask mode, a temporary Quick Mask channel stores the degree of transparency based on the current selection. A semi-transparent red overlay shows areas being masked (i.e., the areas that are not included in the current selection).

You can save a Quick Mask channel as a permanent Alpha channel by dragging the Quick Mask channel onto the New Channel button at the bottom of the panel. This adds a channel named "Quick Mask copy," which remains even if you exit Quick Mask mode. You can then double-click the Alpha channel name in the panel to rename it, as we did in the following image (naming the channel "Lion Head").

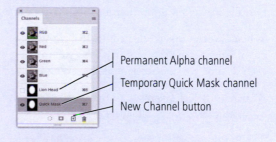

Permanent Alpha channel

Temporary Quick Mask channel

New Channel button

You can change the appearance of an Alpha channel mask by double-clicking a channel thumbnail in the Channels panel. In the top half of the resulting dialog box, you can change the overlay to show selected areas instead of the default masked areas.

Clicking the Color swatch opens a Color Picker, where you can change the color of the Quick Mask overlay.

Quick Masks are useful when you need to work with a temporary selection, or if you are still defining the exact selection area. As long as you stay in Quick Mask mode, the temporary Alpha channel remains in the Channels panel (listed as "Quick Mask"). If you return to Standard mode, the Quick Mask disappears from the window and the panel.

You can also use the Opacity field to change the transparency of the overlay (the default is 50%). Keep in mind that these settings only affect the appearance of the mask in Photoshop; the density of the selection is not affected by changing the overlay opacity.

Select a Color Range and Create a Layer Mask

Many images have both hard and soft edges, and/or very fine detail that needs to be isolated from its background (think of a model's blowing hair overlapping the title on the cover of a magazine). In this type of image, more sophisticated selection tools can be used to create a very detailed selection based on the color in the image.

Rather than simply deleting pixels, as you did for the lightning image, another option for isolating an object with a path is to create a **layer mask** that hides unwanted pixels. Areas outside the mask are hidden, but not deleted, so you can later edit the mask to change the visible part of the image.

1. **With aftermath.psd open, hide all but the Skyline layer. Click the Skyline layer to make it active.**

2. **Choose the Magic Wand tool (under the Object Selection tool). In the Options bar, make sure the New Selection button is active and set the Tolerance field to 32.**

   The Magic Wand tool is an easy way to select large areas of solid color. The first four options in the Options bar are the same as those for the Marquee tools (New Selection, Add to Selection, Subtract from Selection, and Intersect with Selection).

   Tolerance is the degree of variation between the color you click and the colors Photoshop will select. Higher tolerance values select a larger range based on the color you click. If you're trying to select a very mottled background, for example, you should increase the tolerance. Be careful, however, because increasing the tolerance might select too large a range of colors if parts of the foreground object fall within the tolerance range.

   The **Anti-alias** check box, selected by default, allows edges to blend more smoothly into the background, preventing a jagged, stair-stepped appearance.

   When **Contiguous** is selected, the Magic Wand tool only selects adjacent areas of the color. Unchecking this option allows you to select all pixels within the color tolerance, even if some are noncontiguous (for example, inside the shape of the letter Q).

   By default, selections relate to the active layer only. You can check **Sample All Layers** to make a selection of all layers in the file.

   The **Refine Edge** button opens a dialog box where you can use a number of tools to fine-tune the selection edge.

   Note:

   Anti-aliasing is the process of blending shades of pixels to create the illusion of sharp lines in a raster image.

3. **Click anywhere in the blue sky area of the image.**

New Selection is active.

Magic Wand tool

Marching ants indicate the selection area.

Fine detail can't be distinguished by marching ants.

4. **Choose Select>Deselect to turn off the current selection.**

   Although you could keep adding to the selection with the Magic Wand tool, the marching ants can't really show the fine detail.

5. **Choose Select>Color Range.**

6. **Make sure the Localized Color Clusters option is unchecked.**

7. **In the Selection Preview menu, choose White Matte (if it is not already selected).**

   By changing the Selection Preview, you can more easily determine exactly what is selected. You can preview color range selections in the image window as:

   • **None** shows the normal image in the document window.

   • **Grayscale** shows the entire image in shades of gray. Selected areas are solid white and unselected areas are solid black.

   • **Black Matte** shows unselected areas in solid black. Selected areas appear in color.

   • **White Matte** shows unselected areas in solid white. Selected areas appear in color.

   • **Quick Mask** adds a partially transparent overlay to unselected areas.

8. **Set the Fuzziness value to 25 and click anywhere in the blue sky (in the document window).**

   Fuzziness is similar to the Tolerance setting for the Magic Wand tool. Higher Fuzziness values allow you to select more variation from the color you click.

   Depending on where you clicked, your selection might not exactly match what you see in our screen capture. The important thing to notice is that the visible areas indicate the current selection.

Note:

Press Command/ Control-D to deselect the active selection.

Note:

Because the dialog box preview is so small, we prefer to rely on the preview in the document window, which is controlled in the Selection Preview menu at the bottom of the dialog box.

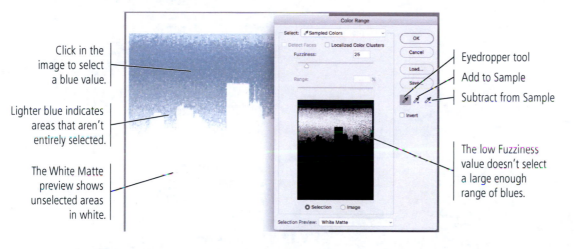

Click in the image to select a blue value.

Lighter blue indicates areas that aren't entirely selected.

The White Matte preview shows unselected areas in white.

Eyedropper tool

Add to Sample

Subtract from Sample

The low Fuzziness value doesn't select a large enough range of blues.

Selecting Localized Color Clusters

The **Localized Color Clusters** option in the Color Range dialog box can be used to select specific areas of a selected color. When this option is checked, the Range slider defines how far away (in physical distance) a color can be located from the point you click, and still be included in the selection.

Using Localized Color Clusters and a reduced Range, we were able to isolate this jellyfish.

We used a number of clicks with different Fuzziness values to sample the colors in this jellyfish.

Selection Presets

The Select menu at the top of the dialog box includes several presets for isolating specific ranges of primary colors (Reds, Yellows, Greens, Cyans, Blues, or Magentas), or specific ranges of color (highlights, midtones, or shadows).

If you select the **Skin Tones** preset, you can then activate the Detect Faces option at the top of the dialog box. By adjusting the Fuzziness slider, you can use this dialog box to make reasonably good selections of people's skin.

As you can see in this example, however, no automatic option is a perfect substitute when subjective decision-making is required. The tones in several of the models' shirts are very close to the color of skin, so some of those areas are included in the selection. This automatic selection method is still a good starting point, though, for making the complex selection of only a person's (or people's) skin.

Choose a preset from this menu.

When you choose the Skin Tones preset, you can also activate the Detect Faces option.

Some colors are close to skin tones, but are not skin. You will have to manually edit the mask to correct these areas.

9. **Change the Fuzziness value to 80 and watch the effect on the dialog box preview.**

Changing the Fuzziness value expands (higher numbers) or contracts (lower numbers) the selection. Be careful, though; higher fuzziness values can eliminate fine lines and detail.

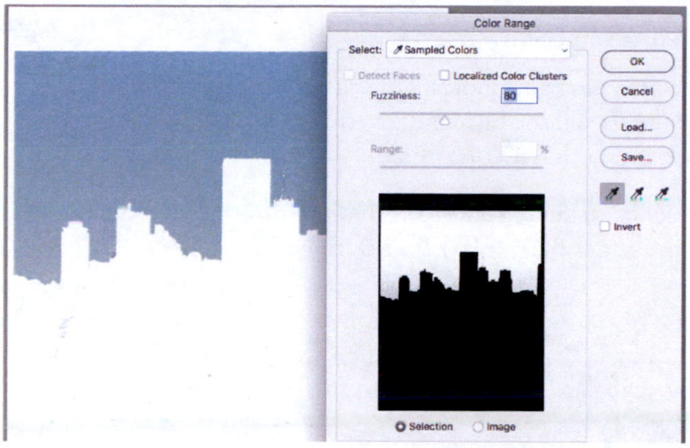

10. **In the Color Range dialog box, click the Add to Sample eyedropper. In the document window, click where parts of the blue sky are not shown in full strength.**

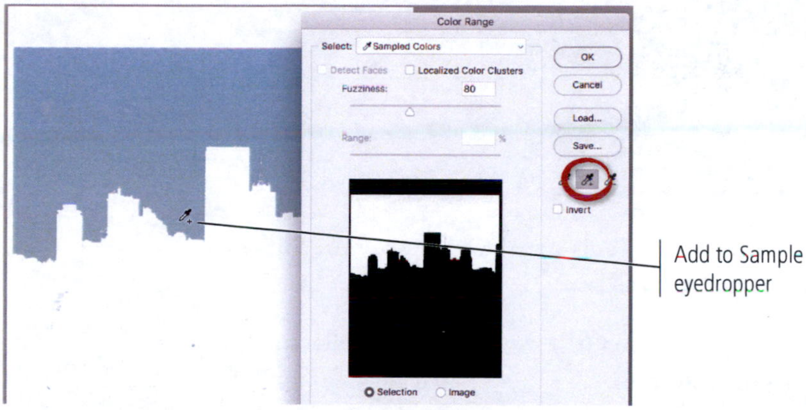

Add to Sample eyedropper

11. **Check the Invert box in the Color Range dialog box.**

Because your goal is to isolate the city and not the sky, it helps to look at what you want to keep instead of what you want to remove.

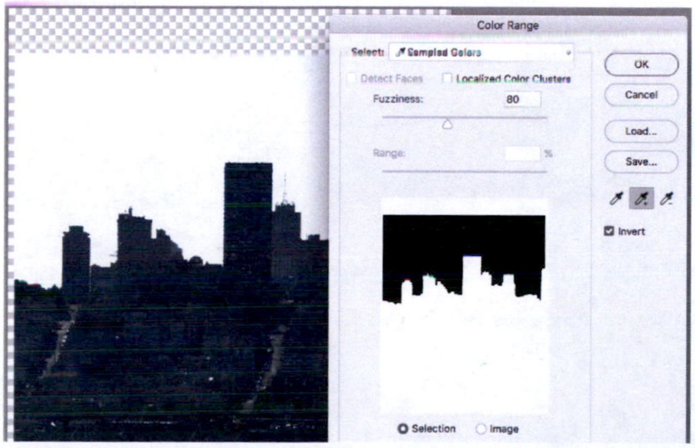

Note:

When the Color Range dialog box is open, you can press Command/Control to switch between the Selection and Image previews within the dialog box.

12. **Continue adding to (or subtracting from, if necessary) your selection until you are satisfied that all the blue sky is gone.**

    You can also adjust the Fuzziness slider if necessary, but be sure you don't adjust it too far to include areas of the city.

13. **Click OK when you're satisfied with your selection.**

    When you return to the image window, the marching ants indicate the current selection. In the Color Range dialog box, you selected the blue and inverted the selection — in other words, your selection is everything that isn't blue.

    If you zoom out to see the entire file, you see the marching ants surround the canvas, as well as the blue sky. Since the transparent area is not blue, it is included in the selection.

Note:

For the purposes of this exercise, don't worry if you have small unselected areas in the city or sky areas. You will fix these in the next exercise.

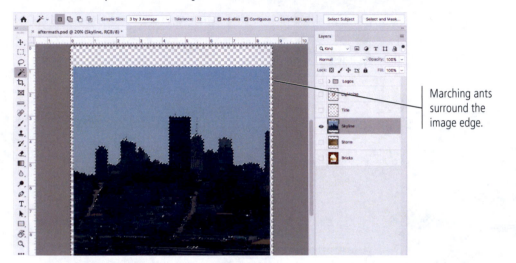

Marching ants surround the image edge.

14. **Choose the Magic Wand tool in the Tools panel and choose the Subtract from Selection option on the Options bar.**

15. **Click anywhere in the transparent area (the gray-and-white checkerboard) to remove that area from the selection.**

Subtract from Selection is active.

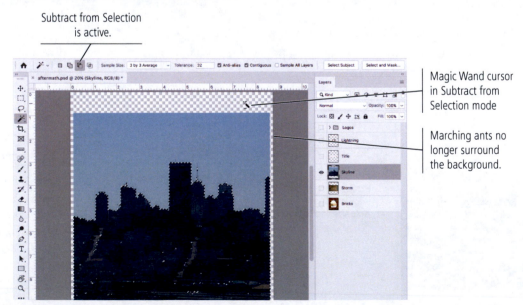

Magic Wand cursor in Subtract from Selection mode

Marching ants no longer surround the background.

16. In the Layers panel, click the Add Layer Mask button.

A **layer mask** is a map of areas that will be visible in the selected layer. The mask you just created is a raster-based pixel mask, based on the active selection when you created the mask. This is a nondestructive way to hide certain elements of a layer, without permanently deleting pixels. You can edit or disable the layer mask at any time.

Note:

A layer mask is basically an Alpha channel connected to a specific layer.

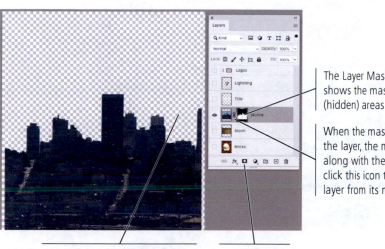

The Layer Mask thumbnail shows the masked (hidden) areas in black.

When the mask is linked to the layer, the mask will move along with the layer. You can click this icon to unlink the layer from its mask.

On the masked layer, pixels outside the original selection are hidden.

Add Layer Mask button

17. Control/right-click the mask thumbnail and choose Disable Layer Mask from the contextual menu.

You have to click the mask thumbnail to open the contextual menu for the mask.

When you disable the mask, the background pixels are again visible. This is one of the advantages of using masks — the background pixels are not permanently removed, they are simply hidden.

Note:

In the Layers panel, the Add Layer Mask option is not available if the Background layer is selected. You can't apply a layer mask to the Background layer of a file, so you first have to convert the Background layer to a regular layer.

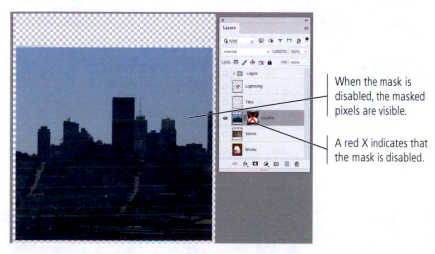

When the mask is disabled, the masked pixels are visible.

A red X indicates that the mask is disabled.

18. **Control/right-click the mask thumbnail and choose Apply Layer Mask from the contextual menu.**

    This option applies the mask to the attached layer, permanently removing the masked pixels from the layer.

The masked pixels are permanently removed from the layer.

The mask is removed from the layer.

19. **Choose Edit>Undo Apply Layer Mask to restore the layer mask.**

    As you saw in the previous step, applying a mask permanently removes the masked pixels. This essentially defeats the purpose of a mask, so you are restoring it in this step.

20. **Control/right-click the mask thumbnail and choose Enable Layer Mask from the contextual menu.**

Note:

Creating selections, reversing them, and then deleting the pixels surrounding an object is a common method for creating silhouettes — but not necessarily the best method. Masks protect the original pixels while providing exactly the same result.

21. **Save the file and continue to the next exercise.**

Edit a Layer Mask

In the previous exercise, you created a mask based on a selected color range. Depending on how you clicked to select the color range, you might have small areas of selected color in the city area, or small areas of unselected color in the sky. Rather than trying to isolate small spots of color in the Color Range dialog box, you can manually edit the mask using the built-in painting tools.

1. **With aftermath.psd open, click the Skyline layer mask thumbnail to select it.**

These corner icons indicate that the base layer is selected.

Clicking the layer mask thumbnail selects the mask so you can edit it.

2. **In the Channels panel (Window>Channels), make the Skyline Mask channel visible.**

    Layer masks are not visible by default; you have to turn them on in the Channels panel to see them. This isn't strictly necessary, since you can paint a mask without seeing it, but it is easier (at least when you're first learning) to be able to see what you're painting. By painting on a layer mask, you're not really "painting" anything; instead, you're actually "painting" the visibility of the associated layer.

Making the mask channel visible allows you to see the red overlay in the image.

3. **In the Channels panel, double-click the Skyline Mask channel thumbnail. Change the Opacity value to 100% in the Layer Mask Display Options dialog box, and then click OK.**

    Remember, this change only affects the transparency of the mask, not the degree of transparency applied to the layer. By setting the mask opacity to 100%, you know that anything solid red will be hidden and anything with no red will be visible.

4. **Carefully review the image to find any problems with the existing mask.**

   Changing the mask opacity makes it easier to find areas in the sky that need to be masked, as well as areas in the city that need to be removed from the mask.

These areas should be added to the mask.

These areas should be removed from the mask.

5. **Choose the Brush tool in the Tools panel.**

6. **Click the Default Foreground and Background Colors button at the bottom of the Tools panel.**

   If you look at the layer mask thumbnail for the layer, you can see it's just a black-and-white shape. White areas of the thumbnail show which parts of the layer are visible in the main document. The black parts of the mask hide the associated areas of the layer. This is an important distinction: painting with black on a layer mask hides those areas, while painting with white on a layer mask reveals those areas.

Click here to open the Brush Preset picker.

Brush tool

Default Foreground and Background Colors button

7. **In the Options bar, open the Brush Preset picker to access the tool options.**

   This panel shows the different brushes that are included with Photoshop. The default brush set includes a number of specific-diameter hard- and soft-edge brushes, as well as some artistic options. A number below a brush icon shows the size of the brush; if you click a specific brush in the panel, the same number displays in the Size field.

8. **In the top half of the Brush Preset picker, change the Size value to** 50 px **and change the Hardness value to** 100%.

Define the brush size and hardness in theses fields.

Note:

If you see anything other than a round brush shape in the top-left corner of the Brush Preset picker, expand the General Brushes folder in the lower half of the Brush Preset picker and choose the Hard Round option.

9. **Press Return/Enter to dismiss the Brush Preset picker.**

10. **With the Brush tool active and Black as the active foreground color, click and drag over those pixels that you want to add to the mask area.**

   The Brush tool paints with whatever is defined as the foreground color, which is black, in this case. Remember — when painting on a mask, black adds to the mask and hides pixels on the masked layer.

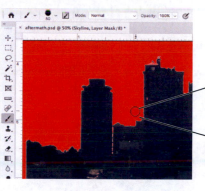

Brush tool cursor

Paint with black to remove pixels from the image (add to the mask).

11. **Click the Switch Foreground and Background Colors button near the bottom of the Tools panel.**

12. **Paint over any masked areas inside the city area.**

   Painting on a mask with white removes from the mask area, revealing the masked layer's pixels.

   As you paint to fine-tune a mask, keep the following points in mind:

   - You can use the bracket keys to enlarge (]) or reduce ([) the brush size.

   - You can press X to switch the current foreground and background colors. This is very useful to remember when you are painting on a mask, because you can reset the default (black and white) colors, and switch them as necessary, depending on what you want to accomplish.

   - You can also use the Eraser tool on a mask. Be careful, though, because erasing an area of the mask when the foreground color is white has the same effect as painting with the background color.

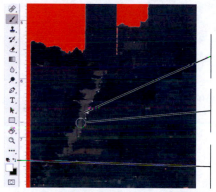

Paint the mask with white to reveal areas.

The Brush tool cursor reflects the size of the brush.

Switch Foreground and Background Colors button

13. **With the layer mask selected in the Layers panel, open the Properties panel (Window>Properties).**

Like the Options bar, the Properties panel is contextual. Different options are available in the panel depending on what is selected in the Layers panel. When a layer mask is selected, you can manipulate a variety of properties related to the selected mask.

The layer mask must be selected in the Layers panel.

The Properties panel can be used to edit the selected mask.

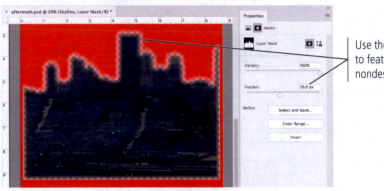

The Density slider changes the opacity of the overall mask. If you reduce the density to 80%, for example, underlying layers will be 20% visible through the mask. (Don't confuse this with the opacity of an alpha channel, which only affects the appearance of the mask on screen.)

14. **In the Properties panel, change the Feather value to 25 px.**

If you feather a selection, and then make a layer mask from that selection, the feathering becomes a permanent part of the mask.

The Properties panel allows you to adjust the feathering of a hard-edge mask, and then later change (or even remove) the feathering if necessary, without painting on the mask.

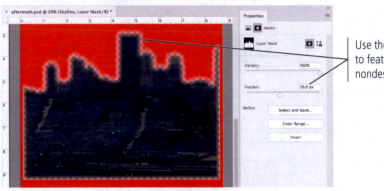

Use the Properties panel to feather the mask edge nondestructively.

15. **Change the Feather value to 1 px.**

This small feathering value will help to remove (or, at least, minimize) any remaining background artifacts around the edges of your mask.

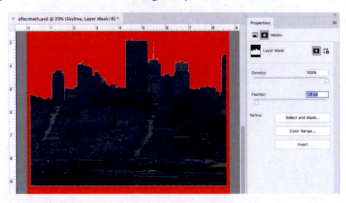

16. **Save the file and continue to the next exercise.**

Make and Refine a Quick Selection

As you just learned, you can make selections based on the color in an image. This technique is useful when you want to select large areas of solid color, or in photos with significant contrast between the foreground and background. When the area you want to select has a complex edge, refining that edge can produce very detailed results.

1. **With aftermath.psd open, hide all but the Bricks layer. Click the Bricks layer to select it as the active layer.**

2. **Choose the Quick Selection tool (nested under the Magic Wand tool).**

3. **In the Options bar, make sure the Sample All Layers option is not checked.**

   You only want to select the area in the bricks layer (the hole in the wall), so you do not want to make a selection based on the content of other layers in the file.

4. **Click at the top area of the hole in the wall and drag down to the bottom edge of the hole.**

   The Quick Selection tool essentially allows you to "paint" a selection. As you drag, the selection expands and automatically finds the edges in the image.

Note:

If you stop dragging and then click in a nearby area, the selection grows to include the new area.

New Selection   Add to Selection   Subtract from Selection   Click to change the brush size and attributes.

Quick Selection tool

Click here...

...and drag to here.

Marching ants surround the selected area.

5. **Click the Select and Mask button in the Options bar.**

The Select and Mask workspace is a specialized workspace that contains only the tools you need to refine a complex selection.

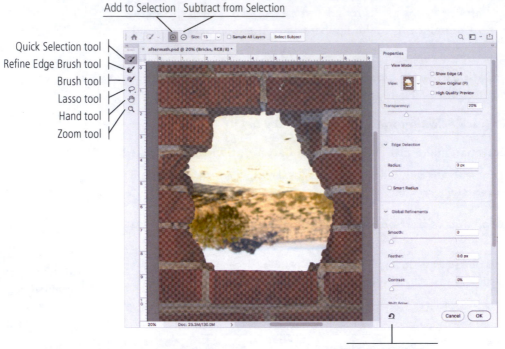

Add to Selection   Subtract from Selection

Quick Selection tool
Refine Edge Brush tool
Brush tool
Lasso tool
Hand tool
Zoom tool

Reset the Workspace

6. **In the Properties panel, open the View menu and click the On White option.**

The different types of preview change the way your image appears while you refine the edges within the workspace.

- **Onion Skin**, the default, shows unselected (masked) areas as semi-transparent, based on the value in the Transparency slider. You can make the masked areas more or less transparent by increasing or decreasing (respectively) the Transparency value.

- **Marching Ants** shows the basic standard selection.

- **Overlay** shows the unselected areas with a Quick Mask overlay.

- **On Black** shows the selection in color against a black background.

- **On White** shows the selection in color against a white background.

- **Black & White** shows the selected area in white and the unselected area in black.

- **On Layers** shows only the selected area. Unselected areas are hidden so that underlying layers are visible in masked areas in the preview.

Note:

If the Show Edge option is checked, only the edge of the selection area will be visible in the preview.

7. **In the Properties panel, change the Opacity slider to 100%.**

Using the default setting, the masked areas appear at 50% opacity in the Select and Mask workspace. By changing this setting to 100%, masked pixels are entirely hidden by the white area.

8. **Experiment with the adjustments in the Properties panel until you're satisfied with the selection edge.**

You want to include a small amount of darkness around the edge so that when you invert the selection to remove the hole in the wall, there is no light halo effect left by the selection edge. We used the Shift Edge slider to slightly expand the selection edge.

- **Radius** is the number of pixels around the edge that are affected. Higher radius values result in softer edges and lower values result in sharper edges.

- **Smart Radius** automatically adjusts the radius for hard and soft edges found in the border region. You should turn off this option if your selection area has all hard edges or all soft edges, or if you prefer to manually control the Radius.

- **Smooth** reduces the number of points that make up your selection and, as the name suggests, makes a smoother edge. You can set smoothness from 0 (very detailed selection) to 100 (very smooth selection).

- **Feather** softens the selection edge, resulting in a transition that does not have a hard edge (in other words, blends into the background). You can feather the selection up to 250 pixels.

- **Contrast** is the degree of variation allowed in the selection edge. Higher Contrast values (up to 100%) mean sharper selection edges.

- **Shift Edge** shrinks or grows the selection edge by the defined percentage (from −100% to 100%).

- **Invert** reverses the mask; selected areas become unselected and vice versa.

Note:

It might help to work with a closer view while you refine edges. You can use the Zoom and Hand tools to change the image preview.

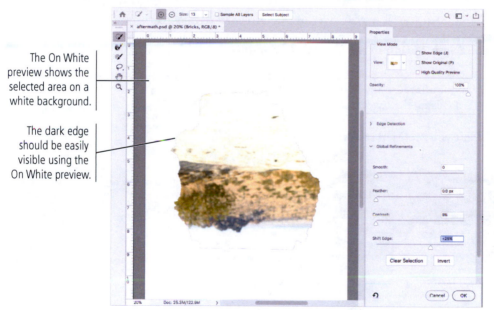

The On White preview shows the selected area on a white background.

The dark edge should be easily visible using the On White preview.

9. **Click the Invert button near the bottom of the Properties panel.**

As you know, you want to remove the hole in the wall — not the wall. You selected the area in the hole to create the mask, but you now need to invert the selection. This button reverses the mask, so now only the bricks are visible.

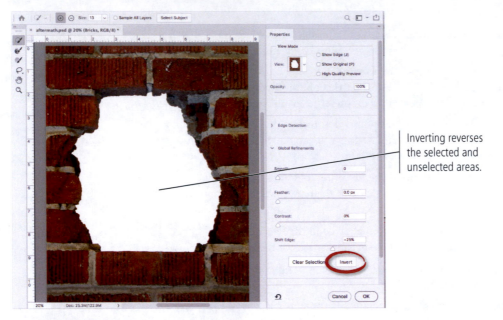

Inverting reverses the selected and unselected areas.

10. **At the bottom of the Properties panel, expand the Output Settings section.**

11. **Choose the Layer Mask option in the Output To menu.**

This menu can be used to create a new layer or file (with or without a mask) from the selection. You want to mask the existing layer, so you are using the Layer Mask option.

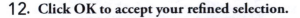

12. **Click OK to accept your refined selection.**

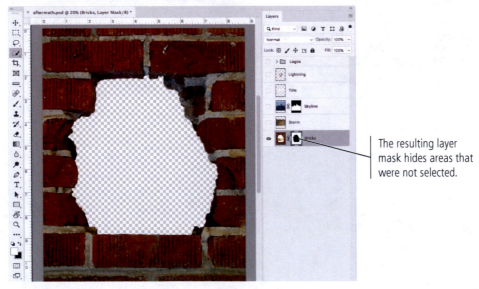

The resulting layer mask hides areas that were not selected.

13. **Save the file and continue to the next exercise.**

Arrange Layer Position and Stacking Order

The ad is almost final, but a few pieces are still not quite in position. You already know you can use the Move tool to move the contents of a layer around on the canvas. You can also move a layer to any position in the **stacking order** (the top-to-bottom position of a layer) by simply dragging it to a new position in the Layers panel.

1. **With aftermath.psd open, make all layers visible.**

2. **Click the Bricks layer in the Layers panel and drag up. When a heavy bar appears below the Title layer, release the mouse button.**

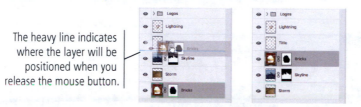

The heavy line indicates where the layer will be positioned when you release the mouse button.

Note:

Press Command/Control-[(left bracket) to move a layer down in the stacking order.

Press Command/Control-] (right bracket) to move a layer up in the stacking order.

Be careful when dragging layers near a layer group. If the border appears around a layer group, releasing the mouse button would place the dragged layer inside that group.

3. **Repeat the process to move the Lightning layer below the Skyline layer.**

4. **Choose the Move tool, and check the Auto-Select option in the Options bar. Open the attached menu (to the right of the Auto-Select check box) and choose Layer.**

When Layer is selected in the Auto-Select menu, only the relevant layer will move, even if it is part of a layer group. If you want all layers in a group containing the selected layer to move, choose Group in the menu.

5. **In the document window, click any pixel in the movie title and drag down until the title appears in the bottom half of the canvas.**

Your layers should appear in the same order as shown in the following image.

Check the Auto-Select option and choose Layer in the menu.

Click any pixel in the title layer content and drag to move that layer's content.

Be careful to not click an area in which the layer is transparent.

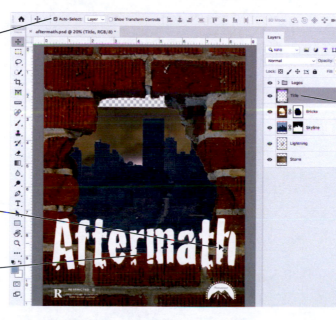

When Auto-Select is active, clicking in the document window automatically selects the relevant layer.

6. **If necessary, drag the Storm layer until the image fills any transparent area behind the bricks and skyline.**

    Make sure you click an area in which no pixels from another layer are visible.

7. **With the Move tool still active, uncheck the Auto-Select option in the Options bar.**

8. **Click the Lightning layer in the Layers panel to select it. Click and drag in the document window to move the layer content so the lightning appears to strike one of the buildings.**

Note:

When the Move tool is active, you can move the selected object or layer 1 pixel by pressing the Arrow keys. Pressing Shift with any of the Arrow keys moves the selected object/layer by 10 pixels.

Uncheck the Auto-Select option.

When Auto-Select is not active, remember to first select the layer you want to move.

9. **Save the file and continue to the final stage of the project.**

STAGE 4 / **Saving Files for Multiple Media**

At the beginning of the project, you saved this file in Photoshop's native format (PSD). However, many Photoshop projects require saving the completed file in at least one other format. Many artists prefer to leave all files in the PSD format because then, there is only one file to track. Others prefer to send only flattened TIFF files of their artwork because the individual elements can't be changed.

Ultimately, the format (or formats, if the file is being used in multiple places) you use will depend on where and how the file is being placed. For this project, you have been asked to create a flattened, high-resolution TIFF file and a low-resolution JPEG file for use on a website.

Save a Flat TIFF File

The printed magazine suggests that ads created in Photoshop be submitted as flat TIFF files. Since you designed the ad to incorporate bleeds for pages up to 8.5″ × 11″, all you have to do for this version is save the file in the appropriate format.

1. With **aftermath.psd** open, choose File>Save As.

2. **Choose File>Save As. In the resulting dialog box, click the Save on Your Computer button.**

3. **If necessary, navigate to your WIP>Movie folder as the target location for saving the final files.**

   The Save As dialog box defaults to the last-used location. If you continued the entire way through this project without stopping, you won't have to navigate.

4. **Open the Format/Save as Type menu and choose TIFF.**

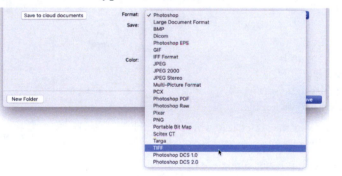

5. In the lower half of the dialog box, uncheck the Layers option.

Because this file contains layers, this option is probably checked by default. If your file contained alpha channels, annotations, or spot colors, those check boxes would also be available. When you uncheck the Layers option, the As a Copy check box is automatically activated.

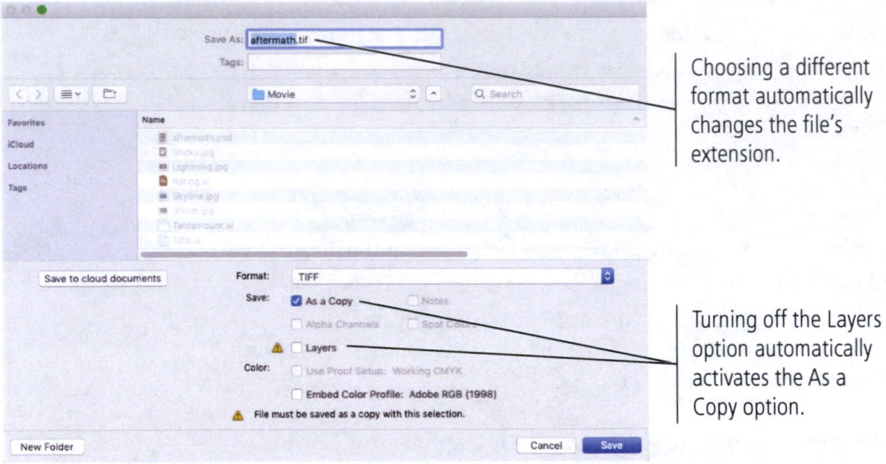

Choosing a different format automatically changes the file's extension.

Turning off the Layers option automatically activates the As a Copy option.

6. Click Save.

Most file formats include additional options, which you should understand before you simply click OK.

7. In the TIFF Options dialog box, make sure the (Image Compression) None radio button is selected.

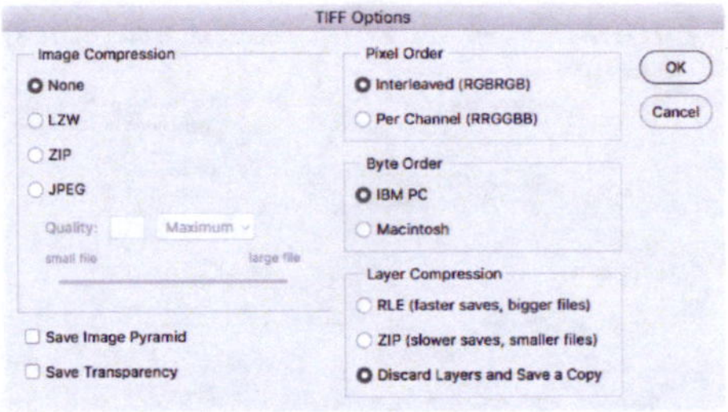

TIFF files can be compressed (made smaller) using several methods:

- **None** (as the name implies) applies no compression to the file. This option is safe if file size is not an issue, but digital file transmission often requires files to be smaller than a full-page, multilayered Photoshop file.

- **LZW** (Lempel-Ziv-Welch) compression is lossless, which means all file data is maintained in the compressed file.

- **ZIP** compression is also lossless, but is not supported by all desktop publishing software (especially older versions).

- **JPEG** is a **lossy** compression scheme, which means some data will be thrown away to reduce the file size. If you choose JPEG compression, the Quality options determine how much data can be discarded. Maximum quality means less data is thrown out and the file is larger. Minimum quality discards the most data and results in the smaller file size.

8. **Leave the Pixel Order and Byte Order options at their default values.**

Pixel Order determines how channel data is encoded. The Interleaved (RGBRGB) option is the default. Per Channel (RRGGBB) is called "planar" order.

Byte Order determines which platform can use the file, although this is somewhat deceptive. Even in older versions of most desktop publishing software, Macintosh systems can read the PC byte order, but Windows couldn't read the Macintosh byte order. If you don't know which platform will ultimately be used, choose IBM PC.

Save Image Pyramid creates a tiered file with multiple resolution versions; this isn't widely used or supported by other applications, so you can typically leave it unchecked.

If your file contains transparency, the Save Transparency check box will be available. If you don't choose this option, transparent areas will be white in the saved file.

Note:

Some experts argue that choosing the order for your system can improve print quality, especially on desktop devices.

9. **Click OK to save the file.**

When you return to the document, the original native Photoshop file is still active. The TIFF file that you just created is saved in the target location, but it is not the active file because the As a Copy option was checked in the Save As dialog box. If you had included layers, and not intentionally checked the As a Copy option, the active file would be the TIFF file that you saved, instead of the original native Photoshop file.

10. **Continue to the next exercise.**

Save a JPEG File for Digital Media

Your client has also requested a low-resolution JPEG file, using the RGB color model. Several extra steps are required to create this file with the required settings.

1. **With aftermath.psd open in Photoshop, choose File>Save As.**

To protect your work, you are saving this file with a different file name *before* making significant destructive changes.

2. **Click the Save on Your Computer button if necessary.**

From this point on throughout this book, you should assume you saving the files to a local drive. We will not continue to repeat the instruction to click the Save on Your Computer button.

3. **Choose JPEG in the Format/Save as Type menu. Change the file name to aftermath-web.jpg, and then click Save.**

JPEG files do not support multiple layers. When you choose the JPEG format, the Layers option is automatically unchecked, and the As a Copy option is automatically activated.

3. **In the JPEG Options dialog box, choose High in the Quality menu and then click OK.**

You can use these options to reduce the weight of the resulting JPEG file. Keep in mind that JPEG is a lossy compression scheme, so the application throws away what it perceives as redundant data to reduce the file weight. Lower quality settings mean more compression and smaller file weight (and thus, shorter download time), but you might notice significant deterioration in image quality.

The right side of the dialog box shows the estimated file size — in this case, just over 1 megabyte.

4. **Close the aftermath.psd file.**

Remember, when the As a Copy option is checked, the file you had open before the save remains active in the document window. You need to manually open the JPEG file so you can make the necessary changes for web distribution.

5. **Open aftermath-web.jpg from your WIP>Movie folder.**

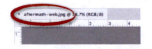

6. **Choose Image>Image Size.**

You created this file at 300 pixels per inch, which is appropriate for commercial print requirements. For web distribution, however, 300 ppi is far more than you need. To further reduce the file weight and resulting download time, you should downsample the file to 72 ppi — an appropriate resolution for most web display requirements.

7. **With the Resample option checked in the Image Size dialog box, change the Resolution field to 72.**

When the Resample option is checked, changing the resolution does not affect the file's physical size; rather, the actual number of pixels is reduced. In this case, at 72 ppi, only 630 × 810 pixels are required for a file that is 8.75″ × 11.25″.

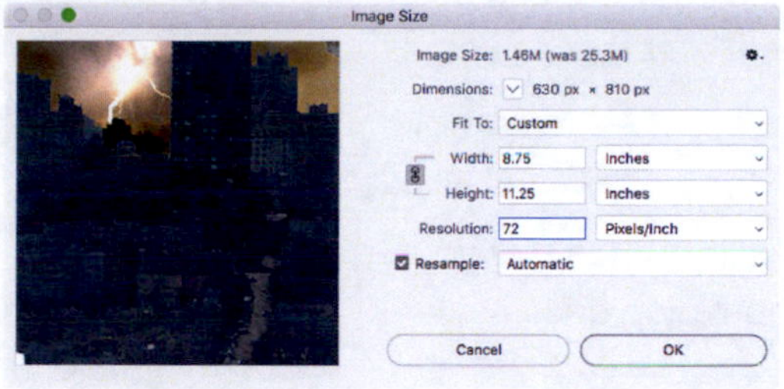

8. **Click OK to finalize the change.**

9. **Choose File>Save As. Leave the options at their default values and click Save.**

You are using the Save As process so that you can review the compression settings that will be applied in the resulting JPEG file.

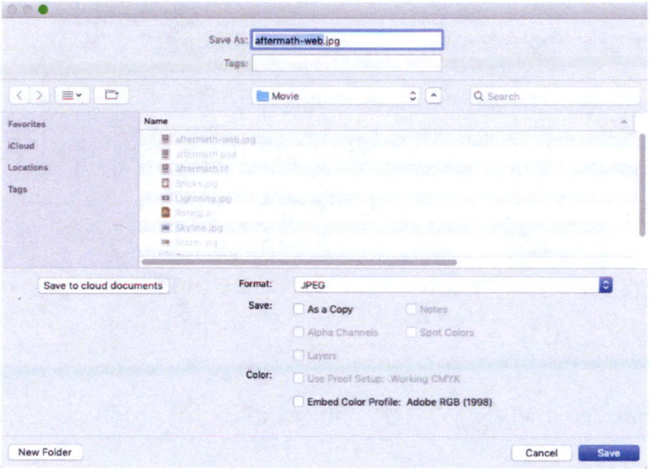

10. **In the resulting warning message, click Replace/Yes.**

Because you did not change the file name, you are asked to confirm whether you want to overwrite the existing JPEG file.

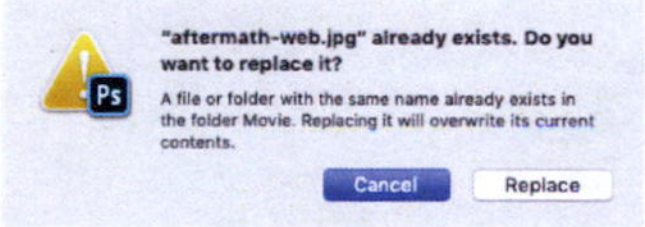

11. **In the JPEG Options dialog box, make sure High is selected in the Quality menu, and then click OK.**

When you first saved the file at the beginning of this exercise, the resulting JPEG file was over 1 megabyte. By reducing the resolution, the file is now approximately 194 kilobytes.

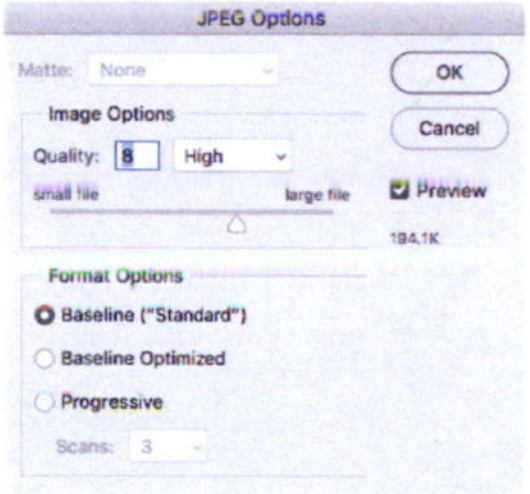

12. **Close the active file.**

PROJECT REVIEW

fill in the blank

1. _____ is likely to cause degradation of a raster image when it's reproduced on a printing press.

2. A _____ is a linked file that you placed into another Photoshop document.

3. The _____ is context sensitive, providing access to different functions depending on which tool is active.

4. The _____ is the final size of a printed page.

5. The _____ tool is used to draw irregular-shaped selection marquees.

6. The _____ tool is used to select areas of similar color by clicking and dragging in the image window.

7. The _____ tool can be used to drag layer contents to another position within the image, or into another open document.

8. When selecting color ranges, the _____ value determines how much of the current color range falls into the selection.

9. A _____ can be used to non-destructively hide certain areas of a layer.

10. _____ is a lossy compression method that is best used when large file size might be a problem.

short answer

1. Briefly describe the difference between raster images and vector graphics.

2. Briefly explain three methods for isolating an image from its background.

3. Briefly explain the concept of a layer mask.

PORTFOLIO BUILDER PROJECT

Use what you have learned in this project to complete the following freeform exercise.
Carefully read the art director and client comments, then create your own design to meet the needs of the project.
Use the space below to sketch ideas. When finished, write a brief explanation of the reasoning behind your final design.

art director comments

Tantamount Studios is pleased with your work on the *Aftermath* ad, and they would like you to create the ad concept and final files for another movie that they're releasing early next year.

To complete this project, you should:

❏ Download the **Airborne_Web20_PB.zip** archive from the Student Files web page to access the client-supplied title artwork and rating placeholder file.

❏ Find appropriate background and foreground images for the movie theme (see the client's comments at right).

❏ Incorporate the title artwork, logos, and rating placeholder that the client provided.

❏ Composite the different elements into a single completed file. Save both a layered version and a flattened version.

client comments

The movie is titled *Above and Beyond*. Although the story is fictionalized, it will focus on the men who led the first U.S. Airborne unit (the 501st), which suffered more than 2,000 casualties in the European theater of World War II.

We don't have any other images in mind, but the final ad should reflect the time period (the 1940s) of the movie. The 501st Airborne was trained to parachute into battle, so you should probably incorporate some kind of parachute image.

This movie is a joint venture between Sun and Tantamount, so both logos need to be included in the new ad. It isn't rated yet, so please use the "This Movie Is Not Yet Rated" artwork as a placeholder.

Create this ad big enough to fit on an 8.5″ × 11″ page, but keep the live area 1″ inside the trim so the ad can be used in different-sized magazines.

project justification

Making selections is one of the most basic — and most important — skills that you will learn in Photoshop. Selections are so important that Photoshop dedicates an entire menu to the process.

As you created the movie ad in this project, you used a number of skills and techniques that you will apply in many (if not all) projects you build in Photoshop. You learned a number of ways to make both simple and complex selections, and you will learn additional methods in later projects. You also learned how to work with multiple layers, which will be an important part of virtually every Photoshop project you create, both in this book and throughout your career.

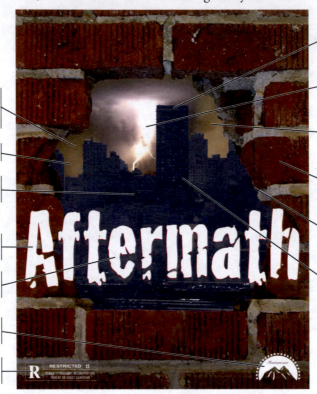

Composite images by dragging from one document to another

Transform a regular layer

Composite images by copying and pasting

Incorporate vector graphics into a raster image

Move layer content around on the canvas

Embed files as Smart Object layers

Transform a Smart Object layer

Make a basic selection with a Marquee tool

Create a feathered selection to blend one layer into another

Create a silhouette using the Select Color Range utility

Create a silhouette using the Quick Selection tool

Refine a selection using the Select and Mask utility

Use a layer mask to hide pixels on a layer

Car Magazine Cover

2

Your client publishes a monthly magazine for car enthusiasts. Your agency has been hired to take over the magazine design and you have been tasked with designing the cover for the next issue.

This project incorporates the following skills:

- ❏ Resizing and resampling supplied images
- ❏ Creating complex vector paths and shape layers
- ❏ Compositing images as Smart Objects
- ❏ Applying nondestructive styles, effects, and filters
- ❏ Developing a custom artistic background

PROJECT MEETING

client comments

Every month, the magazine cover includes one main featured car, and three smaller images related to other articles in the issue. In addition to those images and the magazine title, we also always include several text blurbs with teasers for secondary articles in the issue, and a QR code that links to the website.

We're looking for a new way to present these elements. Once we finalize a general layout, we'll use that layout going forward for every new issue.

The only thing we're fixed on is the trim size, which is 8″ × 10″, with a 1/8″ bleed allowance.

art director comments

The client sent me the main car image for the first redesign. It's a little bit small, so we'll have to do some manipulation to make it large enough to fill the cover space. The car also needs to be knocked out of its background so it can be more prominent. A vector path will work well to meet this goal because you can edit it at any time without losing quality.

You're going to use a combination of styles, filters, and effects on the background and inset images. Photoshop's Smart Object capabilities will be a significant advantage in this task because we can edit the effects and filters if the client isn't thrilled with the initial effort.

I've also already created a template in Illustrator with the magazine nameplate and text elements; we'll repurpose the same file every month with the different text for each issue. You can place that file directly into Photoshop as a linked file so that any last-minute changes in the file will automatically appear in the final composite cover.

project objectives

To complete this project, you will:

- ❏ Resize and resample an existing source image
- ❏ Edit the canvas size
- ❏ Create a vector-based layer mask
- ❏ Create a vector shape layer
- ❏ Create a clipping mask
- ❏ Add texture to a shape layer
- ❏ Apply custom layer effects
- ❏ Use the Filter Gallery
- ❏ Liquify a layer
- ❏ Use the Eyedropper tool
- ❏ Create a custom gradient
- ❏ Print a composite proof

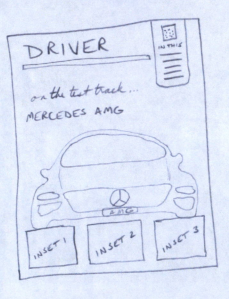

STAGE 1 / Enlarging Source Files

Any project that you build in Photoshop requires some amount of zooming in and out to various view percentages, as well as navigating around the document within its window. As we show you how to complete different stages of the workflow, we usually won't tell you when to change your view percentage because that's largely a matter of personal preference. Nonetheless, you should understand the different options for navigating around a Photoshop file so you can easily and efficiently get to what you want, when you want to get there.

To review information from the Interface chapter, keep in mind that you have a number of options for navigating around a document:

- Click with the Hand tool to drag the image around in the document window.

- Click with the Zoom tool to zoom in; Option/Alt-click to zoom out.

- Use the View Percentage field in the bottom-left corner of the document window.

- Use the options in the View menu (or the corresponding keyboard shortcuts).

- Use the Navigator panel.

Note:

As you complete the exercises in this project, use any of these methods to zoom in or out on different areas of the file.

Resize and Resample the Existing Source Image

This project — like many others you will build throughout your career — starts with an existing image, which you will open and use as the basis for the rest of the project. Whenever you start with an existing file, it's best to evaluate what you already have before you make any changes.

1. **Download Cars_Web20_RF.zip from the Student Files web page.**

2. **Expand the ZIP archive in your WIP folder (Macintosh) or copy the archive contents into your WIP folder (Windows).**

   This results in a folder named **Cars**, which contains the files you need for this project. You should also use this folder to save the files you create in this project.

3. **In Photoshop, choose File>Open. Navigate to the file amg.jpg in your WIP>Cars folder and click Open.**

4. **Choose View>Fit on Screen so you can see the entire image, and make sure rulers are visible (View>Rulers).**

5. **Choose Image>Image Size.**

   The amg.jpg file is 25″ wide by 18.75″ high, with a resolution of 72 pixels/inch. Commercial printing typically requires 300 pixels/inch, so this image would not be considered "print quality" at its current size.

   The first step is to resize the image using the principle of effective resolution to achieve the 300 pixels/inch required for commercial printing.

6. **At the bottom of the dialog box, uncheck the Resample option and change the Resolution field to 300.**

Remember, when resampling is not active, the image retains the same number of pixels when you change the size or resolution fields. The image's physical size is now smaller since you compressed 300 pixels into an inch instead of the original 72 ppi.

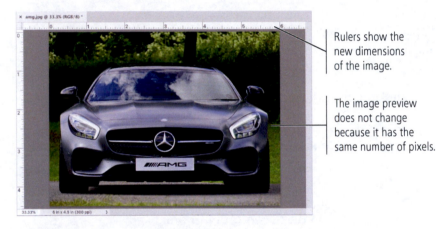

Uncheck the Resample option.

The actual number of pixels in the file is not affected.

Changing the resolution also changes the physical file size.

7. **Click OK to resize the source image.**

As you can see, the image view in the document window does not change because the image still has the same number of pixels. The rulers at the left and top edges of the document window show the new measurements that are associated with the resized image.

Rulers show the new dimensions of the image.

The image preview does not change because it has the same number of pixels.

8. **Choose Image>Image Size again.**

Because you already defined the appropriate resolution for this image, you now need to make the image large enough to meet the overall job requirements.

Resampling adds or removes pixels to create the size you define without affecting the defined resolution.

9. **Click in the Preview window and drag until the logo on the car's grill is visible.**

Areas of greater detail are the most prone to distortion when you enlarge an image. The Image Size preview area allows you to review the results before finalizing the process.

10. **At the bottom of the dialog box, check the Resample option.**

When the Resample option is checked, you can change the actual number of pixels in the image without affecting its resolution.

11. **Open the Resample menu and choose Preserve Details (enlargement).**

Although you should try to capture images at the size you will need them, this is not always possible when working with client-supplied images. The Preserve Details option significantly improves the results of artificially enlarging an existing image.

12. **Make sure the Constrain option is active.**

13. **With the units menus set to Inches, change the Width field to 8.25.**

The overall project requires a finished image that is 8.25″ wide by 10.25″ high. If you enlarged the picture to match the required height, it would be too wide for the entire car to fit into the composition. Instead, you are enlarging the image to match the required width; you will later adjust the canvas to suit the project's height requirement.

As you can see, increasing the image's physical size with resampling adds more pixels to the image. This also significantly increases the file weight (its size in bytes).

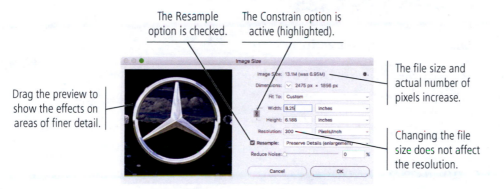

The Resample option is checked.

The Constrain option is active (highlighted).

Drag the preview to show the effects on areas of finer detail.

The file size and actual number of pixels increase.

Changing the file size does not affect the resolution.

14. **Drag in the Preview window to show an area with flat areas of color near a high-contrast edge.**

Artificially enlarging an image often results in small pixels of varying color, especially in areas of solid color and near high-contrast edges. When you choose the Preserve Details option, you can use the Reduce Noise slider to help reduce those artifacts.

15. **Change the Reduce Noise slider to 20%.**

The Preview window shows the results that will be achieved when you finalize the resampling.

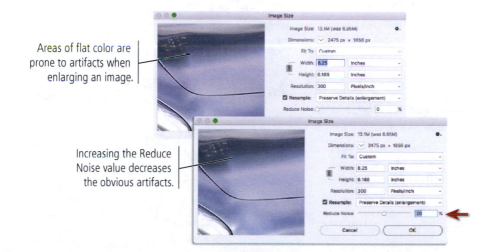

Areas of flat color are prone to artifacts when enlarging an image.

Increasing the Reduce Noise value decreases the obvious artifacts.

16. **Click OK to finalize the resampling.**

    Resampling the image (enlarging) adds pixels to the file. The image no longer fits in the document window at the current view percentage.

The image now has more pixels, so less of the image is visible in the document window.

17. **Choose View>Fit On Screen to show the entire image.**

18. **Choose File>Save As. Save the file as a native Photoshop file named magazine.psd in your WIP>Cars folder.**

19. **Continue to the next exercise.**

Sharpen the Enlarged Image

When you enlarge an image in Photoshop, the application must generate new data. The algorithm underlying the Preserve Details option does a significantly better job of generating new pixels than was available in previous versions, but the pixels are still not original to the image. This can result in a loss of detail, especially near apparent edges or areas of high contrast. Whenever you enlarge an image, **sharpening** can help to restore detail and make the image appear more crisp.

1. **With magazine.psd open, choose Filter>Sharpen>Unsharp Mask.**

2. **Make sure the Preview check box is active in the dialog box.**

   Unsharp masking sharpens an image by increasing contrast along apparent edges in th image.

   Drag here or click in the document window to change the visible area in the preview window.

   - **Amount** determines how much the contrast in edges will increase. Typically, 150–200% creates good results in high-resolution images.

   - **Radius** determines how many pixels will be included in the edge comparison. Higher radius values result in more pronounced edge effects.

   - **Threshold** defines the difference that is required for Photoshop to identify an edge. A threshold of 15 means that colors must be more than 15 levels different.

3. **Change the Amount to 100%, the Radius to 2.0 pixels, and the Threshold to 3 levels.**

4. **Toggle the Preview option off and on to review the results in the document window.**

Sharpening is most obvious in areas of high contrast.

5. **Click OK to apply the Unsharp Mask filter.**

6. **Save the file and continue to the next exercise.**

 Edit the Canvas Size

As you learned in the project meeting, the final artwork for this project needs to be 8.25″ wide by 10.25″ high. You already accomplished the required width when you resampled the source file. In this exercise, you are going to enlarge the canvas to meet the project's height requirement.

1. **With magazine.psd open, make the Layers panel visible.**

   Photos and scans almost always default to exist on the Background layer when you first open them.

2. **Choose Image>Canvas Size.**

   In Photoshop, **canvas** refers to the overall image area — like the surface of a canvas used by traditional artists. It is not directly connected to the content of most layers (except for the Background layer).

   You can use this dialog box to change the size of the canvas to specific measurements.

3. **Choose the top-center anchor option.**

   The Anchor area shows the reference point around which the canvas will be enlarged or cropped. Using this option, all new pixels will be added at the bottom of the image.

4. **Change the Height field to 10.25 [Inches], and choose White in the Canvas Extension Color menu.**

   This menu defines what color will appear in the new pixels on the Background layer.

Anchoring the top edge means new pixels will be added to the bottom of the existing canvas.

Use this menu to define the color of new pixels on the Background layer.

Note:

If you define smaller measurements, you are basically accomplishing the same thing as using the Crop tool.

5. **Click OK to apply the change, then choose View>Fit On Screen.**

   As you can see, new pixels were added to the bottom of the canvas. Because the existing image content exists on the Background layer, and the Background layer cannot contain transparent pixels, the new pixels are filled with white.

Note:

If you reduce the canvas size, clicking OK in the Canvas Size dialog box results in a warning that some clipping will occur.

Content on the Background layer that is outside the new canvas size is permanently removed from the layer. Content on other layers is maintained.

Because the photo existed on the locked Background layer, new pixels are filled with white.

6. **Choose Edit>Undo Canvas Size.**

   Press Command/Control-Z to undo the previous action.

7. **In the Layers panel, click the Lock icon to unlock the Background layer.**

8. **Double-click the Layer 0 name, type Car to rename the layer, then press Return/Enter.**

9. **Choose Image>Canvas Size again. Select the top-center Anchor option, then change the Height field to 10.25 [Inches].**

This menu is not available because the file no longer has a locked Background layer.

Note:

If you check the Relative option, you can change the canvas size by specific amounts. For example, to make the canvas one inch narrower, you would type −1 in the Width field. Photoshop automatically calculates the resulting canvas size based on the selected Anchor position.

10. **Click OK to apply the change.**

Regular layers support transparency, so the new pixels are not filled with a solid color. The gray-and-white checked pattern identifies transparent areas of the visible layer.

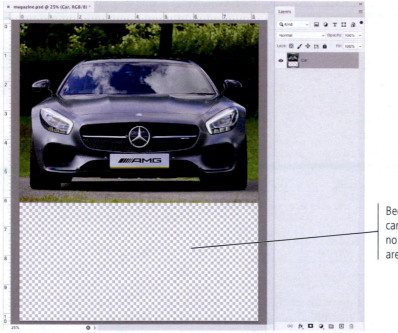

Because regular layers can include transparency, no color appears in the area of the new pixels.

11. **Save the file. With Maximize Compatibility checked, click OK in the Photoshop Format Options dialog box.**

Because you converted the Background layer to a regular image layer, you see the dialog box that asks if you want to maximize compatibility the first time you save the file.

12. **Continue to the next stage of the project.**

Vector paths, also called Bézier curves, are defined mathematically based on the position of anchor points and the length and angle of direction handles that are connected to those anchor points. Unlike the pixels in a raster image, vector paths do not have a defined resolution until they are output. Because of this, vector paths can be edited at any time without any loss of quality.

Photoshop includes a number of tools for creating vector paths:

Note:

The Type tool is also technically a vector-based tool because digital type uses vectors to define the character shapes.

- The **Pen tool** places individual anchor points each time you click; line segments connect each point. If you click and drag, you create a point with direction handles, which precisely control the shape of the connecting segments.

- The **Freeform Pen tool** draws vector paths wherever you drag, just as you would draw with a pencil on paper.

- The **Rectangle** and **Ellipse tools** create shapes that you would expect based on the tool names. If you press Shift while you click and drag, you create a shape with equal height and width (a square or circle, respectively).

- The **Polygon tool** creates a shape with any number of sides. Clicking once opens a dialog box where you can define the number of sides.

    If you check the **Smooth Corners** option, each anchor point has direction handles that make the corners rounded instead of sharp.

    If you choose the **Star** option, the **Indent Sides By** value determines where the inner points of the star appear relative to the overall shape diameter.

    You can also check the **Smooth Indents** option to create smooth curves on the inside points of the shape, instead of corner points.

Polygon created with all options unchecked

Polygon created with the Star option checked

Polygon (star) created with the Smooth Corners option checked

Polygon (star) created with the Smooth Corners and Smooth Indents options checked

- The **Line tool** creates open straight lines with two points — one at each end. When first created, the points have no direction handles and the connecting segment is a straight line.

- The **Custom Shape tool** creates vector-based shapes from built-in or external libraries.

When you use the vector drawing tools, you have the option to create a new shape, path, or pixels.

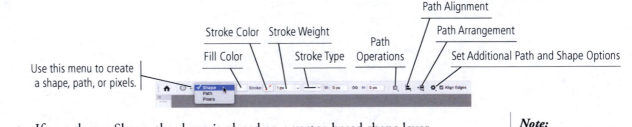

Use this menu to create a shape, path, or pixels.

Fill Color

Stroke Color

Stroke Weight

Stroke Type

Path Operations

Path Alignment

Path Arrangement

Set Additional Path and Shape Options

- If you choose Shape, the shape is placed on a vector-based shape layer.

- If you choose Path, the shape exists only as a work path in the Paths panel.

- If you choose Pixels, the resulting shape is created as pixels on the previously selected layer. No vector path is created.

Note:

The Pixels option is not available when you are using the Pen tools.

Use the Freeform Pen Tool

The Freeform Pen tool creates a vector path based on where you drag the cursor. The application creates anchor points and direction handles as necessary to create the shape that you draw.

1. **With magazine.psd open, show the image at 100% in the document window.**

   Ideally, you should work at 100% while you complete this exercise.

2. **Choose the Freeform Pen tool (nested under the Pen tool) in the Tools panel.**

3. **In the Options bar, choose the Path option in the left menu.**

   When you choose Path in the tool mode menu, the vector path that you draw is stored in the Paths panel.

4. **Open the Path Operations menu and choose the Combine Shapes option.**

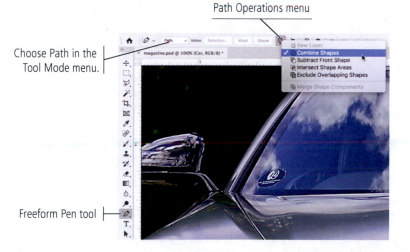

Path Operations menu

Choose Path in the Tool Mode menu.

Freeform Pen tool

Note:

The Pen Pressure option only applies if you have a pressure-sensitive graphics tablet. When this option is turned on, higher pressure decreases the Width tolerance.

These options define how a new path will interact with any existing paths. (Illustrator and InDesign users might recognize these as options from the Pathfinder panel.)

- **New Layer**, available when Layer is selected in the Tool Mode menu, creates a new shape layer every time you draw a new path.

- **Combine Shapes** adds new paths to an already selected path or shape layer. Each path's shape is maintained as a separate vector path. If you want a new path to include only areas inside the path you draw, you should choose this option before you begin drawing a new path.

- **Subtract Front Shape** removes the area of secondary shapes from existing shapes.

- **Intersect Shape Areas** results in a shape that is only the area where a new shape overlaps an existing shape.

- **Exclude Overlapping Shapes** is similar to Subtract; overlapping areas are removed from the existing shape, but non-overlapping areas of the new shape are filled with the shape color.

- The **Merge Shape Components** option, available when a single path contains more than one shape, results in a single (possibly compound) shape. Any overlapping paths are combined into one shape/path.

5. **Check the Magnetic option in the Options bar, then click the Set Additional Path and Shape Options button.**

When you draw with the Pen tool, the default path appears in the document window as a thin, medium blue line. You can use the Thickness and Color options to change the appearance of the path. (The settings here do not affect the actual stroke color and width of a path; they refer only to the appearance of paths in the document window.)

- **Curve Fit** determines how closely the curves will match the path that you drag with the mouse cursor. When the Magnetic option is active, you can also define settings that control how the magnetic function behaves:

- **Width** determines how far from an edge you have to drag (1–256 pixels) for Photoshop to still find the edge.

- **Contrast** determines how much variation (1–100%) must exist between pixels for Photoshop to define an edge.

- **Frequency** determines the rate at which Photoshop places anchor points. Higher values (up to 100) create anchor points faster than lower values (down to 0).

6. **Define the following settings in the pop-up menu, then press Return/Enter to apply them:**

Thickness:	**2 px**
Color:	**Light Red**
Curve Fit:	**2 px**
Width:	**15 px**
Contrast:	**10%**
Frequency:	**25**

Open this menu.   Check this option.

Note:

The default path color is very similar to the colors in the image you're working with; you are changing it to a thicker red path so it will be easier to see as you work through this project.

7. **Click at the corner where the left side mirror meets the car to place the first anchor point. Drag up and around the car shape.**

You don't have to hold down the mouse button when you draw with the Freeform Pen tool in Magnetic mode.

As you drag, the magnetic function creates anchor points to define a vector path around obvious edges where you drag.

Magnetic Freeform Pen tool cursor

The path snaps to the high-contrast edges near where you drag.

Click here to place the first anchor point for the path.

Note:

When you draw by holding down a button (mouse button or the button on a graphics tablet/pen) it is not uncommon for the line to "jump" where you don't want it to jump. If this happens, press Esc to remove your selection or path, and start drawing again.

8. **Continue dragging around the car shape to create the initial outline.**

Skip the tires for now, and don't worry if the path is not perfect as you outline the car shape. You will fine-tune the path in the next few exercises.

9. **If you can't see the entire car in the document window, press the Spacebar to temporarily access the Hand tool, then click and drag to move the image so you can see the edges that you need to follow.**

The Spacebar temporarily switches to the Hand tool, so you can drag the image in the window, even while working on another task. When you release the Spacebar, you return to the previously selected tool, so you can continue drawing the path of the car's shape.

If you drag past the edge of the document window, Photoshop automatically scrolls the visible area of the image. Manually repositioning with the Hand tool gives you better control over exactly what you see.

Note:

Some users report processor-related issues when temporarily switching to the Hand tool while drawing with the Freeform Pen tool in Magnetic mode.

If you experience performance problems, try zooming out and in with the keyboard commands instead of dragging with the Hand tool.

Press the Spacebar to temporarily access the Hand tool.

10. **When you reach an obvious corner in the car's outline, click to place a specific anchor point.**

Although Photoshop automatically creates anchor points based on the defined magnetic behavior, you can also click to place anchor points in specific locations.

Click to manually place an anchor point at apparent corners.

11. **Continue outlining the car shape. When you get back to your original starting point, click to create a closed path.**

When the tool cursor is over the original starting point, a hollow circle in the icon indicates that clicking will close the path.

The hollow circle indicates that clicking will close the path.

12. Open the Layers and Paths panels.

As you can see, no layer has been added. The path you drew is stored in the Paths panel as the Work Path, which is a temporary path that exists only until you create another path.

Some parts of the car are not included inside the path.

No layer is added to the file.

The path you drew is stored as the Work Path.

13. With the Work Path selected in the Paths panel, open the panel Options menu and choose Save Path.

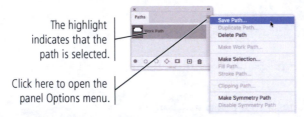

The highlight indicates that the path is selected.

Click here to open the panel Options menu.

More about Working with the Paths Panel

In the Paths panel options menu, you can choose **Make Selection** to make a marching-ants selection based on the path shape. You can use the resulting dialog box to define the details of the selection.

If you choose **Fill Path** in the Options menu, you can use the resulting dialog box to determine how the fill will be created. You can choose a color or pattern, blending mode and opacity, and whether to feather the edge of the fill so it blends smoothly into underlying layers.

If you choose the **Stroke Path** option, you must also choose which tool will create the stroke. The applied stroke will have the last-used settings for the selected tool. In other words, you have to define the tool options (brush size, hardness, etc.) that you want before using this option.

The Fill Path and Stroke Path options add the resulting pixels to the currently active layer — an important distinction from the Shape Layer option, which creates a new layer when you begin drawing the vector path. It is also important to remember that although the path remains a vector path, color applied to the fill or stroke of the path is raster-based and it does not have the same scalability as a vector shape layer.

If you choose the **Clipping Path** option, the selected path will become a clipping path, which is essentially a vector mask that can define the visible area of an image. The white area in the path thumbnail defines the visible areas.

Buttons across the bottom of the panel provide quick access to many of the available options. They are, from left:

- Fill Path with Foreground Color
- Stroke Path with Brush
- Load Path as a Selection
- Make Work Path from Selection
- Add Layer Mask
- Create New Path
- Delete Path

14. **Type Car Outline in the resulting dialog box, then click OK.**

    After you save the path, the new name appears instead of "Work Path;" this path will remain in the file even if you create a different temporary Work Path.

The saved path is permanent.

Understanding Anchor Points and Handles

An **anchor point** marks the end of a line **segment**, and the point **handles** determine the shape of that segment. That's the basic definition of a vector, but there is a bit more to it than that. (The Photoshop Help files refer to handles as direction lines and distinguishes different types of points. Our aim here is to explain the overall concept of vector paths, so we use the generic industry-standard terms. For more information on Adobe's terminology, refer to the Photoshop Help files.)

Each segment in a path has two anchor points and can have two associated handles.

You can create corner points by simply clicking with the Pen tool, instead of clicking and dragging. Corner points do not have their own handles; the connected segments are controlled by the handles of the other associated points.

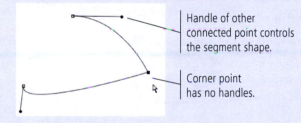

Handle of other connected point controls the segment shape.

Corner point has no handles.

In the image shown here, we first clicked to create Point A and dragged (without releasing the mouse button) to create Handle A1. We then clicked and dragged to create Point B and Handle B1. Handle B2 was automatically created as a reflection of B1. Point B is a **symmetrical point**.

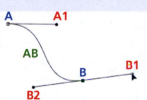

This image shows the result of dragging Handle B1 to the left instead of to the right when we created the initial curve. Notice the difference in the curve here, compared to the curve above. When you drag a handle, the connecting segment arcs away from the direction you drag.

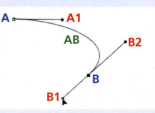

It's important to understand that every line segment is connected to two handles. In this example, Handle A1 and Handle B2 determine the shape of Segment AB. Dragging either handle affects the shape of the connected segment.

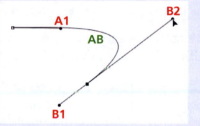

When you use the Pen tool, clicking and dragging a point creates a symmetrical (smooth) point; both handles start out at equal length, directly opposite one another. Changing the angle of one handle of a symmetrical point also changes the opposing handle of that point. In the example here, repositioning Handle B1 also moves Handle B2, which affects the shape of Segment AB. You can, however, change the length of one handle without affecting the length of the other handle.

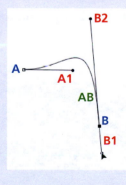

15. Click the bottom area of the Paths panel to deselect the path.

When the path is not selected, you can't see its anchor points and connecting segments in the document window.

When the path is not selected, you can't see it in the document window.

16. Save the file and continue to the next exercise.

Add to an Existing Path

In the previous exercise, you intentionally skipped the wheels in the image because the Freeform Pen tool's magnetic properties perform better with higher-contrast edges than what is evident where the tires meet the pavement. In this exercise, you will use the Pen tool to add the wheels to the existing path.

1. With magazine.psd open, make sure the view percentage is 100% and position the image so the right wheel is entirely visible.

2. Choose the Pen tool (nested under the Freeform Pen tool) in the Tools panel.

When you choose a nested tool, it becomes the default option in that position of the Tools panel. To access the original default tool — the Pen tool, in this case — you have to click the tool and hold down the mouse button to access the nested tools menu.

3. In the Paths panel, click the Car Outline path to make it visible in the document window.

You want to add more shapes to the existing path, so the path needs to be selected and visible in the document window.

4. In the Options bar, choose Path in the Tool Mode menu.

5. Click the Path Operations button and choose Combine Shapes (if it is not already selected).

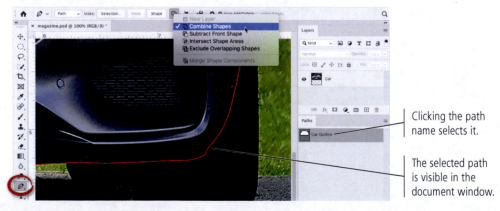

Clicking the path name selects it.

The selected path is visible in the document window.

6. **Click the Pen tool in the Tools panel to hide the anchor points of the existing path (if necessary).**

If the existing path's anchor points are visible, you can use the Pen tool to add anchor points to the existing path. You want to create a second shape in the same path, so you need to turn off the existing path's anchor points.

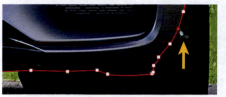

If the existing path's anchor points are visible, clicking would add a new point to the existing path.

If the existing path's anchor points are not visible, clicking creates a new shape that is part of the same path.

7. **Click with the Pen tool cursor where the rear tire meets the car undercarriage.**

Clicking once with the Pen tool creates a corner anchor point with no direction handles.

8. **Move the cursor down and right along the tire edge (as shown in Step 9).**

9. **Click to create an anchor point, hold down the mouse button, and drag down and right to create direction handles for the point.**

Click here to place the first point.

Click and drag to create a new point with direction handles.

Note:

Don't worry if the curve isn't quite perfect — you will learn how to edit anchor points and handles in the next exercise.

10. **When the shape of the connecting segment between the two points matches the shape of the tire, release the mouse button.**

When you click and drag with the Pen tool, you create a smooth point with symmetrical direction handles. As you drag, you can see the handles extend equal distances from both sides of the point you just created. The length and angle of the direction handles control the shape of segments that connect two anchor points.

As long as you hold down the mouse button, you can drag to change the length and angle of the point's handles, which also changes the shape of the connecting segment.

11. **Move the cursor to the right, following the bottom edge of the rear tire. Click and drag to create another anchor point with symmetrical direction handles. When the connecting segment matches the shape of the tire, release the mouse button.**

When you click-drag to create a smooth point, the point is automatically symmetrical. In other words, the handles on each side of the point are the same length.

These handles affect the shape of the connecting segment.

12. **Click without dragging where the rear tire meets the front tire.**

Click without dragging to create a corner point.

13. **Continue adding symmetrical smooth points to the path, placing the final point where the front tire meets the body of the car.**

Add a point where the tire meets the body.

14. **Click and drag to place another smooth point inside the area of the bumper.**

You are intentionally overlapping the new path with the existing one. Later, you will combine the multiple separate shapes into a single path.

15. **Move the cursor over the original starting point. When you see a hollow circle in the cursor icon, click to close the path.**

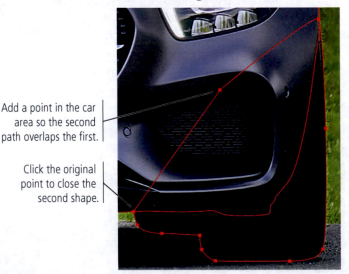

Add a point in the car area so the second path overlaps the first.

Click the original point to close the second shape.

16. **Repeat the process from this exercise to add a path around the left wheels.**

Remember, clicking without dragging creates a corner point, which does not have direction handles.

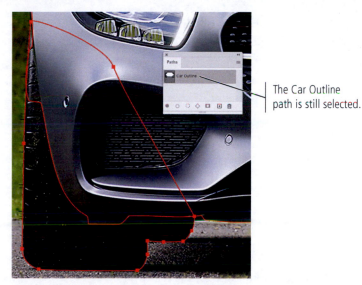

The Car Outline path is still selected.

17. **Change your view percentage so you can see the entire car in the document window.**

18. **With the Car Outline path selected in the Paths panel, make sure the Pen tool is still active.**

19. **Open the Path Operations menu in the Options bar and choose Merge Shape Components.**

The three original paths are combined into a single shape. Photoshop adds anchor points where necessary and removes overlapping segments from the original paths.

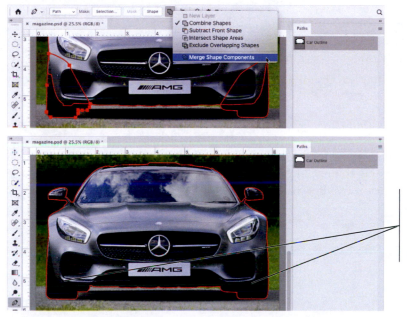

After merging shapes, the three separate paths are combined into a single path that is the outermost path of each component.

20. **Save the file and continue to the next exercise.**

Edit Vector Paths

You probably noticed that the path you created in the previous exercises is not a perfect outline of the car. The Freeform Pen tool can be a very good starting point for creating odd-shaped paths, but you will almost always need to edit and fine-tune the results to accurately reflect the path you want. Fortunately, Photoshop offers a number of options for editing vector paths.

You can use the **Path Selection tool** ( ) to select an entire path or the **Direct Selection tool** ( ) to select a specific anchor point or segment.

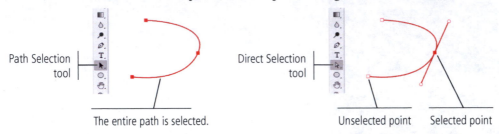

Path Selection tool   Direct Selection tool

The entire path is selected.   Unselected point   Selected point

The **Add Anchor Point tool** ( ) adds a new anchor point to an existing path. Photoshop automatically creates handles for the new point and adjusts handles for existing points to maintain the existing path shape.

You can use the **Delete Anchor Point tool** ( ) to remove an existing point from a path. Photoshop removes the selected point and adjusts the handles of remaining points to try to maintain the original path shape.

Clicking a smooth point with the **Convert Point tool** ( ) converts that point to a corner point by removing its handles (below left). Clicking and dragging from a corner point with this tool converts it to a smooth, symmetrical point (below right).

You can add a handle to only one side of a corner point by Option/Alt-clicking a point with the Convert Point tool and dragging (below left). You can also click a handle with the Convert Point tool and drag to move only one handle of the point, resulting in a corner point with asymmetrical handles (below right).

Note:

When the Pen tool is active, placing the cursor over an existing selected path automatically shows the Add Anchor Point tool cursor.

Note:

When the Pen tool is active, placing the cursor over an existing point on a selected path automatically shows the Delete Anchor Point tool cursor.

Note:

When the Pen tool is active, you can press Option/Alt to temporarily access the Convert Point tool cursor.

1. **With `magazine.psd` open, set your view percentage to at least 100%.**

2. **Drag around the image to review the Car Outline path.**

   Although your results might differ from our screen captures, the path almost certainly does not accurately outline the car. You must use what you learned on Page 107 and Page 112 to edit the path to exactly match the car's shape.

   The Magnetic Freeform Pen tool path excluded some areas that must be inside the path.

   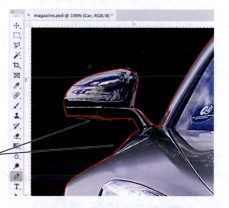

3. **Use the following information to fine-tune your Car Outline path.**

   In this instance, we can't give you specific instructions because everyone's path will be a bit different. Keep the following points in mind as you refine your shape:

   - Use the Direct Selection tool to select and edit specific segments or points on the path. You can move points to a new position by dragging (or using the Arrow keys) or moving their handles to change segment shapes.

   - Use the Add Anchor Point tool to add a point to the path.

   - Use the Delete Anchor Point tool to remove a point from the path.

   - Use the Convert Point tool to change a corner point to a smooth point and vice versa.

   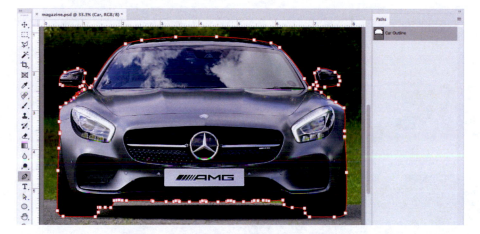

4. **Save the file and continue to the next exercise.**

Create a Vector-Based Layer Mask

Now that your car outline shape is nearly complete, you are going to use the path to create a vector-based layer mask, which will remove the car from the surrounding background. The edges of a vector mask are defined by a vector path, which means they cannot have degrees of transparency. To edit the mask edge, you have to edit the vector path.

1. **With magazine.psd open, set your view percentage so you can see the entire car in the document window.**

2. **Select the Car Outline path in the Paths panel and select the Car layer in the Layers panel.**

3. **Choose Layer>Vector Mask>Current Path.**

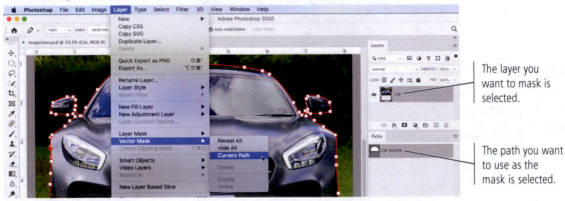

The layer you want to mask is selected.

The path you want to use as the mask is selected.

As you can see, a new path is added to the Paths panel. The name, "Car Vector Mask" identifies this path as a vector mask for the layer named, "Car." This temporary path only appears in the panel when the masked layer is selected.

Nothing is added to the Channels panel because channels are raster-based; they do not store vector-based path information.

The mask thumbnail is added to the masked layer.

The mask path is visible in the Paths panel when the masked layer is selected.

No alpha channel is added to the file.

4. **Click the empty area at the bottom of the Layers panel to deselect the layer.**

   When the masked layer is not selected, the mask path does not appear in the Paths panel. This is an important distinction — if you want to edit the mask path, you have to make sure the correct path is selected first. Editing the original Car Outline path will have no effect on the mask path.

When the masked layer is not selected, the mask path does not appear in the Paths panel.

5. **Save the file and continue to the next exercise.**

Drawing with the Curvature Pen Tool

The Curvature Pen tool, nested under the regular Pen tool, can be used to create and edit complex paths without manually manipulating anchor points.

Using the Curvature Pen tool, begin by clicking to place points in a new path. As you drag after creating the first two points, the software shows a rubber-band preview of the path that will be created by clicking again.

If you don't see the rubber-band behavior, open the Set Additional Pen and Path Options menu in the Options bar and make sure Rubber Band is checked.

As long as the Curvature Pen tool is active, you do not need to change tools to edit the path:

- Option/Alt-click to create a corner point.
- Click anywhere along an existing path to add a new anchor point.
- Double-click any point to toggle it between a smooth and corner point.
- Click a point to select it.
- Drag a selected point to move it.
- Press Delete to remove the selected point. The existing curve is maintained.
- Press the Esc key to stop drawing the current shape.

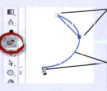

Click to place the first two points.

Rubber-band behavior previews the curve that would be created by clicking again.

Make sure Rubber Band is checked.

Create a Vector Shape Layer

A shape layer is a special type of Photoshop layer that retains vector path information. The vector shape functions as a mask, revealing the defined fill color for the shape. Any vector paths can have defined stroke properties (color, width, and type/style), and can be edited using the same tools that you used to edit the paths in the previous exercises.

In this exercise, you will build a compound vector shape that will provide a background for the magazine's "In This Issue" text.

1. **With `magazine.psd` open, hide the Car layer.**

2. **In the Tools panel, choose the Rounded Rectangle tool (nested under the Rectangle tool).**

3. **In the Options bar, choose Shape in the Tool Mode menu.**

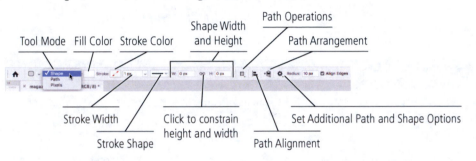

Note:

If a tool is missing from its default spot in the Tools panel, check in the Edit Toolbar menu ••• at the bottom of the Tools panel. You can also reset the Essentials workspace to show all tools in their default locations.

4. **Click the Fill color swatch to open the pop-up Swatches panel. Click the arrow to the left of the CMYK group, then click the CMYK Blue swatch to select it as the fill color.**

You can define separate fill and stroke colors of a vector shape layer, just as you might do for an object you create in Adobe Illustrator or InDesign. Clicking the Fill or Stroke color swatch opens a pop-up panel, where you can select a specific swatch to use as the attribute's color. Four buttons at the top of the panel change the attribute to (from left): None, Solid, a Gradient, or a Pattern. Predefined color swatches are organized into folders by category. You can also click the Color Picker button to define any color that is not already in the Swatches panel.

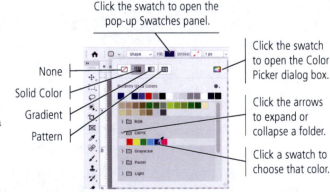

5. **Click the Stroke swatch and choose No Color in the pop-up Swatches panel.**

6. **Change the Radius field to 50 px.**

A rounded-corner rectangle is simply a rectangle with the corners cut at a specific distance from the end (the corner radius). The two sides are connected with one-fourth of a circle, which has a radius equal to the amount of the rounding.

This imaginary circle has a 50-px radius.

7. **Click in the top-right area of the canvas, then drag down and right to create the new shape.**

When you release the mouse button, the shape you drew fills with the defined Fill color. Because you chose None as the Stroke color, the shape you drew has no applied stroke. The red color you see around the shape is the color you defined earlier as the path color when you drew the car path.

When you use the Shape option in the Tool Mode menu, the resulting vector shape exists by default on its own layer.

Note:

The color you are using here is temporary, because you will later apply a built-in graphic style to this shape.

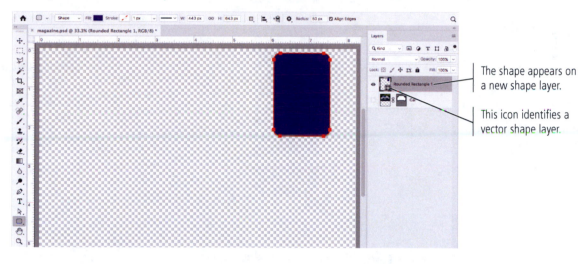

The shape appears on a new shape layer.

This icon identifies a vector shape layer.

8. **Click the empty space at the bottom of the Layers panel to deselect the Rounded Rectangle layer.**

When you deselect the layer, you can see the actual shape without the heavy red vector path. You can now see that the shape you created has no defined stroke color.

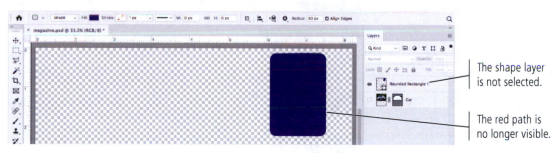

The shape layer is not selected.

The red path is no longer visible.

9. **Click the Rounded Rectangle 1 layer to select it again.**

When the shape layer is selected, you can again see the vector path that makes up the shape.

10. **Make sure the rulers are visible (View>Rulers), then review the information in the Properties panel.**

This panel automatically appears when you create a new shape with one of the vector shape tools. It shows the dimensions and position of the resulting shape, as well as other properties that were not available in the Options bar before you created the shape.

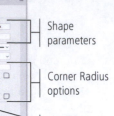

Shape parameters

Align type for stroke

Line cap type for stroke

Line join type for stroke

Corner Radius options

Path Operations

11. **Highlight the current W field and type `500`. Press Tab to highlight the H field, then type `1230`. Press Return/Enter to apply the change.**

The W and H fields define the object's physical dimensions.

The Properties panel defaults to use pixels for shape layers, regardless of the default units for the active file. You can, however, type values in other units of measurement, as long as you include the appropriate unit in the value you type (for example, "2 in" or "4 cm").

Note:

Because you are creating a vector shape, you can edit its properties at any time, without losing quality or pixel integrity (as would happen for pixel-based, raster data).

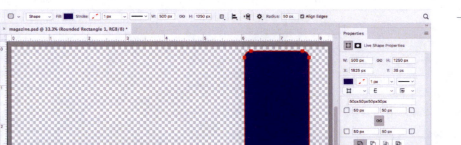

12. **Place the Mouse cursor over the X field until you see the scrubby slider cursor. Click and drag right or left until the X field shows 1865 px (the shape is approximately 3/8″ from the right edge of the canvas).**

The X and Y fields in the Properties panel define the object's position based on its top-left corner. Unlike transforming objects in the Options panel, you cannot select a different reference point around which to anchor the transformation.

Scrubby sliders, available in most Photoshop panels, offer a dynamic way to change field values. You can click the field name and drag left to decrease the value, or drag right to increase the value.

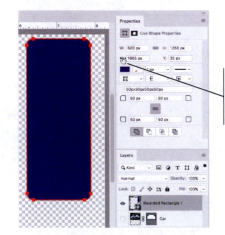

When you see this scrubby slider, click and drag to change the related field value.

13. **Using either the scrubby slider or the field, change the Y position to 0 px.**

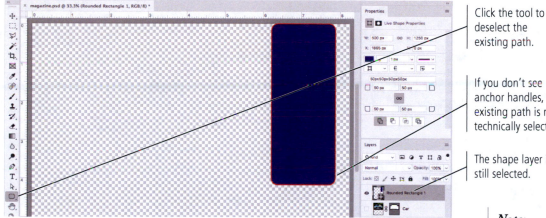

14. **Click the Rounded Rectangle tool in the Tools panel to deselect the existing vector shape and hide the path's anchor handles.**

    Although the actual vector path is deselected, the shape layer is still selected in the Layers panel.

    Click the tool to deselect the existing path.

    If you don't see anchor handles, the existing path is not technically selected.

    The shape layer is still selected.

15. **In the Options bar, open the Path Operations menu and choose Subtract Front Shape.**

    If no shape layer is currently selected, the Path Operations menu defaults to New Layer. As long as a shape layer is selected and one of the shape layer tools is active, the menu retains the last-used option. You can continue subtracting as many new shapes as you like until you switch to a different tool — the Direct Selection tool, for example, to modify a specific anchor point.

Note:

The Path Operations menu retains the last-used selection, as long as the same tool remains active. If you switch to a different tool, the path operation reverts back to the New Layer option.

More about Vector Shape Options

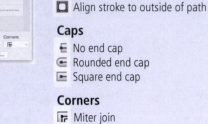

Stroke Types

When a vector drawing tool is active, you can use the Stroke Type menu in the Options bar to choose a preset stroke style (solid, dashed, or dotted).

- The Align menu changes the stroke's alignment relative to the path. The icons in the menu suggest the result.

- The Caps menu determines how the stroke aligns to the ends of the path.

- The Corners menu defines the way the stroke appears at corners on the path.

If you click the More Options button, you can define a custom dash pattern.

Align

- Align stroke to inside of path
- Align stroke to center of path
- Align stroke to outside of path

Caps

- No end cap
- Rounded end cap
- Square end cap

Corners

- Miter join
- Rounded join
- Beveled join

Path Alignment

You can use the **Path Alignment** to align or distribute multiple shapes on the same layer. For these options to work properly, you must use the Path Selection tool to select the paths you want to align, and then choose an option from the menu. When Canvas is selected in the Align To menu, you can align one or more paths in relation to the overall canvas.

Geometry Options

Pen Tool

For the Pen tool, you can check the Rubber Band option in the Geometry Options menu to show a preview of the path curve as you move the cursor.

Rectangle, Rounded Rectangle, and Ellipse Tools

When **Unconstrained** is selected, you can simply click and drag to create a rectangle of any size.

If you choose the **Square** option (or Circle for the Ellipse tool), the shape you draw will be constrained to equal width and height (1:1 aspect ratio).

Rectangle/Rounded Rectangle tool

You can use the **Fixed Size** option to create a shape at a specific width and height. When you click in the canvas, you see a preview of the shape that will be created. You can drag around to determine where the shape will be placed when you release the mouse button.

Ellipse tool

You can also use the **Proportional** option to define the aspect ratio of the shape you will create. When you click and drag, the shape is constrained to the proportions you define.

If you choose the **From Center** option, the center of the shape you create will be placed where you first click.

Polygon Tool

Geometry options for this tool are the same as those that are available when you click the tool to define the shape you want to create (see Page 102).

Line Tool

When you draw with the Line tool, you can use the Geometry Options menu to add arrowheads to the start and/or end of the line. The Width and Length fields define those attributes of the arrowheads as a percentage of the line weight. The Concavity field defines the arrowheads' inset as a percentage of its length.

Custom Shape Tool

The Custom Shape tool makes it easy to create custom vector shapes from one of several defined libraries. You can open the Shape panel in the Options bar to access the built-in libraries of shapes.

Geometry options for the Custom Shape tool are the same as those for the Rectangle and Ellipse tools.

New Layer

When you first choose one of the vector drawing tools — Pen, Freeform Pen, or one of the Shape tools — the Path Operations menu defaults to **New Layer**. When this option is active, every new path will be created on a separate layer.

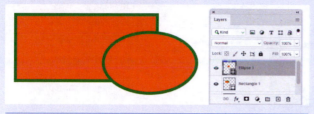

Combining Shapes

Combine Shapes creates the new path on the existing (selected) shape layer.

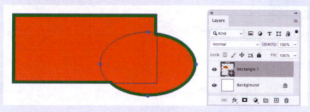

Subtract Front Shape creates the new path on the existing (selected) layer and removes overlapping areas of the new shape from the existing shape.

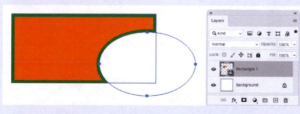

Intersect Shape Areas results in the shape of only overlapping areas in the existing and new shapes.

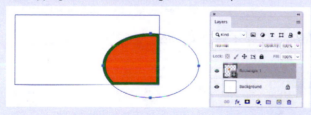

Exclude Overlapping Areas removes overlapping areas between the existing and new shapes.

Merge Shape Components

It is important to note that with the four Combine options explained to the left, the result is the appearance of a single shape, but the original paths of each shape are maintained. You can still manipulate each component path independently.

To make the interaction of overlapping shapes permanent, you can select the paths you want to affect and choose **Merge Shape Components**. This results in a single shape that is the combination of any selected paths; unselected paths are not affected.

The actual result of this command depends on the interaction of the selected paths. In the example below, the top shape has been created with the Intersect Shape Areas operation. After applying the Merge Shape Components operation, anchor points were removed where the original paths did not intersect (as shown in the bottom image).

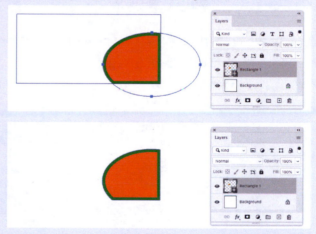

Merging Shape Layers

If multiple shape layers are selected in the Layers panel, you can combine them by choosing Merge Shapes in the Layers panel Options menu.

This command combines the shapes on all selected layers into a single shape layer — basically the same as using the Combine Shapes path operation. The new combined layer adopts the name of the highest layer in the previous selection.

Important note: Don't confuse this Merge option with the Merge Shape Components option in the Path Operations menu. The Merge Shapes option in the Layers panel actually combines the various shapes into a single layer, but maintains all of the existing paths.

16. Click and drag to create another rectangle inside the area of the first.

Using the Subtract Front Shape option, the second shape removes the overlapping area of underlying shapes, creating a compound path that results in a "window" effect.

Options for the basic Shape tools remember the last-used settings, so the new shape automatically has the 50-px corner radius that you defined for the first shape.

Note:

*A **compound path** is any single shape made up of more than one closed path.*

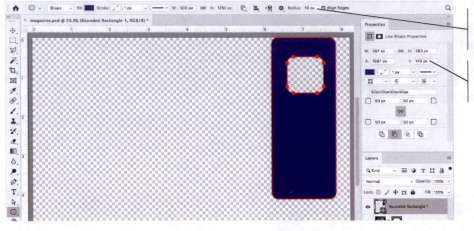

The Options panel shows options for the overall shape layer.

The Properties panel shows options for the selected vector path.

17. In the Properties panel, change the new shape's parameters to:

W: 300 px   H: 300 px
X: 1965 px   Y: 135 px

18. In the lower half of the Properties panel, make sure the four corner radius fields are linked.

When the link icon is highlighted (active), changing any one radius value affects the other three corners.

19. Type 10 in the top-left field, then press Return/Enter to apply your changes.

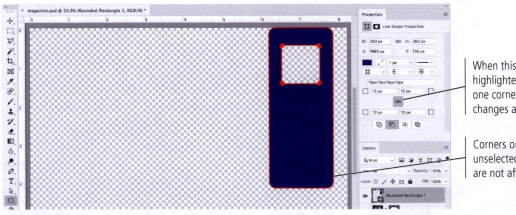

When this icon is highlighted, changing one corner radius changes all four corners.

Corners on the unselected path are not affected.

20. **Choose the Path Selection tool in the Tools panel, then click the outer path of the compound shape to select it.**

Each component path of the overall shape is still an independent vector path, which means you can select and edit its properties in the Properties panel at any time.

21. **Unlink the four corner radius fields, then change the top-left and top-right corner radius fields to field to `0 px`.**

Although rounded-corner shapes always start with four identical corners, you can use this panel to change each corner radius individually.

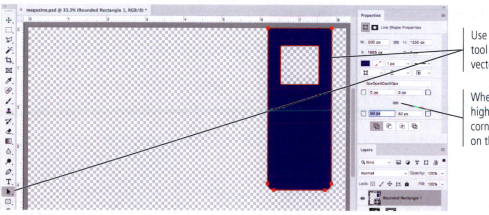

Use the Path Selection tool to select a specific vector path.

When this icon is not highlighted, changing one corner radius has no effect on the other corners.

22. **Save the file and continue to the next exercise.**

Selecting and Modifying Paths

When you draw vector paths, you can use the Path Selection tool to select and move specific paths on a layer.

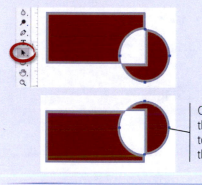

Click and drag with the Path Selection tool to move only the selected path.

You can also select a specific shape to change the path operation that applies to it (in either the Options or Properties panel). In the example below, the rectangle was created first, and then the oval was created with the Combine Shapes path operation. We then used the Path Selection tool to select the oval, and chose the Intersect Front Shape operation. Unless you merge the paths into a single shape, you can always select an individual path and change the way it interacts with underlying shapes.

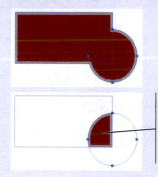

Changing the path operation of the selected path changes the way it interacts with the bottom path.

Because the path operations affect underlying shapes, you should also understand the concept of **stacking order**. When you create multiple shapes on the same shape layer, they exist from bottom-to-top in the order in which you create them — the first shape is on the bottom, and then the next shape is above, and so on, until the last shape created is at the top of the stack. You can use the **Path Arrangement** menu to control the stacking order of selected paths on the same shape layer.

- Bring Shape To Front
- Bring Shape Forward
- Send Shape Backward
- Send Shape To Back

Clone and Align Layers

If you need more than one version of the same layer, you can create a copy by choosing Duplicate Layer in the layer's contextual menu. This command results in a copy of the original layer in exactly the same position as the original.

You can also use the Move tool to **clone** a layer, which results in a duplicate copy of the original, in the position where you drag to make the clone. In this exercise, you will use cloning to create three rectangle shape layers across the bottom of the canvas. You will then distribute those shape layers evenly across the canvas.

Note:

These shapes will be used to hold additional inset photos to enhance the visual interest of the overall composition.

1. **With magazine.psd open, click the empty area at the bottom of the layers panel to deselect the existing shape layer.**

   If you don't first deselect the shape layer, your stroke color changes in the next few steps would affect the existing shape.

2. **Choose the Rectangle tool (nested under the Rounded Rectangle tool if you continued directly from the previous exercise). In the Options bar, define the following settings:**

Fill Color:	**White**
Stroke Color:	**Dark Red (in the Dark folder)**
Stroke Width:	**15 px**

3. **Open the Path Operations menu and review the options.**

   The Path Operations menu defaults to the New Layer option if an existing shape layer is not selected.

4. **Open the Set Additional Shape and Path Options menu. Define a 1 px thickness and use the Default color.**

   Because you are creating a shape with an actual red stroke, the red path you defined earlier is not a good choice. In this case, the thinner Default (blue) option will be far less distracting.

5. **Click and drag to create a rectangle in the lower half of the canvas. Using the Properties panel, define the new shape's parameters as:**

W: 600 px	**H: 500 px**
X: 200 px	**Y: 2430 px**

6. **Choose the Move tool in the Tools panel. Press Option/Alt, then click inside the smaller rectangle shape and drag right to clone it.**

   Pressing Option/Alt while dragging a selection clones that selection. Because the shape layer is the active selection, the entire shape layer is cloned. The Smart Guides help you maintain the cloned layer's horizontal alignment to the original. If you decide to hide Smart Guides, pressing Shift constrains the movement to 45° angles.

   The new cloned layer appears immediately above the original in the Layers panel, with the name, "Rectangle 1 Copy."

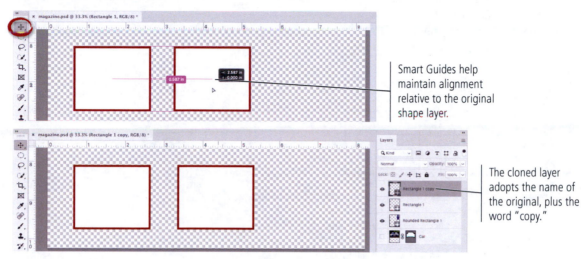

Smart Guides help maintain alignment relative to the original shape layer.

The cloned layer adopts the name of the original, plus the word "copy."

7. **Double-click the name of the Rectangle 1 layer to highlight it. Type** `Left Inset`**, then press Return/Enter to change the layer name.**

   Even though you will have only three copies of this shape layer, it could become very confusing later if you don't use meaningful names to differentiate the layers.

8. **Double-click the name of the cloned layer to highlight it. Type** `Center Inset`**, then press Return/Enter to change the layer name.**

9. **Repeat Step 6 to create a third shape layer at the bottom of the canvas. Name this new layer** `Right Inset`**.**

10. **In the Properties panel, change the X position of the active shape to** `1700 px`**.**

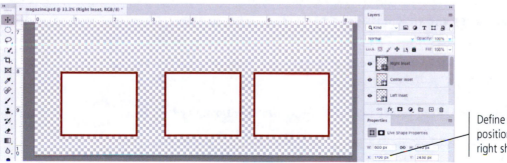

Define the X position of the right shape.

11. **In the Layers panel, Shift-click to select all three Inset shape layers.**

    When multiple layers are selected in the Layers panel, a number of alignment options become available in the Options bar. These are very useful for aligning or distributing the content of multiple layers relative to one another.

12. **With the Move tool active, click the Distribute Horizontally button in the Options bar.**

When the Move tool is active and multiple layers are selected, you can use the Options bar to align the contents of the selected layers relative to one another. The Distribute Horizontal Centers option places an equal amount of space between the center pixel of each selected layer; the positions of layers containing the outermost pixels in the selection are not affected.

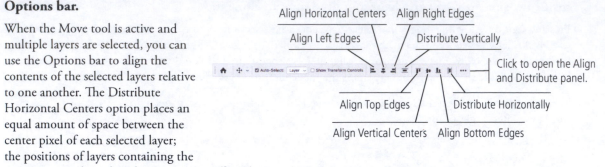

Align Horizontal Centers   Align Right Edges
Align Left Edges   Distribute Vertically
Click to open the Align and Distribute panel.
Align Top Edges   Distribute Horizontally
Align Vertical Centers   Align Bottom Edges

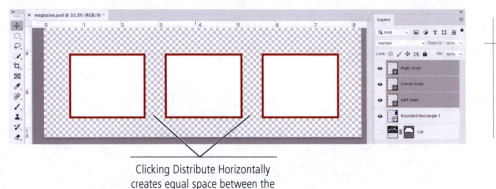

Clicking Distribute Horizontally creates equal space between the content of selected layers.

Note:

You can click the Align and Distribute button to access options for distributing based on specific edges or centers.

13. **Save the file and continue to the next exercise.**

Auto-Select Layers

When your files have more than a few layers — a common occurrence — selecting exactly the layer you want can be difficult. As you already learned, the Move tool defaults to affect the layer that is selected in the Layers panel. Using the Auto-Select option, you can automatically select a specific layer by clicking pixels in the document window, rather than manually selecting a layer in the panel first.

1. **With magazine.psd open, choose File>Place Embedded.**

2. **Navigate to inset1.jpg (in your WIP>Cars folder) and click place. When the image appears on the canvas, press Return/Enter to finalize the placement.**

New Smart Object layers appear immediately above the previously selected layer. In this case, it is at the top of the layer stack.

3. **In the Layers panel, drag inset1 to appear immediately above the Left Inset layer.**

4. **Repeat Steps 1–3 to place inset2.jpg as an embedded file, and position the inset2 layer immediately above the Center Inset layer.**

Unfortunately, you can only select one file at a time in the Place dialog box.

5. Repeat Steps 1–3 to place **inset3.jpg** as an embedded file, and position the inset3 layer immediately above the Right Inset layer.

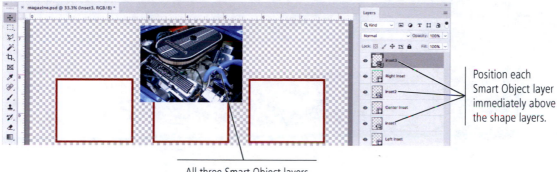

Position each Smart Object layer immediately above the shape layers.

All three Smart Object layers were placed in the center of the document window.

6. **Choose the Move tool in the Tools panel. In the Options bar, check the Auto-Select option.**

7. **Click in the area of the placed images and drag until the inset3 image entirely obscures the bottom-right rectangle shape.**

When Auto-Select is active, clicking in the canvas automatically selects the layer containing the pixel where you clicked. Because the inset3 image is on top of the other two, clicking in the area of the placed images automatically selects the inset3 layer.

Check the Auto-Select option.

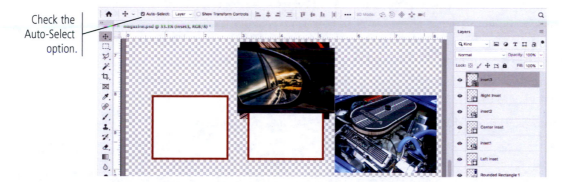

8. **Click again in the original area of the placed images, and drag to move the inset2 image until it entirely obscures the center rectangle.**

Again, clicking automatically selects the relevant layer. Using the Auto-Select option makes it easier to manage layer contents, even when you are not sure which layer contains the pixels you want to affect.

When Auto-Select is checked, clicking automatically selects the layer containing the pixel on which you clicked.

9. **Move the inset1 image until it entirely obscures the left rectangle.**

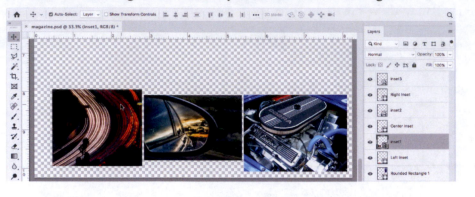

Note:

Remember, if the Auto-Select option is checked in the Options bar, you can simply click pixels of the layer you want to move without first selecting the layer.

10. **Save the file and continue to the next exercise.**

Create Clipping Masks

As you can see, the placed images completely hide the underlying layer content. To make the inset images appear only within the area of the underlying shapes, you need to create clipping masks. This task is relatively easy to accomplish.

1. **With magazine.psd open, Control/right-click the inset1 layer to open the layer's contextual menu.**

   Remember, to access the contextual menu for a specific layer, you have to Control/right-click in the area to the right of the layer name.

2. **Choose Create Clipping Mask from the contextual menu.**

   A clipping mask is another way to show only certain areas of a layer; in this case, using the shape of one layer (Left Inset) to show parts of the layer above it (inset1).

   The Layers panel shows that the inset1 layer is clipped by the Left Inset layer.

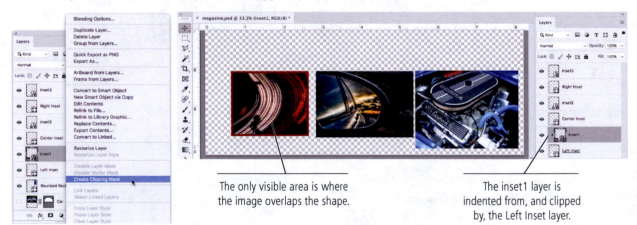

The only visible area is where the image overlaps the shape.

The inset1 layer is indented from, and clipped by, the Left Inset layer.

3. **With the Move tool active, click in the area of the left inset image and drag until you are satisfied with the visible area of the image.**

   Even though a layer is clipped, you can still move it without affecting the position of the clipping layer. Unlike a layer mask, the clipping and clipped layers are not automatically linked.

Use the Move tool to reposition the clipped image.

The clipping layer still defines the visible area of the clipped image.

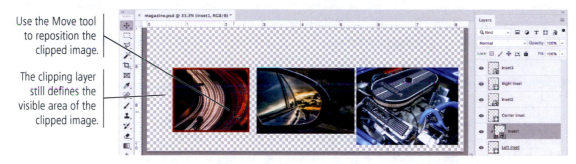

As with layer masks, clipping masks do not permanently modify the pixels in the layer. You can choose Release Clipping Mask in the clipped layer's contextual menu to undo a clipping mask, without altering the affected layers.

4. **Repeat Steps 1–3 to clip the inset2 and inset3 images to their underlying layers.**

5. **In the Layers panel, show the Car layer, and then move it to the top of the layer stack.**

6. **Using the Move tool, position the car so it slightly overlaps the three shape layers at the bottom of the page.**

   Use the following image as a guide.

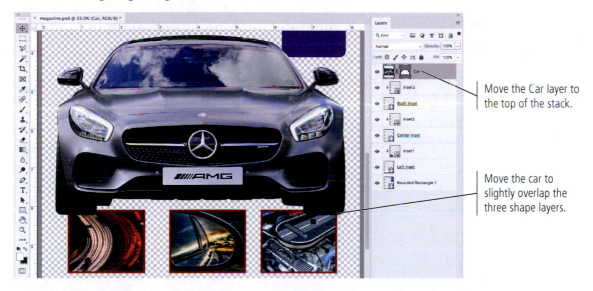

Move the Car layer to the top of the stack.

Move the car to slightly overlap the three shape layers.

7. **Save the file, and then continue to the next stage of the project.**

STAGE 3 / Applying Styles and Filters

Photoshop includes a large number of options for creating artistic effects, including built-in patterns, styles, and filters. You can add texture to the flat fill color of a vector shape layer or apply effects, such as drop shadows or beveling, to add the appearance of depth. You can make images look like pencil sketches, paintings, or any of the dozens of other options. You can even compound these filters and styles to create unique effects that would require extreme skill in traditional art techniques, such as oil painting. In this stage of the project, you will use a number of these options to enhance your overall composition.

Add Texture to a Shape Layer

Aside from their usefulness as scalable vector paths, shape layers can be filled with solid colors (as the background shape is now), with other images (as the smaller inset shapes are now), or with styles or patterns (which you will add in this exercise).

1. **With magazine.psd open, choose Window>Styles to open the Styles panel.**

   This panel shows the predefined styles that can be applied to a shape layer. The icons give you an idea of each style's results.

2. **Click the button in the top-right corner of the Styles panel and choose Small List from the Options menu.**

   After the few default styles that appear at the top of the panel, the built-in styles include a number of sets or **style groups**. You can click the arrow to the left of any group name to expand it and see the individual styles in that group.

   By default, styles appear in the Large Thumbnail view. We prefer the list view because the style names provide a better idea of what the styles do.

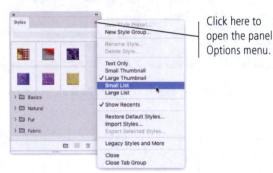

Click here to open the panel Options menu.

3. **Open the Styles panel Options menu again and choose Legacy Styles and More.**

   Photoshop 2020 made significant changes to the way assets such as styles are managed; part of this re-tooling included removing a large number of built-in styles from the default panel. Those styles are still useful, though, and can be accessed by choosing the Legacy Styles and More option.

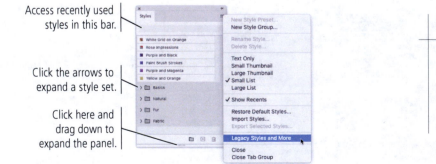

Access recently used styles in this bar.

Click the arrows to expand a style set.

Click here and drag down to expand the panel.

Note:

You can click the bottom edge of the panel and drag to resize the panel, showing more styles and sets at one time.

4. **In the Styles panel, expand the Legacy Styles and More folder, then expand the All Legacy Default Styles and Web Styles subfolders.**

5. **Select the Rounded Rectangle 1 shape layer in the Layers panel, then click the Black Anodized Metal style in the Styles panel to apply the style to the shape layer.**

The layers panel shows that a series of effects (those which make up the style) has been applied to the layer.

Photoshop styles are nondestructive, which means you can change or delete them without affecting the original layer content. You can temporarily disable all effects by clicking the eye icon to the left of the word "Effects" or disable individual effects by clicking the icon for a specific item in the panel.

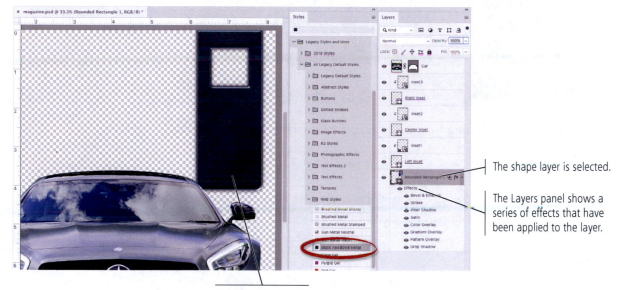

The shape layer is selected.

The Layers panel shows a series of effects that have been applied to the layer.

The selected style fills the shape layer.

6. **In the Layers panel, click the arrow to the right of the fx icon of the Rounded Rectangle 1 layer.**

This collapses the list of applied effects, which helps keep the Layers panel easier to manage.

Click here to collapse or expand the list of applied effects.

7. **Save the file and continue to the next exercise.**

Apply Custom Layer Effects

A style is simply a saved group of effects that can be applied with a single click. You can also create your own styles using the Layer Effects dialog box, which you will do in this exercise.

1. **With magazine.psd open, choose the Left Inset layer.**

2. **Choose Layer>Layer Style>Drop Shadow.**

3. **In the resulting dialog box, make sure the Preview option is checked.**

   The Preview option allows you to see the results of your settings while the dialog box is still open.

4. **In the Layer Style dialog box, make sure the Use Global Light option is checked.**

   This option is checked by default, so you should not have to make any change.

   The Angle field defines the position of the effect in relation to the layer. When the Global Light option is checked, changing the style Angle applies the same change to any other layer for which an effect using the Use Global Light option is applied.

5. **Make the following changes to the default settings in the dialog box:**

Opacity:	**50**%
Distance:	**10** px
Spread:	**5**%
Size:	**10** px

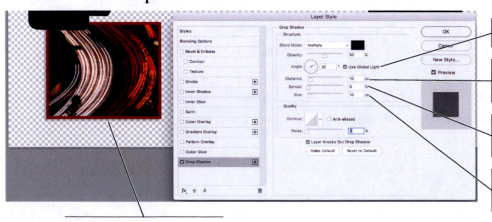

Make sure Use Global Light is checked.

Distance offsets the effect relative to the layer content.

Spread is the percentage the effect expands beyond the layer content.

Size controls the amount of blurring applied to the effect.

When Preview is checked, the effect is visible behind the dialog box.

6. **Click the + button to the right of the Drop Shadow layer style.**

   You can apply more than one instance of certain layer styles (those identified with a "+"). When you click the + button, a new instance of the style appears in the list.

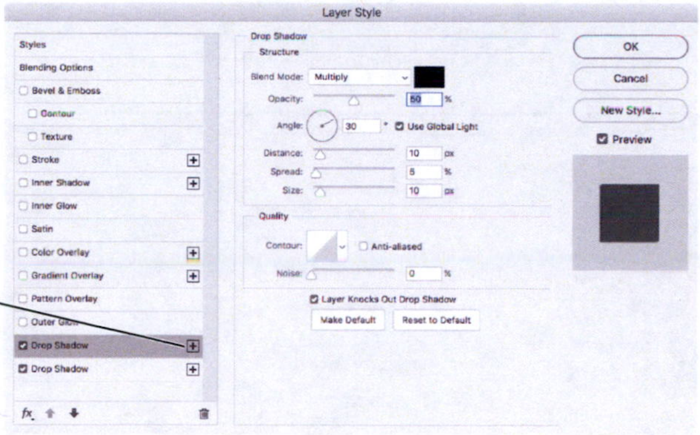

Click the **+** button to add a second instance of the same layer style.

Note:

You can use the buttons at the bottom of the effects list to change the order of applied effects, as well as delete a specific (selected) effect.

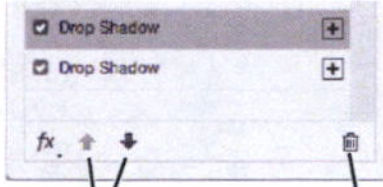

Use these buttons to reorder applied effects.   Delete Effect

7. **With the top Drop Shadow item selected in the list, click the color swatch to the right of the Blend Mode menu.**

8. **When the Color Picker appears, move the mouse cursor over the dark blue color on the car's windshield and click to sample that color. Click OK to close the Color Picker dialog box.**

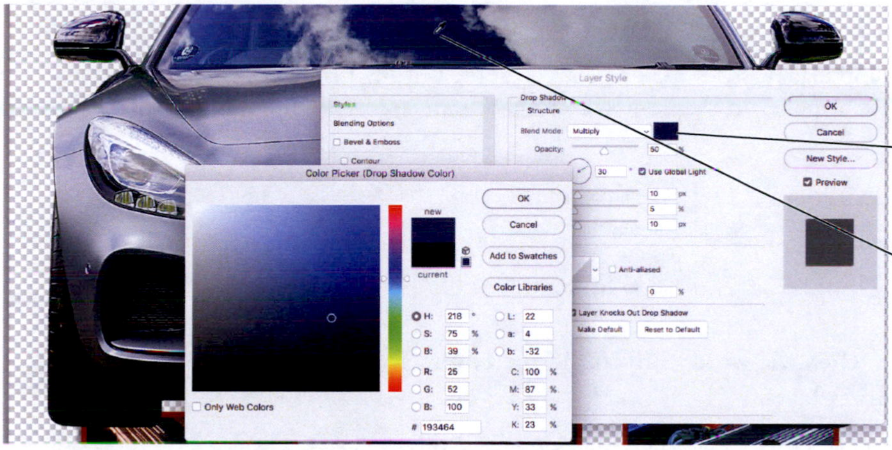

Click the swatch to open the Color Picker for the style.

Click to sample a color that you want to use for the style.

9. **Uncheck the Use Global Light option, then change the Angle field to -150°.**

   If you change the angle field while the Use Global Light option is checked, you would change the global angle and that change would apply to any other applied layer style that uses the global light angle. You want to change the angle for only this style instance, so you must uncheck Use Global Light *before* changing the angle field.

10. **Make the following changes to the settings in the dialog box:**

   Opacity: **75**%
   Distance: **20** px
   Spread: **10**%
   Size: **20** px

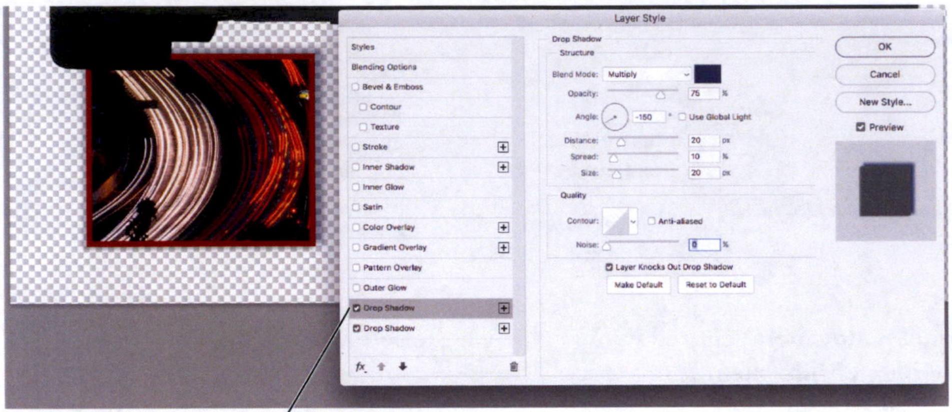

Changes affect only the
selected style instance.

11. **Click OK to apply the layer style.**

   In the Layers panel, the drop shadow styles appear as effects for the Left Inset layer. As with the built-in style you applied in the previous exercise, custom layer styles are nondestructive.

Layer styles are
non-destructive;
use the Eye icons to
turn effects on or off.

12. **Press Option/Alt, then click the word "Effects" in the Layers panel and drag it to the Center Inset layer.**

   Just as you cloned a layer in an earlier exercise, pressing Option/Alt allows you to clone effects from one layer to another. This offers an easy way to apply exactly the same effects to multiple layers in your file.

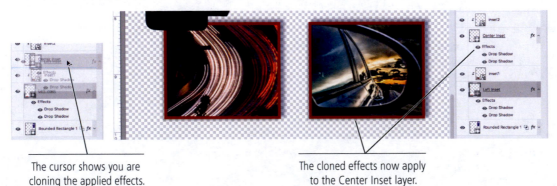

The cursor shows you are
cloning the applied effects.

The cloned effects now apply
to the Center Inset layer.

13. **Repeat Step 12 to add the Drop Shadow effects to the Right Inset layer.**

Bevel and Emboss

This style has five variations:

- **Outer Bevel** creates a bevel on the outside edges of the layer contents.
- **Inner Bevel** creates a bevel on the inside edges.
- **Emboss** creates the effect of embossing the layer contents against the underlying layers.
- **Pillow Emboss** creates the effect of stamping the edges of the layer into the underlying layers.
- **Stroke Emboss** applies an embossed effect to a stroke applied to the layer. (The Stroke Emboss effect is not available if you haven't applied a stroke to the layer.)

Any of these styles can be applied as **Smooth** (blurs the edges of the effect), **Chisel Hard** (creates a distinct edge), or **Chisel Soft** (creates a distinct but slightly blurred edge).

You can change the **Direction** of the bevel effect. **Up** creates the appearance of the layer coming out of the image; **Down** creates the appearance of something stamped into the image.

The **Size** slider makes the effect smaller or larger, and the **Soften** slider blurs the edges of the effect.

In the Shading area, you can control the light source **Angle** and **Altitude** (think of how shadows differ as the sun moves). You can also apply a **Gloss Contour** (see the following explanation of Contours). Finally, you can change the Blending Mode, Opacity, and Color settings of highlights and shadows created in effects.

When a Bevel and Emboss style is applied, you can also apply Contour and Texture effects.

Stroke

The **Stroke** style adds an outline of a specific number of pixels to the layer. The Stroke effect can be added at the outside or inside of the layer edge, or it can be centered over the edge (half the stroke will be inside and half outside the actual layer edge). You can adjust the Blending Mode and Opacity setting of the stroke, and you can also define a specific color, gradient, or pattern to apply as the stroke.

Satin

The Satin options apply interior shading to create a satiny appearance. You can change the Blending Mode, Color, and Opacity settings of the effect, as well as the Angle, Distance, and Size settings.

Drop Shadow and Inner Shadow

Drop Shadow adds a shadow behind the layer. **Inner Shadow** adds a shadow inside the edges of the layer's content. For both types, you can define the blending mode, color, opacity, angle, distance, and size of the shadow.

- **Distance** is the offset of the shadow, or how far away the shadow will be from the original layer.
- **Spread** (for Drop Shadows) is the percentage the shadow expands beyond the original layer.
- **Choke** (for Inner Shadows) is the percentage the shadow shrinks into the original layer.
- **Size** is the blur amount applied to the shadow.

You can also adjust the Contour, Anti-aliasing, and Noise settings in the shadow effect. (See the Contours section later in this discussion for further explanation.)

When checked, the Layer Knocks Out Drop Shadow option removes the drop shadow underneath the original layer area. This is particularly important if you convert a shadow style to a separate layer that you move to a different position, or if the layer is semi-transparent above its shadow.

Global Light. The Use Global Light check box is available for Drop Shadow, Inner Shadow, and Bevel and Emboss styles. When this option is checked, the style is linked to the "master" light source angle for the entire file. Changing the global light affects any linked style applied to any layer in the entire file. You can change the Global Light setting in any of the Layer Style fields, or by choosing Layer>Layer Style>Global Light.

Outer Glow and Inner Glow

Outer Glow and **Inner Glow** styles add glow effects to the outside and inside (respectively) edges of the layer. For either, you can define the Blending Mode, Opacity, and Noise values, as well as whether to use a solid color or a gradient.

- For either kind of glow, you can define the **Technique** as Precise or Softer. **Precise** creates a glow at a specific distance. **Softer** creates a blurred glow and does not preserve detail as well as Precise.
- For Inner Glows, you can also define the **Source** of the glow (Center or Edge). **Center** applies a glow starting from the center of the layer. **Edge** applies the glow starting from the inside edges of the layer.
- The **Spread** and **Choke** sliders affect the percentages of the glow effects.
- The **Size** slider makes the effect smaller or larger.

FOUNDATIONS

Contours

Contour options control the shape of the applied styles. Drop Shadow, Inner Shadow, Inner Glow, Outer Glow, Bevel and Emboss, and Satin styles all include Contour options. The default option for all but the Satin style is Linear, which applies a linear effect from solid to 100% transparent.

The easiest way to understand the Contour options is through examples. In the following series of images, the same Inner Bevel style was applied in all three examples. In the top image, you can clearly see the size and depth of the bevel. In the center and bottom images, the only difference is the applied contour. If you look carefully at the shape edge, you should be able to see how the applied contour shape maps to the beveled edge in the image.

The Linear contour is applied to the bevel.

The Gaussian contour is applied to the same bevel.

The Cone contour is applied to the same bevel.

When you apply a contour, the **Range** slider controls which part of the effect is contoured. For Outer Glow or Inner Glow, you can add variation to the contour color and opacity using the **Jitter** slider.

Textures

The Textures options allow you to create texture effects using the built-in patterns.

* The **Scale** slider varies the size of the applied pattern.
* The **Depth** slider varies the apparent depth of the applied pattern.
* The **Invert** option (as the name implies) inverts the applied pattern.
* If you check the **Link with Layer** option, the pattern's position is locked to the layer so you can move the two together. If this option is unchecked, different parts of the pattern are visible if you move the associated layer.
* When you create a texture, you can drag in the image window (behind the Layer Style dialog box) to move the texture. When the Link with Layer option is checked, clicking the **Snap to Origin** button positions the pattern origin at the upper-left corner of the layer. If Link with Layers is unchecked, clicking the Snap to Origin button positions the pattern at the image origin point.

Color Overlay, Gradient Overlay, Pattern Overlay

A **color overlay** is simply a solid color with a specific Blending Mode and Opacity value applied. A color overlay can be used to change an entire layer to a solid color (with the Normal blending mode at 100% opacity), or to create unique effects using different Blending Mode and Opacity settings.

A **gradient overlay** is basically the same as a color overlay, except you use a gradient instead of a solid color. You can choose an existing gradient or define a new one, change the Blending Mode and Opacity value of the gradient, apply any of the available gradient styles (Linear, Radial, etc.), or change the Angle and Scale values of the gradient.

A **pattern overlay** is similar to the Texture options for a Bevel and Emboss style. You can choose a specific pattern, change the Blending Mode and Opacity value, or change the applied pattern scale. You can also link the pattern to the layer and snap the pattern to the layer or the file origin.

14. Press Option/Alt, then click the second (bottom) instance of the Drop Shadow and drag it to the Car layer.

If you remember, you edited the top instance to use blue as the shadow color. The bottom instance — the one you are cloning here — applies a black shadow at a 30° angle (the global angle).

You can clone an entire set of effects by Option/Alt-dragging the word "Effects," or clone only specific effects by Option/Alt-dragging an individual item in the list.

The cursor shows you are cloning only one drop shadow effect.

The single cloned effect now applies to the Car layer.

15. In the Layers panel, double-click the Drop Shadow effect for the Car layer.

Double-clicking an effect in the panel opens the dialog box, where you can make changes to the settings that define the effect for the active layer.

16. Click in the document window (behind the dialog box) and drag down until the drop shadow is much more prominent behind the car layer.

When you drag in the document window, the dialog box dynamically changes to reflect the new angle and distance for the effect.

As you dynamically change the angle, you should also notice the effect on the three Inset layers. Because the Use Global Light option is checked for all four layers, changing the angle for one of these layers applies the same change to all four layers.

You should also notice, however, that the altered Distance value does not apply to the other three layers in which the Drop Shadow effect is applied. Only the Angle of the effects is synchronized between the various layers.

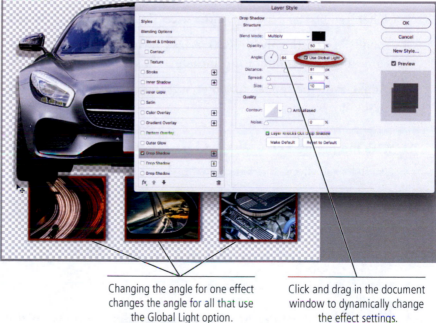

Changing the angle for one effect changes the angle for all that use the Global Light option.

Click and drag in the document window to dynamically change the effect settings.

17. Change the size field to **50 px**, then click OK to apply the changed settings.

18. In the Layers panel, click the arrow buttons to the right of each fx icon to collapse the effects for all layers.

Note:

If you double-click the word "Effects" in the Layers panel, the dialog box opens to the Blending Options: Default screen. Double-clicking a specific effect opens the dialog box directly to the settings for the effect on which you clicked.

19. Save the file and continue to the next exercise.

Use the Filter Gallery

You can apply filters to specific selections, individual layers, or even individual channels depending on what you need to accomplish. If you combine filters with Smart Objects, you can apply nondestructive filters, and then change the settings or turn off the filters to experiment with different results.

In addition to the options in the Filter Gallery, a wide range of other filters can be accessed in the various Filter submenus. We encourage you to explore the various settings. Any filter that includes an ellipsis (...) in the menu command opens a secondary dialog box, where you can control the filter's specific settings.

Keep the following points in mind when you use filters:

- Filters can be applied to the entire selected layer or to an active selection.

- Some filters work only on RGB images. If you are in a different color mode, some (or all) filter options — including the Filter Gallery — will be unavailable.

- All filters can be applied to 8-bit images but options are limited for 16- and 32-bit images.

Note:

Photoshop ships with more than 100 filters divided into 13 categories; some of these are functional while others are purely decorative.

1. With **magazine.psd** open, select the inset3 layer in the Layers panel.

   Like styles and effects, filters apply to the selected layer, not to the entire file.

2. Choose Filter>Filter Gallery.

   If the Filter menu includes the Filter Gallery at the top of the list, the top command applies the last-used filter gallery settings to the selected layer. To open the Filter Gallery dialog box, you have to choose the Filter Gallery command at the third spot in the menu.

This command applies the last-used filter without opening the Filter Gallery dialog box.

This command opens the Filter Gallery dialog box with the last-used settings applied.

3. If necessary, adjust the view percentage and position in the dialog box so you can see the inset3 image.

4. **In the middle pane of the dialog box, expand the Artistic collection of filters and click the Plastic Wrap thumbnail.**

The left side of the dialog box shows a preview of the applied filter(s). You can use the options in the bottom-left corner to change the preview view percentage.

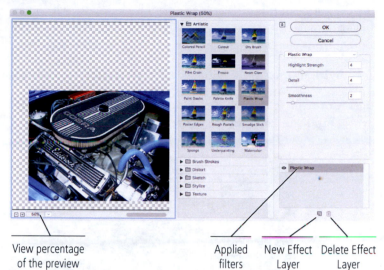

In the middle column, available filters are broken into six categories. Inside each folder, thumbnails show a small preview of each filter.

On the right, the top half shows settings specific to the selected filter (from the middle column). The bottom shows the filters that are applied to the selected layer.

You can apply more than one filter to a layer by clicking the New Effect Layer button in the bottom-right corner of the Filter Gallery dialog box.

View percentage of the preview

Applied filters

New Effect Layer

Delete Effect Layer

5. **Adjust the filter options until you are satisfied with the result, then click OK to apply the filter.**

Because the inset3 layer is a Smart Object layer, the filter is applied nondestructively as a Smart Filter. If you apply a filter to a regular layer, it is destructive, and cannot be changed or turned off.

The filter is applied to the Smart Object layer as a Smart Filter.

6. **Press Option/Alt, then click the Filter Gallery listing in the Layers panel and drag it to the inset2 layer.**

As with layer styles, this method allows you to apply the same Smart Filter to multiple layers, without opening any dialog boxes.

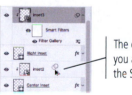

The cursor shows you are cloning the Smart Filter.

7. **Repeat Step 6 to apply the Smart Filter to the inset1 layer.**

The Smart Filters have been cloned, but the lists do not automatically expand in the panel.

8. **Collapse the Smart Filters listing for the inset3 layer.**

9. **Save the file and continue to the next exercise.**

⊕ Duplicate a Layer

The next piece of this project is a custom background, which you will create from a provided image. In this exercise, you will use the Duplicate method to move layer content from one file to another.

1. **With magazine.psd open, open tires.jpg from your WIP>Cars folder.**

2. **Control/right-click the Background layer in the tires.jpg file and choose Duplicate Layer in the contextual menu.**

3. **In the resulting dialog box, choose magazine.psd in the Destination Document menu, then click OK.**

   The Duplicate command provides an easy method for copying an entire layer — either in the current file, any other open file, or a new file. If you choose the current file as the destination, you can define a new name for the duplicated layer.

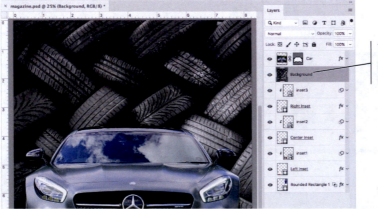

   Choose where you want the duplicate layer in this menu.

4. **Close the tires.jpg file and review the current magazine.psd file.**

   The Background layer from the tires file is copied into the magazine file. It is placed immediately above the previously selected layer. Although it is still named "Background" because of the file from which it was copied, it is neither locked nor placed at the bottom of the layer stack.

   The duplicated layer is placed above the previously selected layer.

5. Click the Background layer in the Layers panel and drag it to the bottom of the layer stack.

6. Double-click the layer name to highlight it. Type **Tires** as the new layer name, then press Return/Enter to finalize the new name.

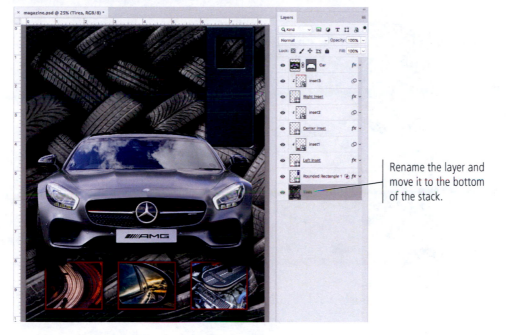

Rename the layer and move it to the bottom of the stack.

7. Save the file and then continue to the next exercise.

Liquify a Layer

Rather than just using the stacked-tires image as the background, you are going to use the Liquify filter to push around layer pixels in a freeform style to create a unique background for the magazine cover.

1. With **magazine.psd** open, hide all but the Tires layer.

   You can Option/Alt-click the eye icon for a layer to hide all other layers.

2. With the Tires layer selected in the Layers panel, choose Filter>Liquify.

   The Liquify filter has its own interface and tools. Depending on which tool you select, different options become available in the right side of the dialog box.

3. In the bottom-left corner of the dialog box, open the View Percentage menu and choose Fit In View.

4. On the left side of the dialog box, choose the Forward Warp tool.

5. On the right side of the dialog box, define a large brush with medium density.

   For any of the distortion tools, you have to define a brush size, density (feathering around the edges), and pressure. Some tools also allow you to define the brush rate (how fast distortions are made).

   For this exercise, we used a 500-pixel brush with 50% density.

6. **Make sure the Pin Edges option is checked.**

   When checked, this option prevents transparent pixels from appearing at the canvas edges.

7. **Click and drag in the preview to warp the tire pattern away from the neat stack in the original image.**

Forward Warp tool

The tool cursor reflects the brush size.

When Pin Edges is active, you can't push pixels away from the canvas edge.

Use this menu to change the view percentage.

Check this option to avoid creating transparent areas at the canvas edges.

8. **Continue clicking and dragging to push pixels until you are satisfied with your results.**

   If necessary, you can press Command/Control-Z to undo your last brush stroke in the Liquify dialog box.

9. **Click OK to return to the image.**

   Depending on the size of the layer you are liquifying, the process might take a while to complete; be patient.

   The Liquify filter is not a smart filter, and cannot be applied to a Smart Object layer; it permanently alters the pixels in the layer to which it is applied.

10. **Save the file and continue to the next exercise.**

More About the Liquify Filter

Tools in the Liquify filter distort the brush area when you drag. The distortion is concentrated at the center of the brush area, and the effect intensifies as you hold down the mouse button or repeatedly drag over an area. (The **Hand** and **Zoom tools** function the same as they do in the main Photoshop interface.)

A. The **Forward Warp tool** pushes pixels as you drag.

B. The **Reconstruct tool** restores distorted pixels.

C. The **Smooth tool** smoothes jagged edges.

D. The **Twirl Clockwise tool** rotates pixels clockwise as you hold down the mouse button or drag. Press Option/Alt to twirl pixels counterclockwise.

E. The **Pucker tool** moves pixels toward the center of the brush, creating a zoomed-out effect if you simply hold down the mouse button without dragging.

F. The **Bloat tool** moves pixels away from the center of the brush, creating a zoomed-in effect.

G. The **Push Left tool** moves pixels left when you drag up, and right when you drag down. You can also drag clockwise around an object to increase its size, or drag counterclockwise to decrease its size.

H. The **Freeze Mask tool** protects areas where you paint.

I. The **Thaw Mask tool** removes the protection created by the Freeze Mask tool.

J. The **Face tool** reveals on-screen controls for changing the shape of various facial features. For example, you can click and drag to change the shape of the forehead, chin height, jawline, and face width when the overall face shape is selected.

Face-Aware Liquify Options

If an image includes faces, the Liquify filter automatically recognizes them, and provides options for manipulating the individual eyes, nose, mouth, and overall face shape. You can use the controls on the right side of the dialog box, or use the Face tool to drag on-screen controls in the preview area.

If more than one face exists in the overall image, you can use the Select Face menu to determine which one you want to edit using the slider controls.

Mask Options

Mask Options allow you to freeze areas in the Liquify preview to protect them from distortion. You can use the Mask options to freeze areas based on existing selections, transparent areas, or layer masks in the original image.

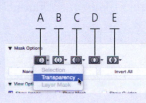

A. **Replace Selection**

B. **Add to Selection**

C. **Subtract from Selection**

D. **Intersect with Selection**

E. **Invert Selection**

You can click the **None** button to thaw all masked areas. Click the **Mask All** button to mask the entire image or the **Invert All** button to reverse the current mask.

Brush Reconstruct Options

When the Liquify dialog box is open, pressing Command/Control-Z undoes your last brush stroke. Clicking **Restore All** has the same effect as using the Undo keyboard shortcut.

You can also use the **Reconstruct** button to affect the last-applied stroke. Rather than undoing the entire stroke, you can use the resulting dialog box to lessen the effect by a specific percentage.

View Options

Show Image, active by default, shows the active layer in the filter's preview area. If you check the **Show Mesh** option, the preview also shows a grid that defaults to small, gray lines. You can use the Mesh Size and Mesh Color menus to change the appearance of the grid.

When **Show Mask** is checked, any mask you paint with the Freeze Mask tool appears in the filter's preview area. You can use the Mask Color menu to change the color of that mask.

When **Show Backdrop** is checked, you can include other layers in the filter's preview area. The Use menu also lists individual layers in the file so you can show only a certain layer in the preview. You can use the Mode and Opacity menus to change how extra layers appear in the preview.

Use the Eyedropper Tool

In Photoshop, there is almost always more than one way to complete a task. In this exercise, you use the Eyedropper tool to change the Foreground and Background colors by sampling from the original car image. You will then use those colors to create a gradient background for the overall composition.

1. **With `magazine.psd` open, hide all but the Car layer.**

   You can hide multiple layers by clicking and dragging over the eye icons of each layer that you want to hide.

2. **Choose the Eyedropper tool in the Tools panel.**

3. **In the Options bar, choose 5 by 5 Average in the Sample Size menu and choose All Layers in the Sample menu. Make sure the Show Sampling Ring option is checked.**

   The default Eyedropper option — Point Sample — selects the color of the single pixel where you click. Using one of the average values avoids the possibility of sampling an errant artifact color because the tool finds the average color in a range of adjacent pixels.

   By default, the sample will be selected from All [visible] Layers. You can choose Current Layer in the Sample menu to choose a color from only the active layer.

4. **Move the cursor over the light silver color near the left edge of the car (as shown in the following image). Click to change the foreground color.**

   When you click with the Eyedropper tool, the sampling ring appears and shows the previous foreground color on the bottom, and the current sample color on the top half.

   If you hold down the mouse button, you can drag around the image to find the color you want. The sampling ring previews which color will be selected if you release the mouse button.

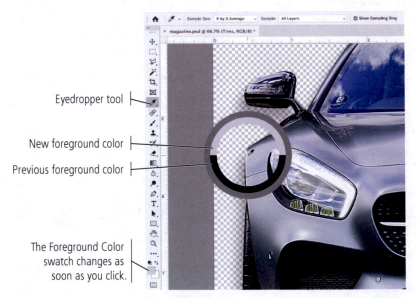

Eyedropper tool

New foreground color

Previous foreground color

The Foreground Color swatch changes as soon as you click.

5. Move the cursor over the yellow/greenish tones in the bottom part of the headlight (as shown in the image below). Option/Alt-click to change the background color.

Pressing Option/Alt while you click with the Eyedropper tool changes the Background color. In this case, the sampling ring shows the previous background color on the bottom and the current selection on the top.

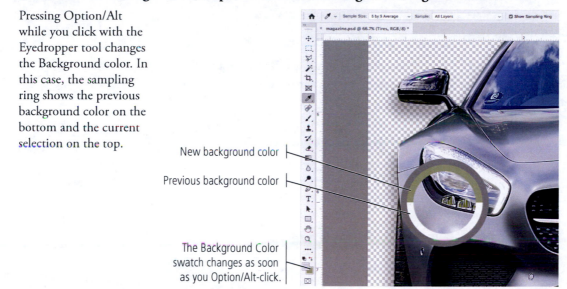

New background color

Previous background color

The Background Color swatch changes as soon as you Option/Alt-click.

6. Save the file and continue to the next exercise.

Create a Custom Gradient

A **gradient** (sometimes called a blend) is a fill that creates a smooth transition from one color to another. Photoshop can create several different kinds of gradients (linear, radial, etc.), and you can access a number of built-in gradients. You can also create your own custom gradients, which you will do in this exercise.

1. With **magazine.psd** open, choose the Gradient tool in the Tools panel.

2. Choose **Window>Gradients** open the Gradients panel.

3. Click the arrow to the left of the Basic folder to expand that set.

4. Click the button in the top-right corner of the Gradients panel, then choose **Small List** view from the panel Options menu.

Note:

You can click the bottom edge of the panel and drag to resize the panel, showing more gradients and sets at one time.

Like the built-in styles, Photoshop includes a number of predefined gradients organized in groups. The Basic set includes foreground-to-background, foreground-to-transparent, and black-to-white. The names are useful for understanding the result of each.

Click here to open the panel Options menu.

Click the arrows to expand individual groups.

Gradient names indicate the result.

Delete Gradient

Create New Gradient

Create New Group

5. **Click the Create New Gradient button at the bottom of the Gradient panel.**

   This button opens the Gradient Editor dialog box, which you can use to edit existing gradients or create new ones.

6. **In the Presets section of the dialog box, expand the Basic set and then click the left gradient swatch to select the Foreground to Background gradient.**

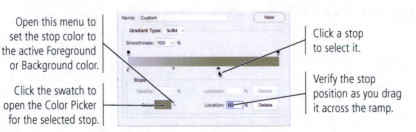

Expand the Basic group, then choose the Foreground to Background gradient.

Gradient ramp

Opacity stop

Color stop

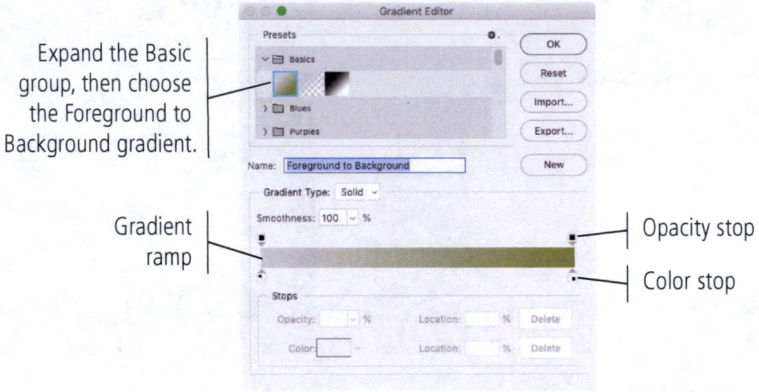

7. **Click the right color stop below the gradient ramp. Drag left until the Location field shows 60%.**

   After you move the color stop, the name changes to Custom because you're defining a custom gradient.

Open this menu to set the stop color to the active Foreground or Background color.

Click the swatch to open the Color Picker for the selected stop.

Click a stop to select it.

Verify the stop position as you drag it across the ramp.

8. **Double-click the moved stop to open the Color Picker dialog box. Change the stop color to C: 25%, M: 40%, Y: 80%, K: 5%, then click OK.**

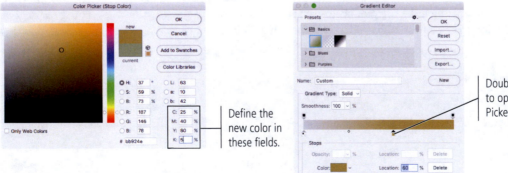

Define the new color in these fields.

Double-click a stop to open the Color Picker for that stop.

9. **Click the left stop to select it. Drag right until the Location field shows 30%.**

10. **Click the small diamond icon between the first and second stops. Drag right until the Location field shows 80%.**

    This point indicates where the colors of the two surrounding stops are equally mixed. Dragging this point extends the gradient on one side of the point and compresses the gradient on the other.

    Drag this icon to change the midpoint between the two surrounding stops.

11. **Click below the right side of the ramp. Drag the new stop until the location field shows 80%.**

    Clicking below the ramp adds a new stop to the gradient, using the same color settings as the last-selected stop.

    Click below the ramp to add a new stop.

    The new stop adopts the color of the last-selected stop.

12. **Click below the left end of the gradient ramp to add a new stop. Set its location to 0%.**

13. **Double-click the new stop to open the Color Picker dialog box. Change the stop color to white (C: 0%, M: 0%, Y: 0%, K: 0%), then click OK.**

    Note:

    Whenever the Color Picker dialog box is open, you can use the Eyedropper cursor to sample a color from the image in the document window.

14. **Click the left stop to select it, then click below the right end of the gradient ramp to add another new stop. Set its location to 100%**

    If you didn't click the leftmost stop first, the new stop from this step would have the same color settings as the last-selected stop (from Step 11).

    Note:

    Drag a stop off the gradient ramp to remove it from the gradient.

15. Type **Car Background** in the Name field and click the New button.

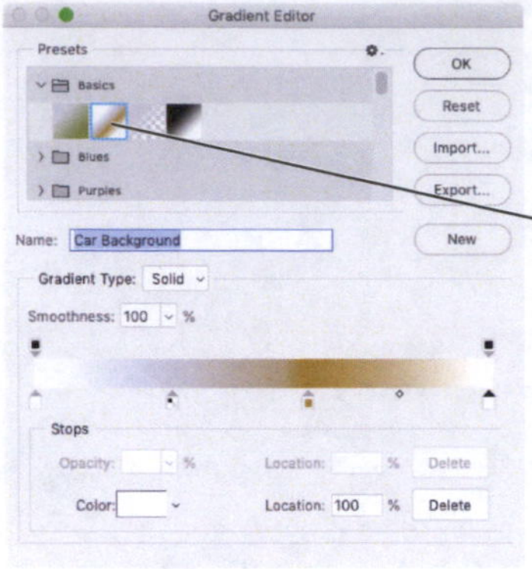

Clicking the New button adds the new swatch to the list of gradient options.

16. Click OK to close the dialog box.

17. Save the file and continue to the next exercise.

Create a Gradient Fill Layer

Once you define the gradient you want, applying it is fairly easy: add a layer (if necessary), select the type of gradient you want to create, and then click and drag.

1. With **magazine.psd** open, make sure the Tires layer is selected.

2. Click the Create a New Layer button at the bottom of the Layers panel. Name the new layer **Shading**.

   When you add a new layer, it is automatically added directly above the selected layer.

Create a New Layer button

3. Choose the Gradient tool in the Tools panel, then review the options in the Options bar.

Click the sample to open the Gradient Editor dialog box.

Click here to open the Gradient Picker panel.

Gradient tool

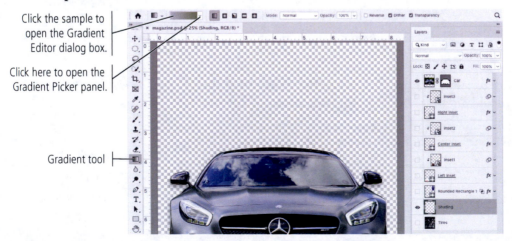

4. **In the Options bar, click the arrow button to open the Gradient Picker panel.**

   The Gradient Picker panel has the same options that are available in the standalone Gradients panel.

5. **Expand the Basics set, then click the Car Background gradient swatch to select it. Make sure the Linear Gradient option is active to the right of the Gradient Picker.**

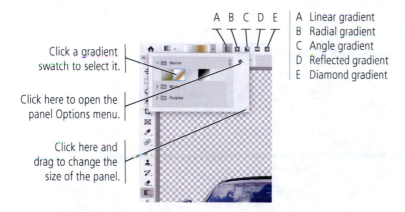

A B C D E   A   Linear gradient
B   Radial gradient
C   Angle gradient
D   Reflected gradient
E   Diamond gradient

Click a gradient swatch to select it.

Click here to open the panel Options menu.

Click here and drag to change the size of the panel.

6. **Click in the top-left area of the canvas drag to the bottom-right area of the canvas (as shown in the following image).**

   When you release the mouse button, the layer fills with the gradient. Areas before and after the line drawn with the Gradient tool fill with the start and stop colors of the gradient (in this case, they're both white).

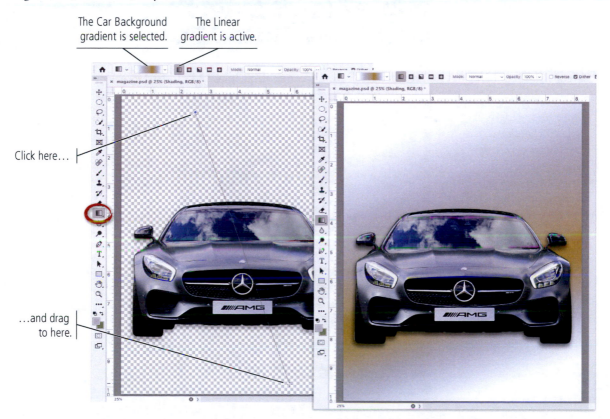

The Car Background gradient is selected.

The Linear gradient is active.

Click here...

...and drag to here.

7. **Save the file and continue to the next exercise.**

Adjust Blending Mode and Layer Opacity

The final step to creating your custom background is to blend the gradient you just created into the liquified tires. Photoshop includes a number of options for making this type of adjustment.

1. **With magazine.psd open, show all layers in the file and then select the Shading layer as the active one.**

2. **Open the Blending Mode menu in the Layers panel and choose Overlay.**

   Photoshop provides access to 27 different layer blending modes; the default is Normal, or no blending applied. As you move your mouse cursor over each option in the menu, the document window shows a dynamic preview of that mode. Using the Overlay mode, colors in the gradient are blended onto the pixels in the underlying Tires layer.

Blending Mode menu

3. **Select the Tires layer in the Layers panel, then change the Opacity field to 10%.**

   Reducing the layer opacity reduces the strength of the layer content so that it no longer overpowers other elements in the composition. You can now better see the effect created by the blended gradient.

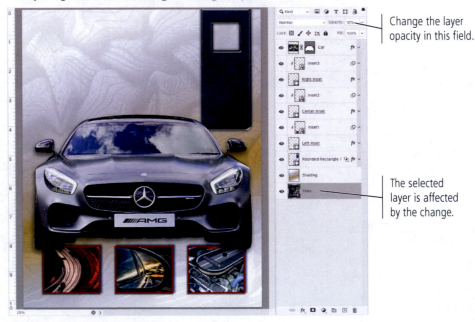

Change the layer opacity in this field.

The selected layer is affected by the change.

4. **Save the file and continue to the next exercise.**

When working with blending modes, think of the top layer as the "blend" layer and the next lowest layer as the "base."

- **Normal** is the default mode (no blending applied).

- **Dissolve** results in a random scattering of pixels of both the blend and base colors.

- **Darken** returns the darker of the blend or base color. Base pixels that are lighter than the blend color are replaced. Base pixels that are darker than the blend color remain unchanged.

- **Multiply** multiplies (hence, the name) the base color by the blend color, resulting in a darker color. Multiplying any color with black produces black. Multiplying any color with white leaves the color unchanged (think of math — any number times 0 equals 0).

- **Color Burn** darkens the base color by increasing the contrast. Blend colors darker than 50% significantly darken the base color by increasing saturation and reducing brightness. Blending with white has no effect.

- **Linear Burn** darkens the base color similar to Color Burn. Using Linear Burn, the brightness is reduced about twice as much for blend colors in the mid-tone range.

- **Darker Color** compares the channel values of the blend and base colors, resulting in the lower value.

- **Lighten** returns whichever is the lighter color (base or blend). Base pixels that are darker than the blend color are replaced. Base pixels that are lighter than the blend color remain unchanged.

- **Screen** is basically the inverse of Multiply, always returning a lighter color. Screening with black has no effect; screening with white produces white.

- **Color Dodge** brightens the base color. Blend colors lighter than 50% significantly increase brightness. Blending with black has no effect.

- **Linear Dodge (Add)** is similar to Color Dodge, but creates smoother transitions from areas of high brightness to areas of low brightness.

- **Lighter Color** compares channel values of the blend and base colors, resulting in the higher value.

- **Overlay** multiplies or screens the blend color to preserve the original lightness or darkness of the base.

- **Soft Light** darkens or lightens base colors depending on the blend color. Blend colors lighter than 50% lighten the base color (as if dodged). Blend colors darker than 50% darken the base color (as if burned).

- **Hard Light** combines the Multiply and Screen modes. Blend colors darker than 50% are multiplied, and blend colors lighter than 50% are screened.

- **Vivid Light** combines the Color Dodge and Color Burn modes. Blend colors lighter than 50% lighten the base by decreasing contrast. Blend colors darker than 50% darken the base by increasing contrast.

- **Linear Light** combines the Linear Dodge and Linear Burn modes. If the blend color is lighter than 50%, the result is lightened by increasing the base brightness. If the blend color is darker than 50%, the result is darkened by decreasing the base brightness.

- **Pin Light** preserves the brightest and darkest areas of the blend color. Blend colors in the mid-tone range have little (if any) effect.

- **Hard Mix** pushes all pixels in the resulting blend to either all or nothing. The base and blend values of each pixel in each channel are added together (e.g., R 45 [blend] + R 230 [base] = R 275). Pixels with totals over 255 are shown at 255; pixels with a total lower than 255 are dropped to 0.

- **Difference** inverts base color values according to the brightness value in the blend layer. Lower brightness values in the blend layer have less of an effect on the result. Blending with black has no effect.

- **Exclusion** is very similar to Difference, except that mid-tone values in the base color are completely desaturated.

- **Subtract** removes the blend color from the base color.

- **Divide** looks at the color information in each channel and divides the blend color from the base color.

- **Hue** results in a color with the luminance and saturation of the base color, and the hue of the blend color.

- **Saturation** results in a color with the luminance and hue of the base color, and the saturation of the blend color.

- **Color** results in a color with the luminance of the base color, and the hue and saturation of the blend color.

- **Luminosity** results in a color with the hue and saturation of the base color, and the luminance of the blend color (basically, the opposite of the Color mode).

Finish the Magazine Cover

The final piece required for this job is the nameplate and text treatment, which is created every month from a template in Adobe Illustrator. In this exercise, you will place and position the required file to complete the project.

1. **With `magazine.psd` open, choose File>Place Linked.**

   You are using the Place Linked option so that any changes in the cover treatment file (a common occurrence in professional design environments) will automatically reflect in your Photoshop file.

2. **Navigate to `driver-mag.ai` (in your WIP>Cars folder) and click Place.**

3. **Choose Bounding Box in the Crop To menu of the Open as Smart Object dialog box, then click OK.**

When you place files in Photoshop, either linked or embedded, they are commonly placed at slightly other than 100%. You should always verify — and correct, if necessary — the scaling of the placed content.

4. **In the Options bar, change the W and H values to `100%`, then press Return/Enter to finalize the placement.**

5. In the Layers panel, move the driver-mag layer to the top of the layer stack.

6. Using the Properties panel, change the position of the placed content to X: **0.375 in**, Y: **0.375 in**.

The Properties panel only displays two decimal values, so after typing the new position, the fields show only "0.38 in". This is a minor flaw in the software, but one that is worth noting.

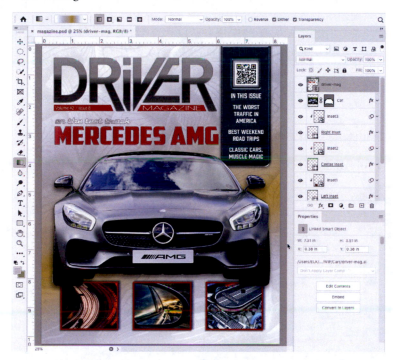

7. Save the file and then continue to the final exercise.

Sharing Photoshop Files

If you are connected to the Internet, you can use the Share an Image button to easily send a JPEG version of your file through a variety of communication media. If you choose Mail in the menu, for example, the image automatically appears in a new mail message in your email client software. If you choose one of the social media outlets, you can create your post directly through a window in the Photoshop interface; you do not need to interact with a browser or separate application to share an image from Photoshop. Keep in mind that you must have defined accounts in your system preferences for each of the various social media outlets. If an account is not defined, you will be prompted to add one before you can use these options in Photoshop.

Print a Composite Proof

The last stage of most jobs — after the client has approved the work — is printing a proof. A printed proof is basically the output provider's roadmap of how the final job should look. As more processes move to all-digital workflows, a printed proof is not always required — especially if you're submitting files digitally. But some output providers still require a printed proof, and you might want to print samples of your work at various stages of development.

To output this file at 100%, you need a sheet at least tabloid size (11″ × 17″). If you don't have that option, you can use the Photoshop Print dialog box to fit the job onto letter-size paper. Keep in mind, however, that many of the effects that you created with filters will lose some of their impact when you reduce the file to fit onto a letter-size page.

1. **With `magazine.psd` open, choose File>Print.**

2. **In the Printer menu of the Print dialog box, choose the printer you're using.**

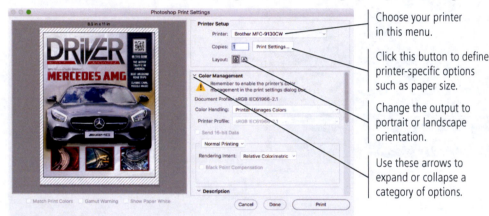

Choose your printer in this menu.

Click this button to define printer-specific options such as paper size.

Change the output to portrait or landscape orientation.

Use these arrows to expand or collapse a category of options.

3. **Choose the Portrait layout option (below the number of copies).**

   Ideally, you should always print proofs at 100%. If this is not possible, however, you can print a sample content proof by scaling the page to fit the available paper size.

4. **Review the options in the scrolling pane below the Printer Setup options.**

   Different types of output jobs require different settings. If you are simply printing a desktop proof, you can leave most of these options at their default values.

   As a general rule, proofs should be printed at 100% of the actual file size. If you are printing a file that is larger than the paper size your printer can handle, you can use the Scaled Print Size options to fit the job on the available paper size. Alternatively, you can use the Print Selected Area option to output different portions of the image onto separate sheets, and then manually assemble the multiple sheets into a single page.

5. **Click Print to output the file.**

6. **When the output process is complete, close the file without saving.**

Note:

If you submit a scaled proof with a print job, make sure you note the scale percentage prominently on the proof.

Color Management Options

- **Color Handling** determines whether color management is applied by the printer or by Photoshop.

- **Printer Profile** defines the known color characteristics of the output device you are using.

- **Normal Printing** simply prints the file to your printer, using no defined output profile for color management.

  - **Rendering Intent** defines how colors are shifted to fit inside the printer's output capabilities.

  - **Black Point Compression** adjusts for differences in the black point (the darkest possible black area) between the file and the output device.

- **Hard Proofing** simulates the color output properties of another printer, based on the defined profile in the Proof Setup menu.

  - **Simulate Paper Color** applies the absolute colorimetric rendering intent to simulate the appearance of color on the actual paper and output device that will be used (for example, newsprint on a web press).

  - **Simulate Black Ink** simulates the brightness of dark colors as they would appear on the defined output device. If not checked, dark colors are printed as dark as possible on the actual printer you are using.

Position and Size Options

- **Position** defines the location of the output on the paper. It is centered by default. You can use the Top and Left fields to position the output at a specific distance from the paper corner. You can also click in the preview area and drag to reposition the image on the paper.

- **Scale** defaults to 100%, creating a full-size print. The **Height** and **Width** fields define the size of the image being printed. If you change the Scale field, the Height and Width fields reflect the proportional size. You can also define a specific size in the Height and Width fields; in this case, the Scale field is adjusted accordingly.

- If you check **Scale to Fit Media**, the image is automatically scaled to fit inside the printable area on the selected paper size.

- **Print Resolution** defines the resolution that will be sent to the output device. Remember the principle of effective resolution: if you print a 300-ppi image at 200%, the printer has only 150 ppi with which to work.

- If you check **Print Selected Area**, handles appear in the preview area. You can drag those handles to define the image area that will be output.

Printing Marks

- **Corner Crop Marks** adds crop marks to show the edges of the image where it should be cut.

- **Center Crop Marks** adds a crop mark at the center of each edge of the image.

- **Registration Marks** adds bulls-eye targets and star targets that are used to align color separations on a printing press. (Calibration bars and star target registration marks require a PostScript printer.)

- **Description** adds description text (from the File>File Info dialog box) outside the trim area in 9-pt Helvetica.

- **Labels** adds the file name above the image.

Functions

- **Emulsion Down** reverses the image on the output. This option is primarily used for output to a filmsetter or imagesetter.

- **Negative** inverts the color values of the entire output. This option is typically used if you are outputting directly to film, which will then be used to image a photo-sensitive printing plate (a slowly disappearing workflow).

- The **Background** option allows you to add a background color that will print outside the image area.

- The **Border** option adds a black border around an image. You can define a specific width (in points) for the border.

- The **Bleed** option moves crop marks inside the image by a specific measurement.

PostScript Options

- **Calibration Bars** adds swatches of black in 10% increments (starting at 0% and ending at 100%).

- The **Interpolation** option can help reduce the jagged appearance of low-resolution images by automatically resampling up when you print. This option is only available on PostScript Level 2 or 3 printers.

- The **Include Vector Data** option sends vector information in the output stream for a PostScript printer, so the vector data can be output at the highest possible resolution of the output device.

If your printer is not PostScript compatible, the PostScript options will not be available.

PROJECT REVIEW

1. _____ sharpens an image by increasing contrast along the edges in an image.

2. _____ refers to the overall image area, like the surface used by traditional painters.

3. The _____ tool is used to draw freeform, vector-based shapes and paths.

4. A _____ is a special type of Photoshop layer that retains vector path information.

5. _____ control the shape of a curve between two anchor points.

6. The _____ option is used to link the angle of styles to the "master" angle for the entire file. Changing it affects any linked style applied to any layer in the entire file.

7. A _____ is a smooth transition from one color to another.

8. The _____ command is used to show only areas of one layer that fall within the area of the underlying layer.

9. In the Liquify filter, the _____ tool can be used to protect specific areas from being liquified.

10. The _____ allows you to experiment with different filters and filter settings, and to compound multiple filters to create unique artistic effects.

1. Briefly explain the difference between vectors and pixels.

2. Briefly describe two different tool modes when using a vector drawing tool.

3. Briefly explain the difference between the Path Selection tool and the Direct Selection tool.

PORTFOLIO BUILDER PROJECT

Use what you have learned in this project to complete the following freeform exercise.

Carefully read the art director and client comments, then create your own design to meet the needs of the project.

Use the space below to sketch ideas. When finished, write a brief explanation of the reasoning behind your final design.

art director comments

Against The Clock is considering a new design for the covers of its *Professional Portfolio* series of books. You have been hired to design a new cover comp for the Photoshop book.

❏ Measure the cover of the existing Photoshop CC book to determine the required trim size.

❏ Incorporate the same elements that currently appear on the book cover — title, logo, and the text in the bottom-right corner. (The logo file is included in the **Covers_Web20_PB.zip** archive on the Student Files web page.)

❏ Create compelling images and artwork to illustrate the concept of the book title.

❏ Design the cover to meet commercial printing requirements.

client comments

We really like the existing cover design, but after nine editions, we're starting to think a fresh look might be a good thing.

Obviously, the most important element of the cover is the title. Keep in mind that Adobe differentiates each software release using the year instead of a version or edition number, so the year needs to be incorporated somewhere in the cover design.

In the last few version of the covers, we've used an urban theme — cityscapes, museum buildings, architectural macros, and so on — as a representation of places where graphic designers find jobs. We don't really have any set ideas for new imagery, but there should be some connection between graphic design and the imagery you choose.

Finally, keep in mind that the design should allow for repurposing for the other titles in the series.

project justification

PROJECT SUMMARY

Vectors offer an advantage over pixel-based images because they can be freely scaled and edited, without losing quality. This project focused on many different options related to working with vectors in Photoshop — drawing paths, creating shape layers, and editing vector shape properties. You used vectors in this project to create a custom layer mask, as well as vector shapes that you filled with other images and a custom artistic pattern.

This project also introduced some of the creative tools that can turn photos and flat colors into painting-like artwork. You learned to use the Filter Gallery, the Liquify filter, custom gradients, and layer blending modes. You will use these options many times in your career as you complete different types of projects in Photoshop.

Create a compound vector shape layer

Edit corner properties of vector shapes

Apply a style to a vector shape layer

Use a vector mask to remove an image from its background

Use gradients to create a custom background

Liquify pixels to create unique effects

Adjust blending mode and opacity to blend one layer into another

Create clipping masks to isolate specific image areas

Apply filters to images to create artistic effects

City Promotion Cards

3

Your client is the Redevelopment Authority for the city of Lancaster, in the California high desert (north of Los Angeles). You have been hired to create a series of promotional postcards featuring the improvements that have been made over the last two years, that will help drive tourism to the area.

This project incorporates the following skills:

❏ Managing missing and mismatched profiles

❏ Working with content-aware tools

❏ Adding effects in the Blur Gallery

❏ Creating and managing different types of text layers

❏ Using paragraph styles to format text

❏ Working in 3D

❏ Creating layer comps

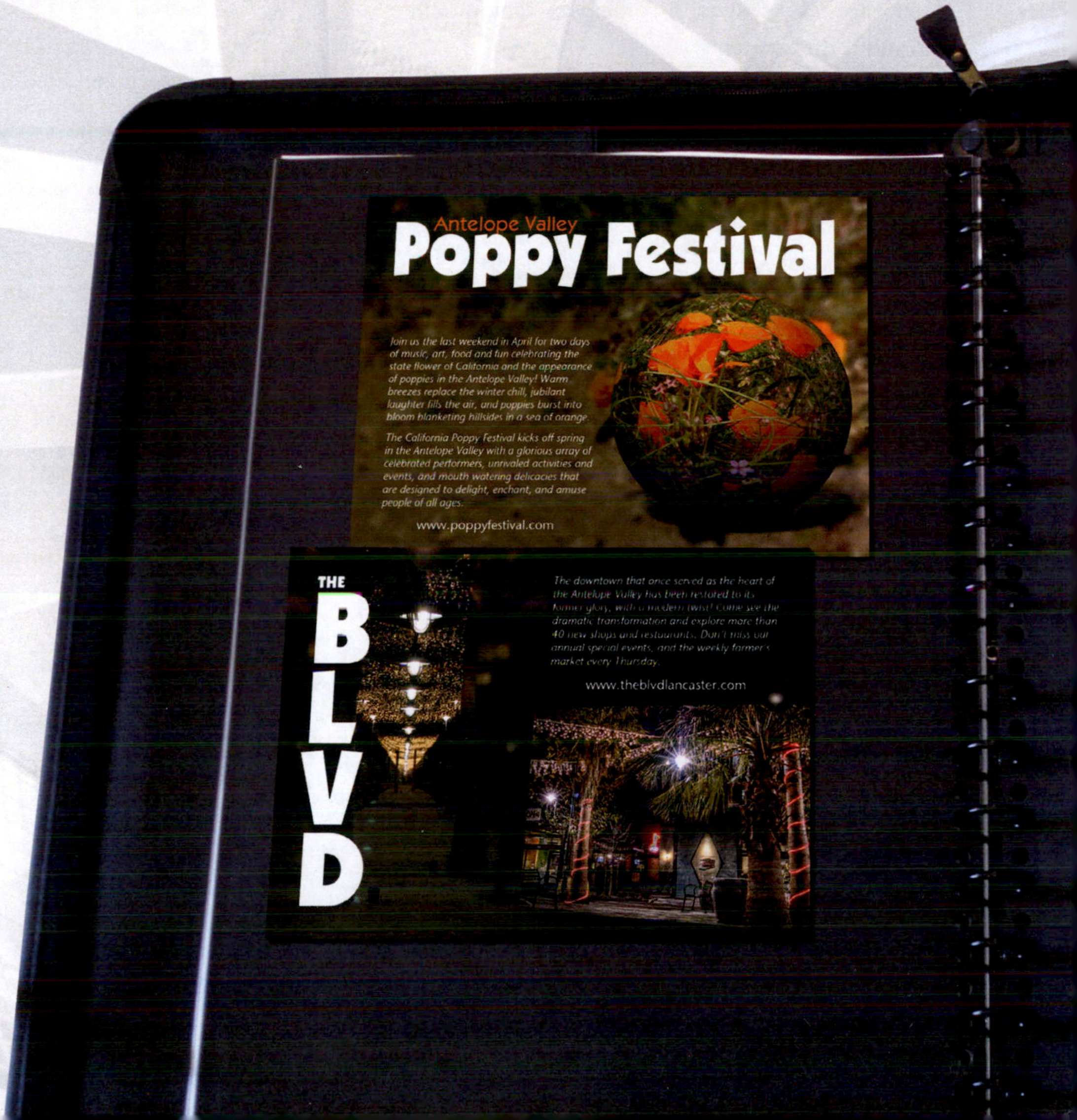

PROJECT MEETING

client comments

We want to feature two of our proudest achievements in a postcard campaign that we're hoping will help drive tourism to the area.

In the past two years, more than $50 million of public and private funding has been spent revitalizing the downtown area. The BLVD, Lancaster's new outdoor shopping and dining destination, is lined with a unique mix of dining, shopping, arts, and entertainment venues.

The Poppy Festival is attended by more than 20,000 visitors over two days. It's an award-winning festival that celebrates California's state flower, which is fitting, since we're also the home of the Antelope Valley Poppy Preserve.

The images you create will be used in digital advertising and on websites, but we also plan to print them for inclusion in a larger promotional package that we send to conference coordinators around the country.

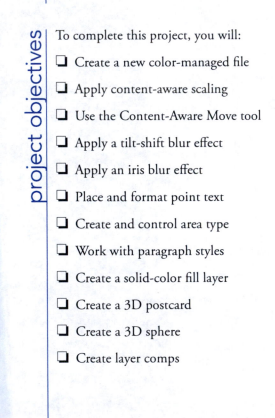

art director comments

The client wants to create these files for both digital and print applications, so you should define the file size to meet the print specs:

Trim: 5″ high × 7″ wide

Bleed requirement: 0.125″ on all four sides

I want each postcard to include two images. Those we have will require some manipulation to work in the overall composition.

Although compositing type and images is typically done in a page layout application, there isn't a lot of text to include on these postcards. You can use the Photoshop type tools to do what you need, without requiring a separate file.

I'd also like to see two different versions of each postcard. The 3D options in Photoshop can create the appearance of depth even in a flat file — which might provide the "pop" the client requested.

When you're finished, save each version as a JPEG that we can email for approval.

project objectives

To complete this project, you will:

❑ Create a new color-managed file

❑ Apply content-aware scaling

❑ Use the Content-Aware Move tool

❑ Apply a tilt-shift blur effect

❑ Apply an iris blur effect

❑ Place and format point text

❑ Create and control area type

❑ Work with paragraph styles

❑ Create a solid-color fill layer

❑ Create a 3D postcard

❑ Create a 3D sphere

❑ Create layer comps

STAGE 1 / Creating New Files

The basic process of creating a new file is relatively easy. However, you have a number of options that affect what you will see when you begin working. The first stage of this project explores a number of these issues, including color management settings and controlling the background layer.

Create a New Color-Managed File

The Color Settings dialog box defines the default working spaces for RGB, CMYK, Gray, and Spot Color spaces. Once you've made your choices in the Color Settings dialog box, those working spaces are automatically applied when you create a new file.

1. Download **Cards_Web20_RF.zip** from the Student Files web page.

2. Expand the ZIP archive in your WIP folder (Macintosh) or copy the archive contents into your WIP folder (Windows).

   This results in a folder named **Cards**, which contains the files you need for this project. You should also use this folder to save the files you create in this project.

3. In Photoshop, choose Edit>Color Settings.

4. In the resulting dialog box, choose the appropriate profile for your monitor in the Working Spaces: RGB menu.

5. Set all three Color Management Policies menus to Preserve Embedded Profiles, and check all three boxes for Profile Mismatches and Missing Profiles.

You can display a warning when opening or pasting an image with an embedded profile that does not match the working profile. You can also display a warning when opening an image that doesn't have an embedded profile.

Choose your monitor profile here.

Check all three of these options.

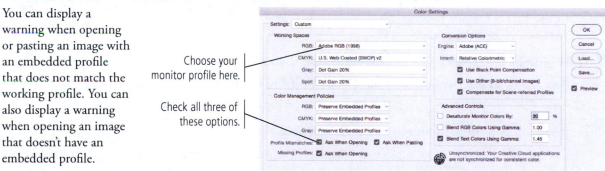

6. Click OK to apply your changes.

7. Choose File>New.

You have several options for creating a new file:

- Choose File>New
- Use the associated keyboard shortcut, Command/Control-N
- Click the New button in the Start workspace

If the Home workspace is visible, click the Create New button to open the New Document dialog box.

8. **Click the Print option at the top of the resulting New Document dialog box.**

9. **Click the bottom edge of the New Document dialog box and drag down until you can see all of the options in the Preset Details section.**

The New Document dialog box presents a number of preset sizes, broken into categories based on the intended output.

When you choose the Print category, you see common page sizes such as Letter. Each preset includes a unit of measurement (for example, 8.5 × 11 in for the Letter preset or 210 × 297 mm for the A4 preset). The defined unit of measurement for each preset is set in the Preset Details section of the dialog box.

The Photo, Print, and Art & Illustration presets all default 300 Pixels/Inch resolution. The Web, Mobile, and Film & Video presets default to 72 Pixels/Inch.

The **color mode** defines the structure of the colors in your file. All presets in all categories default to 8-bit RGB color mode. Although the file will eventually be printed, you are going to work in the RGB space to preserve the widest-possible gamut during the development stage.

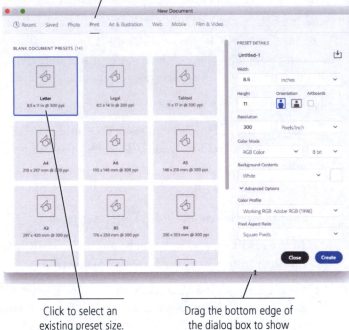

Click a category name to show related presets.

Click to select an existing preset size.

Drag the bottom edge of the dialog box to show all the available options.

10. **In the Preset Details section, type festival in the Name field.**

11. **Highlight the existing Width field value, and then type 7.25.**

Because this file will eventually be printed, you are defining the width to include the required bleed (1/8″) area on each side.

12. **Press Tab two times to highlight the Height field.**

Like most applications, you can press Tab to move through the options and fields in a dialog box. Pressing Shift-Tab moves to the previous field in the dialog box.

13. **Change the highlighted Height field to 5.25.**

Again, this size includes the required 1/8″ bleed for the top and bottom edges.

14. **Choose Transparent in the Background Contents menu.**

If you choose White or Background Color in this menu, the new file will include a default locked Background layer. If you choose Transparent, the new file will have a default, unlocked Layer 1.

15. **Expand the Advanced options (if necessary) and choose Working RGB: [Profile Name] in the Color Profile menu.**

This option defines the working RGB space that you selected in the Color Settings dialog box. Options in the Pixel Aspect Ratio menu are primarily used for editing video. Since this is a print project, you don't want to alter the pixel ratio.

16. Click Create to create the new file.

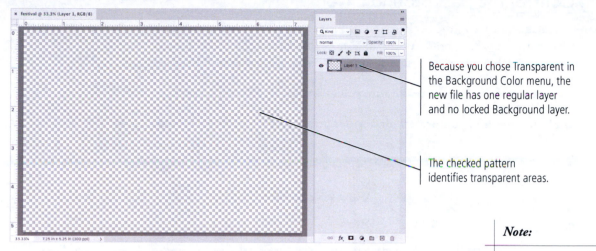

Because you chose Transparent in the Background Color menu, the new file has one regular layer and no locked Background layer.

The checked pattern identifies transparent areas.

17. Choose File>Save As. Navigate to your WIP>Cards folder as the location for saving this file.

Because you named the file when you created it (in the New Document dialog box), the Save As/File Name field is automatically set to the file name you already assigned. The extension is automatically added on both Macintosh and Windows computers.

18. Make sure Photoshop is selected in the Format/Save As Type menu and click Save.

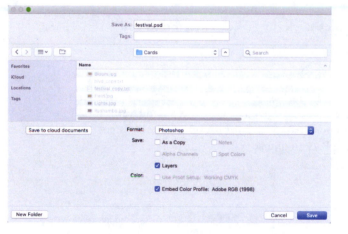

Note:

If you create a file using a profile other than the default working profile for that space, the document tab (or title bar, if you're not using the Macintosh Application frame) shows an asterisk next to the color space information.

19. Read the resulting warning message, then click OK.

This warning appears as soon as a file has at least one regular layer. This file has no locked background layer, so the only layer is a regular layer by default.

Control the Background Layer

When you create a new file, the background of the canvas depends on your selection in the New dialog box. You should understand how that choice affects not only the color of the canvas, but also the existence (or inexistence) of a background layer.

1. **With `festival.psd` open, make sure rulers are visible (View>Rulers).**

2. **Using any method you prefer, place ruler guides 0.125″ from each edge.**

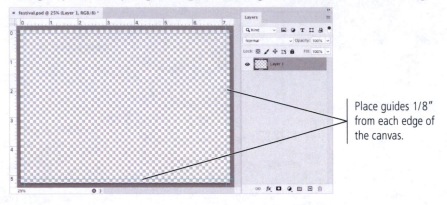

Place guides 1/8″ from each edge of the canvas.

3. **Save the file.**

4. **At the bottom of the Tools panel, click the Default Foreground and Background Colors button.**

5. **At the bottom of the Tools panel, click the Switch Foreground and Background Colors button.**

6. **With the default Layer 1 selected, choose Layer>Flatten Image.**

   When you flatten an image, all layers in the file are flattened into a locked Background layer. Because this file currently has only one layer, the new Background layer is simply a solid white fill. It is important to note that the defined Background color is not applied as the color of the resulting Background layer.

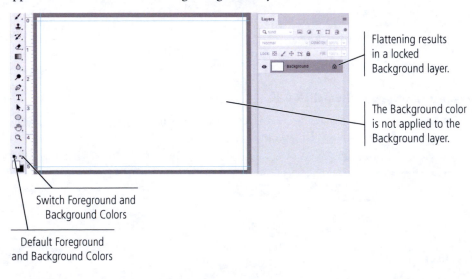

Flattening results in a locked Background layer.

The Background color is not applied to the Background layer.

Switch Foreground and Background Colors

Default Foreground and Background Colors

7. **With the Background layer selected, choose Edit>Fill.**

   You can fill a selection with a number of options:

   - Choose the defined foreground or background color.
   - Choose Color to define a specific color in the Color Picker dialog box.
   - Choose Content Aware to fill an area with pixels from surrounding image areas.
   - Choose Pattern, and then choose a specific pattern in the pop-up menu.
   - Choose History to fill the object with a specific history state (if possible).
   - Choose Black, 50% Gray, or White.

   You can also define a specific blending mode and opacity for the filled pixels. Using layers for different elements, however, is typically a better option than changing the fill transparency settings because you can adjust the layer blending mode and opacity as often as necessary.

Note:

Press Shift-Delete/Back-space to open the Fill dialog box.

8. **In the Fill dialog box, choose Background Color in the Contents menu and then click OK.**

   Because you did not draw a specific selection area, the entire selected layer (the Background layer) is filled.

9. **Choose File>Save As. In the Save As dialog box, change the file name to blvd.psd and click Save.**

10. **Continue to the next exercise.**

Control Missing and Mismatched Profiles

In the Color Settings dialog box, you told Photoshop how to handle images with profiles that don't match your working profiles, as well as images that don't have embedded profiles. These issues become important any time you work with files from more than a single source — and especially with client-supplied images, which often come from a wide variety of sources.

1. **With blvd.psd open, open Lights.jpg from your WIP>Cards folder.**

   This image does not have an embedded profile, so (as you defined in the Color Settings dialog box) Photoshop asks how you want to handle the file.

2. **Choose Leave As Is and click OK.**

3. **With Lights.jpg open, chose Select>All. Choose Edit>Copy, then close the file.**

4. **With blvd.psd active, choose Edit>Paste.**

   Because the file's locked Background layer was selected, the pasted contents are added as a new layer immediately above the existing (selected) layer. Remember, you can't paste content onto a locked layer.

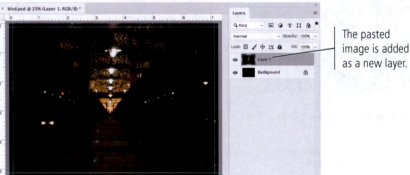

The pasted image is added as a new layer.

5. **In the Layers panel, rename Layer 1 as Lights.**

6. **Choose File>Save. Click OK in the Maximize Compatibility warning.**

   As we already explained, this warning appears the first time you save a file that has at least one regular layer.

7. **Open the file festival.psd from your WIP>Cards folder.**

8. **Open the file `Bloom.jpg`, and read the resulting warning.**

   This file has an embedded profile, but it does not match your defined working RGB profile. Again, you told the application to show a warning when opening a file with a mismatched profile.

   Embedded Profile Mismatch

   ⚠ The document "Bloom.jpg" has an embedded color profile that does not match the current RGB working space.

   Embedded: ColorMatch RGB

   Working: Adobe RGB (1998)

   What would you like to do?

   ⦿ Use the embedded profile (instead of the working space)
   ○ Convert document's colors to the working space
   ○ Discard the embedded profile (don't color manage)

   Cancel   OK

9. **Choose the option to use the embedded profile, then click OK.**

10. **Copy the contents of the file, then close it.**

11. **With `festival.psd` open, choose Edit>Paste.**

   In the Color Settings dialog box, you told the application to warn you if profiles do not match when you paste layer content. Photoshop cannot manage more than one profile for a single color space within the same file.

   Paste Profile Mismatch

   ⚠ You are pasting content copied from a document with a different color profile.

   Source: ColorMatch RGB

   Destination: Working RGB - Adobe RGB (1998)

   What would you like to do?

   ⦿ Convert (preserve color appearance)
   ○ Don't convert (preserve color numbers)

   Cancel   OK

   The Convert option converts the pasted image colors to the color profile of the file into which you're pasting, preserving the color appearance. The Don't Convert option preserves the color data, but not the actual profile, in the pasted information.

12. **In the Paste Profile Mismatch dialog box, choose the Convert option, and then click OK.**

   Because this file has no Background layer, the pasted image is pasted into the active Layer 1.

   The pasted content is added to the selected Layer 1.

13. **In the Layers panel, rename Layer 1 as Bloom.**

14. **Save the file and continue to the next stage of the project.**

STAGE 2 / Manipulating Pixels

Before digital image-editing software, a photo was a photo. If you wanted a different angle or arrangement, you simply took another photo. Digital photo editing makes it much easier to manipulate the actual content of an image — from scaling specific objects to a different size or moving them to a new location, to changing the image's entire focal point. In this stage of the project, you will learn a number of techniques for changing the content in the client's supplied images to better meet the needs of the project.

Apply Content-Aware Scaling

When you scale a selection, you are stretching or squashing the pixels in that selection. This can produce the result you want, but it can also badly distort the image. Content-aware scaling intends to correct this problem by analyzing the image and preserving areas of detail when you scale the image.

1. **Make blvd.psd the active file.**

   The focus of this image is directly down the center. Because you are going to add type and other images to complete the entire postcard composition, you first need to move the image's focal point to create room for the textual elements.

2. **Choose the Move tool in the Tools panel.**

3. **With the Lights layer selected in the Layers panel, click in the document window to activate it. Press Shift, then click and drag to the left until the path in the image is approximately one-third of the way across the canvas.**

   As you can see, moving a layer's contents reveals the underlying layer. The right edge of the path image creates a harsh line.

Note:

The black background does not appear clearly in our screen captures, however, you should be able to see the edge on your monitor.

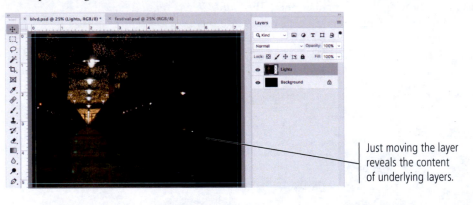

Just moving the layer reveals the content of underlying layers.

4. **Choose Edit>Undo Move.**

   Rather than simply moving the image to the position you want, you are going to scale it to fill the entire space, while moving the lighted path into the left half of the image.

5. **With the Lights layer still selected, choose Edit>Transform>Scale.**

   When you enter into transformation mode by calling any of the Transform submenu options, the selection (or entire layer, if you don't have a specific area selected) is surrounded by a bounding box and handles, which you can use to control the transformation. The Options bar also includes fields for numerically transforming the selection.

6. **Shift-click the left-center handle on the image layer and drag left until the path in the image is approximately one-third of the way across the canvas.**

Remember, you have to hold the Shift key to transform a selection away from its original aspect ratio.

It can be helpful to reduce the view percentage so you can see more area around the defined canvas.

Transformations alter the pixels in the layer. As you can see, the lights are distorted by scaling the layer in only one direction.

Scaling in only one direction distorts the image content.

7. **In the Options bar, click the Cancel Transform button (or press ESC).**

As long as the transformation handles remain visible, you can cancel any changes you made. By cancelling the transformation, the layer is restored to its original state.

8. **With the Lights layer selected, choose Edit>Content-Aware Scale.**

Again, you see the transformation handles. The process is virtually the same as regular scaling, but it identifies and tries to protect areas of detail when you scale the image.

9. **Shift-click the left-center handle on the layer and drag left until the path in the image is approximately one-third of the way across the canvas.**

As you can see, some distortion still occurs. However, the lights hanging over the path — the most obvious point of detail — are not noticeably distorted. Other areas of detail — the trees and bench, for example — are somewhat distorted, but not nearly as badly as they were from the regular scale transformation.

Content-aware scaling attempts to preserve areas of detail.

10. **Press Return/Enter to finalize the transformation.**

11. **Save the file and continue to the next exercise.**

More About Content-Aware Scaling

Content-aware scaling identifies areas of detail when it determines what to protect. In some cases, though, the image focus might have little or no detail within the shape areas, like the white bird in the following images. To solve this problem, you can identify a specific mask area to protect when you use content-aware scaling.

Use this menu to protect a specific mask area.

Click this button to protect skin tones from scaling.

Original image

Image scaled using Transform>Scale mode

Image scaled using Content-Aware Scale mode

Image scaled using Content-Aware Scale mode, but with the bird area protected by a mask.

Use the Content-Aware Move Tool

Photoshop makes it easy to move content around on the canvas. If an entire layer is selected, you can easily use the Move tool to move all the content on that layer to a different location. If you create a specific selection area using one of the marquee or lasso tools, you can also move only the selected area to another location on the active layer. It's important to realize, however, that this process actually removes the area under the original selection area, which might not be what you want. The Content-Aware Move tool allows you to move a selection and fill the original selection area with detail instead of leaving an empty hole.

1. **Make festival.psd the active file.**

   The main focus of the poppy image is nicely centered in the canvas. To make room for the other pieces of the composition, you need the flower to be on the right side of the image.

2. **Choose the Lasso tool in the Tools panel.**

3. **Draw a marquee that roughly selects the flower in the center of the image.**

Lasso tool

Draw a loose selection around the entire flower.

Note:

Make sure your selection area is well away from the flower petals to avoid unwanted remnants after you move the selection.

4. **Choose the Move tool in the Tools panel.**

5. **Click inside the selection area, then drag it to the right side of the canvas.**

    When you use the Move tool with a specific selection marquee, you are moving all of the pixels within that selection area. The area of the original selection is removed from that layer, so you can see underlying layers (or transparent gray-and-white checkerboard, if there is no underlying layer).

Move tool

Moving the selection reveals the underlying layers (or transparent area if there is no underlying layer).

You should notice that the moved pixels remain on the same layer. As long as the selection marquee remains active, you can continue to move the selected pixels around the same layer without affecting the other pixels on that layer. If you deselect, however, the underlying pixels will be permanently replaced by the pixels you moved.

To get around this problem, it's fairly common practice to move selected pixels to another layer before dragging with the Move tool:

1. Make a selection.
2. Choose Edit>Cut to remove the selected pixels from the original layer or choose Edit>Copy to keep the selected pixels on the original layer.
3. Choose Edit>Paste to add the cut/copied pixels onto a new layer.

6. **Choose Edit>Undo Move to restore all the pixels to their original positions.**

7. **With the same marquee still selected, choose the Content-Aware Move tool (nested under the Spot Healing Brush tool).**

    You can draw a new marquee with the Content-Aware Move tool, but in this case it isn't necessary because you already defined the selection area with the Lasso tool.

Note:

If you leave the selection marquee in place before choosing Edit>Paste, the cut/copied pixels are pasted in exactly the same position they were in when you cut/copied them.

8. **In the Options bar, make sure Move is selected in the Mode menu and the Transform On Drop option is selected.**

When the Content-Aware Move tool is active, the Mode menu in

the Options bar determines whether you will move or extend the selection area.

The Adaptation menu determines how closely the software analyzes the structure and color of the image to create the final result. Structure is defined on a 1–7 scale and Color is defined on a 0–10 scale. Higher values mean stricter adaptation; they take longer to process, but can produce more accurate results.

When the Transform On Drop option is active, releasing the mouse button results in a bounding box around the moved selection. You can use the bounding-box handles to adjust the moved selection's size. The movement is not finalized until you press Return/Enter or click the Commit Transform button in the Options bar. If Transform On Drop is *not* checked, the movement is finalized as soon as you release the mouse button.

9. **Click inside the selection area and drag the selected flower to the right side of the canvas.**

Content-Aware
Move tool

Transform On Drop is checked by default.

When you release the mouse button, bounding-box handles are available to transform the moved selection.

Moving the selection does not reveal the underlying layers.

10. **Press Return/Enter to finalize the move.**

When the process is complete, the original selection area is filled with pixels that seamlessly blend into the surrounding area. The edges of the moved area are also blended into their new surrounding area.

The original selection area is filled with information that blends into the image.

Edges of the moved selection area are blended into the surrounding image.

Note:

The process might take a while to complete because Photoshop has to analyze and determine which pixels to create. Be patient.

11. **Turn off the active selection (Select>Deselect).**

12. **Save the file and continue to the next exercise.**

More About the Content-Aware Move Tool

You can also use the Content-Aware Move tool in Extend mode to enlarge objects in a linear direction, as you can see in the images to the right.

Tighter selection marquees generally produce better results than a loose area that includes a lot of background pixels.

Original image | Image after extending the rear building with the Content-Aware Move tool.

Apply a Tilt-Shift Blur Effect

Many of the Blur filters can be used for functional purposes, such as removing noise with the Gaussian Blur filter. Others have more artistic purposes, and include far more specific controls than a simple dialog box interface. Photoshop includes five sophisticated blur filters, which are controlled in a specialized workspace that contains only the tools you need to apply the filters.

1. **Make the blvd.psd file active, and make sure the Lights layer is selected in the Layers panel.**

2. **Choose Filter>Blur Gallery>Tilt-Shift.**

   The Tilt-Shift filter applies a linear blur out from a center line. You can use on-screen controls in the Blur Gallery to change the angle and position of the blur, as well as a number of other options.

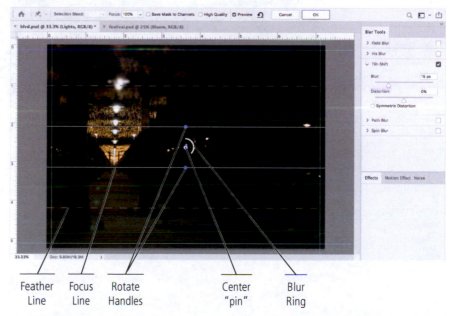

Feather Line | Focus Line | Rotate Handles | Center "pin" | Blur Ring

3. **Move the cursor over either Rotate Handle. Press Shift, then click and drag until the cursor feedback shows the angle of 90°.**

Heads-up display shows the blur rotation angle.

Note:

Pressing Shift constrains the rotation to 22.5° increments.

4. **Click the center "pin" of the blur control and drag left until the row of lights is between the two focus lines.**

Anything between the two focus lines will be preserved without a blur.

5. **Click the left Focus Line (the solid line) away from the Rotate Handle, and drag left until the line is close to the right side of the left palm tree.**

6. **Click the left Feather Line (the dotted line) and drag until the line is just past the left side of the same palm tree.**

The Feather Lines define the distance from unblurred (at the Focus Line) and completely blurred pixels.

Note:

*In the Effects panel, you can control **bokeh** effects — the aesthetic qualities of blurred points of light — for a field, iris, or tilt-shift blur.*

***Light Bokeh** brightens blurred areas of an image.*

***Bokeh Color** changes the color of lightened areas in the image from neutral (0%) to colorful (100%).*

***Light Range** determines which brightness values are affected by the Light Bokeh.*

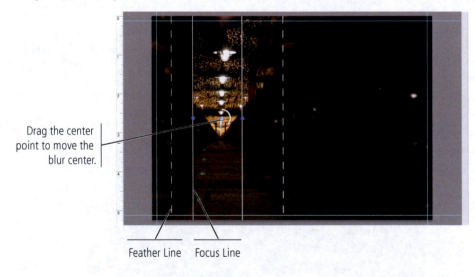

Drag the center point to move the blur center.

Feather Line   Focus Line

7. **Repeat Steps 5–6 to position the right Focus and Feather lines relative to the right palm tree.**

8. **Click the Blur Ring and drag the white area until the cursor feedback shows the Blur: 20.**

Changing intensity of the blur using the on-screen control applies the same change in the Blur field in the Blur Tools panel.

Note:

The Distortion option in the Blur Tools panel defines the shape of the blur that is applied. You can also check the Symmetric Distortion option to apply the distortion amount to both sides of the blur.

Drag the outer ring to change the blur intensity.

9. **Click OK in the Options bar to apply the blur.**

When you finalize the blur, the process can take a while to render. Be patient.

Because the Lights layer is a regular layer, the Blur Gallery filter is applied destructively. If you apply these filters to a Smart Object layer, they are remembered as Smart Filters and can be edited.

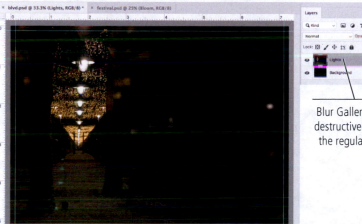

Blur Gallery filters destructively affect the regular layer.

10. **Save the file and continue to the next exercise.**

Apply an Iris Blur Effect

The Iris Blur filter mimics the effect of changing the aperture, focal length, and focus distance with a camera. The blur applies around a central point; you can use on-screen controls to define the shape and size of the blur.

1. **Make the `festival.psd` file active.**

2. **With the Bloom layer selected, choose Filter>Blur Gallery>Iris Blur.**

   The Iris blur is also controlled in the Blur Gallery interface.

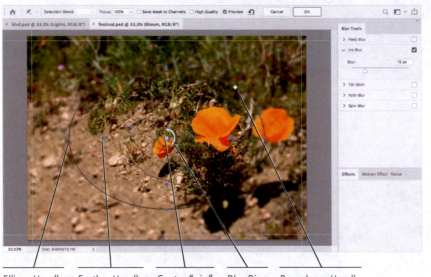

   Ellipse Handle   Feather Handle   Center "pin"   Blur Ring   Roundness Handle

3. **Click the center "pin" and drag to position the blur so it is approximately centered on the flower.**

   You can click away from the existing blur controls to add a new pin, which means you can define more than one focal point on the same layer.

4. **Click the right ellipse handle and drag left to make the ellipse narrower.**

   If you click the ellipse *away* from the handle, you can enlarge or shrink the existing ellipse without affecting its proportional shape.

Drag the pin to move the focal point of the blur.

Drag the Ellipse Handle to rotate or change the shape of the blur ellipse.

Drag the Ellipse to resize the blur without changing its shape.

Note:

You can apply a blur to only certain parts of a layer by drawing a selection marquee before opening the Blur Gallery. In this case, you can use the Selection Bleed option (in the Options bar) to determine how much the selected area blends with the unselected areas.

Note:

Click the Roundness Handle and drag to make the blur shape more or less rectangular.

5. **Click the top Feather Handle and drag down until it is placed at the top edge of the center flower.**

   The distance between the Feather Handle and the outer ellipse defines the length of the blur. When you click and drag one handle, all four move symmetrically.

Drag any Feather Handle to change the distance from unblurred to entirely blurred pixels.

When you drag one Feather Handle, all four move the same distance.

6. **Press Option/Alt, then click the bottom Feather Handle and drag up to increase the blur distance on only the bottom of the flower.**

   Pressing Option/Alt allows you to move one Feather Handle independently of the others.

Option/Alt-drag a Feather Handle to move it independently of the other handles.

Note:

You can use the Save Mask to Channels option (in the Blur Gallery Options bar) to create an alpha channel mask from the defined blur. Solid areas in the mask show areas that are unblurred; white areas of the mask show areas that are entirely blurred.

Note:

The Focus option in the Options bar defines the clarity of the area in the focus zone. For a Tilt-Shift blur, this is the area between the two Focus Lines. For an Iris blur, this is the area inside the Feather Handles.

7. **Click the Blur Ring and drag around to increase the intensity to 20 px.**

8. **Click OK in the Options bar to apply the blur.**

9. **Save the file and continue to the next stage of the project.**

More About the Blur Gallery

Field Blur

The Field Blur filter applies an overall blur that affects the entire layer. Changing the blur intensity changes the amount of blur that is applied to that layer.

You can also place multiple focus points to change the blur in different areas of the layer. In the image to the right, we applied a 25-px blur to the pin at the top of the image and a 0-px blur to the pin in the center portion of the image. The 0-px pin prevents the blur from affecting the entire image, so the front of the bridge appears in focus.

Spin Blur

The Spin Blur filter creates a rotational blur around a defined point. The blur angle controls the amount of blur that is applied.

You can click and drag the rotation point to move the blur's center point. If you Option/Alt-click and drag the rotation point, you can move it away from the center of the blur ring to create an off-center spin blur.

The feather handles define the outer edge of the area affected by the blur.

Clicking and dragging the blur ring away from the ellipse handles resizes the blur ring proportionally. You can also click and drag one of the ellipse handles to resize the blur ring in only one direction.

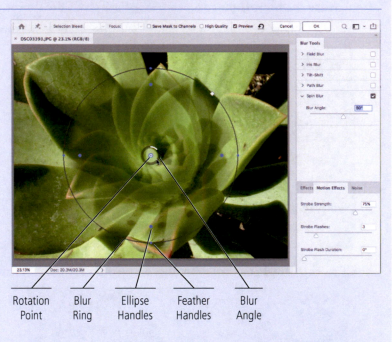

Rotation Point   Blur Ring   Ellipse Handles   Feather Handles   Blur Angle

You can also use the Motion Effects panel to change the strength of the blur:

- **Strobe Flashes** defines the number of exposures that will be visible.
- **Strobe Strength** defines how much blurring is visible between strobe flash exposures. A setting of 0% (the default) means no strobe effect is visible. A setting of 100% results in very little blur between exposures.
- **Strobe Flash Duration** defines the length of the strobe flash exposure in degrees, which controls the distance of the blur around the blur circumference.

Applying a spin blur with an increased Stroke Strength effect creates the appearance of the blade in motion. Because Strobe Flashes effect is set to 3, you can see three ghosted versions of the plant's center leaves in the image above.

Path Blur

The Path Blur filter creates a motion blur based on a path that you define.

Clicking and dragging in the gallery window creates the initial blur path. You can click anywhere along the blue path to create a path midpoint and bend the path in a specific direction.

In the Blur Tools panel, you can use the top menu to define a basic blur or rear sync flash blur (this simulates the effect of a flash fired at the end of an exposure).

The Speed slider defines the overall blur amount for all defined blur paths.

The Taper slider adjusts the edge fading of blurs. Higher values allow the blur to fade gradually.

The Centered Blur option creates stable blurs by centering the blur shape for any pixel on the defined path.

Each end point on the blur path can have a different speed, or the degree of blur that is applied at that point. If **Edit Blur Shapes** is checked in the Blur Tools panel, you can drag a red arrow to change the speed (length) of the blur and bend the red arrow to change the direction of the blur that is applied along the blur path.

In the Motion Effects panel, Strobe Flashes defines the number of exposures of the virtual strobe flash light. Strobe Strength defines how much blurring is visible between strobe flash exposures.

In the above images, we created two separate blur paths. The first defines a curved blur that follows the shape of the lower stairs; the starting point has a rather high blur speed and the end point has a blur speed of 0 px. Because the 0-px blur speed does not eliminate all blurring at the end point, we added a second straight blur path with 0-px blur speeds at both ends to eliminate all blurring in that area (the top of the staircase) of the image.

STAGE 3 / **Working with Type**

Type is a vector-based element. As long as you maintain type as vectors, the letter shapes can be resized and transformed without losing quality. As you know, Photoshop can combine raster and vector objects into a single composition.

Many Photoshop jobs require some kind of type. Although Photoshop is not a typesetting tool by definition, its type capabilities are robust enough for creating and manipulating type in a variety of ways. To complete these postcards, you are going to create and format several type elements.

The Anatomy of Type

Before we jump into the exercises in this section, you should understand the terms that you will often hear when people talk about type:

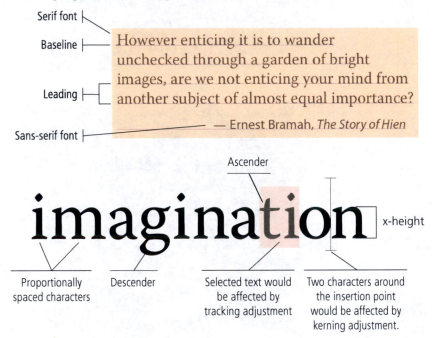

Type is typically divided into two basic categories: serif and sans serif. **Serif type** has small flourishes on the ends of the letterforms; **sans-serif** has no such decorations (*sans* is French for "without"). The actual shape of letters is determined by the specific **font** you use. Each **character** in a font is referred to as a **glyph**.

Fonts can be monospaced or proportionally spaced. In a monospace font, each character takes up the same amount of space on a line. In other words, a lowercase "i" and "w" will occupy the same horizontal width. In a proportionally spaced font, different characters occupy different amounts of horizontal space as necessary.

When you set type in a digital application, the letters rest on a nonprinting line called the **baseline**. If a type element has more than one line in a single paragraph, the distance from one baseline to the next is called **leading** (pronounced, "ledding"). Most applications set the default leading as 120% of the type size, but you can change the leading to any value you prefer.

The **x-height** of type is the height of the lowercase letter "x." Elements that extend below the baseline are called **descenders** (as in, "g," "j," and "p"). Elements that extend above the x-height are called **ascenders** (as in, "b," "d," and "k").

The size of type is usually measured in **points** (there are approximately 72 points in an inch). When you define a specific type size, you determine the distance from the bottom of the descenders to the top of the ascenders, plus a small extra space above the ascenders called the **body clearance**.

Note:

There are other types of special fonts, including script, symbol, dingbat, decorative, and image fonts. These don't fit easily into the serif/sans-serif distinction.

Place and Format Point Type

You can create two basic kinds of type in Photoshop: point type and area type. **Point type** is created by simply clicking in the image window with one of the Type tools. A point type element can exist on one or multiple lines. Point type can continue into apparent infinity without starting a new line. If you want to start a new line, you have to manually tell Photoshop where to create the break.

Note:

You must install the ATC fonts from the Student Files website to complete the rest of this project.

1. **With `festival.psd` active, choose the Horizontal Type tool.**

   You can access the basic type options in the Options bar. Additional options are available in the Character and Paragraph panels.

2. **In the Tools panel, click the Default Foreground and Background Colors button.**

   Type automatically adopts the active foreground color — in this case, black.

3. **In the Options bar, change the Font Size to 28 pt.**

   If you define type settings before you create a type layer, those settings automatically apply to the layer you create.

A Toggle Text Orientation
B Font Family
C Font Style
D Font Size
E Anti-Aliasing Method
F Left Align Text
G Center Align Text
H Right Align Text
I Text Color
J Create Warped Text
K Toggle the Character and Pararaph Panels

Horizontal Type tool

4. **Click anywhere in the canvas to create a type layer.**

   When you create a new type layer, it is automatically filled with placeholder text, which is highlighted. You can immediately see the formatting that is currently applied to the new type layer.

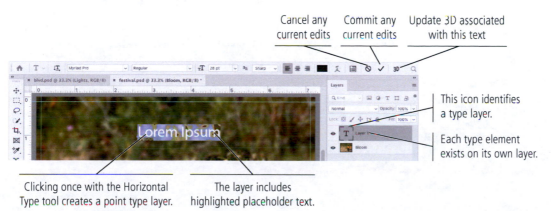

Cancel any current edits
Commit any current edits
Update 3D associated with this text

This icon identifies a type layer.

Each type element exists on its own layer.

Clicking once with the Horizontal Type tool creates a point type layer.

The layer includes highlighted placeholder text.

5. **With the placeholder text selected, type Antelope Valley.**

When text is selected on a type layer, typing replaces the previously highlighted text with whatever you type.

Note:

You can turn off the automatic placeholder text in the Type pane of the Preferences dialog box.

6. **In the Options bar, click the Commit button to finalize your changes to the active the Type layer.**

You can also choose a different tool, or select a different layer to finalize your changes.

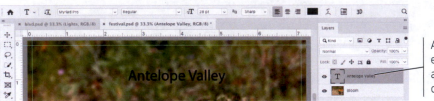

After committing the edits, the type layer adopts its name based on the text in the layer.

7. **With the new type layer selected, click the Font menu to highlight it and type atc g.**

Typing in the Font menu returns a list of all fonts that contain the defined search string. The resulting font names do not need to exactly match the search string. In this case, any fonts that include the characters "atc" and "g" are returned.

8. **Move the mouse cursor over the first font in the resulting list.**

Photoshop includes a live font preview that automatically shows the selected text in the font where your mouse cursor is currently hovering.

Note:

If you're working with the insertion point flashing in a type layer or you have characters on a type layer selected, you can't use the keyboard shortcuts to access different tools.

Type in this field to search for specific fonts.

Click this button to show all fonts that are available on your computer.

The active type layer changes to show the font that is active under the mouse cursor.

Only fonts matching the search criteria appear in the resulting menu.

9. **Click ATC Garnet Medium in the menu to change the font of the active type layer.**

10. **Click with the Horizontal Type tool again (away from the existing type) to create a second type layer, then type Poppy Festival.**

Clicking places the insertion point in a new point type element, creating a new type layer.

The Type tools remember the last formatting options you defined.

Clicking again creates a separate type layer.

11. **With the insertion point flashing in the second type layer, choose Select>All.**

When the insertion point is flashing, this command highlights (selects) all of the text in the active type layer.

You can also click and drag to select specific characters, double-click to select an entire word, triple-click to select an entire line, or quadruple-click to select an entire paragraph.

Note:

If you change the alignment of point type, the text moves around the origin point of the element.

12. **In the Options bar, change the Font Style to Ultra and change the Font Size to 72 pt.**

If you type in the field, you have to Press Return/Enter (or click the Commit button) to finalize the new formatting. If you choose a defined size from the attached menu, you do not need to press Return/Enter.

Character attributes such as font size affect all selected characters.

Point type exists on a single line unless you manually insert a line break.

13. **Press the Left Arrow key to deselect the characters and move the insertion point to the beginning of the type. With the insertion point still flashing in the type, press and hold Command/Control to access the type layer bounding box.**

Pressing Command/Control temporarily switches to the Move tool, so you can move a type layer without switching away from the Horizontal Type tool.

Press Command/Control while the insertion point is flashing to access the layer's transformation bounding box.

14. **Click inside the bounding-box area and drag to move the type until it is centered horizontally on the canvas — approximately 0.25″ from the top ruler guide.**

The pink smart guides identify when the dragged content is centered on the canvas. To find the correct position for the top edge of the type, you might want to turn on page rulers (View>Rulers).

Command/Control-click inside the bounding-box area and drag to move the layer content.

Smart Guides identify when the center of the object aligns to the center of the canvas.

Note:

You could accomplish the same thing by selecting the type layer with the Move tool active, and then choosing Edit>Free Transform.

You can click the arrow to the right of the Font Family menu to open the Font panel, which provides a number of options for finding fonts you want to use in your design. (The same options are available wherever you see a Font Family menu — the Character panel, the Options bar, and the Properties panel.)

The top section of the menu lists up to ten of the most recently used fonts. These appear in the order in which they were used, with the most recent at the top of the menu. You can change the number of displayed fonts in the Type pane of the Preferences dialog box.

The second section lists SVG fonts. The third section lists all other fonts that are available to Photoshop.

Open the Font menu

Click an arrow to show all styles available in a specific font family.

Click a solid star to remove a font from your "favorites" list.

Click a hollow star to add a font to your "favorites" list.

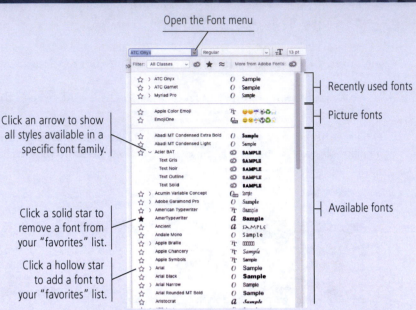

Recently used fonts

Picture fonts

Available fonts

The font family names in each section appear in alphabetical order. An arrow to the left of a font name indicates that a specific font family includes more than one style. You can click the arrow to show all possible styles in the panel.

If you apply a font that includes more than one style, the style you choose appears in the Font Style menu. You can open the Font Style menu to change the style, without changing the font family.

Above the list of fonts in the Font panel, you can use the Filter menu to show only certain classes of fonts. You can also use the three filter buttons to show only certain fonts in the panel. Simply click an active button to turn off that filter.

Show Adobe Fonts

★ Show Favorite Fonts

≈ Show Similar Fonts

The right column in the Font menu shows a sample of the font, as well an icon to identify the type of font:

a **PostScript (Type 1) fonts** have two file components (outline and printer) that are required for output.

T̲T̲ TrueType fonts have a single file, but (until recently) were primarily used on the Windows platform.

O **OpenType fonts** are contained in a single file that can include more than 60,000 glyphs (characters) in a single font. OpenType fonts are cross-platform; they can be used on both Macintosh and Windows systems.

OpenType SVG fonts allow font glyphs to be created as SVG (scalable vector graphics) artwork, which means glyphs can include multiple colors and gradients. These fonts, which are relatively new, are most commonly used for emojis.

OpenType Variable fonts, introduced in 2016, were developed jointly by Adobe, Apple, Google, and Microsoft to allow a single font file to store a continuous range of variants. If you apply a variable font, you can adjust the width and weight of the applied font, without the need for different font files for variations, such as Bold, Black, Condensed, or Extended.

Adobe fonts (previously called Typekit fonts) are those that have been activated from Adobe servers through your Creative Cloud account.

15. **While still holding the Command/Control key, click the bottom-right bounding-box handle, press Shift, and drag down. Resize the type so it is approximately 1.25″ high.**

Unlike transforming a layer in Transform mode, you need to press the Shift key to transform the type layer proportionally while the Type tool is active.

Even though you resized the type layer, it is still live type — you can still place the insertion point and edit as necessary.

Drag the handles to resize or transform the type layer disproportionally.

Note:

Feel free to toggle rulers on and off as necessary while working on this (and all) projects.

16. **When you finish resizing the type, release the Command/Control key.**

17. **If your two type layers overlap in the document, use the Layers panel to hide the Antelope Valley layer.**

This will allow you to better see the effects of your changes in the next few steps.

18. **Click to place the insertion point between the "F" and "e" in the word Festival.**

19. **In the Options bar, click the button to toggle open the Character and Paragraph panels.**

You can also choose Window>Character or Type>Panels>Character to open the Character panel. Changes made in the Character panel apply only to selected text.

20. **In the Character panel, change the Kerning field to -30.**

Kerning and tracking control the spacing between individual characters. **Kerning** adjusts the spacing between two specific characters (called a **kerning pair**). **Tracking** (also called range kerning) is applied over a range of selected type.

Kerning values are based, by default, on the type **metrics** (the values stored in the font data). Professional-quality fonts include predefined kerning and tracking tables in the font data. The **Optical** option in the Kerning menu is useful for fonts that don't have built-in kerning values. Photoshop applies kerning based on how it perceives letter shapes.

You should always check the letter spacing when you set headline type, use All Caps or Small Caps type styles, or apply any other artificial manipulation (such as the stretching you applied in Step 11).

Note:

Kerning and tracking are largely matters of personal taste. In this project, you want the letters to be very tightly spaced, but not touching.

Note:

Press Option/Alt-Left Arrow to apply −20 kerning units or Option/Alt-Right Arrow to apply +20 kerning units at the insertion point.

Click here to toggle the Character and Paragraph panels.

The Font Size shows the change that was created by scaling the type layer.

Kerning applies to the space between two characters, where the insertion point is placed.

Changes to character formatting affect only selected characters. If you make changes before typing, the changes apply to all characters you type from the insertion point.

All of the character formatting options that are available in the Options bar are also available in the Character panel. However, the Character panel includes a number of other options that control the appearance of type in your document.

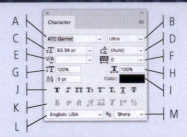

A **Font Family** is the general font that is applied, such as Minion or Warnock Pro.

B **Font Style** is the specific variation of the applied font, such as Italic, Bold, or Light.

C **Font Size** is the size of the type in points.

D **Leading** is the distance from one baseline to the next. Adobe applications treat leading as a character attribute, even though leading controls the space between lines of an individual paragraph. (Space between paragraphs is controlled using the Space Before and Space After options in the Paragraph panel.) To change leading for an entire paragraph, you must first select the entire paragraph.

If you change the leading for only certain characters in a line, keep in mind that the adjusted leading applies to the entire line where adjusted characters exist. For example:

> In this sentence, we changed the leading
>
> for only the <u>underlined</u> word; all text in the same line moves to accommodate the adjusted leading of the characters.

E **Kerning** increases or decreases the space between pairs of letters. Kerning is used in cases in which particular letters in specific fonts need to be manually spread apart or brought together to eliminate a crowded or spread-out appearance. Manual kerning is usually necessary in headlines or other large type elements. Many commercial fonts have built-in kerning pairs, so you won't need to apply much hands-on intervention with kerning. Adobe applications default to the kerning values stored in the **font metrics**.

F **Tracking**, also known as "range kerning," refers to the overall tightness or looseness across a range of characters. Tracking and kerning are applied in thousandths of an **em** — or the amount of space occupied by an uppercase "M," which is usually the widest character in a typeface.

G, H **Vertical Scale** and **Horizontal Scale** artificially stretch or contract the selected characters. This scaling is a quick way of achieving condensed or expanded type if those variations of a font don't exist. (Type that has been artificially condensed or expanded too much looks bad because the scaling destroys the type's metrics. If possible, use a condensed or expanded version of a font before resorting to horizontal or vertical scaling.)

I **Character Color** moves the selected type above or below the baseline by a specific number of points. Positive numbers move the characters up; negative values move the characters down.

J Type Styles — **All Caps**, **Small Caps**, **Superscript**, **Subscript**, **Underline**, and **Strikethrough** — change the appearance of selected characters.

K **OpenType Attributes** change selected characters to alternate glyphs, such as ligatures, stylistic alternates, and fractions. These options are only available if the active font is an OpenType font, which can store more than 65,000 glyphs or characters in a single font. Not all stylistic alternates are available for all OpenType fonts.

L **Language Dictionary** defines the language that is used to check spelling in the story.

M **Anti-Aliasing** can be used to help smooth the apparent edges of type when it is rendered (rasterized) — even if that doesn't happen until the final output. Anti-aliasing produces smooth-edge type by partially filling the edge pixels, which allows the edges of the type to better blend into the background when the type is rendered. (Be aware that anti-aliasing small type might distort the letter shapes.) Photoshop supports the following five options for anti-aliasing type, the effects of which are best viewed at higher zoom percentages:

- None applies no anti-aliasing.
- Sharp creates the sharpest type.
- Crisp makes type appear slightly sharp.
- Strong makes type appear heavier.
- Smooth makes type edges appear very smooth.

21. **Continue adjusting the kerning between the letter pairs until you are satisfied with the results.**

Note:

The only options you can't apply to live text are the Distort and Perspective transformations, custom warps (although you can use the built-in warp shapes), and filters. To use these features, you must rasterize the type layer.

22. **Save the file and continue to the next exercise.**

Use the Move Tool with Type Layers

Type layers in Photoshop are similar to most other layers. You can drag and transform type layers using most of the same tools that you use to transform other kinds of layers. You can scale or skew type layers; change their opacity, fill, and blending mode; apply layer styles; and even add warp effects, while still maintaining the editable type.

1. **With festival.psd active, make sure the Antelope Valley type layer is visible. Click the Antelope Valley layer in the Layers panel to select it.**

2. **Choose the Move tool.**

    Using the Move tool, you can move and manipulate type layers like any other layer, but you can't edit the actual type.

3. **With the Auto-Select option turned off in the Options bar, click and drag to move the type so the first letter in the layer appears just above the "o" in the word "Poppy."**

    If you don't turn off the Auto-Select option, you would have to click exactly on the rather thin letters in the type. When this option is not checked, you can click anywhere in the canvas to drag the selected layer.

    As you can see, the 28-pt text is too large to fit in the space. The type runs directly behind the "F" in the word "Festival" because the "Poppy Festival" type layer is higher in the layer stacking order.

4. **In the Character panel, click the Color swatch to open the Color Picker for the text color.**

The insertion point does not need to be flashing to change the formatting of the active type layer. Keep in mind, however, that any change you make while the insertion point is *not* flashing applies to all type in the layer. If you want to change the formatting of only some type on a layer, you first have to use the Type tool to select the characters you want to affect.

5. **Move the Eyedropper cursor over a bright orange color in the poppy image and click to sample that color. Click OK to change the type color.**

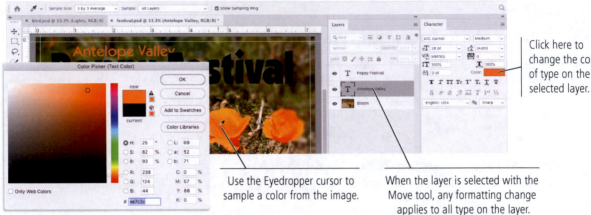

Click here to change the color of type on the selected layer.

Use the Eyedropper cursor to sample a color from the image.

When the layer is selected with the Move tool, any formatting change applies to all type on the layer.

6. **In the Character panel, reduce the font size to 22 pt.**

This layer uses left paragraph alignment, and the origin point of the layer remains in place when you change the formatting.

This type layer is still selected.

7. **Select the Poppy Festival type layer, then use the Character panel to change the type color to white.**

Select the Poppy Festival layer before changing the type color.

8. **Save the file and continue to the next exercise.**

The Paragraph Panel in Depth

You can change a number of paragraph attributes, including alignment and justification, indents, and space above and below paragraphs. The Justification options are only available when you work with area type (which you will do shortly), and some options are not relevant for point type that only occupies a single line.

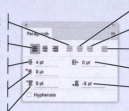

Justify last left
Align left, center, and right
Indent left margin
Indent first line
Add space before paragraph

Justify last center
Justify last right
Justify all (force justify)
Indent right margin
Add space after paragraph

Hyphenation Options

When the Hyphenate option is selected, text in area type hyphenates automatically, based on the Hyphenation options in the Paragraph panel Options menu. You can control the minimum length of a word before it can be hyphenated, as well as the minimum number of characters that must appear before or after a hyphen. Formal rules of typography typically suggest that only words longer than six characters should be hyphenated, and at least three characters should exist before or after a hyphen.

Justification Options

When you work with area type, you can justify paragraphs inside the type area. Justified type stretches horizontally to fill the width of the area. The last line of the paragraph can be aligned left, centered, or right, or it can be stretched based on your choice in the Paragraph panel. When text is justified, it's stretched based on the defined Justification options, which can be changed by choosing Justification in the Paragraph panel Options menu.

The Minimum and Maximum values define the acceptable spacing for justified paragraphs. The Desired value defines the *preferred* spacing for paragraphs:

- The **Word Spacing** fields control the space between words (anywhere you press the space bar). A 100% value means the word spacing remains the same when you justify a paragraph.

- The **Letter Spacing** fields control the space between letters, including kerning and tracking values. A 0% value means the letter spacing remains the same when you justify a paragraph.

- The **Glyph Scaling** fields control the width of individual characters. A 100% value means they are not stretched.

The **Hyphen Limit** field defines how many hyphens can appear at the ends of consecutive lines. Formal rules of typography recommend limiting consecutive hyphens to three, but preferably, no more than two.

The **Hyphenation Zone** determines the distance from the right edge of a type area where automatic hyphens can exist. If this field is set to 1/2″, for example, the automatic hyphen would have to fall within half an inch of the type area edge for a word to be automatically hyphenated.

The final option, **Hyphenate Capitalized Words**, can be turned off to prevent automatic hyphenation in proper nouns such as corporate or product names — many companies seriously frown on their trademarks being split across lines.

The **Auto Leading** field applies to both area type and point type that occupy more than one line. By default, automatic leading is set to 120% of the type size. You can change this automatic value, but it is usually better to change the leading for individual type instances instead.

Create Vertically Oriented Type

Although most type (in English, at least) is oriented left-to-right, row-to-row, there are times when you want to orient type vertically — each character below the next. You can use the Vertical Type tool to accomplish this goal, whether for a foreign-language design or simply for artistic purposes.

1. Make **blvd.psd** the active file, then choose the Vertical Type tool (nested under the Horizontal Type tool).

2. In the Options bar, choose ATC Garnet Ultra as the font, define the size as **72 pt**, choose the Top Align Text option, and choose white as the type color.

3. Click to create a new type layer, then type **BLVD**.

   When you use the Vertical Type tool, each letter appears below the previous one.

   As you can see, the left edges of the letters (especially B and L) do not align. Vertical type orientation does not recognize the edges of lettershapes for the sake of alignment.

   In the Options bar, paragraph alignment options affect the position of type relative to the point at which you click. You can align the type below, centered on, or above the origin point. You cannot, however, align the left or right edges of the letters.

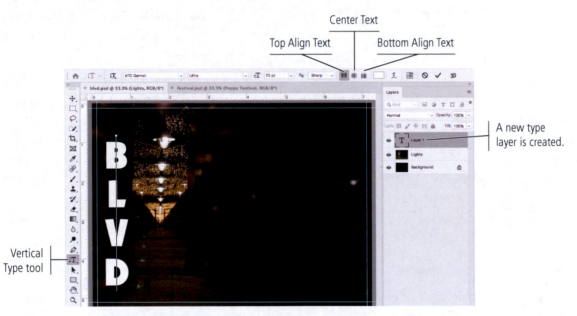

Center Text

Top Align Text   Bottom Align Text

A new type layer is created.

Vertical Type tool

4. Click the new type layer in the Layers panel to select the layer (not the highlighted text), then choose Type>Orientation>Horizontal.

Select the actual type layer to change its orientation.

5. Click to place the insertion point after the "B" and press Return/Enter to start a new paragraph.

6. Repeat this process to move each character onto a separate line.

For horizontally oriented type, the default (auto) leading creates a large space from one baseline to the next.

7. Place the insertion point before the "B." In the Options bar or Character panel, change the type size to 12 pt. Type THE and then press Return/Enter.

Changes to character formatting apply only to the insertion point and the new type that you add from that point.

8. Select the four letters in "BLVD." In the Character panel, change the Leading field to 55 pt.

Although leading appears to apply to paragraphs, it is a character property. To change the leading for an entire paragraph, you have to select all characters in that paragraph.

Changes to character formatting apply only to the highlighted type.

Reduced leading reduces the space from one baseline to the next.

9. Choose the Move tool. With the type layer selected, move it so the type begins in the top-left corner of the canvas, approximately 1/4″ from the ruler guides.

10. **Choose Edit>Free Transform. Click and drag the bottom-right handle until the letters occupy the entire left side of the canvas. Leave approximately 1/4" from the bottom ruler guide, as shown in the following image.**

Remember, you do not need to hold the Shift key to maintain the selection's aspect ratio as you transform it.

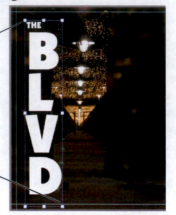

Move the type to be approximately 1/4" from the top-left corner.

Transform the type to occupy the entire left side, leaving a 1/4" margin inside the ruler guides.

11. **Press Return/Enter to finalize the transformation.**

12. **Double-click any of the characters on the type layer to highlight all of it.**

You do not need to manually switch to the Type tool to access the characters in a type layer. Simply double-click the characters to highlight all characters on the layer; the Horizontal Type tool is automatically activated for you.

13. **Click to place the insertion point anywhere in the word "THE" (the first paragraph).**

14. **In the Paragraph panel, change the Indent Left Margin field to 4 pt.**

You can choose Window>Paragraph to open the Paragraph panel, or click the Toggle the Character and Paragraph Panels button in the Options bar.

The Indent values affect the position of the type relative to the layer's orientation point. This better aligns the "T" in "THE" with the left edge of the "B" in "BLVD."

When you work with point type, paragraph attributes apply to all type on a single line. If you have more than one paragraph — as you do in this type layer — you can apply different paragraph format options to each paragraph.

15. **Change the Add Space After Paragraph field to -3 pt.**

Leading affects the space from one baseline to the next, even within a single paragraph. The Space Before Paragraph and Space After Paragraph options relate to an entire paragraph. By reducing this value, you are closing up the space between the first paragraph ("THE") and the second paragraph ("B").

Paragraph formatting options apply to the entire paragraph in which the insertion point is flashing.

16. **Save the file and continue to the next exercise.**

Create and Control Area Type

In many cases, your clients will provide specific text to include in a design; that text might be part of an email message or saved in a word-processing file. If the client-supplied text is only a couple of words, it's easier to retype the text into your Photoshop file. However, when the supplied text is longer, there's no point in making extra work by retyping.

The final type element you need for each postcard is a two- or three-paragraph blurb of promotional copy. You are going to create these as area-type layers so that you can better control the line breaks and alignment, and more easily fit them into a specific amount of space.

1. **On your desktop, double-click the file festival_copy.txt (in your WIP>Cards folder) to open the text file in a text-editing application.**

   You can't place or import external text files directly into a Photoshop file. If you want to use text from an external file, you simply open the file in a text editor, copy it, and paste it into a Photoshop type layer.

Note:

We used Macintosh TextEdit as our word processor.

2. **Select all text in the file, copy it, then close the file.**

3. **With festival.psd active in Photoshop, choose the Horizontal Type tool in the Tools panel.**

4. **Click the empty area at the bottom of the Layers panel to deselect all layers.**

5. **In the Characters panel, define the following type formatting options:**

Font Family:	**ATC Onyx**
Font Style:	**Italic**
Font Size:	**11 pt.**
Leading:	**14 pt.**
Type Color:	**White**

   If you did not deselect any of the existing type layers in Step 4, these changes would affect whatever layer was selected. Instead, these settings will apply to the next type layer you create.

Click here to deselect existing layers.

Define formatting options before creating a new type layer.

6. **Click below the "P" in "Poppy," and drag down and right to create a type area (as shown in the following image).**

When you release the mouse button, a new type layer is created for the type area.

Because you defined the type formatting before you created the type area, placeholder text in the new area is automatically formatted with the settings you defined.

When the insertion point is placed (or text is selected) in a type area, the area shows eight bounding-box handles that you can drag to change the area's shape.

A new type layer is created.

Click and drag to create a type area.

Type is selected in the area, so you can see the area's bounding-box handles.

The formatting you defined applies to placeholder text in the new type area.

7. **With the placeholder text selected, choose Edit>Paste.**

8. **With the Horizontal Type tool still active, click the right-center bounding-box handle of the type area and drag so the right edge of the area is between the "y" in "Poppy" and the "F" in "Festival."**

When you resize the type area by dragging the bounding-box handles, you do not affect the type; you change the type *container*, which allows more (or less, depending on how you drag) of the type to show.

Type also wraps within the type area. You don't have to manually define where new lines begin — simply press Return/Enter to start a new formal paragraph.

9. **Click the bottom-center handle and drag down to the bottom ruler guide.**

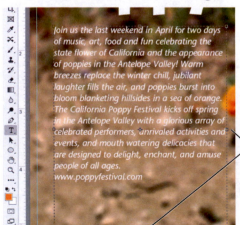

Dragging a type area handle with the Horizontal Type tool changes the size of the area without resizing the type.

Note:

Make sure to use the Horizontal Type tool when you want to change the dimensions of a type area. If you press Command/Control-T or choose Edit>Free Transform, stretching or otherwise resizing the type area bounding box resizes the type it contains.

10. **Click and drag to select at least part of all three paragraphs in the area. In the Paragraph panel, change the Add Space After Paragraph field to 8 pt.**

Paragraph formatting attributes apply to any paragraph that is even partially selected. If no characters are highlighted, any paragraph formatting changes apply to the paragraph in which the insertion point is currently placed.

11. **Drag the top-center handle of the type area until the last paragraph is approximately 1/4″ from the bottom guide.**

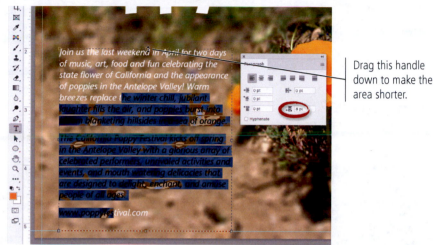

Drag this handle down to make the area shorter.

12. **Select the entire last paragraph in the area. In the Character panel, change the font to ATC Onyx Normal, and change the size to 13 pt. In the Paragraph panel, click the Center Text button.**

Remember that character attributes, such as font and size, apply only to selected characters. To change these for the entire paragraph, you must first select the entire paragraph.

13. **Save the file and continue to the next exercise.**

Create Paragraph Styles

When you work with longer blocks of text, many of the same formatting options are applied to different text elements (such as headings) throughout the story, or to different elements in similar pieces of a campaign. To simplify the workflow, you can use styles to store and apply multiple formatting options with a single click.

Another powerful benefit of styles is that when you change the options applied in a style, any text formatted with that style reflects the newly defined options. In other words, you can change multiple instances of noncontiguous text in a single process, instead of selecting each block and making the same changes repeatedly.

1. **With festival.psd active, select the entire first paragraph in the type area.**

2. **Open the Paragraph Styles panel (Window>Paragraph Styles).**

   The Paragraph Styles panel shows that the selected type is formatted with the Basic Paragraph style.

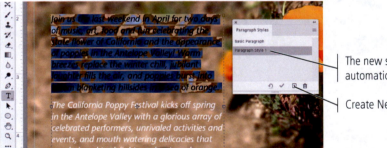

The Basic Paragraph option is included in every file.

3. **Click the Create New Paragraph Style button at the bottom of the panel.**

   When you create a new style, it defaults to include all formatting options that are applied to the currently selected type.

The new style is automatically applied.

Create New Paragraph Style

If you have used type styles in InDesign or Illustrator, you need to be aware of a difference in the way you create styles based on existing formatting. In those applications, a new style adopts the formatting of the current insertion point, which means you do not have to select specific type to create a style.

In Photoshop, however, you do have to select at least part of a paragraph to create a style based on that paragraph's formatting. Also, you cannot select multiple paragraphs with the same formatting to create a style based on those options.

Note:

Photoshop also supports character styles, which can be used to store any character-formatting options that can be applied to selected characters.

Note:

You can delete a style by dragging it to the panel's Delete button. If the style had been applied, you would see a warning message, asking you to confirm the deletion. (You do not have the opportunity to replace the applied style with another, as you do in Adobe InDesign.)

4. **Double-click the new style in the panel to review its settings.**

Double-clicking a style opens the Paragraph Style Options dialog box for that style, so you can edit its stored settings. Different options are available in the right side of the dialog box, depending on what is selected in the list of categories.

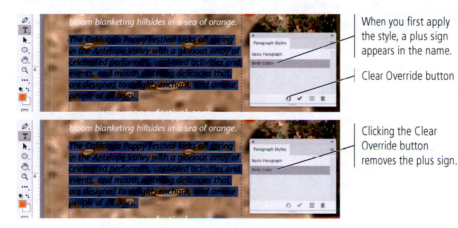

Note:

You can also choose Style Options in the panel Options menu to open this dialog box.

Checking the Preview option allows you to immediately see the effect of your changes in the layout before you finalize them.

5. **Change the style name to Body Copy and click OK.**

6. **Select the entire second paragraph, then click the Body Copy style in the Paragraph Styles panel to apply it to the active paragraph.**

The plus sign next to the style name indicates that formatting other than what is defined by the style is applied. You have to click the Clear Override button to apply only the style's formatting to the selected type.

7. **With the same type selected, click the Clear Override button at the bottom of the Paragraph Styles panel.**

If you do not clear the overrides, later changes to the applied style might not correctly reflect in type formatted with the style. Whenever you work with styles, check the applied styles to see if a plus sign appears where you know it shouldn't.

Note:

You could also choose Clear Override in the Paragraph panel Options menu.

When you first apply the style, a plus sign appears in the name.

Clear Override button

Clicking the Clear Override button removes the plus sign.

Note:

If the applied style shows a plus sign in the name, you can click the Redefine button to change the selected style's formatting to match that of the current text selection.

8. **Repeat this process to create a new paragraph style named Web Address based on the formatting of the last paragraph in the type area.**

9. **Save the file and continue to the next exercise.**

Load Paragraph Styles from Another File

Once you create styles, you can apply them to any text on any layer. You can also import styles from other Photoshop files so they can be used for different projects.

1. On your desktop, open the file **blvd_copy.txt** (from your WIP>Cards folder) in a text editor application.

2. Select all the text in the file, copy it, then close the file.

3. In Photoshop, open the **blvd.psd** file if necessary. Using the Horizontal Type tool, click and drag to create a type area in the top-right corner of the canvas.

4. With the insertion point in the new area, paste the copy from Step 2.

   The pasted type adopts the last-applied formatting options, which is not what you want. Because you already defined paragraph styles for the other card in this same campaign, you can load those styles and apply them to the type in this card.

5. If necessary, adjust the handles of the area so all the type in the story appears in the type area.

Note:

Don't worry if your formatting doesn't match what you see here. You're going to change it in the next few steps.

6. In the Paragraph Styles panel Options menu, choose Load Paragraph Styles. Navigate to **festival.psd** (in your WIP>Cards folder) and click Open/Load.

7. Select the entire first paragraph in the type area. Click Body Copy in the Paragraph Styles panel, then click the Clear Override button.

8. Repeat Step 7 to apply the Web Address style to the second paragraph.

9. Adjust the type area handles until you are satisfied with the text appearance.

Note:

Loading styles from one Photoshop file to another is an all-or-nothing choice; you can't select certain styles to import.

10. Save the file and continue to the next stage of the project.

In some cases, maintaining a type layer with live text is either unnecessary (e.g., you know the book title isn't going to change), or it prevents you from applying certain changes (e.g., you can't apply filters to a type layer). When you find an effect or change that won't work with live text, you must convert the type layer.

You can simply rasterize a type layer by choosing Type>Rasterize Type Layer, which converts the editable, vector-based type to a regular, pixel-based layer. Once rasterized, you can't edit the text, but you can apply filters and use the layer as a clipping mask.

Rasterizing type results in a regular, pixel-based layer.

You should understand that type is fundamentally based on vectors. Rather than simply rasterizing type, you can convert a type layer to a vector-based shape layer by choosing Type>Convert to Shape. Converting a type layer to a shape means the type is no longer editable, but you can still manipulate the letterforms as you would any other vector shape layer. By converting type to a shape layer, you can use the Distort or Perspective transformation to create custom warps for the layer. You still can't apply filters, however, since filters only work on rasterized layers.

The resulting shape layer adopts the original text color as the fill color.

If you need to apply filters, custom warps, or transformations to type, but you want to maintain the type layer as live (editable) text, you can convert the type layer to a Smart Object in the layer's contextual menu. You can apply filters or transformations in the main document, but still edit the text in the Smart Object file.

Convert the type to a Smart Object in the master file.

The Smart Object file maintains the live type.

Finally, you can use the vector information of type to create a work path (Type>Create Work Path), which you can then save as a regular path in the Paths panel. In this case, the type layer is maintained as an editable type layer, but you can use the path for any purpose you choose.

The original type layer is maintained.

The work path appears in the Paths panel.

Creating Type Selections

You can use one of the Type Mask tools (horizontal or vertical) to create a selection in the shape of letters. When you click with one of these tools, you automatically enter a kind of Quick Mask mode; letters you type are removed from the mask to show what will be selected. (If you press Command/Control while the red mask is visible, you can drag the type selection around in the image window.)

When you have finished typing, switching to the Move tool shows the marching ants that make up the type-shaped selection. No layer, path, or channel is automatically created when you use the Type Mask tools.

To complete the rest of this project, you will learn several new techniques for adding visual interest to layers, including creating a solid-color overlay and applying layer effects.

Create a Solid-Color Fill Layer

A solid-color fill layer is exactly what it sounds like — a layer of colored pixels, which obscure all underlying layers. Like a vector shape layer (which you used in Project 2: Car Magazine Cover), the fill layer's thumbnail shows a swatch of the current fill color; you can double-click that swatch to change the color. A fill layer also has an attached (pixel-based) layer mask, which you can use to define where the fill color will be visible.

1. **With** `festival.psd` **open, select the Bloom layer in the Layers panel.**

2. **Click the Create New Fill or Adjustment Layer button at the bottom of the Layers panel and choose Solid Color in the resulting menu.**

The new layer will be created immediately above the selected layer.

Create new fill or adjustment layer

3. **Click OK in the Color Picker dialog box to accept the default color value.**

    The fill color defaults to the active foreground color. Don't worry if yours is different than what you see in our images; you will change the color in the next few steps.

The solid color of the fill obscures the underlying image layer.

The Color Picker automatically opens when you add a solid-color fill layer.

4. **In the Layers panel, click the eye icon to hide the Color Fill layer.**

To sample a color from the underlying image, you first have to hide the fill layer.

5. **Double-click the Color Fill 1 layer's thumbnail to reopen the Color Picker dialog box.**

You can change the Color Fill layer color even though it isn't currently visible.

6. **With the Color Picker dialog box open, click in the image (behind the dialog box) with the eyedropper cursor to sample a medium-dark green area of the image as the layer's fill color.**

Because the Color Fill layer is hidden, you can sample a color from the underlying layer.

Double-click the color icon to change the layer's fill color.

7. **Click OK to close the Color Picker dialog box, then make the Color Fill layer visible again.**

8. **In the Layers panel, click to select the mask thumbnail for the Color Fill layer.**

Fill and adjustment layers automatically include a mask, which you can use to define where the fill is visible. This is similar to the vector shape layers, where the vector path(s) define where the color is visible. The fill layer's mask, however, is pixel-based, which means it can include shades of gray.

Remember, black areas of a mask are transparent and white areas are opaque. In this case, white areas of the mask result in full strength of the fill layer's color. Shades of gray indicate varying degrees of the fill color.

Note:

You could have accomplished the same basic goal by creating a new layer, filling it with a solid color, and then manually adding a pixel mask. When you add a solid-color fill layer, the mask is automatically added for you. You can also double-click the color swatch in the layer icon to change the color that fills the layer.

9. **Choose the Gradient tool in the Tools panel. Reset the foreground and background colors (so that white is the Foreground and black is the Background Color), then choose the Foreground to Background gradient in the Options bar.**

Choose the Linear Gradient option.

Click here to choose the gradient you want to use.

Use this menu to view the gradients as a list instead of swatches.

Default foreground and background colors for a mask are white and black, respectively.

The mask is selected.

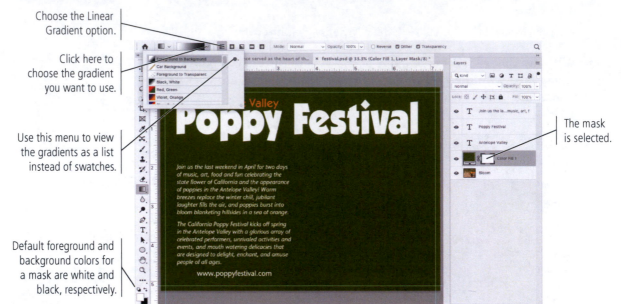

10. **Make sure the Linear Gradient option is selected. Click near the right edge of the type area (with the body copy), then drag right to the right edge of the canvas.**

We dragged the gradient from here...

...to here.

11. Choose Multiply in the Blending Mode menu at the top of the Layers panel.

Multiplying the dark color with the underlying image allows the white type to stand out more clearly against the background. The result, however, is too dark — it almost entirely obscures the underlying image.

The Multiply blending mode mixes the color of the fill layer with colors in the underlying layer.

12. Change the layer's opacity to 75%.

Reducing the fill layer's opacity allows more of the underlying image to show through. You can type the new value in the field, use the attached menu, or use the scrubby slider for the field's label.

The **Opacity** percentage changes the opacity of the entire layer, including applied effects and styles. The **Fill** percentage changes the opacity of the actual layer pixels, but none of the applied effects or styles. In this case, the layer doesn't yet have any applied styles or effects, so both controls would have the same effect.

Note:

If the Opacity field is unavailable, check the Lock options. When you use the Lock All option, you can't change the layer opacity.

Reducing the fill layer's opacity reduces the darkness created by the multiplied colors.

Note:

When a layer is selected and the insertion point is not flashing in a Type layer, you can press the number keys to change the active layer's opacity in 10% increments:

1 = 10%	*6 = 60%*
2 = 20%	*7 = 70%*
3 = 30%	*8 = 80%*
4 = 40%	*9 = 90%*
5 = 50%	*0 = 100%*

13. **Select the Bloom layer in the Layers panel, then click the Lock All button at the top of the Layers panel.**

The Bloom layer is technically the postcard background, even though it is not a formal Background layer. By locking all properties, you prevent the layer from being moved, painted on, or otherwise edited.

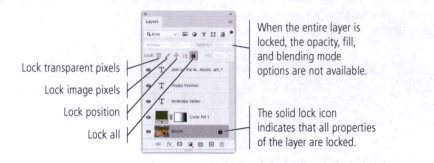

Lock transparent pixels
Lock image pixels
Lock position
Lock all

When the entire layer is locked, the opacity, fill, and blending mode options are not available.

The solid lock icon indicates that all properties of the layer are locked.

Note:

For all but type layers, you can lock three different attributes individually, or you can lock the entire layer at once.

14. **Select the three type layers, then click the Lock Position button.**

By locking the layers' positions, you prevent them from accidentally being moved as you continue working. Since only the position is locked, however, you can still apply effects that do not affect the position of the layer content.

You cannot, by definition, lock the image pixels or transparent pixels of a type layer. If you activate the Lock All button for a Type layer, you will not be able to apply styles to those layers in the next steps.

The hollow lock icon indicates that some, but not all, properties of the layer are locked.

15. **Save the file, then make blvd.psd active.**

16. **Choose File>Place Embedded. Select the file Roshambo.jpg (in your WIP>Cards folder) and click Place.**

17. **Click inside the bounding box of the placed image and drag to move the placed layer to the empty area in the bottom-right corner of the canvas. Press Return/Enter to finalize the placement.**

18. **Save the file and continue to the final stage of the project.**

STAGE 5 / **Working in 3D**

Photoshop includes the ability to create real-time, three-dimensional artwork. You can create these from scratch, or by importing wire frames and rendered artwork from industry-standard 3D applications, such as Maya or 3D Studio Max.

The following is a brief introduction to Photoshop's 3D functionality. If you have never worked in real three dimensions before, you will almost certainly have to spend some extra time learning the related terminology. We also encourage you to experiment with the various 3D options until you are comfortable manipulating objects in digital space.

You should already be familiar with the concept of the X and Y axes. When you work with 3D files, you also need to understand the concept of the Z axis, which creates the illusion of depth.

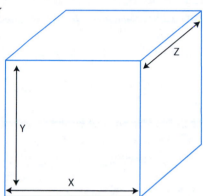

3D objects in Photoshop include a number of special attributes:

- **Meshes** (sometimes called **wireframes**) are the basic skeletons of three-dimensional objects. The mesh defines the underlying shape of the 3D object.

- **Materials** refer to the physical surface of an object (for example, the aluminum of a soda can or the felt of a fedora hat). Photoshop uses a number of texture-map characteristics to create the material appearance of a 3D object. You can also define existing, two-dimensional Photoshop layers as the material for a mesh.

- **Lighting** affects the way highlights and shadows are created, on and by, a 3D object. Photoshop supports four types of lighting — infinite, spot, point, and image — to create different lighting effects.

- **Camera position** refers to the point of view relative to the object. Photoshop includes the ability to move the camera around an object on all three axes.

Note:

*In 3D terminology, moving an object in 3D space (near to far) is called a **translation**. Rotating an object in 3D space is called a **transformation**.*

To understand digital 3D modeling, think about the way you interact with the world at large. When you walk around a car, for example, you are able to see the different sides of it, and they all look different.

Also, consider that what you see depends not only on your position relative to an object, but also on the position of the object. For example, if you stand still, but someone backs a car into a parking space, you see a different aspect of the car.

Finally, what you see on a 3D object also depends on the position of the light. When the garage light shines behind you, for example, you might see your own reflection in the car's window. When the interior lights are on, you see more of the car's interior than your reflection.

Keep in mind that 3D modeling considers the physical shape and position of an object, your position relative to the object, and the position of light sources relative to the object.

It is also important to realize that entire books are written about Photoshop's 3D features. The exercises in this stage were designed to introduce you to the possibilities relative to enhancing a static image, such as the postcards in this project.

Create a 3D Postcard

Photoshop can open existing 3D files created in other applications and import 3D objects as new 3D Photoshop layers. You can also use built-in functionality to create some 3D objects from scratch. In this case, you're going to create a new 3D object from the simplest built-in shape preset — a postcard. In the final exercise of this project, you will use Layer Comps to export two separate versions of the file using these two separate layers.

Important note: If, after first launching the application, you saw a warning about insufficient vRAM, you will not be able to complete this stage of the project. Your finished project will consist of one version of each postcard, which you should save as flattened JPEG files for client approval.

1. **Open the Performance pane of the Preferences dialog box. Make sure the Use Graphics Processor option is checked and click OK.**

   If this option is not available (grayed out) on your computer, your video card and/or driver does not support OpenGL. If you cannot use OpenGL, your 3D options and functionality will be very limited and very slow; all processes will be performed (if possible) by the Photoshop application instead of the video card in your computer.

2. **With blvd.psd active, drag the Roshambo layer to the Create a New Layer button at the bottom of the panel.**

   This is an easy way to duplicate a layer. You could also Control/right-click the layer name and choose Duplicate Layer from the contextual menu.

   3D extrusions permanently change the layer to a special 3D layer. To maintain the originally placed "flat" image and a 3D version of it, you have to use two separate layers.

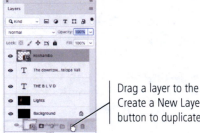

   Drag a layer to the Create a New Layer button to duplicate it.

3. **Change the name of the Roshambo copy layer to Roshambo 3D.**

   This step is simply to make it easier to distinguish one layer from the other. You do not need to include the "3D" tag in a layer that you are using for 3D effects.

4. **Hide the Roshambo layer, then select Roshambo 3D as the active layer.**

5. **Choose View>Show>Guides to hide the ruler guides.**

   The 3D workspace has a number of on-screen controls. The ruler guides are no longer necessary, and would simply confuse the visual clarity of the 3D controllers.

6. **Choose 3D>New Mesh from Layer>Postcard.**

   Photoshop includes a number of prebuilt meshes, which you can add to any file. The most basic mesh — a "postcard" — is simply a two-sided representation of the selected layer. Just like a physical postcard, it has no real depth, but it can be moved in three dimensions to show different aspects of the card.

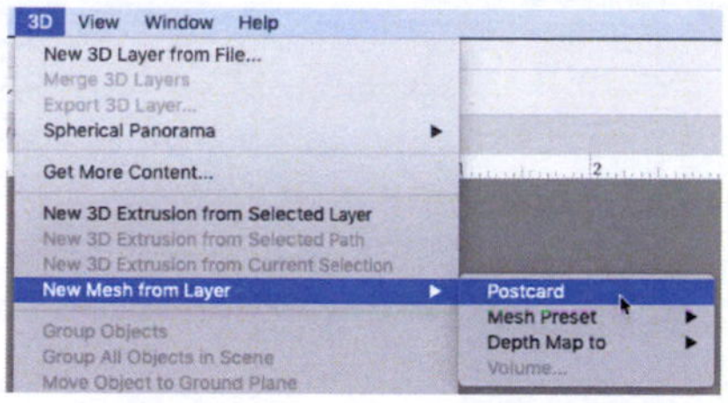

   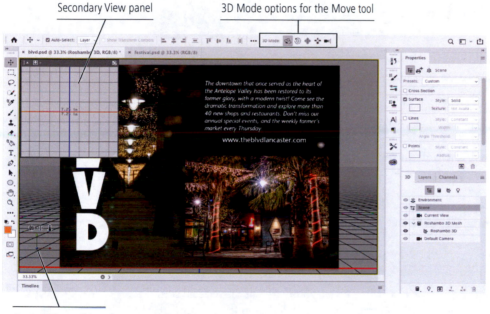

7. **Read the resulting message, then click Yes to automatically switch to the 3D workspace.**

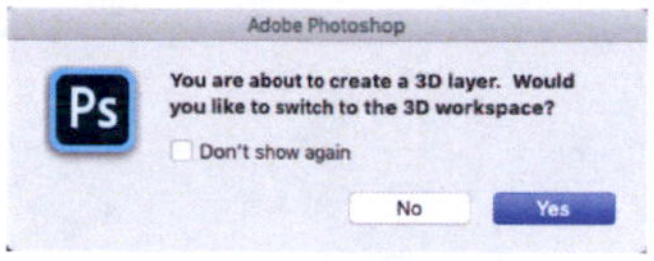

   Photoshop's built-in 3D workspace includes a number of tools that are useful in controlling a 3D layer. Some of these tools might be intimidating the first time you use the 3D workspace, but they will make more sense when you begin to manipulate the 3D object.

   Note:

   If you don't see the Secondary View panel, choose View>Show>3D Secondary View.

   Secondary View panel   3D Mode options for the Move tool

   Ground Plane widget

8. **With blvd.psd active, review the Roshambo 3D layer in the Layers panel.**

   When you create a 3D mesh from an existing layer, that layer shows a number of special attributes. The layer thumbnail includes a 3D icon, and the previous layer content is converted to a material for the active mesh.

   This icon identifies a 3D layer.

   The selected layer content is converted to a material for the 3D object.

9. **Save the file and continue to the next exercise.**

Move an Object in 3D

One advantage to working with 3D is the ability to move objects in three directions — left or right, up or down, near or far. You can also rotate the mesh around any axis to change the visible portion of the object.

1. **With blvd.psd open, open the menu in the Secondary View panel and choose Default.**

   The Default view is the same as what you see in the main document window when you first create the 3D object.

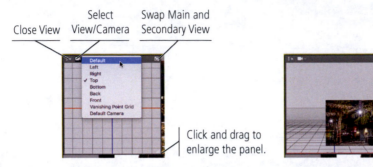

2. **Click the Close View button in the top-left corner of the panel to hide the Secondary View panel.**

This panel is a good way to review other aspects of a 3D object without affecting what appears on the canvas. In addition to the options in the menu, you can also click and drag around the panel to change the secondary view. If you find a view you like, you can click the Swap Main and Secondary View button in the top-right corner of the panel to replace the current view on canvas with what you see in the secondary view.

Note:

Press Option, and drag in the Secondary View panel to zoom in or out.

3. **In the Tools panel, make sure the Move tool is selected. Choose the Orbit the 3D Camera mode in the Options bar.**

The 3D tool modes can be used to change various properties of the selected scene attribute (the current view or a specific mesh). The modes, from left to right, are:

- **Orbit the 3D Camera.** Drag up-down to rotate the object around the X axis, or left-right to rotate around the Y axis. Press Option/Alt to rotate the object around the Z axis.

- **Roll the 3D Camera.** Drag left-right to rotate the object around the Z axis.

- **Pan the 3D Camera.** Drag left-right to move the object horizontally, or up-down to move the object vertically, without affecting its depth or rotation. Press Option/Alt and drag up-down to move the object along the X/Z axis (horizontally far to near).

- **Slide the 3D Camera.** Drag left-right to move the object horizontally, or up-down to move the object on the X/Z axis (horizontally far to near). Press Option/Alt and drag up/down to move the object along the X and Y axes simultaneously.

- **Zoom the 3D Camera.** Drag up-down to make the object proportionally larger or smaller. Press Option/Alt to scale the object along the Z axis only.

Note:

You can toggle the visibility of all the 3D on-screen widgets in the View>Show submenu.

Note:

You can save a specific view preset by choosing Save in the Current View menu.

4. In the 3D panel, select Current View. In the document window, click the 3D Ground Plane and drag to reposition the ground plane.

As you drag, you can see the ground-plane grid move. The red line in the grid represents the X axis and the blue line represents the Z axis.

You should also notice that the 3D object moves along with the ground plane. Basically, rotating the ground plane is like moving the camera to a different location; if you walk around an object with a camera in your hand, the visible area of the object changes with your relative position. In the Properties panel (3D Camera mode), the View menu automatically switches to "Custom View."

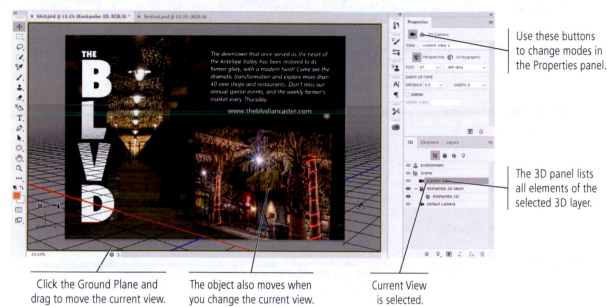

Use these buttons to change modes in the Properties panel.

The 3D panel lists all elements of the selected 3D layer.

Click the Ground Plane and drag to move the current view.

The object also moves when you change the current view.

Current View is selected.

5. With 3D Camera options visible in the Properties panel, choose Default in the View menu to reset the camera view.

The Properties panel has a number of different modes, depending on what is selected in the 3D panel. The Coordinates mode shows the current position of the camera relative to its original (default) position.

It's important to realize that the changes you make — whether to the scene or to the mesh — are nondestructive; you can reposition either as much as you like, at any time.

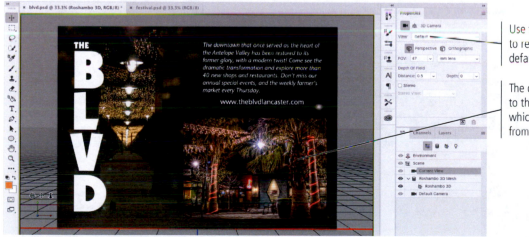

Use this menu to restore the default view.

The object returns to the default view, which is directly from the front.

6. In the 3D panel, click the Roshambo 3D Mesh.

You could also simply click the mesh on the canvas to select the object.

The gray rectangle represents the edge of the mesh object.

When the mesh object is selected, the 3D Axis widget appears on-screen.

You can apply virtually any changes to the object position using the 3D Axis widget. Each axis in the widget has three different controls:

- **Move On Axis** changes the position of the object along the selected axis.

- **Rotate Around Axis** changes the rotation of the object around the perpendicular axis. In other words, the control on the red (X) axis rotates the mesh around the green (Y) axis.

- **Scale Along Axis** changes the size of the object along the selected axis.

You can also click the center cube in the widget and drag to scale the object uniformly (on all three axes).

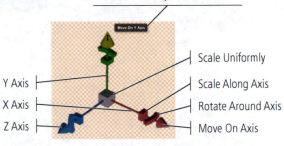

Cursor feedback shows the name of the active (yellow) control.

Scale Uniformly
Scale Along Axis
Rotate Around Axis
Move On Axis

Y Axis
X Axis
Z Axis

7. In the Properties panel, click the Coordinates button to show the numeric position of the mesh.

8. In the 3D Axis widget, click the Rotate Around Y Axis control (on the red axis) and drag right to rotate the mesh.

When you make changes using the on-screen controls, those changes are reflected in the Coordinates pane of the Properties panel. You can use either method to move, rotate, and scale the selected mesh.

Note:

Press V to cycle through the modes of the Properties panel.

Cursor feedback shows the specific transformation as you drag.

The gray mesh wireframe shows how the object is changing.

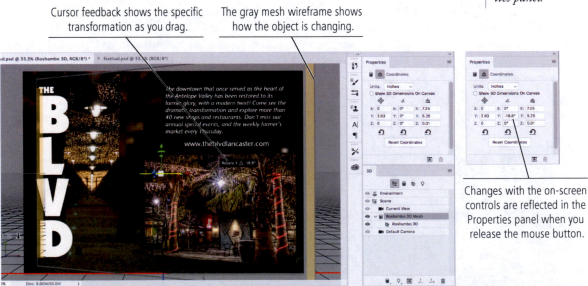

Changes with the on-screen controls are reflected in the Properties panel when you release the mouse button.

9. **Place the cursor over the center cube in the 3D Axis widget. Press Shift, then click and drag up to enlarge the icon.**

Before rotating the mesh in the previous step, it was difficult to see all of the controls in the widget. Making the icon larger makes it easier to access the individual controls.

Shift-drag the Scale Uniformly control to enlarge the widget.

Note:

In the 3D Axis widget, the Y axis is green, the X axis is red, and the Z axis is blue.

10. **In the Z Axis (blue) of the widget, click the Rotate Around X Axis control and drag up to rotate the mesh.**

This rotation tilts the mesh front to back.

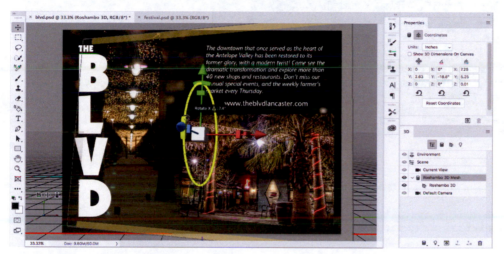

11. **In the X Axis (red) of the widget, click the Move on X Axis control and drag right to move the mesh until the right edge of the image is past the canvas edge.**

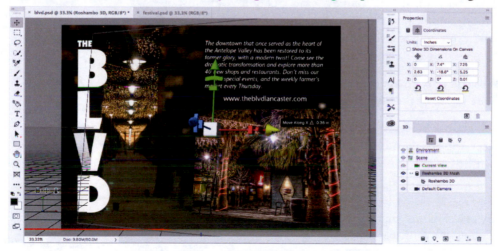

12. Click the Render button at the bottom of the Properties panel.

While you work with the 3D mesh, the preview is simply an on-screen representation. Rendering the 3D creates the final, full-resolution version of your 3D object.

The complete rendering process takes a long time, depending on the power of your computer processor. Be patient! The status area at the bottom-left corner of your document window shows the time remaining to complete the rendering process.

Note:

You can press the ESC key to cancel the rendering process.

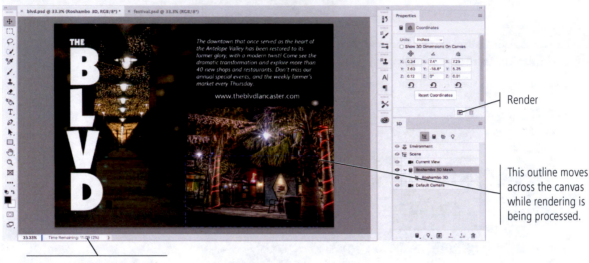

Render

This outline moves across the canvas while rendering is being processed.

Time remaining to complete the rendering process appears here.

13. Save the file and continue to the next exercise.

Create a 3D Sphere

In the previous exercises, you worked with a simple "flat" 3D object. Photoshop includes a number of more complex meshes that allow more flexibility and creativity than a simple postcard. In this exercise, you are going to add a sphere to the festival postcard, with another poppy image as the material on that mesh.

1. With `festival.psd` active, create a new empty layer at the top of the layer stack. Change the name of the new layer to Globe.

2. In the 3D panel, choose Selected Layer(s) in the Source menu. Choose the Mesh from Preset option, then choose Sphere in the attached menu. Click Create at the bottom of the panel.

This has the same general effect as choosing 3D>New Mesh from Layer>Mesh Preset>Sphere. Try to be aware of your options for accomplishing any particular goal and determine which is best suited to your personal working preferences.

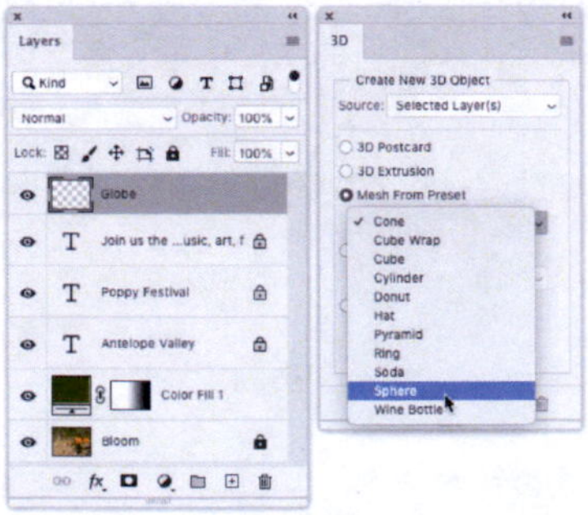

Note:

If you are not already using the built-in 3D workspace, you will be asked if you want to switch to that workspace before proceeding.

3. **If you get an Embedded Profile Mismatch warning, choose Convert Document's Colors to the Working Space, then click OK.**

4. **If necessary, close the Secondary View panel.**

    Although the 3D workspace elements all serve useful purposes, they can be distracting at times. You can turn specific interface elements off or on in the View>Show submenu.

5. **In the 3D panel, select the Sphere_Material.**

    If you don't see Sphere Material listed in the panel, choose the Move tool and then click the globe shape on the screen to select it.

6. **In the Properties panel, open the menu next to the Base Color option and choose Replace Texture.**

    This option defines an image that will appear on the surface of the 3D object.

Sphere_Material is selected.

7. **Navigate to Field.jpg (in your WIP>Cards folder) and click Open.**
    If you see a warning about mismatched color profiles, use the embedded profile.

The selected image becomes the material on the sphere surface.

8. **Click the sphere on the canvas to select the mesh object.**

Mesh cage

Cursor feedback shows you can move the object by dragging the mesh edge.

Move the cursor over different parts of the mesh cage to move or rotate the mesh.

9. **Click one of the gray lines that represents the mesh edge, and drag to move the object into the bottom-right corner (approximately covering the poppy in the background image).**

When the mesh is selected, it is surrounded on the screen by a cage that represents the outer 3D "box" shape. In addition to using the 3D Axis widget, you can also use the mesh cage to make specific changes. Cursor feedback shows what you can accomplish by clicking a specific location on the mesh preview.

Click one of the wireframe edges and drag to move the mesh.

Moving the mesh does not affect the ground plane.

10. **In the Properties panel, click the Coordinates button to show the numeric position of the mesh object.**

11. **Move the cursor near the vertical edge of the mesh cage. When the cursor feedback shows "Rotate Around Y Axis," click and drag right until the large cluster of poppies is visible on the sphere.**

We liked the content that appears when the sphere is rotated approximately −26°, as you can see in the cursor feedback while dragging and in the Properties panel when you release the mouse button.

Change the panel to Coordinates mode.

When you release the mouse button, the new Y rotation angle appears in the Properties: Coordinates panel.

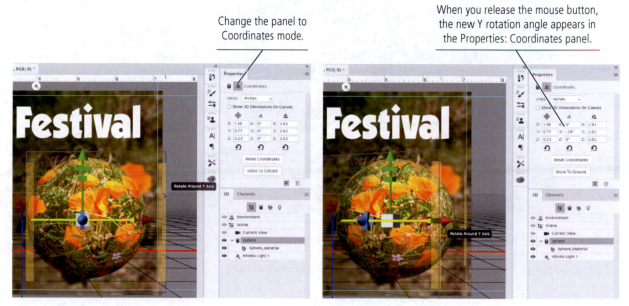

12. **Move the cursor near the top horizontal edge of the mesh cage. When the cursor feedback shows, "Rotate Around X Axis," click and drag down until you are satisfied with the image that appears on the sphere's surface.**

13. **Click the Scale Uniformly control and drag up to enlarge the sphere proportionally.**

14. **In the Properties panel, show the Coordinates options and then click the Move to Ground button.**

This snaps the object to create the appearance of sitting on the ground plane, which is represented by the red line.

15. **In the 3D panel, click the Current View to select it.**

16. **Choose the Pan the 3D Camera button in the Options bar.**

17. **Click and drag until the sphere is back in the same relative position as before you snapped it to the ground plane.**

When the Current View is selected in the 3D panel, you can drag the ground plane and change the view of the object without changing the actual mesh. The object retains its position relative to the ground plane so it does move, but the actual mesh and mesh texture do not change.

Note:

The Move to Ground button has the same effect as choosing 3D>Move Object to Ground Plane.

Pan the 3D Camera

When you move the ground plane, you also move the object mesh.

Current View is selected.

18. Click Infinite Light 1 in the 3D panel to show the light widget in the document window.

The light sources related to a 3D object determine how shadows are cast. The Sphere preset mesh includes one infinite light source, which is a light that shines from a single point far away (like the sun).

Note:

You could also click the Infinite Light 1 option in the 3D panel to select the light.

19. Click the light handle in the on-screen preview and drag until the shadow on the bottom of the sphere is strongest on the bottom-right side of the mesh.

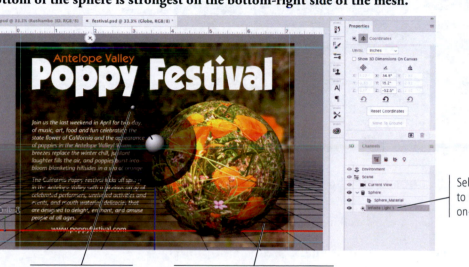

Select the light to show the on-screen widget.

Drag the light handle to change the direction of the light source.

Changing the light direction changes the shadows on the sphere, and those cast on the ground plane.

20. In the Properties panel, show the Infinite Light options. Change the light Intensity to 60% and change the Shadow Softness to 30%.

Now that you can better see the shadow, you can make more informed changes. The Softness option creates a blurrier edge on the ground-plane shadow.

Click to show specific Infinite Light properties.

Use this option to change the strength of the light.

Use this option to soften the shadow edges.

21. **Select the Environment in the 3D panel. In the Properties panel, change the Ground Plane Shadows Opacity to 85%.**

This darkens the shadow that is cast by the sphere onto the ground plane, but does not affect the shadow on the surface of the sphere.

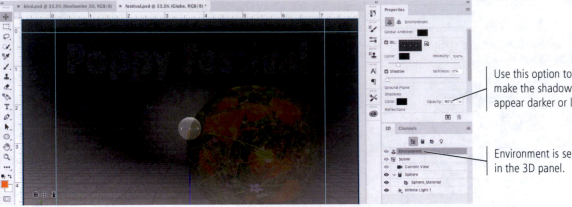

Use this option to make the shadow appear darker or lighter.

Environment is selected in the 3D panel.

22. **Click the Render button at the bottom of the Properties panel.**

When the rendering is complete, the sphere edges and the ground-plane shadow show a distinct improvement over the working on-screen preview.

23. **Save the file, then continue to the final exercise of the project.**

Create Layer Comps

A layer comp can store the position and visibility of individual layers, as well as any effects applied. This feature is useful when you want to experiment with the position of specific layers, but you want to keep a record of earlier positions of the layers. In this case, you want to present two versions of a file — one with a layer visible and one with a layer hidden.

1. **With festival.psd open, select any layer other than the Globe layer.**

Deselecting the 3D layer turns off all of the 3D visual aids (such as the ground plane).

2. **Open the Layer Comps panel (Window>Layer Comps).**

When no layer comps exist in the file, or you make changes that do not match what is saved as an existing layer comp, the panel shows the Last Document State as active. Buttons at the bottom of the panel enable a number of options:

- A   Apply Next Selected Layer Comp
- B   Update Visibilities of Selected Layer Comps and Layers
- C   Update Positions of Selected Layer Comps and Layers
- D   Update Appearances of Selected Layer Comps and Layers
- E   Update Layer Comp Selection for Smart Objects of Selected Layer Comps and Layers
- F   Update Layer Comp
- G   Create New Layer Comp
- H   Delete Layer Comp

Note:

Layer comps do not store pixel information; modifying the actual pixel data on a layer will not be undone by reverting to an earlier layer comp. To undo that kind of change, you must use the History panel and snapshots (assuming you haven't closed the file since you created the snapshots).

3. **Click the Create New Layer Comp button at the bottom of the Layer Comps panel.**

4. **In the New Layer Comp dialog box, name the comp Final 3D. Make sure the Visibility option is checked, and then click OK.**

When you choose the Visibility option, only the currently visible layers (in this case, all of them) will be included in the comp.

When you close the dialog box, the new comp has been added to the panel. It is active because you haven't made any changes to layers since saving the layer comp.

Icons to the right of the layer comp identify which attributes — visibility, position, and appearance — are stored in the layer comp. If an icon is grayed out, it is not part of that comp. You can click these icons to toggle each attribute on or off for a selected comp.

This icon shows the currently active comp.

Only the Visibility property is stored in this layer comp.

5. **In the Layers panel, hide the Globe layer.**

When you make changes in the file after creating a layer comp, the Active icon on the left side of the panel automatically switches to Last Document State.

6. **Create another new layer comp named Final Flat, again including only the layer visibility attributes in the comp.**

Remember, you hid the Globe layer in Step 5; checking the visibility option means that layer will not be visible if you activate the Final Flat layer comp.

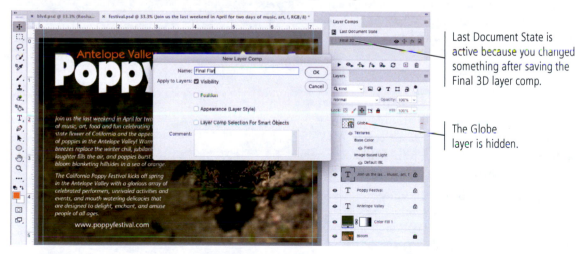

Last Document State is active because you changed something after saving the Final 3D layer comp.

The Globe layer is hidden.

7. **Choose File>Export>Layer Comps to Files.**

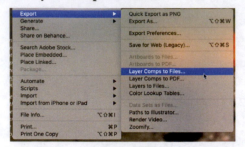

8. **In the Layer Comps to Files dialog box, make sure the WIP>Cards folder is selected in the Destination field, and make sure festival appears in the File Name Prefix field.**

   This script creates separate files for each layer comp. The target location defaults to the same location as the working file, and the file name defaults to the current file name.

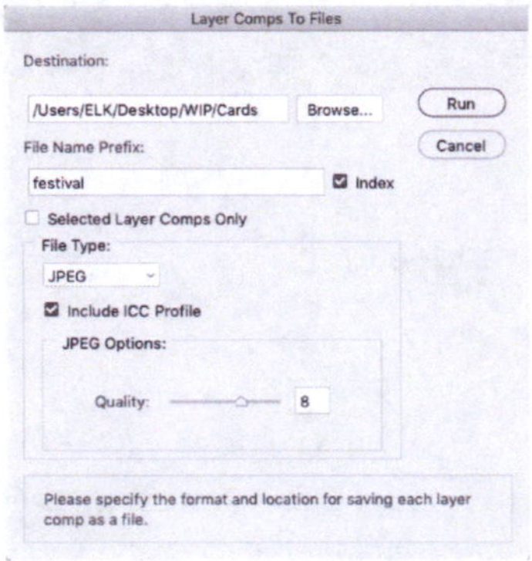

Note:

You can select a specific layer comp in the panel and click the buttons at the bottom to change the layer properties that are stored in that comp. The first three buttons affect only one attribute (visibility, position, or appearance); the Update Layer Comp button updates all three attributes at once.

9. **Choose JPEG in the File Type menu, and leave the remaining options at their default values.**

10. **Click Run.**

    The process could take a while to complete; don't panic and don't get impatient. When the file is done, you will see the message shown here.

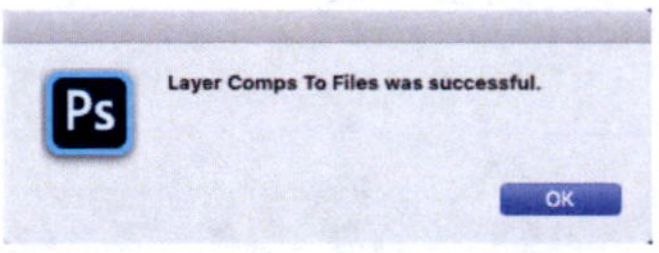

11. **Click OK to close the message, and then save and close the Photoshop file.**

12. **Repeat this process to create two versions of the BLVD postcard. Make sure you show the Roshambo layer when you create the "flat" layer comp. Also, make sure the File Name Prefix field accurately reflects the files that you are exporting.**

    There appears to be a bug in the software — when you open this dialog box the second time, the file name defaults to the last-used option. If you don't change it to "blvd," you will overwrite the festival postcard versions.

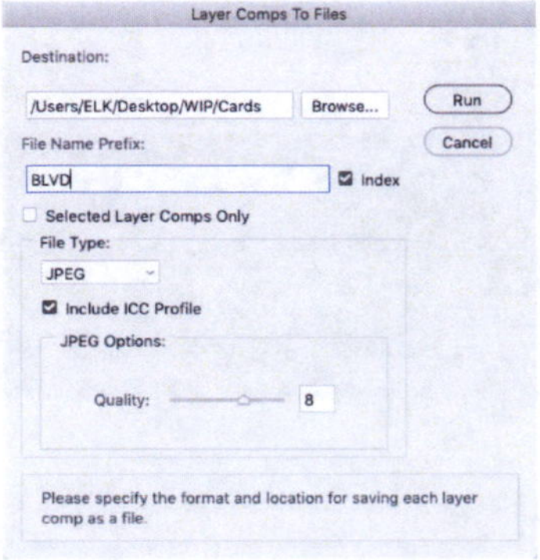

13. **Save and close the blvd.psd file.**

PROJECT REVIEW

fill in the blank

1. _______________ identifies and tries to protect areas of detail when you scale the image.

2. _______________ allows you to move a selection, filling the original selection area with detail, instead of leaving an empty hole.

3. A _______________ effect applies a consistent blur over the entire selected layer.

4. _______________ is created by simply clicking (without dragging) with one of the Type tools.

5. _______________ is the distance from one baseline to the next in a paragraph of type.

6. The _______________ tools can be used to create selections in the shape of individual characters or entire words.

7. _______________ describes the space between individual type characters (where the insertion point is placed).

8. _______________ cannot be applied to type layers; you must first rasterize a type layer to apply them.

9. A(n) _______________ light source shines as a single point from a seemingly far distance.

10. A(n) _______________ stores the visibility of specific layers at a given point.

short answer

1. Briefly describe the result of moving a selection with the Move tool.

2. Briefly explain the difference between point type and area type.

3. Briefly explain the concept of a material as it relates to a 3D object.

Use what you have learned in this project to complete the following freeform exercise.
Carefully read the art director and client comments, then create your own design to meet the needs of the project.
Use the space below to sketch ideas. When finished, write a brief explanation of the reasoning behind your final design.

art director comments

As a freelance designer, you have been hired by the band Midnight Sun to create a logo and cover artwork for their forthcoming CD release.

To complete this project, you should:

❑ Design an interesting logotype for the band.

❑ Determine the appropriate size for the cover that is inserted into a CD jewel case.

❑ Locate or create artwork or images to illustrate the CD title.

❑ Create the CD cover art for commercial printing requirements.

client comments

We're originally from Alaska. We all had full-time jobs when we first started, so we practiced late at night (no surprise!) until we decided we would get more exposure in Seattle. Since we spent so much time awake in the middle of the night, we named the band Midnight Sun.

We haven't had much luck yet finding a label, so we're going to self-publish an EP to help promote the band and, hopefully, raise some money. We're calling the disc "The Lower 48," because all of the songs are about our journey to where we are now.

We want the cover art to represent the type of music we play — primarily rock, but with other genres thrown in. Blues, international beats, and even orchestrated undertones all make an appearance.

We have a very unique sound, and we're an eclectic group of people. We're hoping you can create cover art that says who we are, without using a boring group photo.

project justification

_____
_____
_____
_____
_____
_____
_____
_____
_____
_____
_____
_____
_____

PROJECT SUMMARY

Completing this project required a number of new skills for manipulating layer content — scaling and moving selections, applying blur effects, and working with layer styles. By now you should understand the difference between working with an entire layer and working with only a selected area, and be able to choose the appropriate tools to affect only what you want to change.

You also did a considerable amount of work with type, which can be either created from scratch or pasted from a text editor. Although the type controls in Photoshop are not quite as robust as those in formal page layout applications — which are specifically designed to create and control large blocks of type — they are certainly useful for a range of different applications.

You learned how to create both point and area type, as well as the different formatting options that are available for selected characters or entire paragraphs. You also worked with a number of tools that create unique artistic effects from a Photoshop type layer — sampling colors from an image to format type, applying styles to type layers, and changing layer opacity and blending modes.

Finally, you learned the basics of working with 3D objects. As we already stated, we didn't even come close to explaining everything there is to know about 3D. However, you did experiment with a number of the options that are most relevant to print designers.

Create and control a point-type layer

Create and control an area-type layer

Use the Content-Aware Move tool to reposition specific areas of a layer

Use a 3D mesh to add the appearance of depth

Use paragraph styles to move formatting from one file to another

Use content-aware scaling to resize a layer

Use layer comps to create multiple versions of a file

Web Page Design

4

Your client is a costume designer who is launching a new online presence to grow her business. Your job is to take the first draft, and add a number of finishing touches to add visual appeal to the overall site. You must then generate the required pieces that will be used by a web developer to create the functioning HTML.

This project incorporates the following skills:

❏ Using actions and batches to automate repetitive processes and improve productivity

❏ Adding depth and visual interest with puppet warping

❏ Generating image assets from Photoshop layers and layer groups, as required by the HTML developer

❏ Communicating design intent using cascading style sheets

PROJECT MEETING

My business model has largely been word-of-mouth until now, but I've finally decided to take the next step and formalize a plan with all the requisite professional elements.

I'm naming my new company, "Silk Road Costume Design." I have very little for you to work with, other than photos of the work I've done in the past. Those are really the best way to communicate what I do, so I want them to be included in a digital slideshow somewhere on the new website.

I don't want a lot of text, especially not on the site's Welcome page — probably just a heading and one or two short paragraphs. I haven't written the text yet, so can you just use some nonsense text to come up with a design?

First, the web designer tells me that the images for the slideshow should be optimized to no more than 1,000 pixels high. Since there are so many of them (and likely to be more, over time), you should develop an action to resize the images automatically, without having to manually open each one.

The client liked the initial Welcome page comp, but I think there is some room for improvement.

Although we only spec'd space for one image, the client selected three that she wants to feature on the Welcome page. You'll need to break up the defined space to fit the three feature images.

Finally, the silk pattern is too straight. Try warping it to create more of a "flowing cloth" feel, and to help break up the overall blockiness of the page.

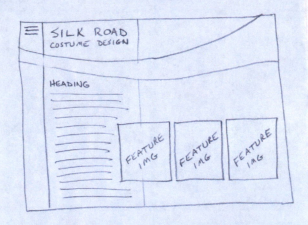

To complete this project, you will:

- ❏ Save an action set
- ❏ Create a new action
- ❏ Batch-process files
- ❏ Use frames to define image position and size
- ❏ Use Puppet Warp to transform a layer
- ❏ Generate image assets from layers
- ❏ Copy CSS for text layers
- ❏ Create alternate layers with artboards

STAGE 1 / **Automating Repetitive Tasks**

Actions are some of the most powerful (yet underused) productivity tools in Photoshop. In the simplest terms, actions are miniature programs that run a sequence of commands on a particular image or selected area. An action can initiate most of the commands available in Photoshop — alone or in sequence — to automate repetitive, and potentially time-consuming tasks.

Running an action is a fairly simple process: highlight the appropriate action in the Actions panel, and then click the Play button at the bottom of the panel. Some actions work on an entire image, while others require some initial selection. If you use the actions that shipped with the Photoshop application, the action name tells you (in parentheses) what type of element the action was designed to affect. In most cases, however, you can run an action on other elements without a problem.

The Actions Panel in Depth

The default **Actions panel** (Window> Actions) shows the Default Actions set, which contains several pre-built actions. A folder icon indicates an **action set**, which is used to create logical groupings of actions. You can expand an action set to show the actions contained within that set, and you can expand a specific action to show the steps that are saved in that action. Any step in an action marked with an arrow can be further expanded to see the details of that step.

The left column of the Actions panel shows a check mark next to each action set, individual action, and step within an expanded action. All elements of prerecorded actions are active by default, which means that playing an action initiates each step within that action. You can deactivate specific steps of an action by clicking the related check mark. If the check mark next to an action is black, all elements of that action are active. If the check mark is red, one or more steps of that action are inactive.

Modal Controls

The second column in the Actions panel controls the degree of user interaction required when running an action. If an icon appears in this column, the Photoshop dialog box relevant to that step opens when the action runs. These are called **modal controls**; the action pauses until you take some required action. You can deactivate modal controls by clicking the dialog box icon for an entire action set, a specific action, or a single step within an action.

If the modal controls are turned off, Photoshop applies the values that were used when the action was recorded. This increases the automatic functionality of the action, but also offers less control over the action's behavior.

Some actions require a certain degree of user interaction, in which case modal controls can't be entirely deactivated. In this case, the dialog box icon appears grayed out in the panel, even when the remaining modal controls are turned off. If an action shows a black dialog box icon, all modal controls within that action are active. If an action shows a red dialog box icon, one or more modal controls within that action have been turned off.

Button Mode

Choosing Button Mode at the top of the panel Options menu makes running an action one step easier. Each action is represented as a colored button, which you can simply click to run the action.

Save an Action Set

Whenever you need to perform the same task more than twice, it's a good idea to automate as much of the process as possible. This project requires you to create thumbnails from a number of images, which requires multiple steps. Rather than performing each step for each image, you can streamline the process using an action, which you have to record only once.

1. **Download `Silk_Web20_RF.zip` from the Student Files web page.**

2. **Expand the ZIP archive in your WIP folder (Macintosh) or copy the archive contents into your WIP folder (Windows).**

    This results in a folder named **Silk**, which contains all of the files you need for this project. You should also use this folder to save the files you create in this project.

3. **In Photoshop with no file open, click the Photoshop icon in the top-left corner of the Home screen.**

    Clicking this icon enters into the Photoshop workspace so you can access the various panels, even when no file is open.

Click this icon to enter the Photoshop workspace.

4. **Open the Actions panel (Window>Actions).**

5. **Choose Clear All Actions from the Actions panel Options menu.**

    Rather than editing an existing action set, you are going to create your own action set to store the action you define. If you did not clear the existing actions, the set you define would include all of the default actions, as well as the one you create.

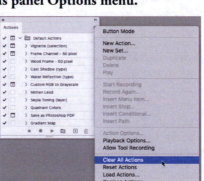

6. **Click OK in the warning message dialog box.**

    Clear All Actions removes everything from the Actions panel. You can also remove a specific action or set from the panel by highlighting the item in the panel, and then clicking the Delete button, or by choosing Delete from the Actions panel Options menu. These commands remove the actions or sets from the panel, but they do not permanently delete saved actions or sets. If you delete an action from one of the built-in sets, you can reload the set to restore all items that originally existed in the set.

7. **Click the Create New Set button at the bottom of the Actions panel.**

Note:

It's important to remember when creating actions that, "just because you can, doesn't mean you should." There are many powerful tools in Photoshop that require human judgment and intervention if they are to be effective. Color correction, for example, is different for every image, and should never be left entirely to a computer to implement.

Note:

*You can add actions to the Actions panel by choosing a defined set, or by choosing **Load Actions** in the panel Options menu.*

Reset Actions *restores the default set to the Actions panel. You have the option to replace the existing actions, or append the default set to the current sets.*

Replace Actions *replaces the current action sets with the set you load in the resulting dialog box.*

8. **In the New Set dialog box, name the new set Portfolio Actions, and then click OK.**

   You can name the set whatever you prefer, but it should indicate what the set contains, whether it's a set of actions for a specific type of project, for a specific client, or any other logical group.

Create New Set

9. **Continue to the next exercise.**

Create a New Action

Recording an action is a fairly simple process: open a file, click the Record button in the Actions panel, and then perform the steps you want to save in the action. Click the Stop button to stop recording. If you stop recording, you can later select the last step in the existing action, and start recording again by clicking the Record button.

1. **In Photoshop, open culture1.jpg from your WIP>Silk>costumes folder. If you get a profile mismatch warning, use the embedded profile.**

   When you apply this action in the next exercise, you can determine how color profile problems are managed by the automated batch processing.

Stop Playing/Recording

Begin Recording

Play Selection

Create New Action

2. **Open the Actions panel if necessary, and click the Create New Action button at the bottom of the panel.**

3. **In the New Action dialog box, type Optimize For Slides in the Name field.**

   By default, new actions are added to the currently selected set. You can add the action to any open set by choosing from the Set menu. The Function Key menu allows you to assign a keyboard shortcut to the action, so, for example, an "F" key (with or without modifiers) can initiate that action. The Color menu defines the color of the button when the Actions panel is viewed in Button mode.

4. **Click Record to close the dialog box.**

   In the Actions panel, the Record button automatically becomes red, indicating that you are now recording. Anything you do from this point forward is recorded as a step in the action until you intentionally stop the recording by clicking the Stop button at the bottom of the Actions panel.

The red button indicates that the action is currently being recorded.

5. **With culture1.jpg open, choose Image>Image Size.**

6. **Make sure the Resample option is checked.**

   You want the slides to be proportionally sized, and you want them to remain at 72 ppi.

7. **With the Constrain Aspect Ratio option active, choose Pixels in the Height Units menu, and then change the Pixel Dimensions height to 1000 pixels.**

   Because the Resample option is active, reducing the number of pixels results in a proportionally smaller document size.

Make sure the Resample option is checked.

Change this value to 1000 pixels.

The image's physical dimensions are reduced proprtionally.

8. **Click OK to close the Image Size dialog box and apply the change.**

9. **In the Actions panel, click the Stop Playing/Recording button.**

10. **Expand the Image Size item in the Optimize for Slides action.**

The things you did in Steps 5–8 are included in the action.

11. **Click Portfolio Actions in the Actions panel to select the set, and then choose Save Actions in the panel Options menu.**

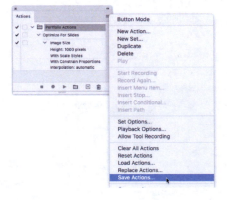

12. In the Save dialog box, review the options and then click Save.

The dialog box defaults to the application's Presets>Actions folder. The extension (.atn) is automatically added for you.

If you are using a shared computer, you might not be able to save files in the application's default location. Saving the file directly to your WIP folder makes it readily available whenever you need it.

Note:

The default file name is the same as the set name that you defined when you created the set.

Note:

Action sets are stored by default in the Presets>Actions folder in the Photoshop Application folder on your computer. You can also load an action from another location, such as when someone sends you an action that was created on another computer.

If you make changes to a set — whether you delete an existing action from the set or add your own custom actions — without saving the altered set, you will have to repeat your work the next time you launch Photoshop.

13. Close the culture1.jpg file without saving.

You don't need to save the changes, as this file will be processed when you run the action on the entire images folder.

14. Continue to the next exercise.

Batch-Process Files

The ability to batch-process files further enhances and automates productivity. If you have a large group of files that all require the same adjustments, you can build an action, set up a batch, and go to lunch (or, depending on your computer processor and number of files, go home for the night).

For example, when we write the Portfolio books, we take screen shots in RGB mode at 100%. Before the books are laid out for print production, the screen captures are converted to the U.S. Web Coated (SWOP) v2 CMYK profile, and resized (not resampled) to 40%. As you have probably noticed, there are a lot of screen captures in these books. Rather than sitting for several days and modifying each file (or even sitting for one full day and running an action on each file), we set up a batch that converts all screen captures for an entire book in about 25 minutes.

1. In Photoshop, choose File>Automate>Batch.

At the top of the Batch dialog box, the Set and Action menus default to the active selection in the Actions panel. In this case, there is only one available choice, so the Optimize for Slides action is already selected. You can choose to run a batch for any action in any open set.

Action Stops

When you record actions, you can insert an intentional pause by choosing **Insert Stop** from the Actions panel Options menu. When you insert a stop, the Record Stop dialog box allows you to type a message — for example, specific instructions or reminders to the user — that displays when the action runs.

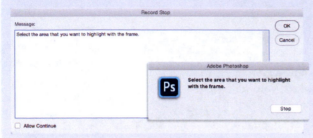

When a user runs the action and the action reaches a stop, the message you entered into the Record Stop dialog box appears. The user must click Stop, perform the required step, and then click the Play button in the Actions panel to complete the rest of the action. If you check the Allow Continue option when you define the Stop, the resulting message includes a Continue button; if the user clicks Continue, the action resumes.

Menu Items

You can cause an action to open a specific dialog box or execute a menu command by choosing **Insert Menu Item** from the Actions panel Options menu. When the Insert Menu Item dialog box appears, you can make a selection from the application menus, and then click OK. When a user runs the action, the specified dialog box opens or the menu command executes.

When you insert a menu item that opens a dialog box (such as, Select>Color Range), you are adding a modal command that can't be turned off. When a user runs the action, even with modal commands turned off, the dialog box opens and requires user interaction. Although an action can automate many steps in a repetitive process, there are still some things that can't be entirely automatic.

Conditional Actions

You can also define steps in an action that occur if a specific condition is met by choosing **Insert Conditional** from the Actions panel Options menu. In the Conditional Actions dialog box:

- If Current defines the condition that will be evaluated. You can choose from the available list conditions.

- Then Play Action menu defines what will occur if the condition is true. You can choose any action that exists in the same set as the action you are recording.

- Else Play Action defines what happens if the condition is *not* true. You can choose any action that exists in the same set as the action you are recording.

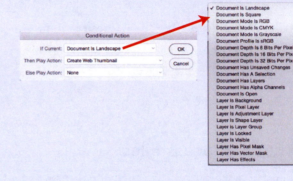

2. **Choose Folder in the Source menu.**

   The Source menu allows you to choose which files are batched:

   - **Folder** processes a complete group of images arranged within a single folder on your computer.
   - **Import** acquires and processes a group of images from a scanner or digital camera.
   - **Open Files** processes all files currently open in the application.
   - **File Browser** processes files selected in the File Browser.

   When Folder is selected, you can also choose to override "Open" commands that are recorded in the selected action, include subfolders within the selected folder, and suppress color profile warnings for the files being processed.

3. **Click the Choose button and navigate to the WIP>Silk>costumes folder. Click Choose/Select Folder to return to the Batch dialog box.**

4. **Make sure the Suppress Color Profile Warnings option is checked to prevent the batch from stopping if color management policies are violated.**

   This is a matter of some debate, but when processing images for the web, color management is not considered as critical as it is for print.

5. **Choose Folder in the Destination menu.**

   The Destination menu in the Batch dialog box presents three options:

   - **None** simply means that the action will run. If the action saves and closes the files, those commands will be completed. If the action does not save and close the files, you might end up with a large number of open files and, eventually, crash your computer.
   - **Save and Close** saves the modified file in the same location with the same name, overwriting the original file.
   - **Folder** allows you to specify a target folder for the files after they have been processed. This option is particularly useful because it saves the processed files as copies of the originals in the defined folder; the original files remain intact.

6. **Click the Choose button (in the Destination area), navigate to the WIP>Silk>slides folder, and click Choose/Select Folder.**

7. **In the File Naming area, open the menu for the first field and choose document name (lowercase) from the menu.**

    The File Naming fields, available when Folder is selected in the Destination menu, allow you to redefine file names for the modified files. You can choose a variable from the pop-up menu, type specific text in a field, or use a combination of both. The example in the File Naming area shows the result of your choices in these menus.

Note:

*You can create a **droplet**, which allows you to run an action using a basic drag-and-drop technique (as long as Photoshop is running). The Create Droplet dialog box (File>Automate>Create Droplet) presents most of the same options as the Batch dialog box, with a few exceptions. Clicking Choose at the top of the dialog box allows you to define the name of the droplet and the location in which to save it. The dialog box does not include Source options because the source is defined when you drag files onto the droplet.*

8. **In the second field (below "document name"), type -slide.**

    This identifies the images as the versions for the slideshow, differentiating them from the full-size images with the same names.

9. **Choose extension (lowercase) from the menu for the third field.**

10. **Click OK to run the batch.**

    When the process is complete, you will have 14 images in your WIP>Silk>slides folder.

Note:

*The Errors section of the Batch dialog box determines what happens if an error occurs during a batch. **Stop for Errors** (the default setting) interrupts the batch and displays a warning dialog box. **Log Errors to File** batch-processes every file and saves a record of all problems.*

11. **Continue to the next stage of the project.**

STAGE 2 / Editing Layers for Visual Effect

At the meeting, your art director defined three tasks that need to be completed in the client's Welcome page design. Photoshop offers a number of tools for manipulating layers, from simple transformations to liquifying pixels. If you completed the other projects in this book, you have already used many of these techniques to fulfill specific project goals. In this stage of the project, you use three more options for managing and transforming layer content to achieve effects that can't easily be created with other methods.

Use Frames to Place Images

The Frame tool offers another option for defining the visible area of a placed image. If you have used a page-layout application such as Adobe InDesign, you should be familiar with the concept of frames.

In this exercise, you will create frames to present three images that the client wants to feature on her site's Welcome page. Rather than simply placing the feature images into the layout, you will use frames to define the image areas, so that you can more easily change the images inside the frames without affecting the actual frames that define the location for those images.

1. **Open the file silk-road.psd from your WIP>Silk folder.**

2. **Make sure rulers are visible (View>Rulers).**

3. **Control/right-click the horizontal ruler at the top of the document window and make sure Pixels is checked as the unit of measurement.**

4. **In the Layers panel, Command/Control-click to select all five pixel-based (non-type) layers: Menu Icon, SILK ROAD, Silk, Text Background, and Background Image.**

5. **With those five layers selected, click the Lock All button at the top of the Layers panel.**

When you draw a new frame, it automatically applies to the topmost pixel-based layer in the file. Because you don't want the new frame to affect the existing layers, you are locking those layers to prevent them from becoming attached to the frame.

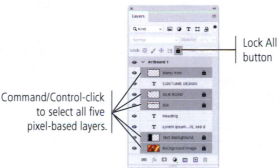

Command/Control-click to select all five pixel-based layers.

Lock All button

6. **Choose the Frame tool in the Tools panel. In the Options bar, make sure the Rectangle option is selected.**

   When the Frame tool is active, you can use the Options bar to determine whether you are creating a rectangle or ellipse frame.

7. **Click at the top-left corner where the ruler guides meet, and drag down and right to the bottom-right intersection of the ruler guides.**

   If you don't see the page guides, choose View>Show>Guides.

   Clicking and dragging creates the selected frame shape. A new layer for the frame shape is added to the Layers panel.

Note:

If you don't see the Frame tool in the main Tools panel, check in the Edit Toolbar menu *at the bottom of the Tools panel.*

Create a new rectangular frame.   Create a new elliptical frame.

Frame tool

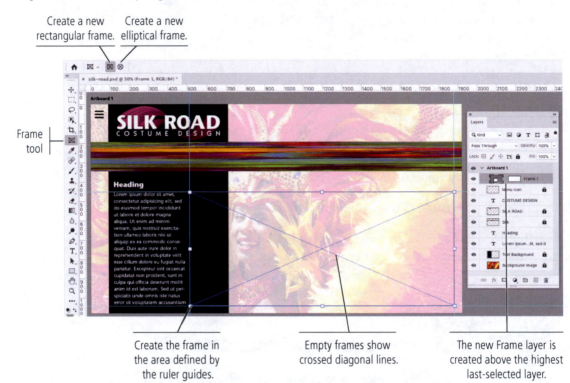

Create the frame in the area defined by the ruler guides.

Empty frames show crossed diagonal lines.

The new Frame layer is created above the highest last-selected layer.

8. **In the Properties panel, open the Inset Image menu and choose Place from Local Disk - Embedded.**

   You can use this menu to place an image directly from the Adobe Stock library, from an open CC Library file, or from your local drive as an Embedded or Linked Smart object. You can also drag images into a frame from the Libraries panel or from a Finder window.

   You can also create a frame from an existing layer. For vector-based layers, Control/right-click the layer name and choose Convert to Frame. For regular layers, choose Frame from Layers in the contextual menu; in this case, you can define the new frame name, as well as change the frame dimensions away from the existing frame content.

Note:

If you place a file that includes layer comps, you can use the Properties panel to determine which comp should be used in the frame.

9. **In the resulting dialog box, navigate to the file feature1.jpg in the WIP>Silk>costumes folder and click Place.**

After you define the image to inset into a frame, the frame layer shows two thumbnails — the actual frame on the left and the inset image on the right. Brackets surround the thumbnail of the active element. Be sure to check which is active before you make changes.

By default, the placed image is automatically scaled to fill the frame. Image areas outside the frame dimensions are hidden, but they are not permanently removed.

You can use the Properties panel to change the X and Y position of the image relative to the top-left corner of the canvas. Keep in mind, these values do not refer to the image's position within the containing frame.

The image in the frame is active.

The image is scaled to fill the frame.

Image areas outside the frame are not visible.

The light boundary shows the actual image dimensions.

10. **In the Layers panel, click the Frame thumbnail to select the actual frame, then review the Properties panel. Note the frame height.**

When the frame is selected and the Frame tool or Move tool is active, bounding-box handles surround the frame. You can drag those handles to change the frame size. You can also use the Properties panel to define the frame height, width, and position relative to the overall canvas.

The actual frame is selected.

The Properties panel shows the frame's dimensions.

Handles surround the edges of the selected frame.

11. **In the Layers panel, click the placed image thumbnail to select the image inside the frame.**

12. **With the placed image selected in the Layers panel, press Command/Control-T to enter Free Transform mode.**

When the frame content is active, you can simply click and drag to change the visible portion of the placed image. You can also enter Free Transform mode to scale or otherwise transform the placed content.

13. **In the Options bar, make sure the Maintain Aspect Ratio option is active. Highlight the existing H field value and type 590 px, then press Return/Enter to finalize the change.**

The final result will probably be slightly different than 590 px after you press Return/Enter. This appears to be a minor bug in the software, but it should not affect the end result of your work in this project.

Note:

You can use the Edit Contents button to open the Smart Object file, or use the Convert To Linked button to save the embedded file on your computer and link that content to that file as a linked Smart Object.

Maintain Aspect Ratio should be active.

Change the image height to match the frame height.

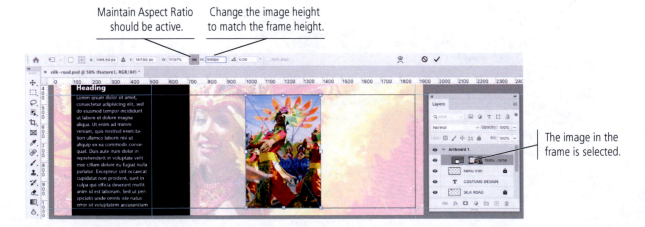

The image in the frame is selected.

14. In the Layers panel, click to select the containing frame.

15. Click the left-center handle and drag right until the frame edge meets the edge of the placed content.

16. Click the right-center handle and drag left until the frame edge meets the edge of the placed content.

The actual frame is again selected.

Drag the handles to match the size of the placed image.

17. In the Layers panel, click the name of the frame layer to select the entire layer (frame and content).

18. Click inside the frame boundaries and drag left until the frame snaps to the left ruler guide.

Because you selected the entire layer before dragging, both the frame and its contents move.

The entire layer (frame and content) is selected.

Click inside the frame boundary and drag to move the frame and its content.

19. Using the Frame tool, click to the right of the existing frame and drag to create a second empty frame. Drag the frame's bounding-box handles to match the height of the space defined by the ruler guides.

You can't click inside an existing frame's boundaries to create a new frame.

20. Using the Properties panel, place the file `feature2.jpg` into the frame as an embedded image.

21. Repeat the process from Steps 10–16 to resize the placed content to fit the frame height, then adjust the frame to fit the resized content.

22. In the Layers panel, click the name of the frame layer to select the entire layer (frame and content). Click inside the frame area and drag left until the second frame meets the right edge of the first frame.

23. Repeat the entire frame-creation process to add a third frame with the image `feature3.jpg`. Position this frame so its right edge snaps to the right edge of the space defined by the ruler guides.

Align the third frame to the right ruler guide.

24. **In the Layers panel, Shift-click to select all three Frame layers.**

25. **Choose the Move tool. In the Options bar, click the Align Top Edges button and then click the Distribute Horizontally button.**

    Align and distribute buttons are available in the Options bar when the Move tool is active, and more than one layer is selected. The Align Top Edges button ensures that all three frames are exactly aligned (making up for any slight movement that occurred when you move the frame layers). The Distribute Horizontally button places an equal amount of space between the content of selected layers.

    Align Top Edges   Distribute Horizontally

    All three frame layers are selected.

26. **Save the file, then continue to the next exercise.**

Use Puppet Warp to Transform a Layer

Puppet Warp provides a way to transform and distort specific areas of a layer, without affecting other areas of the same layer. It is called "puppet" warp because it's based on the concept of pinning certain areas in place, and then bending other areas around those pin locations — mimicking the way a puppet's joints pivot. In this exercise, you use puppet warping to bend and distort the top Silk image layer.

1. **With silk-road.psd open, choose View>Show>Guides to hide page guides.**

    The guides are not necessary for this stage of the project; hiding them helps to minimize unnecessary elements on the screen.

2. **Unlock the Silk layer in the Layers panel.**

3. **Control/right-click the Silk layer in the Layers panel. Choose Convert to Smart Object from the contextual menu.**

    By first converting this layer to a Smart Object, you can apply the puppet warp non-destructively.

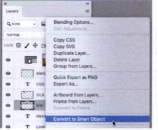

Note:

Puppet warping can be applied to image, shape, and text layers, as well as layer and vector masks.

4. **With the Silk Smart Object layer selected in the Layers panel, choose Edit>Puppet Warp.**

   When you enter Puppet Warp mode, a mesh overlays the active layer content. This mesh represents the joints in the shape that can bend when you warp the layer content.

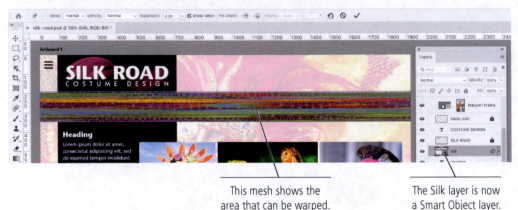

This mesh shows the
area that can be warped.

The Silk layer is now
a Smart Object layer.

5. **In the Options bar, make sure Show Mesh is checked. Choose Distort in the Mode menu and choose Fewer Points in the Density menu.**

Choose the
Distort mode.

Choose
Fewer Points.

6. **Click the mesh near the center of the Silk layer content to place an anchoring pin.**

   Clicking the mesh places a pin, which anchors the layer at that location.

7. **Click the top-right corner of the mesh and, without releasing the mouse button, drag up above the top edge of the image.**

   Clicking and dragging places a new pin, and rotates the image around the location of the existing pin. Because you have placed one other pin on the layer, the entire shape rotates around the first pin location.

Clicking and dragging
places a new pin, and
rotates the layer
around the existing pin.

This is the pin you
placed in Step 6.

8. **Click near the top-left corner of the Silk image and drag up to bend the layer content around the center pin.**

Note:

Pressing Command/ Control-Z while working in Puppet Warp mode undoes the last action you performed inside the puppet warp mesh. You can only undo one action; after you finalize the warp, the Undo command undoes the entire warp — everything you did since you entered Puppet Warp mode.

9. **Add another pin to the bottom-right corner of the layer. Drag the new point until the pin is just past the canvas edge (as shown here).**

10. **Click the center pin and drag left to change the distorted shape.**

   Moving a pin changes the distortion shape because of the distance between various pins on the shape.

   Moving a pin changes the overall shape distortion.

11. **Continue manipulating the filmstrip warp until you are satisfied with the result. Keep the following points in mind:**

- **Click to add new pins at any point in the process.**
- **Option/Alt-click an existing, selected pin to remove it from the mesh.**
- **Press Option/Alt to change the selected pin from an Auto rotation angle to a Fixed rotation angle.**
- **With a specific pin selected, press Option/Alt, click the rotation proxy, and drag to change the angle of that pin.**
- **Uncheck the Show Mesh option to get a better preview of your warp.**

Our solution is shown here.

Note:

The Expansion option in the Options bar determines how far the mesh extends beyond the edge of the layer content.

Note:

If you warp a layer so that the mesh overlaps, you can use the Pin Depth buttons in the Options bar to show pins on underlying layers.

12. **Press Return/Enter to finalize the warp.**

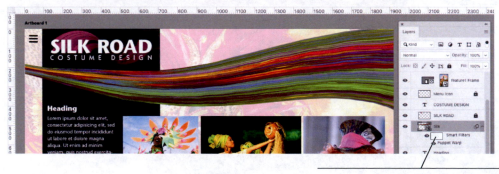

Because you converted the layer to a Smart Object, you can double-click the Puppet Warp effect to change the warp settings.

13. **Click the arrow button in the Layers panel to collapse the Smart Filters for the Silk layer.**

Click here to collapse the Smart Filters.

14. **Save the file, then continue to the next stage of the project.**

STAGE 3 / Generating Web-Ready Assets

It is common practice to create the look and feel of a website in Photoshop, and then hand off the pieces for a programmer to assemble in a web design application, such as Adobe Dreamweaver. In this stage of the project, you complete a number of tasks to create the necessary pieces for the final website, including the different styles that will be used to properly format various elements in the resulting HTML page.

This site is a very simple example, using only a few elements to illustrate the process of properly mapping Photoshop objects to create the pieces that are necessary in an HTML page. We kept the site design basic to minimize the amount of repetition required to complete the project. The skills and concepts you complete in this project would apply equally to more complex sites.

Examine a Photoshop Artboard

Responsive design is a term used to describe how page layouts change based on the size of display being used to show a specific web page. This technique typically requires different settings for various elements (type size, alignment, etc.), and even different content that will — or will not — appear in different-size displays (for example, removing images from extra-small or phone display sizes).

Photoshop artboards are a special type of layer group that make it easier to manage content for multiple display sizes within a single Photoshop file. In this exercise, you are going to examine the artboard concept in the silk-road.psd file, which was designed specifically for large display sizes. In a later exercise, you will duplicate and modify the existing layout elements to create the required files for a different size display.

1. **With silk-road.psd open, unlock all layers in the Layers panel.**

2. **Choose the Artboard tool (nested under the Move tool).**

    If you don't see the Artboard tool, call and reset the Essentials workspace in the Workspace switcher. Some of the built-in workspaces, such as the 3D workspace, do not include the 3D tool.

    When you create a new document using any of the Mobile or Web presets, the file automatically includes an Artboard that matches the defined canvas size.

    This layout was created using the Web Large preset in the New Document dialog box. When the Artboard tool is active, you can see the artboard size and orientation. If you change the size away from one of the built-in presets, or define a custom size when you create the file, the size menu shows "Custom," indicating that the artboard is no longer one of the predefined web or mobile sizes.

3. **Review the Layers panel.**

In the Layers panel, a special Artboard folder contains all the layers with content that appears, at least partially, within the artboard bounds.

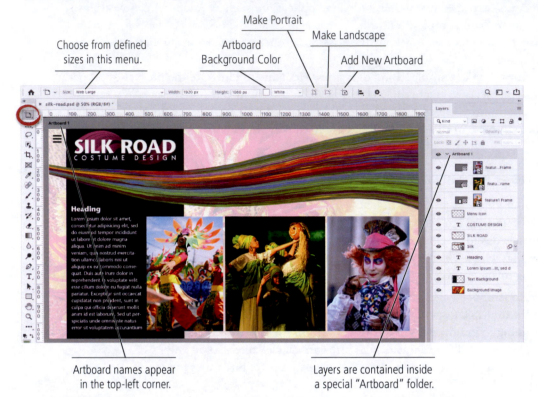

Choose from defined sizes in this menu.

Make Portrait

Make Landscape

Artboard Background Color

Add New Artboard

Artboard names appear in the top-left corner.

Layers are contained inside a special "Artboard" folder.

4. **In the Layer panel, double-click the Artboard 1 name to highlight it. Type Web Large, then press Return/Enter to finalize the new artboard name.**

Like other assets, meaningful artboard names are more useful than the default "Artboard 1."

The artboard name tag changes to show the new name you just defined.

Rename an artboard just as you would rename a layer.

5. **Save the file, then continue to the next exercise.**

Generate Image Assets from Layers

Adobe Generator is a Photoshop plug-in that makes it easy to create the required web-ready assets from layers in any Photoshop file. Any transformations applied to layer content are processed and become a permanent part of the generated asset.

Three image formats are primarily used for digital delivery:

- **JPEG** (Joint Photographic Experts Group), which supports 24-bit color, is used primarily for continuous-tone images, with subtle changes in color, such as photographs or other images that are created in Adobe Photoshop. The JPEG format incorporates **lossy compression**, which means that pixels are thrown away in order to reduce file size. When areas of flat color are highly compressed, speckles of other colors (called artifacts) often appear, which negatively impacts the quality of the design.

- **GIF** (Graphics Interchange Format), which supports only 8-bit color and basic, on-or-off transparency, is best used for graphics with areas of solid color, such as logos or other basic illustrations. The GIF format uses **lossless compression** to reduce file size, while ensuring that no information is lost during the compression.

- **PNG** (Portable Network Graphics), which supports 8- and 24-bit color, as well as a special 32-bit format allowing support for various degrees of transparency, can be used for both illustrations and continuous-tone images. The PNG format uses lossless compression to create smaller file size without losing image data.

In this exercise, you will create the required assets for images that were manipulated or created directly in Adobe Photoshop. You do not need to export the three feature images. Those files already exist in the client's supplied files. Even though you scaled them into the Photoshop frames, the web developer who implements the site in HTML can use code to adjust the images to fit into the necessary spaces.

1. **With silk-road.psd open, open the Plug-Ins pane of the Preferences dialog box.**

2. **Make sure the Enable Generator option is checked (active), then click OK.**

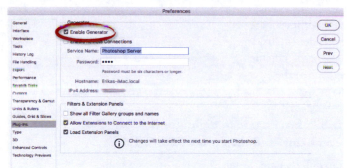

3. **Choose File>Generate>Image Assets to activate that option.**

If this menu item is already checked, simply move your mouse cursor away and click to close the menu.

Note:

Bit depth refers to how many bits define the color value of a particular pixel. A bit is a unit of information that is either on or off (represented as 1 and 0, respectively). One bit has two states, or colors; eight bits have 256 possible colors (2×2×2×2×2×2 ×2×2=256); and 24 bits have 16,777,216 (2^{24}) possible colors.

In an RGB photograph, three color channels define how much of each primary color (red, green, and blue) makes up each pixel. Each channel requires 8 bits, resulting in a total of 24 bits for each pixel ("true color").

4. **In the Layers panel, select both the COSTUME DESIGN and SILK ROAD type layers. Click the Create a New Group button at the bottom of the Layers panel.**

You want the two layers to function together as a single logo in the web page, so you are grouping them together.

Create a New Group button

Selected layers are automatically placed in the new group.

5. **Double-click the new layer group name to select it. Type logotype.png as the new name, and then press Return/Enter.**

Renaming a layer group is the same process as renaming a layer.

Note:

If you are using Adobe Dreamweaver to build a site's HTML files, you can use the Extract functionality inside of Dreamweaver to create the assets you need directly from native Photoshop layers. The Generator functionality is useful if the required assets will be needed in some other web design environment.

6. **On your desktop, open the WIP>Silk folder.**

Adobe Generator creates new web assets as soon as you define a layer name that includes an appropriate extension (.jpg, .gif, or .png). A new folder — silk-road-assets — has been added. The logotype.png file, which was generated as soon as you defined the layer group name, exists inside that folder.

7. **In Photoshop, double-click the Silk layer name to highlight it. Type silk-lg.png as the new layer name, and then press Return/Enter.**

You are using the "-lg" designation to differentiate this file from the one you will create for a smaller display in a later exercise.

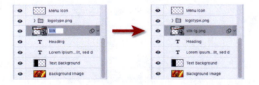

8. **Repeat Step 7 for the following layers:**

Layer	Rename as:
Menu Icon:	menu-icon.gif
Text Background:	text-bkg.jpg
Background Image:	body-bkg.jpg

9. **On your desktop, review the contents of the silk-road-assets folder.**

Note:

To disable image asset generation for the active file, deselect File> Generate>Image Assets.

To disable image asset generation for all Photoshop files, uncheck the Enable Generator option in the Plug-Ins pane of the Preferences dialog box.

10. **In Photoshop, save silk-road.psd and then continue to the next exercise.**

More about Adobe Generator

Creating Multiple Files

You can also use Generator to create multiple files from a single layer by separating asset names with a comma in the Layers panel. For example, the layer name:

menu-bar.jpg, menu-bar.png

creates two separate files in the metro-site-assets folder.

Changing Asset Size Settings

You can also use layer names to define a specific size for the generated assets. Simply add the desired output size — relative or specific — as a prefix to the asset name. Remember to add a space character between the prefix and the asset name. For example:

200% menu-bar.jpg

10in x 2in logotype.png

50 x 25 menu-icon.gif

If you specify the size in pixels, you can omit the unit; other units must be included in the layer name prefix.

Creating Asset Subfolders

If you want to create subfolders inside the main assets folder, simply include the subfolder name and a forward slash in the modified layer name. For example:

thumbnails/bridge_small.jpg

Changing Asset Quality Settings

You can use complex layer/layer group names to define different compression, quality, and size options in the generated assets. By default:

- JPG assets are generated at 90% quality.
- PNG assets are generated as 32-bit images.
- GIF assets are generated with basic alpha transparency.

While renaming layers or layer groups in preparation for asset generation, you can customize quality and size.

For JPEG files, you can define a different quality setting by appending a number to the end of the layer name, such as filename.jpg(1-10) or filename.jpg(1-100%). For example:

menu-bar.jpg50%

creates a JPEG file with medium image quality.

For PNG files, you can change the output quality by appending the number 8, 24, or 32 to the layer name. For example:

filmstrip.png24

creates a 24-bit PNG file, instead of the default 32-bit file.

Copy CSS for Text and Shape Layers

You do not need to be a web programmer to design a site in Photoshop. However, to best take advantage of some of the tools that are available for moving your work into a functional HTML page, you should understand at least the basics of HTML:

- An HTML page contains code that defines the **elements** making up that page.

- Individual page elements are defined with **tags**. For example, a <div> tag identifies a division or area of the page, and a <p> tag identifies a paragraph. Available tags are defined by HTML; you can't simply make them up.

- Specific elements can be identified with user-defined classes, which helps to differentiate them from other same-type elements. For example:

    <div class="feature-image">

- Cascading Style Sheets (CSS) are used to define the properties of HTML elements. CSS files define **selectors**, which contain **property:value pairs** to control the appearance of specific elements in an HTML page. For example:

    header {
       width: 780px;
    }

- Two types of CSS selectors are relevant to site design in Photoshop:

    - **Tag selectors** define the appearance of HTML tags. These selectors simply use the tag name as the selector name; for example, the **div** selector defines the appearance of all **<div>** tags.

    - **Class selectors** define the appearance of any tag that is identified with the defined class. These selector names always begin with a period. For example, the **.text-area** selector would apply to any element that has the **class="text-area"** attribute.

In this exercise, you will use Photoshop to create CSS classes, which the web designer can apply to various page elements, so that your design choices are maintained in the final HTML page.

1. **With silk-road.psd open in Photoshop, change the Heading type layer name to h1-lg.**

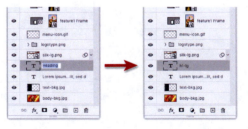

2. **Control/right-click the h1-lg type layer and choose Copy CSS from the contextual menu.**

3. **Using any text-editing application, open the file `type-styles.css` from the WIP>Silk folder.**

We use TextEdit on a Macintosh in our screen captures, but you can use any text editor to complete the following steps.

4. **Place the insertion point on the first empty line at the end of the file, then press Command/Control-V to paste the CSS that was copied in Step 2.**

All CSS copied from Photoshop is created as a class. The selector name, beginning with a period, is taken from the relevant Photoshop layer.

These lines are included in the original file.

These lines create a new class selector based on the settings applied to the h1-lg type layer in the Photoshop file.

5. **Repeat Steps 1–4 to rename the remaining type layer ("Lorem...") as `body-copy-lg` in the Photoshop file. Add the required CSS for that layer to the type-styles.css file.**

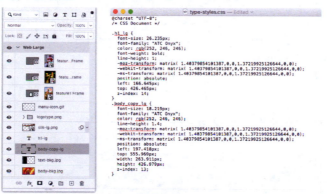

6. **Save type-styles.css, then close it.**

7. **In Photoshop, collapse the Web Large artboard in the Layers panel.**

8. **Save the file, then continue to the next exercise.**

Although the **Slice tool** was intended to cut apart pieces of a web page comp for reassembly in a web design application, it can be used for any situation in which you need to cut a single image into multiple bits.

In addition to creating image assets from layers and layer groups, you can also create image slices. All visible layers in the slice area are included in the resulting images.

Photoshop offers a number of options for creating slices in your artwork:

- Manually draw a slice area with the Slice tool.
- When the Slice tool is active, click Slices from Guides in the Options bar to automatically slice the file based on existing ruler guides.
- When the Slice Select tool is active and a specific slice is selected in the file, click Divide in the Options bar to divide the slice horizontally or vertically into a specific number of equal-size slices.
- Create a new slice based on specific layer content by selecting one or more layers in the Layers panel, and then choosing Layer>New Layer Based Slice.

Once slices are created, you can double-click to select a specific slice with the Slice Selection tool to edit its settings. In the resulting dialog box:

- Name is the file name of the image that is created from the slice.
- URL is the file that opens if a user clicks the slice.
- Target is the location where the URL opens when a user clicks the slice.
- Message Text appears in the browser's status bar.
- Alt Tag appears if image display is disabled.

URL, Target, and Message are better handled in a web design application such as Adobe Dreamweaver.

Dimensions fields are automatically filled with the size of the selected slice. You can also change the slice background type and color if the slice contains areas of transparency.

Copy and Edit Artboard Sizes

As we explained earlier, a Photoshop artboard is basically a way of organizing and managing layers so you can create more than one layout in the same Photoshop file. In this exercise, you are going to create a second artboard to manage the elements you need for an iPhone display.

1. **With silk-road.psd open, make sure the Web Large artboard is selected in the Layers panel and then activate the Artboard tool in the Tools panel.**

Artboard bounding-box handles

Add New Artboard icons

2. **Option/Alt-click the Add New Artboard icon to the right of the existing artboard.**

   When the Artboard tool is active, the Add New Artboard icons appear on all four sides of the active artboard. Clicking one of these icons adds a new, blank artboard adjacent to the existing one (the new artboard appears on the same side as the icon you click).

   If you Option/Alt-click one of the icons, the new artboard is a duplicate of the existing one, including all the layers that existed on the previous artboard.

3. **In the Layers panel, expand the Web Large copy artboard.**

Layers on the original artboard are duplicated in the new artboard.

4. **In the Layers panel, change the name of the Web Large copy artboard to iPhone V.**

   Renaming artboards uses the same process as renaming layers and layer groups — double-click the existing name in the Layers panel, and then type the new name.

5. **With the iPhone V artboard active, choose iPhone 8/7/6 in the Options bar Size menu. Click the Make Portrait button to change the artboard orientation.**

   When you change the size of an artboard, any layers that no longer have content within the bounds of the artboard are automatically moved outside the artboard group in the Layers panel.

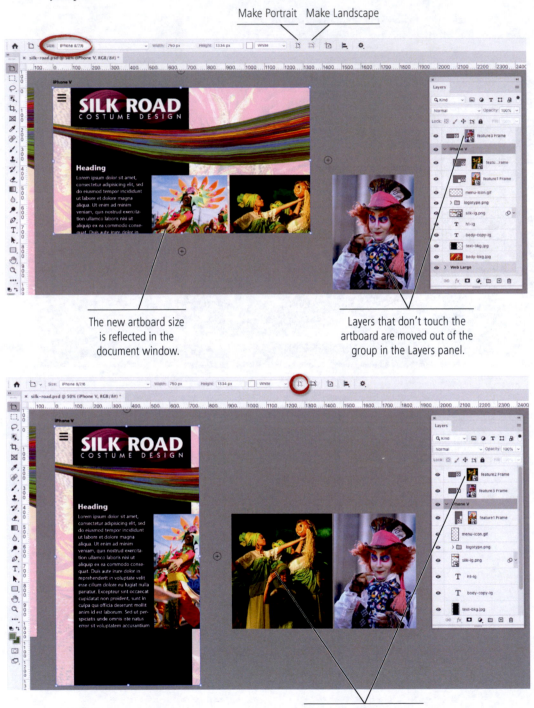

Make Portrait   Make Landscape

The new artboard size is reflected in the document window.

Layers that don't touch the artboard are moved out of the group in the Layers panel.

Artboard size changes can affect which layers are part of the artboard group.

6. **Save the file and continue to the next exercise.**

Adjust Content for the Alternate Display Size

As you might have already guessed, the different sizes and orientations of various displays mean you will often have to define different content positions, sizes, and settings for different displays. In this exercise, you will make several necessary adjustments to the elements in the vertical iPhone layout.

1. With **silk-road.psd** open, Shift-click to select the feature2 Frame and feature3 Frame layers in the Layers panel.

2. With both layers selected, click the panel's Delete button. Click Yes to confirm the deletion.

   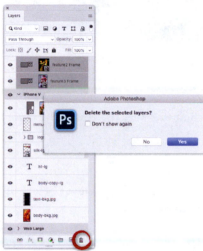

   On a small display size, such as an iPhone, it is common to use fewer images on a page than on a larger physical display. In this case, you will include only a single feature image on the vertical iPhone layout, instead of the row of three, that is more appropriate in the large, horizontal display size.

3. In the Layers panel, rename the silk-lg.png file in the iPhone V artboard as **silk-iphone.png**.

   When you use Generator to export image assets, only the visible portion of the layer is included in the exported image (the resulting image is cropped at the artboard edges).

   In this case, the right half of the puppet-warped layer will not be part of the exported file. If you transformed the layer to fit entirely in horizontal space, it would be much smaller and might lose some of the effect. The left half of the layer that is currently visible in the iPhone V artboard still creates the desired "flowing silk" appearance, so it is sufficient to meet the visual needs of the project.

   The exported asset includes only what you see in the artboard bounds.

4. **Using the Type tool, click to place the insertion point in the body-copy-lg type layer. Adjust the bottom-right type area handle until the cursor feedback shows W: 570 px, H: 250 px.**

Place the insertion point in the type area to access its bounding-box handles.

Drag the bottom-right handle until the area's dimensions are W: 570 px, H: 250 px.

Note:

You might need to zoom in to adjust the frame to the correct size.

5. **Activate the Move tool in the Tools panel. Turn off the Auto Select option in the Options bar.**

6. **In the Layers panel, click to select the feature1 Frame layer.**

   Make sure you click the layer name to select the entire layer, instead of only the frame or only the contents.

7. **Using the Move tool, move the selected layer below the adjusted type area (as shown in the following image).**

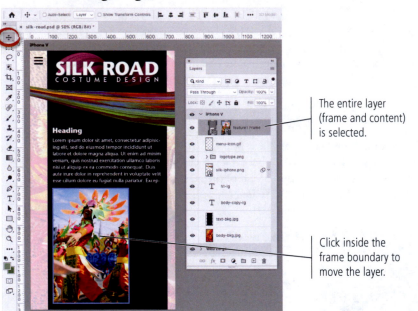

The entire layer (frame and content) is selected.

Click inside the frame boundary to move the layer.

8. **Press Command/Control-T to enter Free Transform mode. Shift-click the bottom-right handle and drag down until only a small amount of the black background shows to the right of the frame.**

Because the entire layer is selected, you are transforming both the frame and the frame's contents.

Note:

You have to press the Shift key while dragging a handle to scale a frame proportionally.

The entire layer is still selected.

Free Transform mode scales the frame and its content.

9. **In the Layers panel, click to select only the frame on the layer you just transformed. Drag up the bottom-center bounding-box handle of the frame until a small area of the black background is visible below the frame.**

Remember, when the actual frame is selected in the Layers panel, the frame's bounding-box handles automatically appear in the document window if the Frame or Move tool is active.

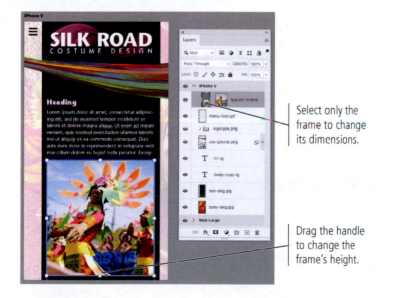

Note:

You do not need to generate the image for this frame because it will be placed and scaled in the web page code.

Select only the frame to change its dimensions.

Drag the handle to change the frame's height.

10. **Click the body-copy-lg layer name to select the layer.**

11. **Using the Character or Properties panel, define a 32 pt font size with 44 pt leading.**

    Remember: When the layer is selected and the insertion point is not placed, changing type settings affects all text on the selected layer.

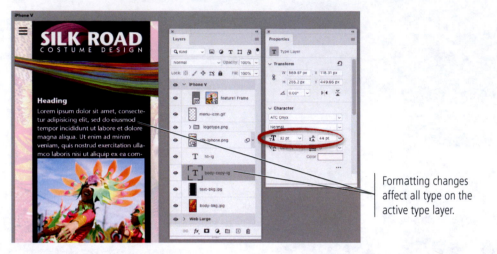

Formatting changes affect all type on the active type layer.

12. **In the Layers panel, change the body-copy-lg layer name to `body-copy-iphone`.**

13. **Control/right-click the body-copy-iphone layer and choose Copy CSS in the contextual menu.**

14. **If necessary, open `type-styles.css` (from your WIP>Silk folder) in a text-editing application.**

15. **Place the insertion point at the end of the existing copy and press Command/Control-V to paste the CSS from Step 13.**

```
@charset "utf-8";
/* CSS Document */

.h1_lg {
	font-size: 26.235px;
	font-family: "ATC Onyx";
	color: rgb(252, 246, 246);
	font-weight: bold;
	line-height: 1;
	-moz-transform: matrix( 1.40379854101387,0,0,1.37219925126644,0,0);
	-webkit-transform: matrix( 1.40379854101387,0,0,1.37219925126644,0,0);
	-ms-transform: matrix( 1.40379854101387,0,0,1.37219925126644,0,0);
	position: absolute;
	left: 166.645px;
	top: 426.465px;
	z-index: 14;
}
.body_copy_lg {
	font-size: 18.219px;
	font-family: "ATC Onyx";
	color: rgb(252, 246, 246);
	line-height: 1.4;
	-moz-transform: matrix( 1.40379854101387,0,0,1.37219925126644,0,0);
	-webkit-transform: matrix( 1.40379854101387,0,0,1.37219925126644,0,0);
	-ms-transform: matrix( 1.40379854101387,0,0,1.37219925126644,0,0);
	position: absolute;
	left: 197.418px;
	top: 555.969px;
	width: 263.911px;
	height: 426.979px;
	z-index: 13;
}
.body_copy_iphone {
	font-size: 23.32px;
	font-family: "ATC Onyx";
	color: rgb(252, 246, 246);
	line-height: 1.375;
	-moz-transform: matrix( 1.40379854101387,0,0,1.37219925126644,0,0);
	-webkit-transform: matrix( 1.40379854101387,0,0,1.37219925126644,0,0);
	-ms-transform: matrix( 1.40379854101387,0,0,1.37219925126644,0,0);
	position: absolute;
	left: 2244.149px;
	top: 517.079px;
	width: 394.579px;
	height: 184.201px;
	z-index: 28;
}
```

16. **Repeat Steps 10–15 to change the font size on the h1-lg layer to** 48 pt **with** 48 pt **leading. Change the layer name to** h1-iphone**, then copy and paste the layer's CSS into the** `type-styles.css` **file.**

17. **Save and close** `text-styles.css`.

18. **Save and close** `silk-road.psd`.

PROJECT REVIEW

fill in the blank

1. The _______________ command can be used to run an action on all files in a specific folder without user intervention.

2. Align options are available in the _______________ when multiple layers are selected in the Layers panel.

3. True or False: A Puppet Warp is always destructive; you cannot edit the original, pre-warp pixels. _______________

4. The _______________ tool can be used to create more than one canvas in a single Photoshop file.

5. The _______________ image format allows lossy compression and does not support transparency; it is best used for photos.

6. The _______________ format supports only 8-bit color; it is best used for artwork or graphics with large areas of solid color.

7. The _______________ format supports both continuous-tone color and degrees of transparency.

8. _______________ are used to define the properties of HTML elements.

9. CSS files define _______________, which contain property:value pairs to control the appearance of elements in an HTML page.

10. All CSS copied from Photoshop is created as a _______________. The selector name, beginning with a period, is taken from the relevant Photoshop layer.

short answer

1. Briefly explain how actions can be used to improve workflow.

2. Briefly explain three file formats that are used for images on the web.

3. Briefly explain the concept of CSS in relation to web design.

Use what you have learned in this project to complete the following freeform exercise.
Carefully read the art director and client comments, then create your own design to meet the needs of the project.
Use the space below to sketch ideas. When finished, write a brief explanation of the reasoning behind your final design.

art director comments

As part of the annual International Classic Surfing Competition, the Honolulu Marketing Group (a major event sponsor) is holding a surfboard decoration contest.

To complete this project, you should:

❏ Use the file **surfboard.psd** (in the **Boards_Web20_PB.zip** on the Student Files web page) as the basis for your work.

❏ Create a custom digital painting to decorate the surfboard shape.

❏ If necessary, rotate the surfboard canvas to paint your design vertically.

client comments

This year is the 30th anniversary of the Classic, and we're planning a contest for people to submit personal, custom surfboard designs.

In addition to people who will paint actual surfboards and send photos, we're allowing people to create virtual entries using the surfboard vector shape in the provided file.

There isn't really a theme, but we will divide the entries into several groups: fantasy, graffiti-style, abstract, and realistic. The winner of each category will win a gift certificate from the ATC Board Company and be entered in the best-of-show judging round.

The best-of-show winner will receive an all-expenses-paid trip for two to Honolulu to attend the International Classic, as well as a custom surfboard handpainted with the winning design.

project justification

PROJECT SUMMARY

The graphic design workflow typically revolves around extremely short turnaround times, which means that any possible automation will only be a benefit. Photoshop actions can be useful whenever you need to apply the same sets of options to more than one or two images. Every click you save will allow you to do other work, meet tight deadlines, and satisfy your clients. In the case of running a batch on multiple images, you are completely freed to work on other projects, be in other places, or even (technically) "work" while you're gone for the evening.

Although many developers use dedicated web design software, like Adobe Dreamweaver, to build sophisticated websites, the images for those sites have to come from somewhere. It is very common for a designer to build the "look and feel" of a site in Photoshop, and then generate the pieces so the developer can more easily reassemble them in the web design application. As you saw by completing this project, Photoshop can even be used to create cascading style sheets (CSS) to communicate the type and object formatting that you define in Photoshop.

Create a 3D extrusion from a type layer

Use puppet warping to distort a layer

Define an action to resize images

Run a batch to resize and rename multiple images

Use artboards to create multiple versions in one file

Create CSS from type layers

Generate web assets based on layers and layer groups

THE DREAMWEAVER USER INTERFACE

Typical Dreamweaver work ranges from static HTML pages with hyperlinks to complex, dynamic, database-driven sites, where pages are generated on-the-fly based on individual user requests. Mastering the tools and techniques of the application can significantly improve your potential career options. Our goal in this book is to teach you how to use the available tools to create different types of work that you might encounter in your professional career.

The basic exercises in this introduction are designed to let you explore the Dreamweaver user interface. Whether you are new to the application or upgrading from a previous version, we recommend you follow these steps to click around and become familiar with the basic workspace.

Launch the Dreamweaver Application

The first time you launch Dreamweaver, you see a series of setup screens that determine what is included in the initial user interface (UI). In this exercise, we walk you step-by-step through the initial setup process.

1. **Macintosh users:**

   While holding down the Command-Option-Shift keys, launch Dreamweaver.

   Windows users:

   — **Locate the Dreamweaver application folder on your system (probably C:/Program Files/Adobe/Adobe Dreamweaver [version]).**

   — **Press and hold the Control-Shift-Windows keys and double-click Dreamweaver.exe.**

2. **Click Yes when asked if you want to reset preferences and settings.**

   Steps 1–2 reset the application to its original "out-of-the-box" state, resulting in Dreamweaver launching as if for the first time.

3. **When you see the setup screen asking if you have used Dreamweaver previously, click the Yes, I Have button.**

   This book is designed to teach you how to use the software; clicking the "Yes" button allows you to more quickly move on to the exercises in this book.

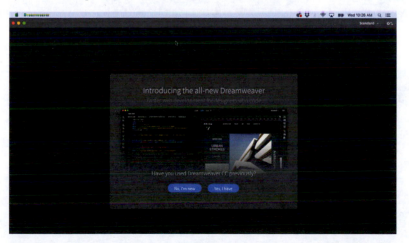

Note:

If you click the No, I'm New button, you will see a series of introductory videos before you can use the software.

4. In the second setup screen, choose the color theme you prefer.

The color theme defines the basic appearance of your overall workspace, including the darkness or lightness of various panels and panes throughout the application. The screen captures throughout this book use the lightest option because they reproduce better on a printed page. Feel free to use whichever theme you prefer.

Note:

You can change the color theme of your work-space at any time in the Interface pane of the Preferences dialog box.

5. In the third setup screen, choose the Standard Workspace option.

These options define what you see when you first begin using the application. Regardless of which option you choose here, the workspace is highly customizable. You will learn how to personalize your individual workspace in the next exercise.

6. Click the Close button in the final setup screen to dismiss it.

You can use the arrow buttons to navigate through the featured new options, or simply close the screen to begin working in Dreamweaver.

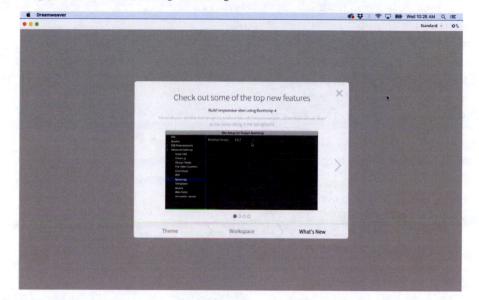

7. If you see a message about syncing settings, click the Advanced button.

As part of your individual-user Adobe Creative Cloud (CC) membership, you can use the Sync Settings options to share certain settings between different computers. This means you can access those same settings and assets on any computer when you are logged in to your CC account.

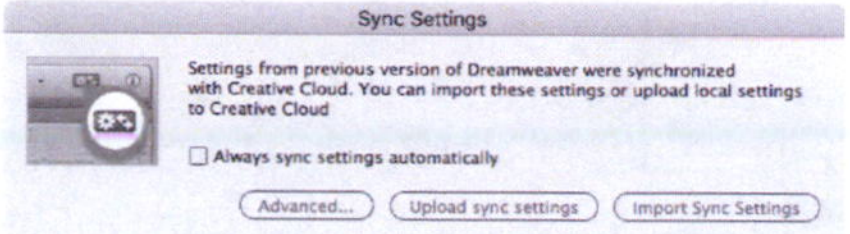

Clicking the Advanced button in the warning dialog box opens the Sync Settings pane of the Preferences dialog box, where you can customize which settings are synced.

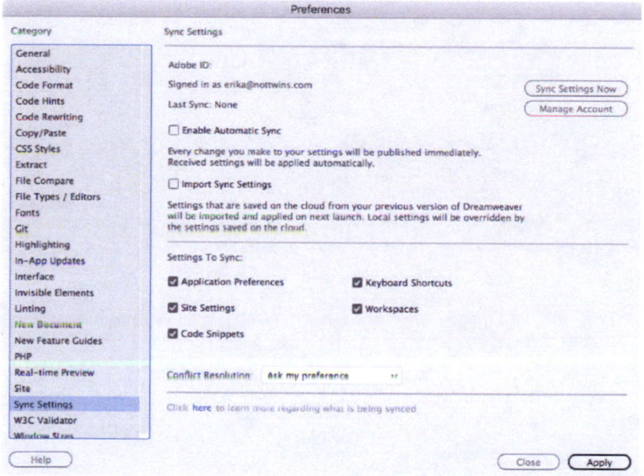

If you check Enable Automatic Sync, changes to the settings in your desktop application automatically upload to your CC account, and those changes automatically apply whenever and wherever you use the application.

8. Click Close to dismiss the Preferences dialog box.

9. Continue to the next exercise.

Note:

You must be logged into your CC account and connected to the internet for the sync process to work. You can open the Help menu to verify that you are signed in to your account.

Note:

If you do not enable automatic syncing, you can click the Sync Settings button in the top-right corner of the user interface to initiate the sync process at any time.

Explore the Dreamweaver Workspace

After making your initial choices in the setup screens, you will see the default workspace settings defined by Adobe. When you relaunch the application after you or another user has quit, the workspace defaults to the last-used settings — including specific open panels and their position on your screen.

Much of the Dreamweaver interface functions in the same way as the Photoshop and Flash user interface. Panels can be opened, moved, and grouped in the same manner, and you can save custom workspaces. In this exercise, you import an existing site into Dreamweaver and explore some of the options for looking at files.

1. **Macintosh users: Open the Window menu and make sure the Application Frame option is checked (toggled on).**

   Many menu commands and options in Dreamweaver are **toggles**, which means they are either on or off. When an option is already checked, that option is toggled on (visible, or active). You can toggle an active option off by choosing the checked menu command, or toggle an inactive option on by choosing the unchecked menu command.

   This option should be checked.

2. **Review the various elements of the workspace.**

   Because you chose the Standard workspace in the previous exercise, the default UI includes the Common Toolbar on the left and a set of docked, expanded panels on the right side of the workspace.

   When no file is open, you see a stored "Home" workspace that provides one-click access to a list of recently opened files (if any), buttons to create a new file or open an existing one, and links to additional functionality provided by the CC suite.

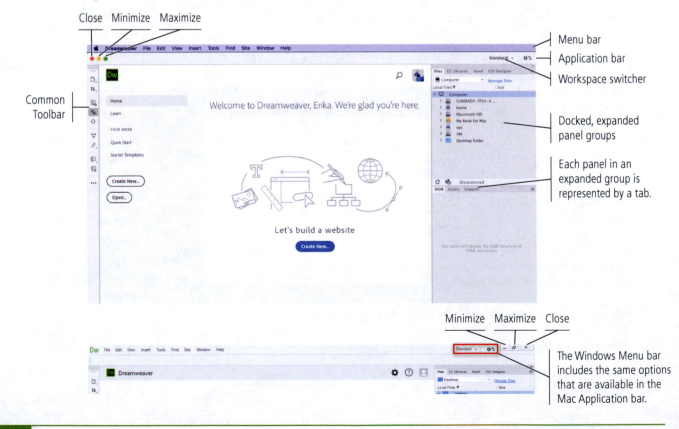

Close   Minimize   Maximize

Common Toolbar

Menu bar
Application bar
Workspace switcher

Docked, expanded panel groups

Each panel in an expanded group is represented by a tab.

Minimize   Maximize   Close

The Windows Menu bar includes the same options that are available in the Mac Application bar.

Understanding the Common Toolbar

The Common Toolbar, which you can toggle on or off in the Window>Toolbars submenu, appears by default on the left side of the UI when you use the Standard workspace. It provides easy access to a number of useful options. (These options will make more sense as you complete the projects in this book, and are explained more clearly in context.)

The Open Documents menu (⌂) lists all open files. Choosing a file in this list makes that file active in the document window.

The File Management menu (⇅) includes options for managing files that are uploaded on a remote server. You can get files from, or put files onto, the server, and check files in or out to view or make changes in a team setting.

The Live View Options menu (⧉) includes a number of options for managing what you see in the document window when the Live view is active.

The Toggle Visual Media Queries Bar button (⇶) can be used to show or hide that element, which appears by default at the top of the document window whenever the Live view is active.

The Inspect button (◇) activates Live view and Inspect mode in the document window.

The Expand All button (⮙) can be used to expand any code blocks that have been collapsed in the Code pane.

The Format Source Code menu (⌁) includes a number of options for formatting code in the Code pane.

The Apply Comment menu (▣) includes several options for adding comments to code in the Code pane.

The Remove Comment button (▣) removes commenting identifiers from the selected code in the Code view.

The Customize Toolbar button (⋯) opens a dialog box that you can use to add or remove various options from the toolbar. If you make changes, you can always reopen the dialog box and click the Restore Defaults button to reset the toolbar to its original state.

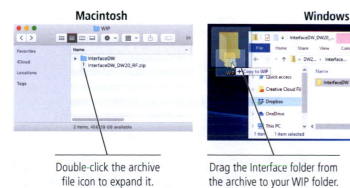

3. Download the `InterfaceDW_Web20_RF.zip` archive from the Student Files web page.

4. Macintosh users: Place the ZIP archive in your WIP folder, and then double-click the file icon to expand it.

   Windows users: Double-click the ZIP archive file to open it. Click the folder inside the archive and drag it into your primary WIP folder.

   The resulting **InterfaceDW** folder contains all the files you need to complete this introduction.

Macintosh

Double-click the archive file icon to expand it.

Windows

Drag the Interface folder from the archive to your WIP folder.

5. **In Dreamweaver, click the Manage Sites link in the Files panel. If you don't see the Manage Sites link, open the Directory menu and choose Manage Sites from the bottom of the list.**

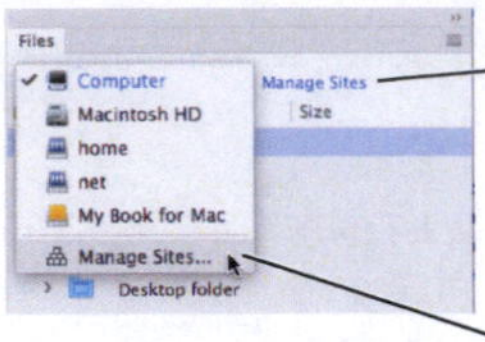

If no sites are currently open in Dreamweaver, click the hot-text link to open the Manage Sites dialog box.

If the Manage Sites link is not available, open the Directory menu and choose the Manage Sites option.

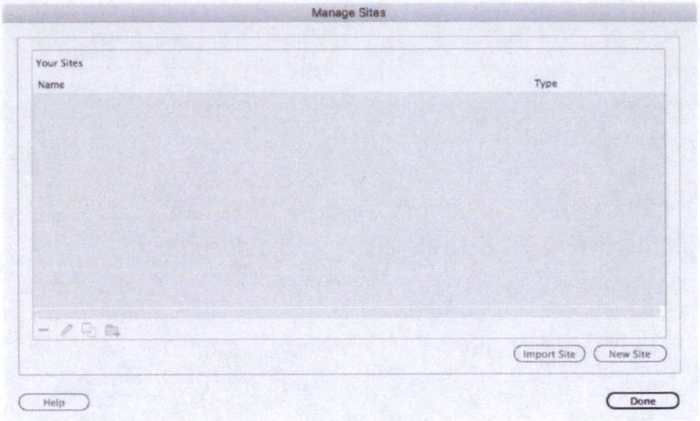

Although Dreamweaver can be used to build individual HTML pages with no links to external files, the application is more commonly used to build entire sites. The Manage Sites dialog box is used to create new sites or import existing ones into Dreamweaver. (You can also open the Manage Sites dialog box by choosing Site>Manage Sites.)

6. **Click the Import Site button in the Manage Sites dialog box. Navigate to your WIP>InterfaceDW folder, select sf-arts.ste in the list of available files, and click Open.**

The ".ste" extension identifies a Dreamweaver site file, which stores information about the site such as URL, FTP login information, etc. By importing this file into Dreamweaver, you can work with an existing site.

Note:

Depending on your system settings, the extension might not appear in your file list.

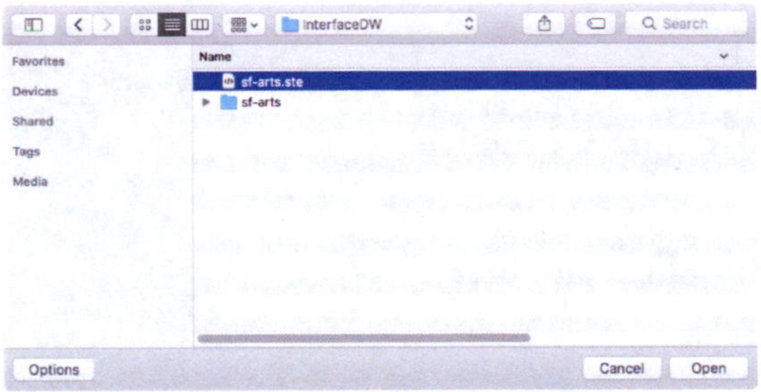

Macintosh 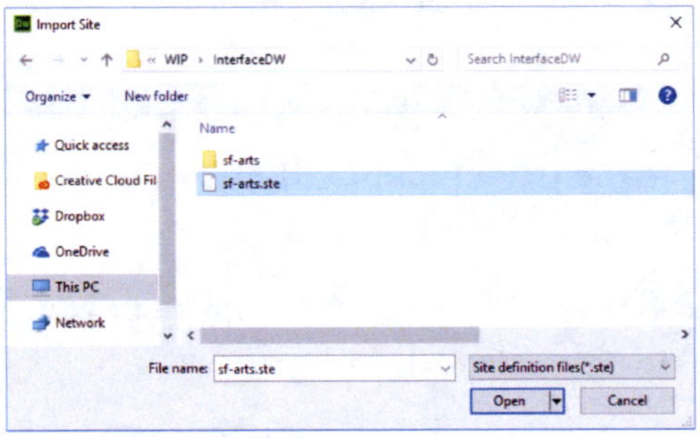   Windows

7. **When asked to select the local root folder of the site, navigate to and open the sf-arts folder (in your WIP>InterfaceDW folder), and then click Open/Select.**

The **root folder** is simply the base folder that contains the files of your site. This is referred to as the "local" root folder because it is on your computer system. When you upload site files to a web server, you place the files in the remote root folder.

Unfortunately the Macintosh dialog box does not include a header telling you what you need to do in this window. When you import an existing site into Dreamweaver, use the first navigation dialog box (after identifying the site file) to identify the site root folder.

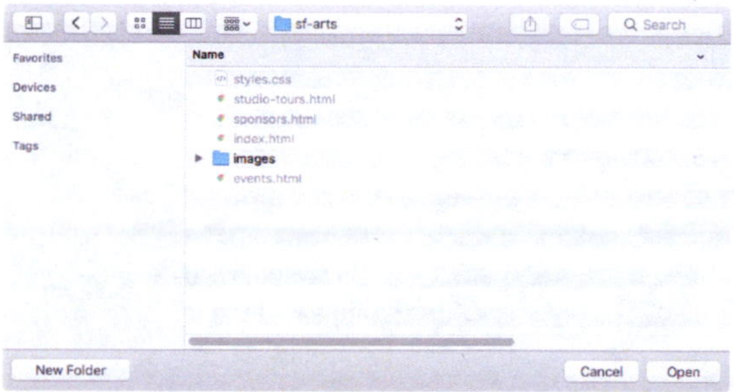

Macintosh 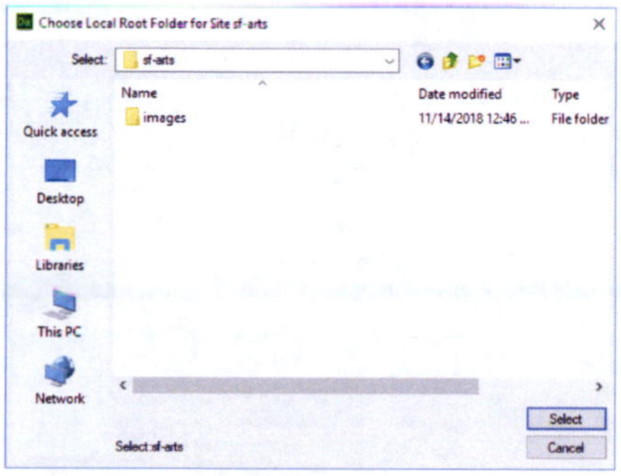   Windows

8. **When asked to select the local images folder for the imported site, navigate to and open the sf-arts>images folder, then click Open/Select.**

Again, the Macintosh dialog box does not include a header telling you what need to do in this window. When you import an existing site into Dreamweaver, use the second navigation dialog box (after identifying the site file) to identify the site images folder.

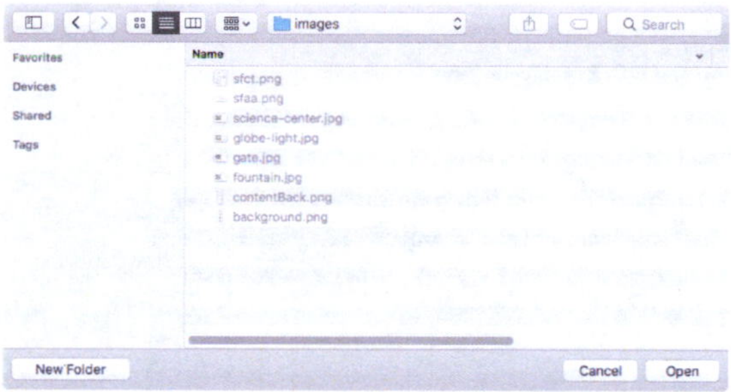

Macintosh 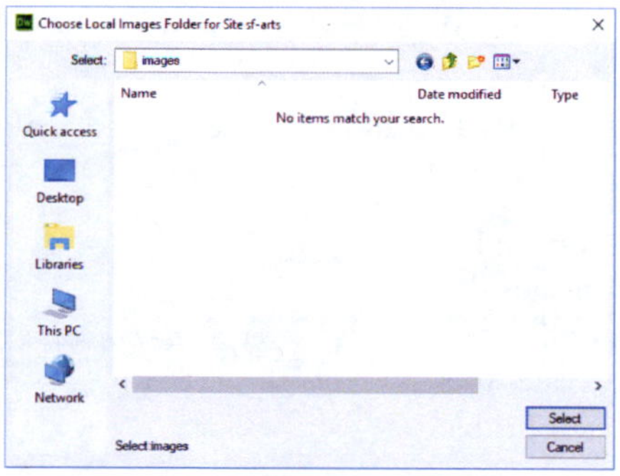   Windows

After you identify the local images folder, files in the site are processed, and then the site is listed in the Manage Sites dialog box. The name of the site (in this case, "sf-arts") is used for internal purposes only; it has no relation to the file names in the live HTML files.

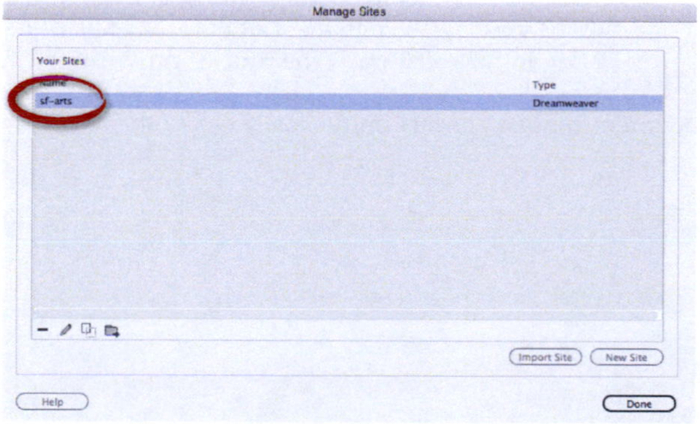

9. **Click Done to close the Manage Sites dialog box.**

A Dreamweaver site typically includes links — from HTML pages to images, from one HTML page to another, and so on — which are the heart of interactive websites. When you import a site into Dreamweaver, the application processes the files in the site to identify links and other information required to maintain the integrity of the overall site.

10. **In the Files panel, click the arrow to expand the site folder.**

The Files panel provides access to all the elements that make up a website, including page files (whether HTML, PHP, or some other format), images, downloadable PDFs, and anything else required for the site to display properly.

Note:

Depending on the number of files in a site, you might see a progress bar indicating that Dreamweaver is processing the files and creating a site cache, which helps the application manage the links between various files in the site.

Click and drag the line between columns to make a column wider or narrower in the panel.

Click any column heading in the panel to sort the files by that category.

Click these arrows to expand or collapse a folder.

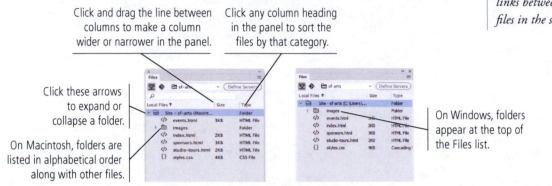

On Windows, folders appear at the top of the Files list.

On Macintosh, folders are listed in alphabetical order along with other files.

11. **In the Files panel, double-click the `index.html` file.**

Double-clicking a file in the Files panel opens it in the document window.

For Dreamweaver to effectively monitor and manage the various links to required supporting files (images, scripts, etc.), you should only open and change site files from within the Files panel. If you open and change a file outside the context of the Files panel, Dreamweaver can't keep track of those changes, which can result in broken links.

Note:

We closed all unnecessary panels and toolbars for this exercise so we could better focus on the issues related to viewing documents.

12. **Open the Window>Toolbars submenu and make sure the Document option is checked.**

Many menu commands are toggles, which means they are either on or off. The check mark indicates that an option is active/visible.

Keyboard shortcuts (if available) are listed on the right side of the menu.

This option should be checked.

On Macintosh, the Document toolbar options appear in the Application bar. An important note for Macintosh users: If you close the Application frame, the Document toolbar options do not appear, even when the Window>Toolbars>Document option is checked. This appears to be a bug in the software at the time of this writing.

On Windows, the Document toolbar appears immediately below the Menu bar.

Note:

The design for this site is based on the "Barren Savannah" template by Bryant Smith. The original template was found at www.free-templates.me, one of many online sources for web design templates that are free to use and modify to meet your specific needs.

13. Review the open file in the document window.

All open files are represented
by document tabs.

Document
toolbar options

The Files panel provides
access to all files in the site.

Related Files bar

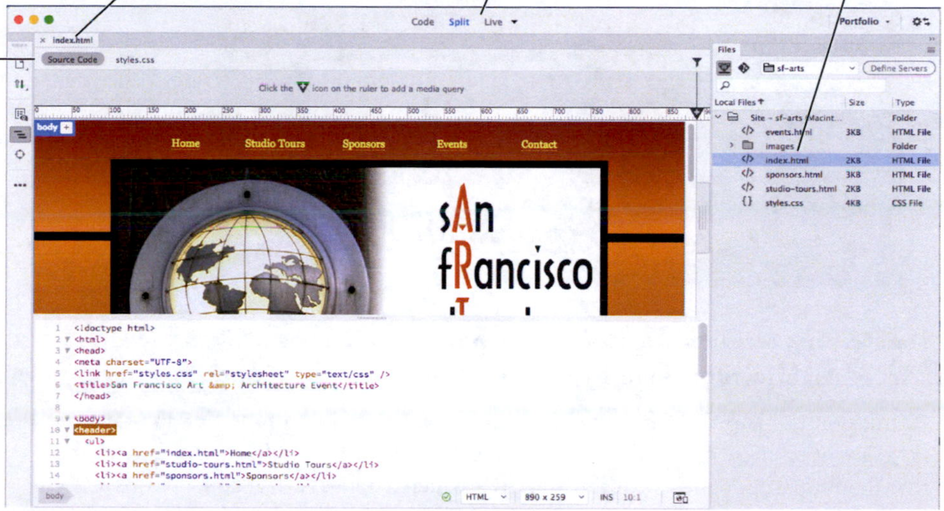

On Windows, the
Document toolbar
appears below
the menu bar.

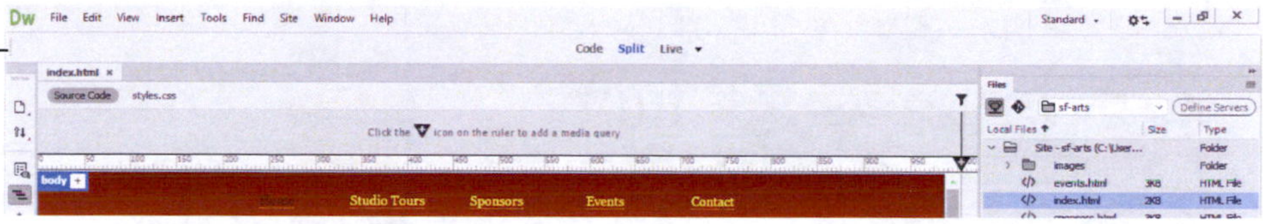

**14. In the Document toolbar, click the Arrow button to the right of the Live
button. Choose Design from the resulting menu.**

Design view is useful for visually-oriented
site design, providing a fairly accurate
visual preview of the file that is similar
to the way it will appear in a browser
window. Live view (the default) will be
explained in the next exercise.

The button shows
whether Design or
Live view is active.

Use this menu to switch
between the Design
and Live [Design] views.

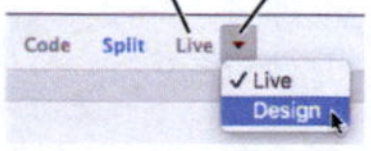

Understanding New Feature Guides

As you begin to work in
Dreamweaver, you will see pop-
up messages with tips and/or
links to videos explaining various
features. Each message appears
only once, so you will not see a
specific message twice after you
close it. To show all of these
messages again, open the New
Feature Guides pane of the
Preferences dialog box and click
the Reset button. The messages
will appear again after you restart the application.

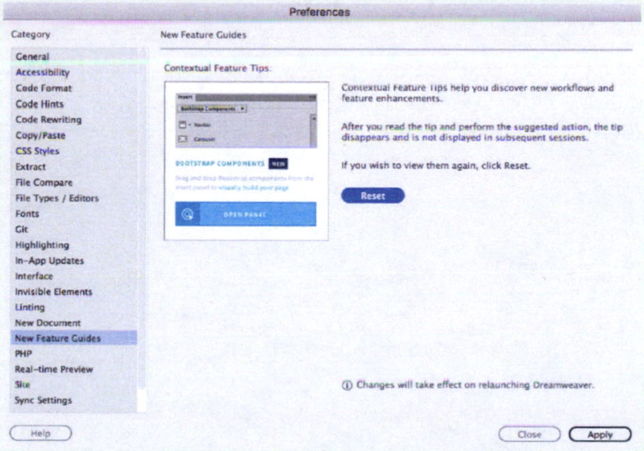

15. Click the Design button to show only the Design view in the document window.

Click these buttons to change which panes are visible in the document window.

16. If necessary, scroll down to show the bottom of the page. Click the "Art & Architecture" logo to select it, then review the Properties panel.

At this point, it isn't necessary to understand what the various properties do — you learn about all these options in later projects. For now, you should simply understand that the Properties panel is context sensitive, which means the available options depend on what is currently selected.

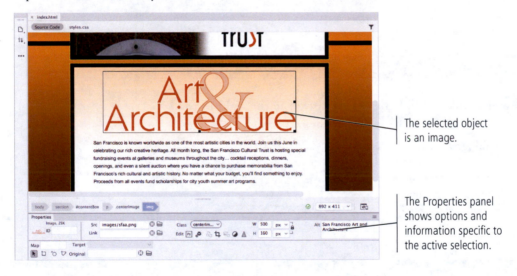

The selected object is an image.

The Properties panel shows options and information specific to the active selection.

17. **Double-click the word "Francisco" (in the first line of text below the logo) to select the entire word, and then review the Properties panel.**

Unlike many design applications, in Dreamweaver you don't have to choose a specific tool to select objects in a document.

The selected word is editable text.

The Properties panel shows options and information related to the selected text.

18. **Click the Split button in the Document toolbar.**

Split view shows both the Code and Design view windows. When working in Split view, selecting an object in the Design view highlights the related code in the Code view.

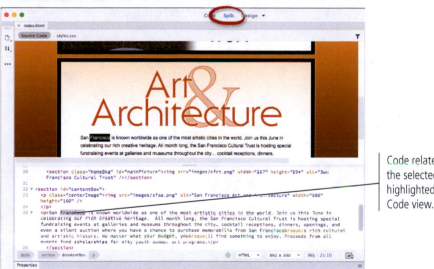

Code related to the selected text is highlighted in the Code view.

Note:

Macintosh users: Code related to the selected element might not appear highlighted in the Code view. This is a bug at the time of this writing.

Note:

You can also choose View>Split>Code-Code to show the page code in two panes at the same time. This view can be useful if you need to write code in one area that specifically relates, or refers to, code at another point in the page.

When the Split view is active, you can use the View>Split submenu to change where the various panes appear in the document window. When the window is split vertically (as it is by default), you can toggle the Design View on Top option to switch the positions of the Design and Code panes. If you choose the Split Horizontally option, you can toggle the Design View on Left option to swap the two panes.

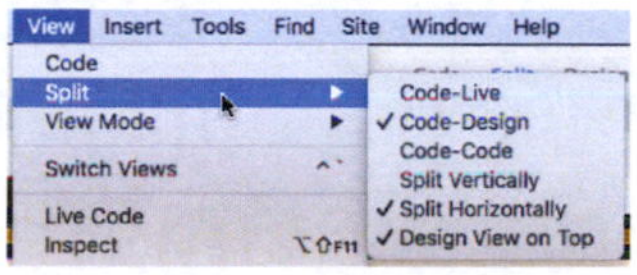

19. **Click the Code button in the Document toolbar.**

The Code view allows you to (temporarily) ignore the visual design and work solely on the code. Dreamweaver includes a number of helpful features for working directly in the page code; you will learn about those as you complete the exercises in this book.

20. **Click the Design button in the Document toolbar to return to only the Design view.**

21. **Continue to the next exercise.**

Preview Files in Dreamweaver Live View

Dreamweaver's Design view does a reasonably good job of allowing you to design web pages visually, but some common design elements, such as rollovers and multimedia files, are not enabled in the Design view. The Live view provides an internal method for checking many of these elements without leaving the Dreamweaver environment.

1. **With the sf-arts site open in the Files panel, make sure index.html is open.**

2. **In the Files panel, double-click studio-tours.html to open that page.**

Each open file is represented by a tab at the top of the document window. You can click any tab to make the associated file active in the document window.

Each open file is represented by a document tab.

Various lines indicate the boundaries of specific objects, such as each link in the menu.

3. **Choose View>Design View Options>Visual Aids>Hide All.**

Visual aids make it easier to identify the various elements (such as page divisions) used to create structure, but which do not necessarily have a tangible physical appearance. While certainly useful, these visual aids interfere with the physical layout of the site, so what you see in the document window is *not* what you get in the browser window.

This option should be checked.

Turning off visual aids is a good first step in previewing the page as it will actually appear to users.

4. **In the Document toolbar, click the arrow button to the right of the Design button. Choose Live from the resulting menu.**

5. **Move your mouse cursor over the Events link at the top of the page.**

Rollover elements do not function properly in Dreamweaver's Design view. The Live view provides a way to test interactive elements (such as rollovers) within the Dreamweaver environment.

In Live view, the rollover button displays as it would in a browser.

6. **Press Command/Control and click the Events link.**

One final reminder: Throughout this book, we list differing commands in the Macintosh/Windows format. On Macintosh, you need to press the Command key; on Windows, press the Control key.

In Live view, pressing the Command/Control key lets you click to preview linked files directly in the Dreamweaver document window.

The active file does not change even though you navigated to a link in the Live view.

Different images and text show that the Events page is visible.

7. **In the Document toolbar, open the menu to the right of the Live button and choose Design to return to the regular Design view.**

Navigating in the Live view does not technically open the linked pages. When you return to the regular Design view, the previously active page — in this case, studio-tours.html — is still the active one.

8. **Click the Close button on the studio-tours.html tab to close that file.**

Each document has its own Close button.

9. **Click the Close button on the index.html document tab to close that file.**

On Macintosh systems, clicking the Close button on the document window closes all open files but does not quit the application.

On Windows systems, clicking the Close (X) button on the Application frame closes all open files and quits the application.

10. **Continue to the next exercise.**

Preview a File in a Browser

The Live view can be used to verify the appearance of many common web design elements. Of course, site users will not be using Dreamweaver to view your pages, so it is always a good idea to test pages using the same method that will actually be used to display your pages — namely, the various browsers that are in common use.

Although there are some standards that govern the way browsers display web page code, the various browsers do have some different capabilities. Different operating systems also introduce display variables, so what you see in Google Chrome on a Macintosh might appear different than Chrome on Windows. As a general rule, you should test your pages on as many browsers as possible — on both Macintosh and Windows.

1. **Macintosh: Choose Dreamweaver>Preferences. Windows: Choose Edit>Preferences.**

   On the left side of the Preferences dialog box, click Real-Time Preview to display the related options.

   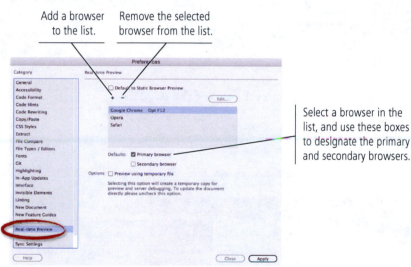

   Add a browser to the list. Remove the selected browser from the list.

   Select a browser in the list, and use these boxes to designate the primary and secondary browsers.

2. **Review the list of browsers that are identified by Dreamweaver.**

   When installed, Dreamweaver scans your computer for available browser applications. You likely have at least one browser in this list — probably more than one.

3. **If a browser is available on your system, but not in Dreamweaver, click the "+" button above the list of browsers.**

4. **In the resulting Add Browser dialog box, click the Browse button and identify the location of the browser you want to add.**

5. **Click OK to return to the Preferences dialog box.**

6. **Repeat Steps 3–5 as necessary to add all available browsers to Dreamweaver.**

Note:

The list of browsers shows the defined primary and secondary browsers, which you can invoke using the associated keyboard shortcuts. To change the defaults, you can simply select a browser in the list and check the related Defaults options.

Note:

Press Option-F12/F12 to preview a page in your primary browser. Press Command/Control-F12 to preview the page in your secondary browser.

If you are using a laptop, you also have to press the Function (FN) key to use the F key shortcuts.

7. **Click Apply in the Preferences dialog box to finalize your changes, and then click Close to close the dialog box.**

8. **In the Files panel, double-click the index.html file to open it.**

9. **Click the Preview button in the bottom-right corner of the document window and choose one of the listed browsers.**

Preview button

Note:

You can also scan the QR code with a smart-phone or tablet, or type the listed http address to preview the file directly on that device. (In this case, you will be asked to sign in to your Adobe Creative Cloud account before you can preview the file.)

10. **In the resulting browser window, click the links at the top of the page to test them.**

The Contact link on the right side of the menu opens a new, pre-addressed mail message in your default email application.

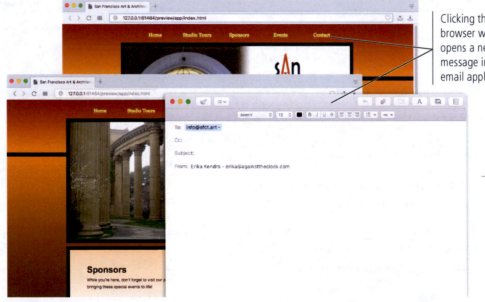

Clicking this link in a browser window correctly opens a new email message in your default email application.

11. **Close the mail message without sending.**

12. **Close the browser window and return to Dreamweaver.**

13. **Close index.html, and then continue to the next exercise.**

Note:

A mailto: link opens a new mail message in the user's default email application. If a user does not have an email client, or has not specified one as the default option, clicking a mailto: link might open a message asking which application to use to send the email.

Remove a Site from Dreamweaver

As you gain experience designing and developing websites, your site definition list will continue to grow. To keep your list under control, you can export site definitions and remove certain sites from the list. When you remove a site from Dreamweaver, you are not deleting the actual files and folders from your computer, you are simply removing them from Dreamweaver's view.

1. **In the Files panel, open the Directory menu and choose Manage Sites at the bottom of the list.**

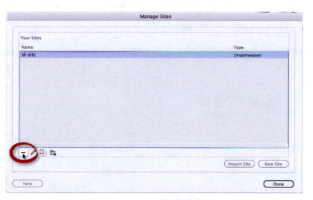

2. **In the resulting Manage Sites dialog box, select the sf-arts site in the list and then click the "–" button below the list of available sites.**

   In this case, you made no changes to the site definitions or files. Because you already have an STE file with the correct information, it is not necessary to re-export the site definition.

3. **Click Yes in the Warning dialog box, and then click Done to close the Manage Sites dialog box.**

   The site no longer appears in the list of sites.

Bistro Site Organization

5

Your client has a successful farm-to-table restaurant in a popular vacation-destination community in California. She has already designed the pages for her new site, but has hired you to make sure everything works properly and then make the site available to the browsing public.

This project incorporates the following skills:

❏ Creating, exporting, and removing site definitions in Dreamweaver

❏ Moving files around in a site root folder

❏ Creating relative links between pages in a site

❏ Defining absolute links to external sites and email addresses

❏ Improving search engine optimization (SEO) with file names and titles

❏ Cloaking site files from a web server

HOME   ABOUT   MENUS   SPECIAL EVENTS

Frank & Burgman

FRESH BISTRO

Site design by Against The Clock, Inc.

I already created the pages for our site, but I don't know which links to use, and I'm not sure how to create them. I've also heard that there are certain things you should do to improve a site's search engine rating — which is obviously important for a small business like mine.

The more pages you add to a site, the more complex it becomes, until it's almost impossible to make sense of what you have and where it is located. Websites — even those with only a few pages — should be designed with a good organizational plan, making it easier to modify pages later.

Once you have a handle on the organization, make sure the pages link to each other properly. Visitors get frustrated very quickly when they're forced to return to the home page every time they want to jump to a different set of pages.

The last thing you should do is add page titles and change file names to give a better indication of what's on each page. Doing so will make the site more accessible to people with screen-reader software, and it will also improve the site's results on search engines.

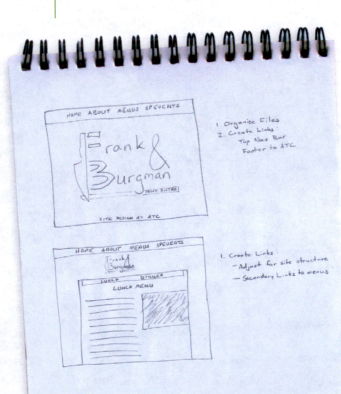

To complete this project, you will:

- ❑ Create a Dreamweaver site definition
- ❑ Create new folders within the site root folder
- ❑ Use various methods to move files from one place to another within the site
- ❑ Create links between pages using several techniques available in Dreamweaver
- ❑ Differentiate between relative and absolute links
- ❑ Copy and paste links from one page to another
- ❑ Improve searchability and usability using page names and titles
- ❑ Cloak site files to hide them from the web server
- ❑ Upload the site files to a server so they can be viewed online

STAGE 1 / Exploring Site Structure

When you start a new project that involves updating an existing site, your first task is to assess the file and folder structure. Doing so gives you a good idea of what the site contains.

A small site with only a few pages requires very little organization. In fact, you *can* place all of the files — web pages and image files — in one folder, although even a small site benefits from a dedicated folder for images. Larger sites, however, require careful organization of file names, pages, and image files. A good site design with excellent organization speeds up development now, and makes it much easier to update later.

Create a New Site Definition

Websites are designed so all of the pages, image files, style sheets, and other resources are stored on your local drive in a folder called the **root folder**. Other folders can be placed inside (below) the root folder to make it easier to manage and organize files.

1. **Download Bistro_Web20_RF.zip from the Student Files web page.**

2. **Expand the ZIP archive in your WIP folder (Macintosh) or copy the archive contents into your WIP folder (Windows).**

   This results in a folder named **Bistro**, which contains all the files you need to complete this project.

3. **In Dreamweaver, set up your workspace so the Files, Insert, and Properties panels are visible.**

   It doesn't matter which saved workspace you use. The primary tools you need for this project are the Files, Insert, and Properties panels. We have closed all other panels to maximize the available space in our screen captures.

4. **In the Files panel, click the Manage Sites link or open the Directory menu and then choose Manage Sites from the bottom of the list.**

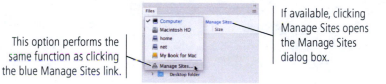

This option performs the same function as clicking the blue Manage Sites link.

If available, clicking Manage Sites opens the Manage Sites dialog box.

Note:

When a site is defined in Dreamweaver, the Manage Sites link at the top of the Files panel is replaced by a menu that defaults to Local view.

5. **Click the New Site button in the Manage Sites dialog box.**

Note:

Ellipses in a menu or button name indicate that clicking will open a dialog box. We do not include the ellipses in our instructions.

6. **In the Site Setup dialog box, make sure Site is selected in the category list.**

7. **Type FB Bistro in the Site Name field.**

   The site name can be anything that will allow you to easily recognize the project, and is only for identification within Dreamweaver. For example, you could use "Eve's site" as the name within Dreamweaver to describe the website (www.evelynsmith.biz) that you are creating for your friend.

8. **Click the Browse for Folder button to the right of the Local Site Folder field. Navigate to the WIP>Bistro folder and click Choose/Select Folder to return to the Site Setup dialog box.**

   Part of the process of defining a site within Dreamweaver is to specify a particular folder as the site root folder of the website. Clicking the Local Site Folder button opens a navigation dialog box where you can find the folder you want to use.

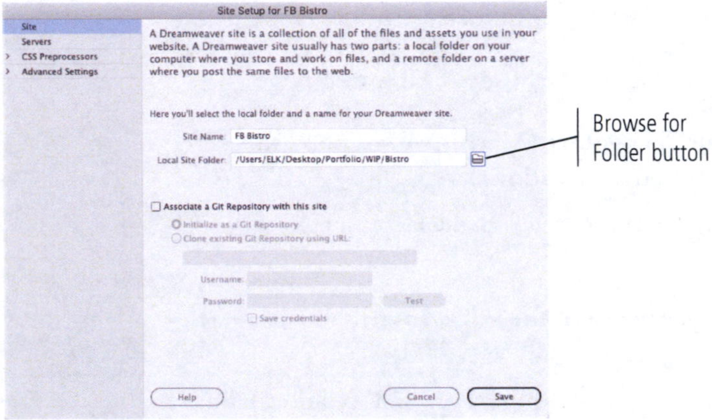

Browse for Folder button

Note:

You will learn about other options in the Site Setup dialog box later in this book.

9. **Click Save to close the Site Setup dialog box.**

10. **In the Manage Sites dialog box, make sure the FB Bistro site appears in the list of sites, and then click Done.**

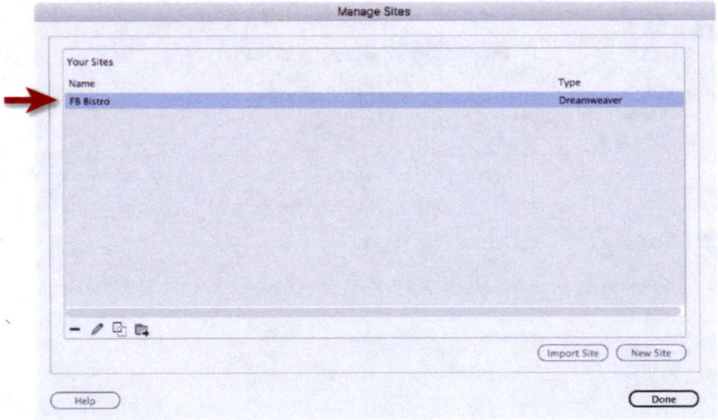

11. **Continue to the next exercise.**

Examine the Site Files

There are a number of files in the FB Bistro site folder. The first step in organizing the files is to examine the web page files and understand what they contain.

1. **With FB Bistro showing in the Directory menu of the Files panel, expand the site folder (if necessary) and examine the files in the site.**

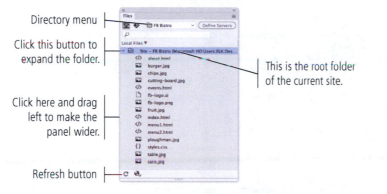

Directory menu

Click this button to expand the folder.

Click here and drag left to make the panel wider.

Refresh button

This is the root folder of the current site.

Note:

If more than one site is defined, you can switch between them using the Directory menu of the Files panel.

2. **Double-click index.html in the Files panel to open the file in Dreamweaver.**

   Using the options in the Document toolbar, close the Code pane, if necessary, and make the Live view active. The regular Design view should be turned off.

   All of the pages in this site use the same basic design. The links at the top of each page need to navigate between the pages. The site designer information at the bottom (in the footer area) needs to navigate to that company's website, which is external to your client's site.

Click this button to show only the Live view.

Choose Live in this menu to show the Live view.

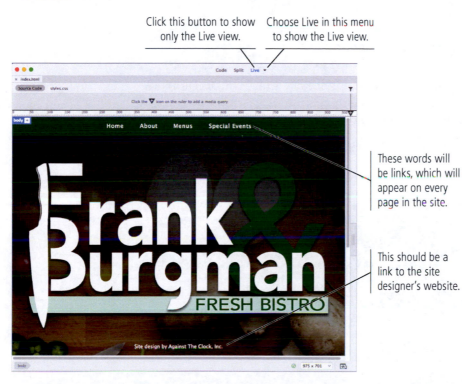

These words will be links, which will appear on every page in the site.

This should be a link to the site designer's website.

3. **Close index.html, and then open `about.html`.**

As you can see, this page uses a slightly different design than the index page, but the navigation links at the top and the footer content at the bottom are the same as on the index page. The specific page content for about.html also includes an email link, which you need to define so users can click it to send your client an email message.

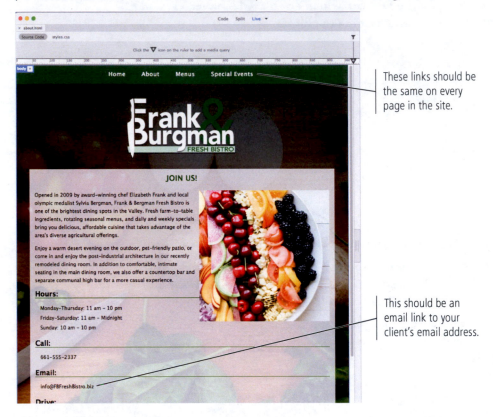

These links should be the same on every page in the site.

This should be an email link to your client's email address.

4. **Close about.html, and then open `menu1.html`.**

This page uses the same basic layout as the other secondary pages in the site. The top area of this page's primary content indicates that there are actually two menus — Dinner and Lunch. As you can see in the Files panel, two separate menu files exist. You will use the two headings at the top of the page to create links to each menu.

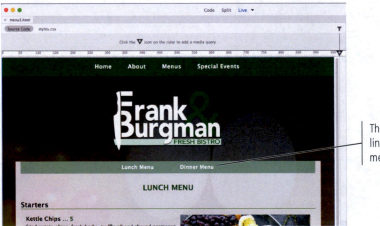

These words should link to the relevant menu page.

5. **Close menu1.html, and then continue to the next exercise.**

Plan Folder Organization

When all files are dumped into the main site folder, it can be challenging to manage your work. A well-organized site is an easy-to-manage site. Ideally, organization occurs before the site is constructed, but Dreamweaver makes it easy to reorganize files and folders at any point in the process.

There are no absolute rules to follow for organizing files and folders, other than the general principle of keeping related components together, so you know where to find certain files when you need them.

1. **With the FB Bistro site open in the Files panel, scroll to the top of the Files panel (if necessary). Control/right-click the site name and choose New Folder from the contextual menu.**

   The basic pages (home, about, contact, etc.) form the root of the site, and should, therefore, appear within the root folder of the site. Other pages are better kept in folders that are named based on what they contain.

2. **Type resources and press Return/Enter to apply the new folder name.**

   If the folder name remains untitled after pressing Return/Enter, Control/right-click the untitled folder, choose Edit>Rename in the contextual menu (or press the F2 key), and then retype the new folder name.

3. **Click the Refresh button in the Files panel.**

   When the Files panel is sorted by name, folders on Macintosh are alphabetized along with all other files and folders after refreshing the file list. On Windows, folders are moved to and alphabetized at the top of the list, above individual files.

   Note:

   Press F5 to refresh the file list in the Files panel.

On Macintosh, folders are alphabetized along with all other files in the site.

Refresh button

On Windows, folders are alphabetized at the top of the site list, above individual files.

4. **Control/right-click the main site folder again and choose New Folder from the contextual menu.**

   You want another folder at the same level as the resources folder — in the main level of the site root — so you first have to use the contextual menu for the site root folder.

5. **Type images and press Return/Enter to apply the new folder name.**

   Web design convention dictates image files be placed in a folder named "images" for easier organization. If you have many photos in various categories, you might want to create additional, nested folders inside the main images folder.

6. **Repeat Steps 4–5 to create another new folder named menus in the site root folder.**

7. Refresh the list in the Files panel.

Note:

You can create a new folder inside an existing folder (called nesting) by Control/right-clicking the existing folder — instead of the root folder — and choosing New Folder from the contextual menu.

8. Continue to the next exercise.

Sort and Move Site Files

When you define a site in Dreamweaver, the application reads all of the pages in the site (a process that can take a few minutes in a large site), notes the links between pages, and identifies which images are used in which pages. These associations between files are stored in a cache that Dreamweaver creates when a new site is defined.

When files are moved or renamed within the site, Dreamweaver recognizes that other files are related to the moved or renamed files, and prompts you to update the links in all of the affected files.

1. With the FB Bistro site open in the Files panel, Control/right-click the Local Files heading and choose Type in the contextual menu.

In addition to the file names and icons, you can show a variety of options in the Files panel, including any notes about the files, the file size, type (format), modification date, and whether the file has been checked out by another user.

Click and drag the header edge to make a column wider or narrower.

2. In the Files panel, click and drag burger.jpg into the images folder.

Make sure you drag the file directly over the name of the folder or folder icon. If you drag the file too far to the left or right, Dreamweaver will not move it.

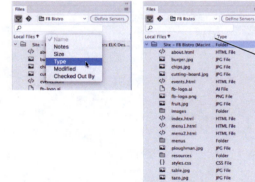

3. **When prompted, click Update to update the affected pages with the new location for the burger.jpg image file.**

When a browser downloads a web page, it reads the page code, requests the image files from the defined locations, and then displays the images within the page. You should understand that images in web pages are not embedded; they are merged into the page by the browser.

Files being updated do not need to be open for Dreamweaver to change the required link information. If pages *are* open, links in those pages are updated, but the changes are not automatically saved — you have to manually save each open file to make the updates permanent.

If you choose Don't Update in the Update Links dialog box, the image will not appear in the page that calls for that file. If you had moved the image file using Windows Explorer or the Macintosh Finder, Dreamweaver would not have been aware of the movement, and you would not have had the opportunity to adjust the path to the image file in pages that link to that image.

The burger.jpg file is now stored in the main images folder. When you move files into a folder, that folder automatically expands in the Files panel.

Note:

To avoid potential problems if you accidentally close a file without saving, you might want to close open files before moving or renaming files in the Files panel.

4. **In the Files panel, click the Type column heading to sort the site files by type.**

By default, site files are sorted by name. You can sort by another criteria by clicking the column headings in the Files panel. Sorting by type allows you to easily find all of the images that are used in this site.

5. **Click the first JPG file in the list (`chips.jpg`) to select that file. Press Shift and click `fb-logo.png` to select all consecutive files between the first and the last ones you selected.**

Press Shift to select multiple consecutive files in the panel. Press Command/Control and click to select multiple, nonconsecutive files.

You can also Command/Control-click to deselect a selected file. For example, if you select a file by accident, you can deselect it by Command/Control-clicking the file name.

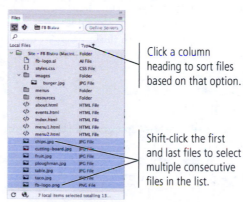

Click a column heading to sort files based on that option.

Shift-click the first and last files to select multiple consecutive files in the list.

Note:

Images in websites typically have a GIF, JPG, or PNG extension.

6. **Click the icon of any of the selected files and drag them into the images folder. When asked, click Update to update all links to all of the moved files.**

7. **Click the down-facing arrow to the left of the images folder name to collapse the folder.**

8. **Click the Local Files column header to re-sort the files by name.**

9. **Select menu1.html and menu2.html, and move them into the menus folder. Update the links when asked.**

This is a relatively small site, so nesting files in subfolders isn't strictly necessary. However, when you work with larger files, clearly organized subfolders can be extremely helpful in maintaining a site that is easy to update as often as necessary.

Note:

You can also copy and paste files into a folder using the Edit options in the contextual menus, or the standard keyboard shortcuts:

Cut: Command/Control-X

Copy: Command/Control-C

Paste: Command/Control-V

10. **Collapse the menus folder.**

11. **Select and move the file fb-logo.ai into the resources folder.**

In this case, you are not asked to update links. This is the original Adobe Illustrator file that was used to export the client's logo as a PNG file. It is not part of the actual website, but it's a good idea to keep this type of file in the site folder in case you need to make changes later. Later in this project, you will learn how to prevent this file from being uploaded as part of the site.

12. **Collapse the resources folder.**

From the folder structure alone, the website appears to be better organized. You now know what to expect when you open each folder.

13. **Continue to the next stage of the project.**

Changing the Update Preferences

As you have seen, Dreamweaver automatically asks you to update links when you move a file in the Files panel. You can change this behavior in the General pane of the Preferences dialog box.

If you choose Always in the Update Links... menu, the affected links are automatically updated without user intervention. In other words, you do not see the Update Files dialog box during the process.

If you choose Never, links are not automatically updated when you move files in the Files panel. If you do not manually correct links, they will result in an error when clicked by a user.

STAGE 2 / Organizing the Site Navigation

Hyperlinks (the official term for links) can be created to link pages on a site to other pages within the same site, or to pages on other sites. A well-designed site includes links that make it easy to get to any part of the site from any other. You should carefully plan the flow of links and connections between pages — always keeping the reader's usability in mind.

Organizing links is a simple application of a science called **information architecture**, which is the organization of a website to support both usability and "findability." As you organize site links, remember that your goal is to enable visitors to see a pattern in your links, which will assist them in navigating through your site. Keep the following points in mind when you plan a site's link structure:

- You can't know how visitors will enter your site. The primary site pages (home, about us, etc.) should be accessible from every page on the site.

- When linking secondary pages, such as different menus for different mealtimes, don't make users constantly click the browser's Back button. Links should allow users to navigate all sibling pages (at the same level) as easily as navigating the primary structure. For example, users should be able to access the dinner or lunch menus in the restaurant's site without first going back to a main "Menu" page.

Using the terms "parent," "child," and "sibling" is simply a way of describing relationships between pages. By grouping pages, you create relationships of equality between pages that are grouped together, as well as between groups that are grouped together.

When you plan a new site, you should create this type of flowchart to make sure you create all the necessary links that make the site as user-friendly as possible. A flowchart of the required Bistro site link structure is shown to the right.

In this stage of the project, you will learn various techniques to create the necessary links on the Bistro site pages.

Fresh Bistro Site Navigation

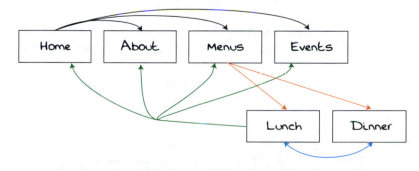

Create Hyperlinks Within the Site

Dreamweaver offers a number of options for creating the necessary links for any website structure.

- **Hyperlink Button in the HTML Insert Panel.** Clicking the Hyperlink button in the HTML Insert panel opens the Hyperlink dialog box, where you define the specific parameters of the link.

- **Insert>Hyperlink menu.** This menu command opens the same dialog box that you see when you click the Hyperlink button in the Insert panel.

- **Properties Panel Fields.** You can also simply define the specifics of a hyperlink in the Properties panel. This method offers the same options as those in the Hyperlink dialog box, but does not require the dialog box interface.

- **Point to File button in the Properties panel.** To create a link using this method, simply click the Point to File button, hold down the mouse button, and drag to a file in the Files panel; Dreamweaver automatically creates a link.

- **Browse for File button in the Properties panel.** The Browse for File button opens a navigation dialog box where you can select the file that will open when a user clicks on the link.

- **Shift-Drag Method.** You can create a link directly from the document window by pressing Shift, and then clicking and dragging from the link source to the destination page in the Files panel. This method only works for text — you can't Shift-drag to create a link for an image.

- **Quick Property Inspector in Live View.** When the Live view is active, you can use the Link button in the Quick Property Inspector, which appears attached to the selected item in the document window, to create a hyperlink.

Note:

Dreamweaver often includes several different ways to achieve the same result. You should use the method that is most efficient at the time.

1. With the **FB Bistro** site open in the Files panel, open **index.html**.

2. In the Document toolbar, click the arrow to the right of the Live button and choose Design from the menu to turn off the Live view.

3. At the top of the page, double-click the word "Home" to select it.

4. If your Insert panel is docked above the document window, click the HTML tab at the top of the panel.

    If your Insert panel is docked on the right side of the screen, or if it is floating as a separate panel, choose HTML in the menu at the top of the panel.

If the panel is in standard mode, use the menu at the top to access different categories of options.

If docked in tabbed mode, use the tabs at the top of the panel to access different categories of options.

5. Click the Hyperlink button in the HTML Insert panel.

The HTML Insert panel contains many of the common functions you use to create web pages. If a different Insert panel is showing, you can return to the HTML Insert panel by choosing HTML in the panel menu.

Note:

From this point on, we will leave our Insert panel docked on the right side of the workspace. Feel free to organize your workspace however you prefer.

If docked in standard mode, buttons in the panel are identified by icon and name.

If docked in tabbed mode, hover your mouse over a button to find its name.

The regular Design view is active.

This word is selected.

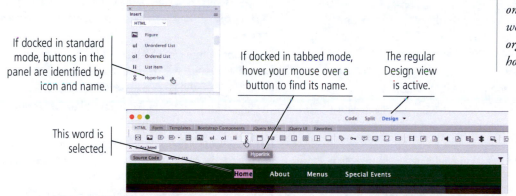

6. In the Hyperlink dialog box, click the Browse button to the right of the Link field.

The text selected in the document appears in the Text field by default. If an image is selected, this field defaults to be blank.

Text selected in the document is automatically entered in the Text field.

Browse button

7. Navigate to your WIP>Bistro folder, select index.html, and then click Open/OK to return to the Hyperlink dialog box.

In the Link field, you can either type the URL of a location outside the site you're building, or you can click the Browse button to select a file within the current site.

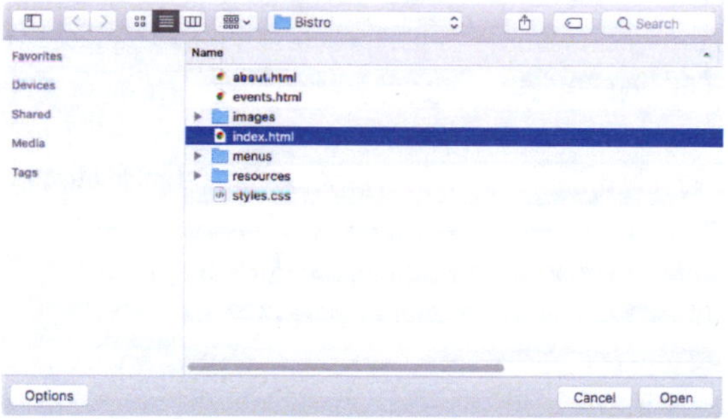

Note:

Remember, when commands are different for different operating systems, we list them as Macintosh/Windows.

The HTML Insert panel contains buttons for inserting frequently used items. Some of the terms and functions in the following descriptions will make more sense as you use those tools to complete later projects.

- **Div** inserts sections (divisions) in a page, which are useful for inserting blocks of content that you want to format independently from other blocks. You will work extensively with div tags in later projects.

- **Image** opens a dialog box where you can define the source for the image you want to insert.

- **Paragraph** surrounds each selected paragraph with <p></p> tags, which is the proper HTML structure for a paragraph of text.

- **Heading** is used to assign predefined HTML heading levels (h1 through h6) to selected text.

- **Table** inserts an HTML table into the page.

- **Figure** inserts a properly structured HTML figure, including the appropriate tags for the figure and a caption.

- **Unordered List** creates a bulleted list from the selected paragraphs. Each selected paragraph is automatically tagged as a list item.

- **Ordered List** creates a numbered list from the selected paragraphs. Each selected paragraph is automatically tagged as a list item.

- **List Item** creates a new list item at the location of the insertion point. No ordered or unordered list is created to surround the list item.

- **Hyperlink** opens a dialog box where you can create text or image links to another file, either in the same website or an external one.

- **Header**, **Navigation**, **Main**, **Aside**, **Article**, **Section**, and **Footer** add the related HTML5 tags to the page. You have the option to determine exactly how the tags are applied in relation to selected text, as well as defining an ID or class attribute for the resulting tag.

- **Meta** opens a dialog box where you define a variety of page head information. When you type specific values in the name and content fields, the appropriate information is added to the page head using the following structure:

    <meta name="test" content="123">

- **Keywords** opens a dialog box where you can define keywords in the page head. The keywords are added using the following structure:

    <meta name="keywords" content="words">

- **Description** opens a dialog box where you can define a text-based description to the page head. The description is added using the following structure:

    <meta name="description" content="Text">

- **Viewport** sets the width of the visible area of a web page on a user's device to match the width of the device screen.

- The **Script** button can be used to add code from an external file, which will be used by the browser to perform an action when the page is accessed.

- The **Email Link** button opens a dialog box where you can create links to email addresses.

- **HTML5 Video** inserts a video element, which allows a video file to be played directly in an HTML5 page without the need for external browser plug-ins.

- **Canvas** inserts a canvas element, which is a container for graphics that are created directly in the page using scripts.

- **Animate Composition** places a defined Animate composition (OAM file) into the HTML page at the location of the cursor.

- **HTML5 Audio** inserts an audio element, which allows an audio file to be played directly in an HTML5 page without the need for external browser plug-ins.

- **Flash SWF** allows you to place an SWF file created from a Flash animation. Keep in mind that SWF files require the Flash Player browser plug-in to function properly.

- **Flash Video** allows you to place an FLV file, which is a video format created from Flash professional. Again, this format requires the Flash Player browser plug-in to function properly.

- **Plugin** embeds a user-defined plug-in file into the page.

- **Rollover Image** opens a dialog box where you can define the default image, as well as a different image that will appear when a user's mouse cursor enters into the image area.

- **iFrame** inserts an iFrame element, which allows you to embed one document into another.

- **Horizontal Rule** inserts a solid line across the width of the page. This can be useful for visually separating sections of text.

- The **Date** button inserts the current date and time. In the resulting dialog box, you can choose the date format, as well as an option to update the date and time whenever the file is saved.

- **Non-Breaking Space** adds a special character that prevents a line break from appearing between specific words in a paragraph.

- **Character** is used to insert special characters, such as copyright symbols and foreign currency characters.

8. **Open the Target menu and choose _self.**

This option determines where the linked file will open:

- **_blank** opens every linked file in a new, unnamed browser window.

- **new** creates a new browser window with the name "_new". Every link assigned the _new target will open in that same _new browser window.

- **_parent** is relevant if a page includes nested frames. This option opens the link in the frame or window that contains the frame with the link.

- **_self** opens the link in the same frame or browser window as the link. This is the default behavior if you do not choose an option in the Target menu.

- **_top** opens the link in the same browser window, regardless of frames.

9. **In the Title field, type FB Fresh Bistro home page.**

The Title field defines text that appears when the cursor is placed over the link text. Defining a descriptive title for links can help a page achieve better search engine results.

Note:

You can use the Access Key field to define a keyboard shortcut for the link. Use the Tab Index field to specify the number of times a user needs to press the Tab key to select the link.

10. **Click OK in the Hyperlink dialog box to create the link.**

11. **Click the Split button in the Document toolbar to review both the design and code views at once.**

A web page is basically a page full of code. A browser reads the code to determine how to treat various elements of the page. HTML code largely revolves around tags, which tell a browser how to interpret specific objects on the page.

A hyperlink is identified by the **a** element, which starts with the opening **<a>** tag. The link destination and target are defined as attributes of that tag (**href="index.html" target="_self"**). After the link text, the closing tag (**</a>**) identifies the end of the link.

The selected text is now a link.

In the code view, the link text is surrounded by opening and closing <a> tags, which identify the text as a link.

The link destination now appears in the Link field of the Properties panel.

12. **Select the word "About" at the top of the page.**

13. **Click the Browse for File button to the right of the Link field in the Properties panel.**

    If you don't see the Properties panel, choose Window>Properties. The Properties panel's primary purpose is to review and change the properties of the selected HTML element (such as a heading, paragraph, or table cell).

The word ABOUT is selected.

Browse for File button

14. **In the resulting dialog box, select about.html, and then click Open/OK.**

The link destination now appears in the Link field of the Properties panel.

15. **Select the word "Menus" at the top of the page.**

16. **Expand the menus folder in the Files panel.**

17. **Click the Point to File button in the Properties panel, hold down the mouse button, and drag to menus/menu1.html in the Files panel.**

The word MENUS is selected.

Point to File button

Note:

You should expand and collapse Files panel folders as necessary, depending on your available screen space. We will not repeat instructions to collapse or expand folders, unless it is necessary to perform a specific function.

18. **Select the words "Special Events" at the top of the page.**

19. **Macintosh: Press the Shift key, and then click the selected text and drag to events.html in the Files panel.**

    You have to press the Shift key, and then click and drag to the link destination. If you try to click and drag before pressing the Shift key, this technique will fail.

    Windows: Use any method you already learned to link the words "Special Events" to the events.html file in the site root folder.

    The Shift-drag method does not work on the Windows operating system.

20. **In the Document toolbar, click the arrow to the right of the Design button and choose Live from the menu to turn on the Live view.**

    You should become familiar with the process of turning the Live view on or off. We will not continue to repeat these specific instructions as you move throughout the projects in this book.

    In the Live view, you can accurately see how the CSS will be rendered by web browsers.

Note:

You can remove a link by selecting the linked text or object and deleting it from the Link field in the Properties panel.

The Live view is active.

In the Live view, CSS is properly rendered.

21. **In the Design window with the Live view active, click in the footer paragraph below the client's logo to place the insertion point.**

You can place the insertion point and edit text directly in the Live view. (You might have to look closely to see the insertion point, in this case.)

When the Live view is active, the Element Display shows the active HTML element. If an element has a defined ID or class attribute, those also appear in the Element Display. You will learn about IDs and classes in later projects. In this case, you can see that the selected element is a **p** element, which is a paragraph.

Note:

At the time of this writing, a minor bug might require you to click two times (not double-click) in an element to place the insertion point.

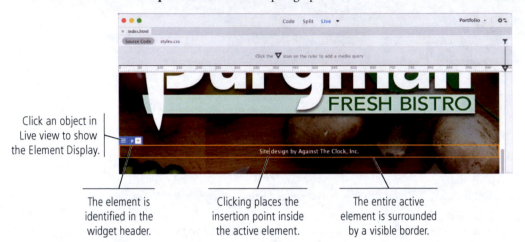

Click an object in Live view to show the Element Display.

The element is identified in the widget header.

Clicking places the insertion point inside the active element.

The entire active element is surrounded by a visible border.

22. **Click and drag to select the words "Against The Clock, Inc." within the active paragraph.**

In the Live view, the Quick Property Inspector shows options related to the selected text. You can use the B and I buttons to apply the **<strong>** and **<em>** tags (respectively). You can also click the Hyperlink button to define a link destination for the selected text.

Quick Property Inspector

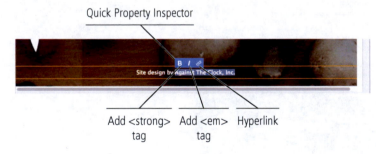

Add <strong> tag

Add <em> tag

Hyperlink

Note:

The strong and em tags are explained in Project 2: HTML Book Chapter.

23. In the Quick Property Inspector, click the Hyperlink button. In the resulting Link field, type **http://www.againsttheclock.com** as the link destination.

Dreamweaver can't help you create an external URL link because it's outside the site definition. You have to simply type or paste the address into the Link field.

An external **URL link** must begin with the "http://" protocol, followed by the domain name and, if relevant, the folder path and file name of the page to which you are linking.

Note:

To minimize the repetitive work required, we already defined this link for you on the other pages in the site. In a professional environment, you would need to add this link to every page in the site.

Clicking the Hyperlink button opens the Link field for the selected text.

You can click the Browse for File button to define an existing file as the link.

24. Press Return/Enter to finalize the hyperlink you defined in Step 23.

25. Using the Document toolbar, turn off the Live view.

26. Choose File>Save to save your changes, then continue to the next exercise.

Copy and Paste Links

Rather than manually creating the same links on every page, you can now simply copy and paste them from one page to another.

1. With **index.html** open (from the FB Bistro site) in the regular Design view, click in any of the text links to place the insertion point.

The insertion point is the location in which text will appear if you type.

2. Review the Tag Selector below the document window.

The Tag Selector, located in the status bar of the document window, shows the nesting order of HTML tags (the "path of tags") based on the current selection or the current location of the insertion point.

Insertion point

Tag Selector

Active tag

3. **Click the <ul> tag in the Tag Selector.**

   The **<ul>** tag identifies an unordered list, which is how this navigation structure was created. Each link is a separate list item (using the **<li>** tag).

   Clicking a tag in the Tag Selector selects that HTML element and all of its content. In the document window, the associated content is highlighted.

   The entire unordered list (all of the links) is selected.

   Selected tag

4. **Choose Edit>Copy (or press Command/Control-C) to copy the selected content to the Clipboard.**

5. **Close index.html and open `about.html`.**

6. **Click to place the insertion point anywhere in the list of links at the top of the page, and then click the <ul> tag in the Tag Selector to select the entire unlinked list.**

   The selected list does not yet include links.

7. **Choose Edit>Paste (or press Command/Control-V) to paste the copied content from the Clipboard.**

8. **Place the insertion point in any of the links and review the Tag Selector.**

   The Tag Selector now shows the **<a>** tag for the current insertion point (in our example, the ABOUT link). The Properties panel also shows the destination of the active link.

   The pasted content includes the links.

9. **Save the changes to about.html and close the file.**

10. **Repeat Steps 6–9 to paste the copied content (the links) into all HTML pages in the site root level, as well as the two HTML pages in the menus folder.**

11. **Save and close any open file, and then continue to the next exercise.**

Adjust Relative Link Paths

A **path** is the route taken through the folder structure to link one page to another. By default, Dreamweaver uses **relative paths** when creating links (the application refers to this as "relative to the document"). The alternative is to create **absolute paths** ("relative to the site"), but unless your site is running on a web server, you can't test links that use absolute paths.

As an example, consider creating a link from index.html to about.html, both of which reside in the root folder (as shown in the figure to the right). In this case, the source and destination pages are in the same folder. The relative-path link simply states the file name of the destination page:

<a href="menu2.html">Link Text</a>

ROOT
  index.html
  about.html
  events.html
  MENUS
    menu1.html
    menu2.html

When you drill down into nested levels of folders, the source folder is not identified in the path — the link automatically works starting from the location of the link. To link from index.html to menu1.html, for example, you have to include the nested menus folder in the path:

<a href="menus/menu1.html">Link Text</a>

When the link is in an upward direction, the ../ notation says, "go up one folder." To link from menu1.html to index.html in the site root folder means that the link needs to take the visitor up one folder level:

<a href="../index.html">Link Text</a>

Each step up in the folder structure requires another command to "go one step up" in the folder structure. If you had another level of nesting inside the menus folder, for example, a link would have to take the visitor up two folder levels to return to the main index page:

<a href="../../index.html">Link Text</a>

1. **With the FB Bistro site open in the Files panel, open menu1.html.**

   In this exercise, you are going to adjust the various links so they work properly on all pages in the site.

2. **Double-click the word HOME at the top of the page to select that element.**

3. **In the Link field of the Properties panel, type ../ before the existing link. Press Return/Enter to finalize the change.**

Type **../** before the existing link.

4. **Repeat Steps 2–3 for the ABOUT and SPECIAL EVENTS links.**

5. **Select the word MENUS at the top of the page.**

   In this case, the link is still a problem because it directs the browser to look for a folder named "menus" inside the same folder as the active page. You need to remove the folder part of the path to prevent an error if a user clicks this link from the menu1.html page.

The active file is in the **menus** folder.

This link causes a browser to look for a **menus** folder at the same level as the active file.

6. **In the Link field of the Properties Inspector, delete menus/ (including the forward slash) from the existing link.**

Delete the folder path from the existing link.

7. **Scroll down if necessary to locate the top of the main content area.**

8. **Using any method you have learned, link "Lunch Menu" (in the main content area) to menu1.html and link "Dinner Menu" to menu2.html.**

Link this to **menu1.html**.   Link this to **menu2.html**.

9. **Repeat the process from Steps 1–8 to adjust the top links and add the necessary secondary links in the menu2.html file.**

10. **Save and close any open files, then continue to the next exercise.**

    You can save each file individually, or choose File>Save All to save all open files at once.

Create an Email Link

Most websites include one or more external links — including email links — which require the appropriate protocol to tell the browser which type of link is present.

An **email link** requires the "mailto:" protocol, followed by the appropriate email address. This instructs the browser to open a new mail message with the defined address already in the To line.

1. **With the FB Bistro site open in the Files panel, open about.html. Make sure the Live view is not active.**

2. **Select the words "info@FBFreshBistro.biz" in the main content area.**

3. **In the HTML Insert panel, click the Email Link button.**

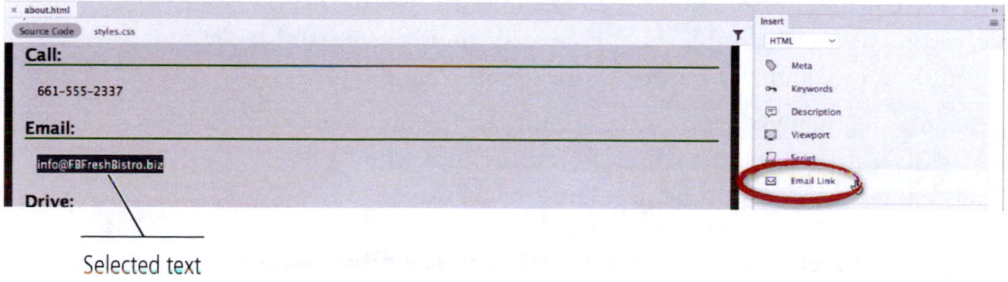

Selected text

4. **Review the resulting dialog box.**

   If you select text before clicking the Email Link icon, the Text field is completed for you. Dreamweaver also recognizes that the selected text is an email address, so the Email field is filled in for you.

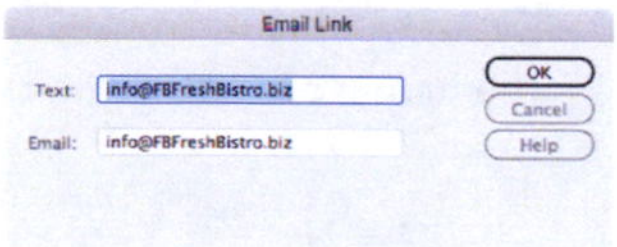

   If the selected text is not recognized as an email address, the Email field defaults to the last address that was defined in the field.

5. **Click OK to create the email link.**

Note:

You can access the same Email Link dialog box by choosing Insert>HTML>Email Link.

6. **Review the link field in the Properties panel.**

   An email link must begin with "mailto:" followed by the address. When you use the Email Link dialog box, Dreamweaver automatically inserts the mailto: protocol.

7. **Save the file and close it, then continue to the next stage of the project.**

STAGE 3 / Naming and Titling Documents

When a **web server** (a computer that stores and delivers web pages) receives a request for a folder, but not a specific page, it delivers the default page for that folder — usually named index.html or index.htm. There is no practical difference between the two extensions, and most web servers can serve files with either. (If you do not have an index file in that folder, the link will result in an error.)

To create links to the default page in a specific folder, you do not need to include the file name if you use the index naming convention. Both **www.fbfreshbistro.com/** and **www.fbfreshbistro.com/index.html** refer to the same page.

Rename Pages for Search Engine Optimization

Search engine optimization (SEO) is the process of improving the ranking of a web page on search engine results pages (SERPs). Search engines certainly use the content of a page for ranking purposes, but the names of folders and files also affect rankings.

Descriptive folder and file names improve usability. You can use **m/menu1.html** for the path to the dinner menu page, for example, but **/menus/dinner-menu.html** is much easier for visitors to understand, and will improve your search engine ranking.

In this exercise, you rename the menu pages to more accurately describe what is contained in the files. As with moving files, the application recognizes when a file name has been changed and knows that links to the page must be adjusted.

1. **With the FB Bistro site open, click menus/menu1.html in the Files panel to select that file.**

2. **Click the selected filename again to highlight it.**

   This highlights the existing filename, excluding the extension.

Note:

You can also Control/ right-click a file in the Files panel and choose Edit>Rename to rename a specific file.

3. **Type lunch-menu, then press Return/Enter. In the resulting dialog box, click Update to update all pages that link to this one.**

Typing when the file name is highlighted replaces the previous file name. Pressing Return/Enter finalizes the change.

As with moving files, Dreamweaver recognizes that all links to the renamed page need to point to the new file name.

4. **Repeat Steps 1–3 to rename menu2.html as dinner-menu.html.**

5. Continue to the next exercise.

Because different servers run on different operating systems, the safest way to name pages is to use only characters that are guaranteed to work perfectly:

• a through z (use only lowercase letters)
• 0 through 9
• Hyphen (great-site.html)
• Underscore (great_site.html)

Consider everything else to be "illegal," including:

• Spaces
• Brackets of all kinds, including ( ), [ ], { }, and < >
• Symbols, including #, @, %, &, |, *, and ~
• Quotation marks, both double (" ") and single (' ')
• Slashes, both back slashes (\) and forward slashes (/)
• Commas, periods, question marks, and exclamation points
• Uppercase characters

Some designers use **CamelCase** — uppercase letters at the beginning of each word within a file name, such as UniversalStudios.html. The problem with mixing the lettercase is that some web server software is case-sensitive and some is not. Most Windows-based web server software is not case-sensitive, but UNIX- and Linux-based web servers are. Considering that many web servers run on UNIX- or Linux-based computers, it's best to use only lowercase file and folder names.

Create Document Titles for Individual Pages

Appropriate document titles are an important concern for both search engines and site visitors. While the document title does not appear within the body of a web page, it does appear in the title bar of the browser, as the default name of the page in the Bookmarks or Favorites list, and as the page name in search-engine results pages.

Page titles should be relatively short — around 70 characters or so — to avoid being truncated in various locations (such as a user's Bookmarks/Favorites list). You should separate the components of the title with some type of divider, such as a colon (:) or pipe (|) character.

In this exercise, you add document titles to the new pages to increase search engine rankings, and improve usability in search engines and bookmarks. You also learn to use the Find and Replace function, which can greatly reduce the amount of effort required to create all of the document titles.

1. **With the FB Bistro site open in the Files panel, open index.html.**

2. **Click the Split button in the Document toolbar to show both the Code and Design views at once.**

3. **Examine the Document Title field in the Properties panel.**

   When you create a new page in Dreamweaver, the default title is "Untitled Document." That text appears in the Document Title field by default, and in the title element in the Code pane (wrapped in the opening and closing **\<title\>** tags).

Note:

When you use the Split view, feel free to arrange the pane however you prefer. We arrange them to best suit what we are trying to show in our screen captures.

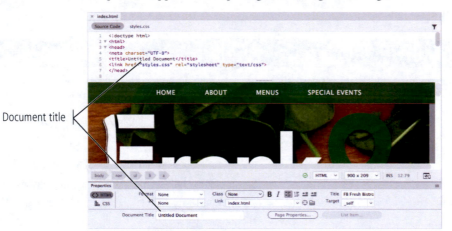

Document title

4. **Choose Find>Find and Replace in Files.**

   This command opens the Find and Replace dialog box, which offers a number of options for searching and replacing specific text.

Note:

At least one file must be open to use the Find and Replace functionality.

5. **In the Find field, type Untitled Document.**

6. Make sure Entire Current Local Site is active in the [Find] In menu.

This option allows you to affect all files in the active site. You can also search only the current (active) document, all open documents, only files in a specific folder, or only selected files in the active site.

7. In the Replace field, type **Frank & Burgman Fresh Bistro | Lancaster, California |** **. Include a space after the final pipe character.**

All pages in the site will include this block of text at the beginning of the document title. Further detail about individual pages will be added to the right of this information.

Unlike file names, document titles can use mixed lettercases and include spaces and other characters. However, you should avoid both single and double quotation marks.

Enter the text you want to find in this field.

Enter the text you want to replace it with in this field.

Note:

Some experts disagree whether the company name should come before or after the specific page information in a title. However, putting the company name at the beginning can help with search engine results, as it is an important keyword.

8. Click Replace All. When prompted to confirm whether you want to proceed with this function, click Yes.

Like most applications, Dreamweaver has an Undo function that allows you to undo the most recently completed actions; however, this function only works if the document is open. Since you are using the Find and Replace function on the entire folder, and not only on an open page, you are making changes in closed documents, which means you cannot use the Undo command.

After completing the Find and Replace function, Dreamweaver displays the results in the Search panel.

9. Examine the title in the Properties panel and the Code pane again for the open file (index.html).

As a result of the Find and Replace function, the document title has been changed. The same change has been made in all pages in the site. Because the **title** tag of the open page is active in the Code pane, the Properties panel now shows only options for that active element.

10. **Control/right-click the Search panel tab and choose Close Tab Group.**

11. **Click in the Code pane to make it active.**

    Making a specific pane active is called "bringing it into focus."

12. **Click at the end of the existing page title to place the insertion point immediately before the closing </title> tag, then type Gourmet Casual Dining.**

    You can edit the page title in the Document Title field of the Properties panel, or in the Code pane. Changes in either place are automatically applied to the other.

Type the new information immediately
before the closing </title> tag.

Note:

If you choose Find>Find/Replace in Current Document, a pop-up panel appears at the bottom of the document window with a field to define the text you want to identify and/or change.

As soon as you enter text in the Find field of the pop-up panel, all instances of that text are highlighted in the Code pane. You can use the left- and right-arrow buttons to navigate through the various instances.

13. **Save index.html and close it.**

14. **Open about.html. Using either the Code pane or the Document Title field in the Properties panel, add Hours and Contact Information to the end of the existing page title.**

15. **Save about.html and close it.**

16. **Repeat this process (Steps 14–15) to change the page titles of the remaining pages as follows:**

File	Title
events.html	Special Event Facilities
menus/dinner-menu.html	Dinner Menu
menus/lunch-menu.html	Lunch Menu

17. **Continue to the next exercise.**

Understanding Find and Replace Options

Options in the Find and Replace dialog box allow you to conduct very specific and targeted searches.

The **[Find] In** menu determines where you want to perform the search. You can search only the current (active) document, all open documents, only files in a specific folder, only selected files in the active site, or all files in the current local site folder.

You can also use the **Tag** menu to limit where you want to search. For example, you can find the text "jpeg" only within an <img> tag and change those instances to the correct extension "jpg".

The **Find Previous** (◀) and **Find Next** (▶) buttons navigate to sequential instances of the text you enter in the Find field.

You can use the **Replace** button to change the active instance of text in the Find field, or use the Replace All button to change all instances.

Clicking the **Find All** button lists all instances of the search text in the Output panel. Double-clicking an item in the Output panel navigates to that instance in the document window.

Clicking the **Replace All** button changes all instances of the Find text to the Replace text. Changes are reported in the Output panel, but changes in files that are not currently open cannot be undone.

If you check the **Exceptions** option in the Find and Replace dialog box, clicking the Replace All button opens the Search panel with a list of each identified instance. You can use the check boxes on the left to determine which instances will be changed, and then click the Replace button in the panel to replace only certain instances.

Use these checkboxes to determine which will be changed.

Click Replace to change only selected instances.

You can also click the **Filters** button (◥) to define specific parameters for a search.

- **Match Case** limits the search to text that exactly matches the case of the text you want to find. For example, a search for "Untitled Document" will not find instances of "untitled document."

- **Use Regular Expressions** causes certain characters to function as operators, so that you can search for non-specific text.

  For example, when this option is not active, a search for the period character will identify actual periods in the document.

  When Use Regular Expressions is checked, the period character is considered a wildcard that identifies any single character. A search for "p.p" would identify any instance in which two ps are separated by one other character (pop, pap, puppy, etc.).

  Possible wildcard characters include:

.	Any character (except a newline character)
\d	Any digit (0-9)
\D	Any non-digit character
\w	Any alphanumeric character or the underscore
\W	Any character, except an alphanumeric character or the underscore
\s	Any white-space character (space, tab, etc.)
\S	Any character, except a white-space character
\t	Tab character

- **Match Whole Word** restricts the search to text that matches one or more complete words.

- **Ignore White Spaces** treats consecutive white space as a single space for the purposes of matching.

  For example, with this option selected, a search for My Portfolio would return instances of My Portfolio and My   Portfolio, but not MyPortfolio.

- **Find in Selected Text** (only available in the Find in Current Document mode) allows you to search only within text that is currently highlighted in the document window.

- **Search Text Only** (available only in the Find and Replace dialog box) allows you to search only text, ignoring any code within the text. When toggled off, your search will include the source code in the document, as well.

Hide Files from a Web Server

As you learned when you created the folders for the new site, not all of the new files are meant to be uploaded to the web server — specifically, the Photoshop file in the resources folder. (You should, however, store such files locally as source files or documentation for the work you completed.) Dreamweaver provides a very useful function — called **cloaking** — that allows you to prevent certain files from uploading. You can cloak an individual file, all files with the same extension (for example, all native Photoshop files with the PSD extension), or a folder (which also cloaks all files in that folder).

1. **With the FB Bistro site open in the Files panel, open the Directory menu and click the FB Bistro site name in the menu.**

   This opens the Site Setup dialog box for the selected site. You do not need to go through the Manage Sites dialog box to edit the settings for the active site.

Click the site name in the Directory menu to open the Site Setup dialog box for the selected site.

2. **In the Site Setup dialog box, expand the Advanced Settings menu on the left side and click Cloaking to show the related options.**

3. **Make sure the Enable Cloaking check box is active.**

   When Enable Cloaking is checked, you can hide selected files and folders from a web server. You can also use the Cloak Files Ending With option to hide all files with the extensions that are listed in the field.

4. **Click Save to close the Site Setup dialog box.**

5. **In the Files panel, collapse all open folders and expand only the resources folder.**

6. Control/right-click the resources folder and choose Cloaking>Cloak.

Notice the red slashes through the resources folder icon and the icon for the file in the resources folder. The red slash refers to the cloaking function only; it does not prevent you from working with the files, adding more, or deleting any of the existing files.

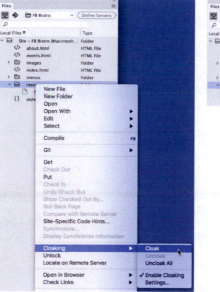

Note:

You can also cloak a specific file by Control/right clicking it in the Files panel and choosing Cloaking>Cloak.

7. Continue to the next exercise.

Export and Remove the Site Definition

To reduce the potential for confusion, it's a good idea to remove the defined sites of completed projects, leaving only those of current projects.

As stated in the Interface chapter, removing a site from Dreamweaver does not delete the actual files and folders from your computer — it simply removes them from Dreamweaver. Rather than removing a site, however, you can export a site definition file, which you can later import to restore the same settings and options you already defined (as you did in the Interface chapter when you imported the sf-arts site).

As you work through the projects in this book, you will export and remove site definitions for completed projects, so your site list remains manageable. You should get into this habit, so you can quickly reinstate site definitions if necessary.

1. With the FB Bistro site open in the Files panel, choose Manage Sites at the bottom of the Directory menu.

You can access this menu even when the Files panel is in expanded mode.

2. **In the Manage Sites dialog box, choose the FB Bistro site name, and then click the Export button.**

This function creates a ".ste" file that stores the Dreamweaver site definition settings.

3. **Navigate to WIP>Bistro and click Save.**

Macintosh users: The first time you open the Export Site dialog box, you might have to expand it to show all the navigation options.

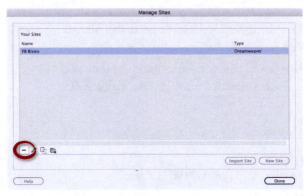

Click here to expand the dialog box.

Note:

If you have defined server information, including passwords, Dreamweaver asks if you want to include that login information in the site file.

If you are sharing site files with other users, you might want to exclude login and password information. Each user should have his or her own password and login information.

4. **In the Manage Sites dialog box, make sure the FB Bistro site is selected and click the "–" button to remove it from the list.**

5. **Click Yes to the warning to confirm the removal of the FB Bistro site definition.**

Remember, you are not deleting the files from the site — you are simply removing the site definition from Dreamweaver.

6. **At the bottom of the Manage Sites dialog box, click Done.**

Uploading Files to a Server

To make files available to other users, you must upload them to a server. When a user types your URL into a browser, the browser software retrieves the required files from a server and displays them for the user.

As a web designer, you should consider signing up for a web hosting service, both for testing your work and displaying your completed work to potential employers. Many online companies offer hosting for a low monthly fee, and some even offer a limited-time free trial for students.

Until you define a server for a specific site, the Files panel includes a Define Server button, which automatically opens the Servers pane of the Site Setup dialog box.

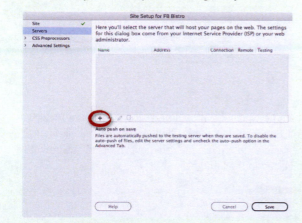

Clicking the Add New Server button opens a secondary window, where you define specific settings for your server.

Our example, shown below, uses the information required by the specific hosting company we are using. You should consult your host's documentation to learn exactly what information you should enter in most of these fields.

Server Name simply identifies the host in Dreamweaver.

Connect Using determines the type of connection protocol. For most online hosting companies, you will choose FTP in this menu. If you are using a local server, consult your network administrator for the settings to use.

FTP Address is the hostname for your server. In many cases, the FTP host is the same as the server name. Check your hosting account documentation for your FTP hostname and account information.

Username and **Password** are the settings for your specific account. If you are working on a shared computer, you might want to uncheck the Save option. You will have to retype your username and password every time you upload files.

Root Directory is the location of the folder in which you want the files to be placed. Some hosting providers require you to place public files inside a specific folder, such as public_html or www. When users navigate to your URL, they see the index page located in the designated folder.

Web URL is the URL with which users will access the site. This should generally not include any of the extra "public_html" or other folders in the Root Directory field.

You can click the Test button to make sure you have the correct information. You must receive a message stating that Dreamweaver successfully connected to the web server. If a connection cannot be established, check your entries, make sure your Internet connection is active, then try again.

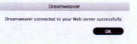

Clicking Save in the Basic Server dialog box returns you to the Site Setup dialog box. The Remote Site option is toggled by default for the first server you define. You can also define a Testing server, which is used to manage files during development, but is not available to the general public.

After you define a remote or testing server for a site, the Files panel includes a number of additional options.

A **Connect to Remote Server** establishes a connection with the defined remote server.

B **Get Files from Remote Server** copies the selected files from a remote server to the local folder.

C **Put Files to Remote Server** copies the selected files from the local folder to the remote server.

D **Synchronize with Remote Server** synchronizes files between the local folder and remote server, so the same version appears in both places.

In the Synchronize menu you can choose to synchronize the entire site, or only selected local files.

In the Direction menu, you can choose how files will be synchronized:

- **Put Newer Files to Remote** uploads local files only if they are newer than identically named files on the remote site.

- **Get Newer Files from Remote** downloads remote files only if they are newer than identically named files on the remote site.

- **Get and Put Newer Files** moves files in whichever direction is necessary, so that the latest version of each is on both the remote and local sites.

E **Expand/Collapse** shows both local files and the remote site (if one has been defined). The expanded Files panel has two panes: one displays the files on the remote or test server, and one displays the local site files.

To collapse the panel back to its normal state, simply click the Collapse button.

When you click the Preview button in the Synchronize with Remote Server dialog box, Dreamweaver shows a list of all files that will be affected by the process.

When you upload files to the remote server, Dreamweaver keeps a log of affected files. The Background File Activity dialog box shows a list of each file, including any potential problems encountered during the transfer process. Clicking the Details button expands the dialog box and shows the progression of the synchronization.

When the synchronization process is complete, the local site files appear in the left side of the expanded Files panel (the remote site). Those files are now visible to any browser connected to the Internet.

PROJECT REVIEW

fill in the blank

1. The _____ extension identifies a Dreamweaver site definition file.

2. The _____ is the primary folder that contains all files and subfolders of a website.

3. The _____ is used to view and manage files that make up a site in Dreamweaver.

4. _____ is the process of improving a page's ranking in search engine results pages.

5. A(n) _____ is a path from one file to another, beginning from the current location and moving up or down through folder paths to the target image.

6. The notation _____ tells Dreamweaver to move up one folder from the current location.

7. The _____ shows the nested order of HTML tags to the currently selected object.

8. The _____ protocol is used to define an email link.

9. _____ is the process of hiding certain files in the site so they are not uploaded to the web server.

10. The _____ pane of the Site Setup dialog box defines the settings you need to upload site files through Dreamweaver's Files panel.

short answer

1. Briefly explain why it is important to define a Dreamweaver site file.

2. Briefly explain the importance of creating a site flowchart.

3. Explain three different methods for creating a link to a page in the current site.

PORTFOLIO BUILDER PROJECT

Use what you have learned in this project to complete the following freeform exercise.
Carefully read the art director and client comments, then create your own design to meet the needs of the project.
Use the space below to sketch ideas. When finished, write a brief explanation of the reasoning behind your final design.

art director comments

Romana Place Town Homes is adding a photo tour to its website. The owner is fairly competent at building web pages, but is having trouble finalizing the new site. Your job is to finish what he started in a professional, organized manner.

To complete this project, you should:

❏ Import the site files into Dreamweaver (from the **Rentals_Web20_PB.zip** archive on the Student Files web page).

❏ Analyze the content of the different pages. Create a flowchart to map the direction of links from one page to another in the site.

❏ Organize the site folder into a clear, understandable structure.

❏ Create the links from one page to another throughout the entire site.

client comments

When I started working with our site files I noticed that none of the links exist anymore. I might have worked from an earlier version of the site files, but I'm not sure. Can you fix this for me? Other than the navigation in the middle of the pages, there are a number of other places where links are necessary:

• Users should be able to navigate between the different property pages, without going back to the main Properties page.

• There should be a link to our main information email address (info@romana-atc.biz) on every page.

• The original design company's name in the footer should link to its website.

project justification

PROJECT SUMMARY

This project focused on two of the foundational elements of website design — organizing files and creating links. A well-organized site structure includes links that make it easy for users to navigate throughout the entire site. Dreamweaver makes it easy to manage the files in a site — renaming and moving them, while maintaining the links between pages within the site. You also learned a number of ways to create links, whether to other pages in the site, to an external URL, or to an email address. The skills you used in this project will be required to complete virtually any site you create in Dreamweaver.

Define descriptive document titles

Create navigation links to site pages

Organize site files in Dreamweaver

Create a link to an external URL

Copy and paste a list of links

Create an email link

Adjust relative link paths to work on nested pages

HTML
Book Chapter

6

In addition to application-specific books, Against The Clock Inc. (ATC) has a series of "companion" titles that discuss concepts underlying the use of design software — basic design principles, type, color, and so on. You were hired to create individual HTML pages for various chapters from the Companion books, which ATC will make available on its corporate website.

This project incorporates the following skills:

❏ Adding text from external sources

❏ Working in both Design and Code views to add semantically appropriate HTML tags

❏ Organizing content with appropriate heading tags

❏ Properly formatting block quotes and citations

❏ Adding special characters that work in HTML code

❏ Creating lists and tables within text-based content

❏ Attaching a CSS file to new pages

ATC HOME   COMPANION SERIES   PROJECTS   PORTFOLIOS

> You may think that I exaggerate the importance of good typography. You may ask if I have ever heard a housewife say that she bought a new detergent because the advertisement was set in Caslon. No. But do you think an advertisement can sell if nobody can read it? As Mies van der Rohe said of architecture, "God is in the details."
>
> David Ogilvy, *Ogilvy on Advertising*

Special Characters In Typography

QUOTES AND RELATED CHARACTERS

While the typewriter keyboard constrains us to using only the prime and double prime, our computers give us access to quotation marks, apostrophes and inch marks as well.

Quotation Marks

Quotation are used to enclose the exact words of a speaker or writer; they may be used in either double or single form. In general practice in the United States, double quotation marks are used for a standard quotation, and single quotation marks are used for a quote within a quote. If the inner quotation ends the sentence, then a thin space should be inserted between the inner and outer quotes. For example, Erin said, "The Gettysburg Address begins 'Fourscore and seven years ago.' "

Apostrophes

QUOTATION CHARACTERS	
Character Description	Character
Double Curly Quotes	" "
Single Curly Quotes	' '
Double Prime (Inches or Seconds)	"
Single Prime (Feet or Minutes)	'

PROJECT MEETING

We publish a series of books that are designed as companion titles to our application-specific training books (which is why it's called *The Companion Series*). The companion titles cover general topics that are important to graphic designers — basic design principles, color, writing, and web design concepts — but don't quite fit into an application-specific book.

These books have been available for several years, but we haven't done any serious marketing of them. When we talk to people about *The Companion Series*, they ask, "Why haven't I heard about these books before?" We're hoping the sample chapters that we post on our site will help get the word out about these books and dramatically improve sales.

We want to be sure of two things: first, this web page needs to be instantly recognizable as part of our existing site, with the same layout and formatting, and second, the page must include searchable text.

The publisher sent the text she wants to offer on the site. When you have this much text on a web page — which isn't uncommon — it's very important to format it with the proper structural tags. If you use Heading 2 because you think Heading 1 is too big, for example, you're causing problems for search engines and anyone with screen-reader software.

As you know, the client already has a corporate website. To create the new page, you can use the existing CSS file that defines the appearance of the various structural elements. Once you apply the correct structural tags to the text in the new pages, you can attach the existing CSS file. This will ensure that the existing format maps to the structural tags in your new page.

To complete this project, you will:

❏ Paste text content from a text-only email

❏ Apply the appropriate heading and paragraph tags throughout the text

❏ Create block quotes and define quote citations

❏ Mark up abbreviations for improved usability and accessibility

❏ Use the correct HTML tags to show emphasis

❏ Add special HTML characters throughout the text

❏ Use a table to present well-organized content

❏ Create ordered and unordered lists

❏ Attach an existing CSS file to the new page

STAGE 1 / Preparing the Workspace

In many web design jobs, you need to create new HTML files in addition to working with existing files. The first step in any new project, however, is to define the Dreamweaver site, so the application can accurately manage the various files and folders that make up the site. Once the site is defined, it's relatively easy to create as many new files as necessary to complete the job.

Define the ATC Site

The procedure for defining the ATC site is essentially the same as it was for the site you built in Project 5: Bistro Site Organization.

1. Download `Chapter_Web20_RF.zip` from the Student Files web page.

2. Expand the ZIP archive in your WIP folder (Macintosh) or copy the archive contents into your WIP folder (Windows).

   This results in a folder named **Chapter**, which contains the files you need for this project.

3. From the Files panel, choose **Manage Sites** at the bottom of the Directory menu (or click the link, if it is available).

4. In the Manage Sites dialog box, click the **New Site** button.

5. In the resulting Site Setup dialog box, type **ATC** in the Site Name field.

6. Click the Browse icon to the right of the Local Site Folder field, navigate to your **WIP>Chapter** folder, and then click Choose/Select.

7. Click Save to accept the Site Setup definition.

8. In the Manage Sites dialog box, make sure the ATC site appears in the list of sites, and then click Done.

9. Continue to the next exercise.

Create a New HTML Document

The content for the new page was sent to you by the client in an email. You need to create a new HTML page, and then move the supplied text into the page so you can apply the necessary HTML structure.

HTML was created as a coding language used to apply structure (paragraphs, headings, and lists) to online documents. By 1996, the modern methods of document markup had outgrown the inflexible HTML, so the extensibility concept from XML (eXtensible Markup Language) was added to HTML 4.01 and referred to as XHTML.

HTML5 is the current revision of the HTML standard, and it is the default document type in Dreamweaver CC. Officially published in 2014, HTML5 replaced both HTML 4 and XHTML.

1. **With the ATC site open in the Files panel, choose File>New.**

2. **In the New Document dialog box, choose New Document in the left pane and choose HTML in the Document Type list.**

   When you create a new HTML page, the Doc Type menu defaults to HTML5 — the current version of the standard.

3. **In the Title field, type Against The Clock | Special Characters in Typography.**

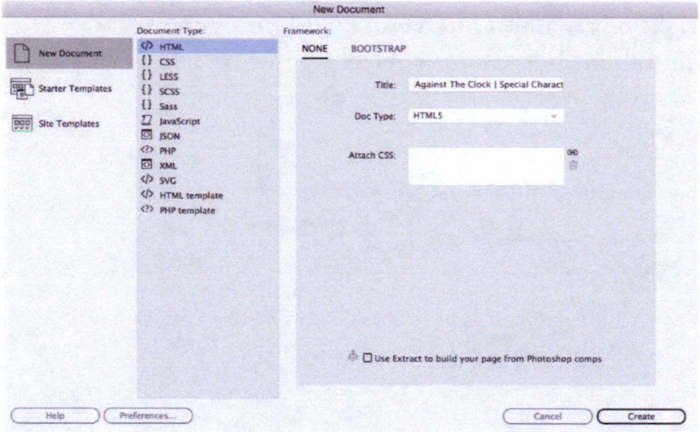

4. **Click Create to create the new blank file.**

5. **Choose File>Save As. Navigate to your WIP>Chapter folder (the root of the ATC site) as the target location and save the document as an HTML file named typography.html.**

After the file is saved, it automatically appears in the Files panel.

6. **If only the Design pane is visible, click the Split button in the Document toolbar.**

Even though the document appears to be blank in Design view, it already contains some code in the background, which you can see in Code view.

7. **Examine the code in the document window.**

The first line — <!doctype html> — is the document type definition, or DTD, which tells the browser which version of HTML is being used. For an HTML5 page — the default type in Dreamweaver CC — the doctype statement simply says "html" without a specific version number.

Content within the **head** element — between the opening **<head>** and closing **</head>** tags — is not visible to the user, except for the content enclosed in the **<title>** tags, which appears in the title bar of a browser, as the title of a bookmark, and as the text in search engine results. Visible web page content is created within the body section, between the opening **<html><body>** and closing **</body></html>** tags.

Document Type Definition (DTD)

Opening <html> tag

Opening <head> tag

Closing <head> tag

Opening and closing <body> tags

Closing <html> tag

```
1  <!doctype html>
2  <html>
3  <head>
4  <meta charset="UTF-8">
5  <title>Against The Clock | Special Characters in Typography</title>
6  </head>
7
8  <body>
9  </body>
10 </html>
11
```

There is no content in the <body> element of this HTML document, so nothing appears in the Design pane.

Note:

Feel free to use whichever Split mode you prefer in your workspace.

8. **Continue to the next stage of the project.**

STAGE 2 / Working with Semantic Markup

Many documents, including those created in word processing applications, like Microsoft Word, are not properly structured by their authors. The user enters text, and then applies **local formatting**, such as bold type style or a larger font size to make certain text appear as headings, subheadings, and so on. While this kind of formatting makes text look readable to human users, these documents have no structure that makes sense to a computer — specifically, not to a web server or search engine.

Properly structured HTML documents use tags to identify various types of text, called **semantic markup**. Semantic markup provides a wide range of benefits: it is more accessible, it loads quickly in a browser, it reduces bandwidth cost for high-traffic websites, it achieves higher search-engine rankings, and it is easy to style. As a web designer, you should take full advantage of these benefits by properly structuring HTML documents. Dreamweaver makes it easy to do this.

Paste Text Content in Design View

HTML is a coding language that defines the structure of elements in a page. Web browsers depend on the structural markup of HTML to properly display a web page, so headings stand out from regular text and paragraphs are separated from one another. Without structure, all text on a page would appear as a single, large block of text.

Clients often supply content as plain-text without structural markup (paragraph returns do not qualify as structure). When people read text that doesn't have structural markup, they are able to make logical inferences about the intended structure — for example, they can assume that a short block of text is a heading and a long block is a paragraph. Browsers, however, can't make assumptions — they require structure to correctly display content.

Although not all lines in a text document are paragraphs (some are headings and some are list items, for example), marking up each line as a paragraph provides a starting point that you can modify later.

> **Note:**
>
> *Web browsers (and Dreamweaver) ignore extra spaces between words and paragraph returns between lines of text. Properly displaying web page text requires structural markup.*

1. **With typography.html (from the ATC site) open in Split view, make the regular Design view active (turn off the Live view).**

2. **Double-click typography.txt in the Files panel to open that file.**

   Text (.txt) files only appear in Code view because there is no "design."

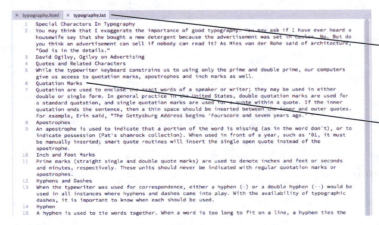

Each open file is accessible in a separate tab.

Although there are smaller and larger blocks of text, there are no codes or styles to separate headings from paragraphs.

3. **Choose Edit>Select All, and then copy the selected content to the Clipboard.**

   Choose Edit>Copy or press Command/Control-C to copy the selected text.

4. **Close typography.txt.**

5. **In typography.html, click to place the insertion point in the Design pane, and then paste the copied text into the Design pane.**

   If you pasted the text into the Code pane, the line-break characters would not be included. You will use those bits of codes in the next few steps to apply the proper structure to the paragraphs of text.

Note:

Press Command/Control-A to select all content in an open file or document.

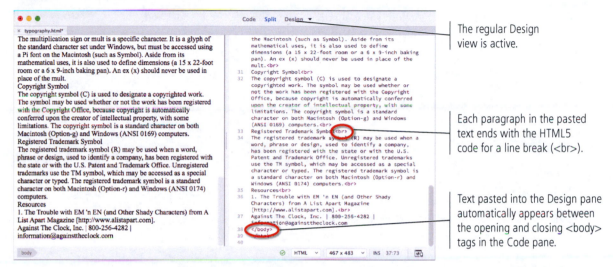

The regular Design view is active.

Each paragraph in the pasted text ends with the HTML5 code for a line break (<br>).

Text pasted into the Design pane automatically appears between the opening and closing <body> tags in the Code pane.

6. **Press Command/Control-A to select all the text in the Design pane, and then choose Paragraph in the Format menu of the Properties panel.**

   An HTML paragraph is surrounded by opening **<p>** and closing **</p>** paragraph tags. Because the paragraphs of pasted text are separated by the code for a forced line break (**
**), the entire block of copy is treated as a single paragraph.

   When you apply the paragraph structure to the selected text, the entire block is surrounded by a single set of paragraph tags in the Code pane.

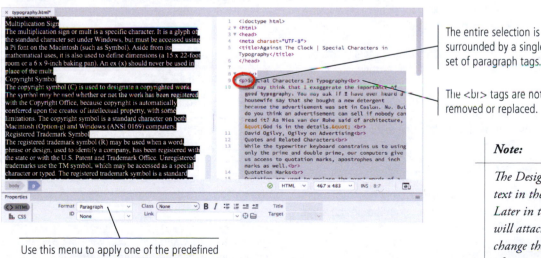

The entire selection is surrounded by a single set of paragraph tags.

The <br> tags are not removed or replaced.

Use this menu to apply one of the predefined structural tags to the selected text.

Note:

The Design pane shows text in the default font. Later in this project, you will attach a CSS file to change the formatting of various elements in the file.

7. **Choose Find>Find and Replace in Files.**

8. **Choose Current Document in the [Find] In menu.**

9. **In the Find field, type `<br>`. In the Replace field, type `</p><p>`.**

    Do not press Return/Enter when typing in the Replace field because the dialog box will prematurely run the Find and Replace operation.

    Each line in the text currently ends with the line-break tag (**`<br>`**) when it should end with a closing paragraph tag (**`</p>`**). Each line should also begin with the opening paragraph tag (**`<p>`**), where nothing currently exists.

    Using the search and replace function, you can remove all of the line-break codes and place the necessary closing and opening paragraph tags in a single click.

Note:

You cannot undo a Find and Replace in documents that are not open. When doing a Find and Replace that includes files that aren't currently open, you might want to back up the site's root folder outside of Dreamweaver before continuing.

10. **Click Replace All.**

11. **Review the Search panel, and then close the tab group.**

Understanding Element Names, Tags, and Attributes

The **element name** is the text that identifies the tag, such as meta, title, head, or body.

A **tag** consists of the element name, surrounded by angle brackets, such as <head> or <body>.

An **element** is the tag plus its containing content, such as the title element <title>Untitled Document</title>.

Container tags consist of an opening tag (<title>) and a closing tag (</title>). The closing tag is the same as the opening tag, with the addition of the initial forward slash. For example:

    <title>"Weather Forecast"</title>

Empty tags do not have a separate closing tag. In an empty tag, the closing forward slash appears with the closing angle bracket of the tag. For example:

    <img src="sun.gif" alt="sunny day" />

Attributes add properties to HTML elements. For example, the id attribute defines a unique identity for an HTML element. Attributes appear in the opening tag only; they consist of the attribute name and the attribute value in quotation marks:

    <section id="sidebar-right">Content here</id>

In this example, the attribute name is id and the attribute value is "sidebar-right".

Some attributes, such as the id attribute, are optional. Some are required, such as the alt attribute, which describes the content of an <img> tag for visually impaired visitors.

A third type of attribute is a **boolean** attribute, which does not require a value. Simply placing this type of attribute in an opening tag makes it active:

    <p hidden>You can't see me!</p>

In the example here, the paragraph will not be visible in the browser window because the hidden attribute is present in the opening <p> tag.

12. **Click the Refresh button in the Properties panel if necessary, and then review the results in both panes of the document window.**

In many cases, changes in the Code pane are automatically reflected in the Design pane. If the changes do not automatically take effect (as in the case

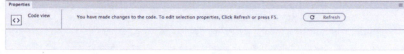

of changing the page code using the Find and Replace dialog box), you can use several techniques to manually refresh the Design view:

- Click the Refresh button in the Properties panel.
- Press F5.
- Simply click in the Design pane to bring it into focus, and refresh at the same time.

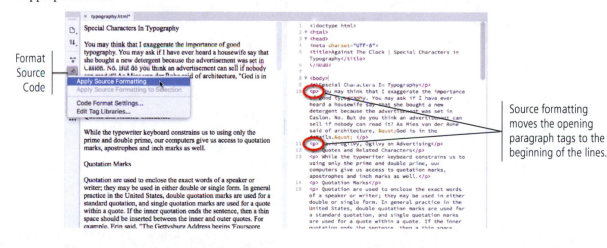

After refreshing the Design view, each paragraph in the Design pane is now separated.

The closing and opening paragraph tags replace the <br> code at the end of each paragraph.

13. **Choose Window>Toolbars>Common to open the Common toolbar (if it is not already open).**

14. **Make sure the insertion point is placed in the Code pane. Click the Format Source Code button in the Common toolbar and choose Apply Source Formatting from the menu.**

This command cleans up the code, moving the opening **<p>** tags to the beginning of each line of copy. Nothing changes in the Design pane when the tags are moved to the appropriate lines.

Source formatting moves the opening paragraph tags to the beginning of the lines.

15. **Save the file and continue to the next exercise.**

Formatting Text with the Properties Panel

You can use the Properties panel in HTML mode to view and modify a number of different properties for selected text:

- The **Format** menu contains the default HTML paragraph and heading styles. The Preformatted option lets you include more than one space between words and does not automatically wrap the contents.

- The **ID** menu contains the list of IDs defined in the page or the attached style sheet.

- The **Class** menu contains the list of defined style classes in the related CSS.

- The **Link** field displays the URL to which the selected text is linked. You can use the Point to File and Browse for File buttons to identify link targets.

- You can use the **B** and **I** buttons to apply the <strong> and <em> tags (respectively).

- The **Unordered List** button formats selected paragraphs as items in a bulleted list.

- The **Ordered List** button arranges the paragraphs in a numbered list.

- The **Remove Blockquote** button removes the indent (and blockquote tags) from selected paragraphs.

- The **Blockquote** button indents paragraphs, wrapping those paragraphs in the opening and closing <blockquote> tags.

- The **Title** field specifies the textual tool tip for a text link.

- The **Target** menu determines where a linked file opens (new window, parent frame, etc.).

Format Headings in Design View

Headings help readers (both human and digital) find the information they need. Screen-reading software and some browsers enable users to skip forward and backward through headings. Also, when reviewing the content of a page and its relevance to a particular topic, search engine software uses headings and heading levels (among other criteria) to make evaluations. For these reasons, it is important to use properly structured headings rather than styled paragraphs.

There are six predefined heading levels in HTML: **<h1>**, **<h2>**, **<h3>**, and so on to **<h6>**. Heading level 1 is the largest and most important; it should be used only once per page to describe the purpose or title of the web page. The rest of the headings can be used multiple times, but they should be used in a branch-like pattern, or hierarchy.

Many new web designers complain that heading level 1 appears too large, so they apply heading level 2 or 3, instead. This is a mistake. In a later project, you will learn to use cascading style sheets (CSS) to define the appearance of different elements on a web page — including different levels of headings.

The special characters described in the text in this project are divided into related groups and subgroups. Your task is to determine which heading level is appropriate for each section. In professional situations, some client-supplied copy will be well-written and well-formatted, enabling you to quickly determine appropriate heading levels, called **editorial hierarchy** or **editorial priority**. Other copy will be poorly structured and difficult to decipher; in such a case, you will need to contact the author for clarification or make a best-guess assessment yourself.

1. **With `typography.html` (from your ATC site) open in Split view, click in the Design pane to place the insertion point in the first paragraph.**

   You should be working with the paragraph "Special Characters In Typography."

2. **In the Properties panel, open the Format menu and choose Heading 1.**

   In the Code pane, the opening and closing **\<p\>** tags automatically change to the **\<h1\>** tags that identify the paragraph as heading level 1.

The \<p\> tags are replaced by the appropriate heading tags (\<h1\> and \</h1\>).

> **Note:**
>
> When you're working in Design view, you can apply paragraph structure and heading levels by choosing from the Format>Paragraph Format menu, or in the Heading menu of the HTML Insert panel.

3. **Move the insertion point to the "Quotes and Related Characters" paragraph and use the Properties panel Format menu to apply the Heading 2 tag.**

   After choosing a format in the Properties panel, the Code pane shows that the **\<p\>** and **\</p\>** tags have been replaced with **\<h2\>** and **\</h2\>** tags, respectively.

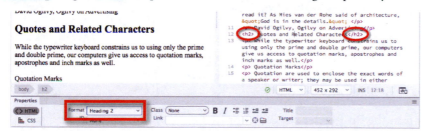

> **Note:**
>
> You can also use keyboard shortcuts to apply common tags:
>
> *Paragraph*
> Command/Control-Shift-p
>
> *Heading 1*
> Command/Control-1
>
> *Heading 2*
> Command/Control-2
>
> *Heading 3*
> Command/Control-3
>
> *Heading 4*
> Command/Control-4
>
> *Heading 5*
> Command/Control-5
>
> *Heading 6*
> Command/Control-6

4. **Using the same technique from Step 3, format "Quotation Marks," "Apostrophes," and "Inch and Foot Marks" as Heading 3.**

5. Apply heading levels to the rest of the document as follows:

Code Line	Content	Heading Level
20	Hyphens and Dashes	2
22	Hyphen	3
24	En Dash	3
26	Em Dash	3
28	Special Characters	2
29	Multiplication Sign	3
31	Copyright Symbol	3
33	Registered Trademark Symbol	3
35	Resources	2

6. Save the file and continue to the next exercise.

Format a Blockquote and Inline Quote

The **blockquote element** formats a quotation as a block of text that is indented from the left and right margins, with extra white space above and below it. The blockquote element requires at least one paragraph element to be nested within it.

The **q element** defines a short quotation, commonly appearing inline with other text, and therefore, called an "inline quote."

The **cite element** can be used to define the name of a work (book, movie, etc.). This should not be confused with the cite attribute of the blockquote and q elements. The **cite attribute** defines the source of a quote for screen-reading software.

1. With **typography.html** open in Split view, make the Design pane active. Select the first and second paragraphs immediately below the heading 1 text (from "You may think..." to "...on Advertising").

2. Click the Blockquote button in the Properties panel to apply the blockquote element to the selected paragraph.

   In the Design pane, the blockquote has been indented from the left and right margins. The first **<p>** tag appears after the opening **<blockquote>** tag and the second closing **</p>** tag appears before the closing **</blockquote>** tag. The **<p>** tags have been nested within the **<blockquote>** tag.

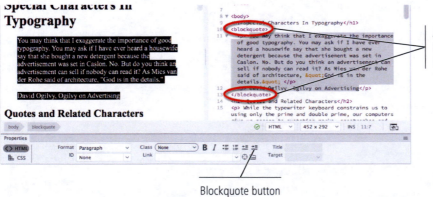

A single set of blockquote tags encloses both selected paragraphs.

Blockquote button

3. **Select "Ogilvy on Advertising" at the end of the second paragraph in the blockquote.**

    Remember, the cite element defines the source of a quote. This is the actual title of a work, not the author's name.

4. **Control/right-click the selected text in the Design pane and choose Wrap Tag from the contextual menu.**

    The Wrap Tag command opens the Quick Tag Editor, which allows you to temporarily work with code while still working in Design view.

Note:

You can also open the Quick Tag Editor by pressing Command/Control-T.

5. **Type cit.**

    As you type the code in the Quick Tag Editor, Dreamweaver provides Code Hints (a list of HTML tags) to assist you. The Code Hint list scrolls to the first HTML tag beginning with the letters "cit" — cite, which is the tag you want.

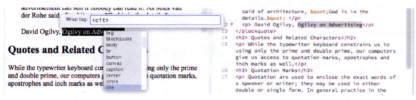

6. **Press Return/Enter to choose cite from the list of tags.**

    When a Code Hint menu is visible, pressing Return/Enter applies the item that is highlighted in the list.

7. **Press Return/Enter again to apply the cite tags to the selected text.**

    The default appearance of cite element text is italic. As you can see in the Code pane, using the Quick Tag Editor automatically adds the appropriate opening and closing tags, wrapped around the text that was selected (hence, the menu command, "Wrap Tag").

Opening and closing cite tags are added around the selected text.

8. **In the Design pane, select the words "God is in the details." at the end of the first paragraph in the blockquote. Include the period, but not the quotation marks.**

9. **Control/right-click the selected text and choose Wrap Tag in the contextual menu.**

10. **In the Quick Tag Editor, type q. Press Return/Enter to accept the q tag, then press Return/Enter again to add the tag around the selected text.**

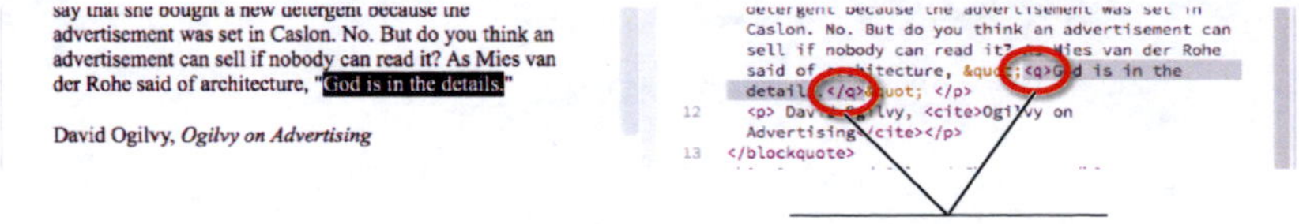

Opening and closing q tags are added around the selected text.

11. **Using the Document toolbar, turn on the Live view.**

As you can see in the Design pane, the q element adds quotation marks around the tag content. This means that the quotation marks included in the actual text are unnecessary.

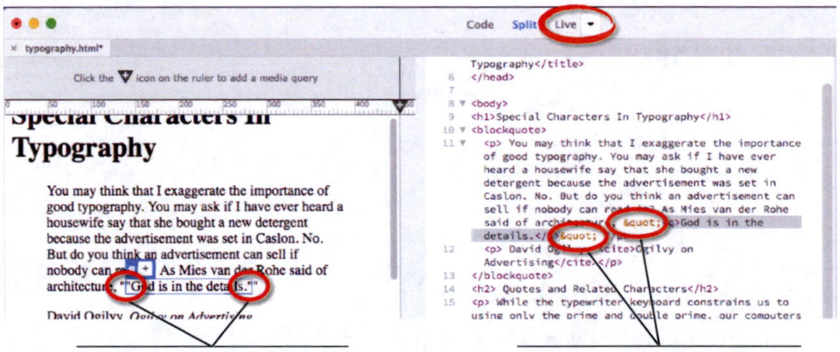

The q element adds quotation marks around the tag content.

This code adds the unnecessary quotation mark characters.

All current browsers automatically place quotation marks around q element text, eliminating the need to insert them as characters in the page content. However, different browsers use different types of quotes (straight quotes vs. curly quotes).

12. **In the Code pane, delete the code for the quote characters (") from around the "God is in the details." text.**

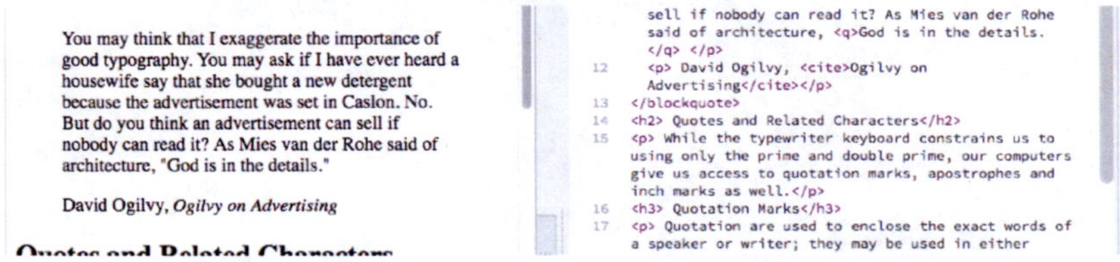

13. **Turn off the Live view, then save the file and continue to the next exercise.**

Mark up Abbreviations in Code View

Both abbreviations and acronyms are shortened forms of words or phrases. If you spell out the short form, such as HTML, it is an abbreviation. If you pronounce it like a word, such as NATO, it is an acronym. HTML5 uses the **abbr** element for both of these types of text.

The title attribute plays a useful role in the **abbr** element. Any text you insert into the title attribute — for example, the full text of the abbreviation or acronym — appears as a tool tip when you hover the mouse over the titled element. People who use screen-reader software also benefit from the title attribute because the software can be set up to read the title text in place of the abbreviation.

In this exercise, you will type directly in the Code pane, using Dreamweaver's code hints to add the necessary tags and attributes.

1. **With typography.html open, open the Preferences dialog box (in the Dreamweaver menu on Macintosh or the Edit menu on Windows).**

2. **Click in the left column to show the Code Hints preferences. On the right side of the dialog box, choose the After Typing "</" radio button.**

   Code hints display by default when you type code in Dreamweaver. You can use the Code Hints pane of the Preferences dialog box to control how code hints display.

   The Close Tags options can be used to close tags automatically:

   - If **After Typing "</"** is checked, the nearest open tag closes when you type the forward slash after the opening carat. This option is selected by default.

   - If **After Typing the Open Tags ">"** is checked, Dreamweaver automatically closes a tag as soon as it opens.

   - Select **Never** if you don't want tags to close automatically.

   You can disable code hints by deselecting the Enable Code Hints check box.

3. **Click Apply, then click the Close button to dismiss the Preferences dialog box.**

4. **In the Design pane, select "ANSI" in the paragraph following the Copyright Symbol heading.**

   The text selected in the Design pane is also selected in the Code pane. This is a useful way to locate specific text in code (or vice versa).

Copyright Symbol

The copyright symbol (C) is used to designate a copyrighted work. The symbol may be used whether or not the work has been registered with the Copyright Office, because copyright is automatically conferred upon the creator of intellectual property, with some limitations. The copyright symbol is a standard character on both Macintosh (Option-g) and Windows (ANSI) 0169) computers.

Registered Trademark Symbol

```
      mult.</p>
33   <h3> Copyright Symbol</h3>
34 ▼ <p> The copyright symbol (C) is used to designate a
      copyrighted work. The symbol may be used whether or
      not the work has been registered with the Copyright
      Office, because copyright is automatically conferred
      upon the creator of intellectual property, with some
      limitations. The copyright symbol is a standard
      character on both Macintosh (Option-g) and Windows
      (ANSI) 0169) computers.</p>
35   <h3> Registered Trademark Symbol</h3>
36   <p> The registered trademark symbol (R) may be used
```

5. In the Code pane, click to place the insertion point before the ANSI text, and then type `<ab`.

The abbr tag is selected in the code hint list.

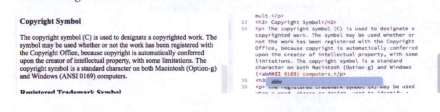

6. Press Return/Enter to accept abbr.

By pressing Return/Enter, you select the **<abbr>** tag. Once you add the tag, the insertion point flashes after it, where you can enter attributes of the new tag.

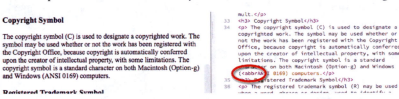

7. Press the Spacebar, and then type `t`.

Inserting a space after the abbr element name within the tag prompts Dreamweaver to open code hints and present a list of valid attributes for the current tag.

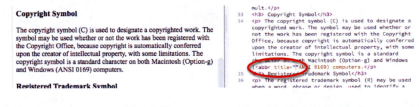

8. Press Return/Enter to accept the title attribute.

When you select the attribute in the code hint list, Dreamweaver follows the attribute with =" " and places the insertion point between the two quotation marks, so you can immediately type a value for the attribute.

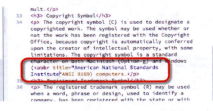

9. Type American National Standards Institute between the quotation marks.

Attribute values must always be surrounded by quotation marks.

Note:

All current browsers display title text as a tool tip when the mouse hovers over the element text.

10. **Move the insertion point to the right of the closing quotation mark and type > to close the tag.**

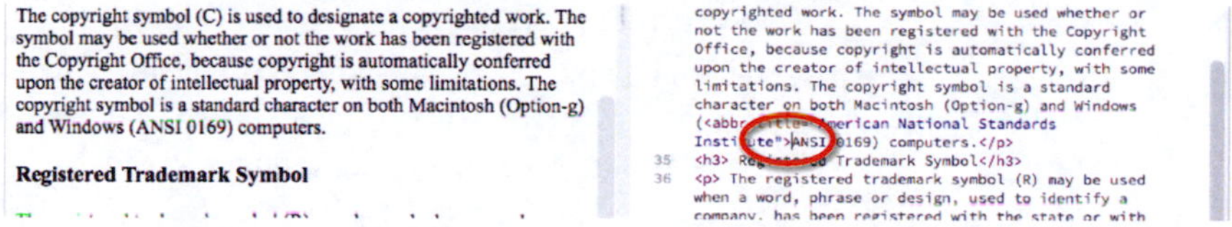

11. **Move the insertion point to the right of the text "ANSI," then type </.**

In opening tags, the HTML element name is specified between opening and closing angle brackets. In closing tags, the forward slash precedes the element name.

This step shows you another of Dreamweaver's code assistance functions, which is to automatically close the nearest unclosed tag when you type "</". In this case, Dreamweaver closes the abbr tag for you.

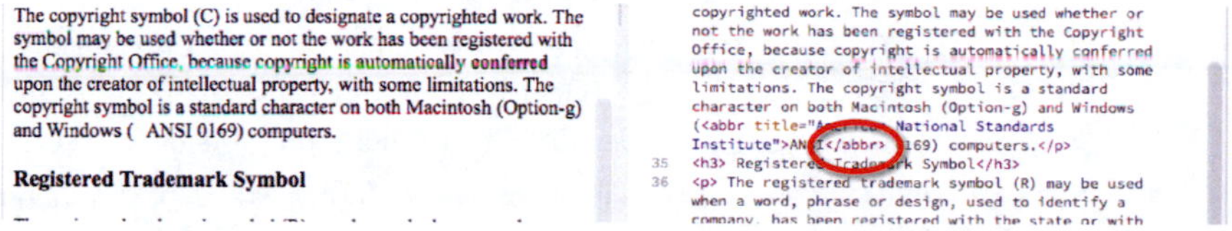

12. **In the Code pane, click in the opening <abbr> tag to place the insertion point.**

When the insertion point is placed in an opening tag in the Code pane, the application automatically highlights all code related to that tag, including the associated closing tag (in this case, </abbr>). Notice, however, that text contained in the tag is not highlighted.

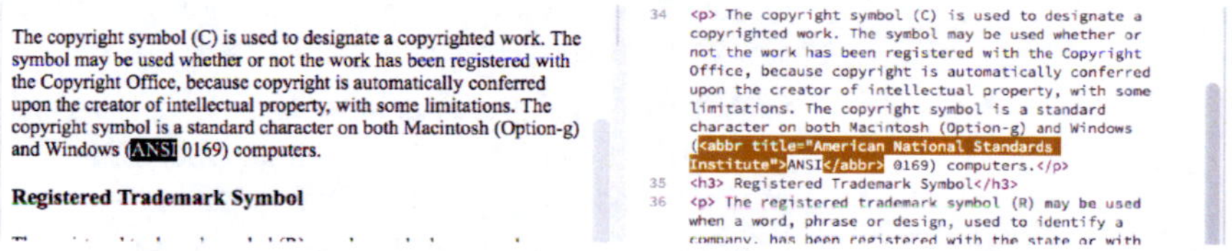

13. **Select all of the code related to the ANSI abbreviation, including the contained text, then choose Edit>Copy.**

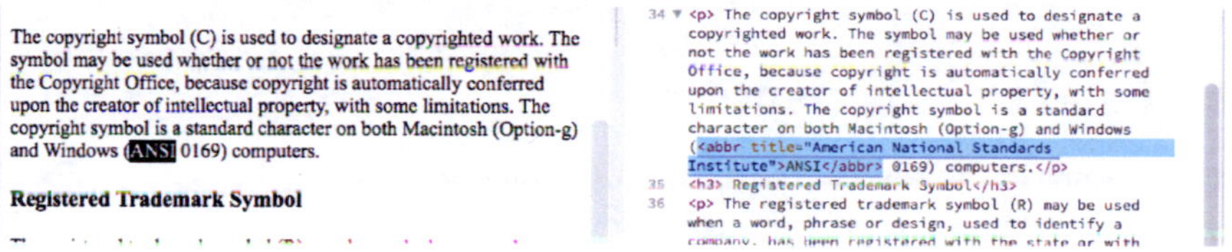

14. **In the Code pane, highlight the instance of "ANSI" near the end of line 36. Choose Edit>Paste to replace the highlighted text with the copied code (including the abbr tags and title attribute).**

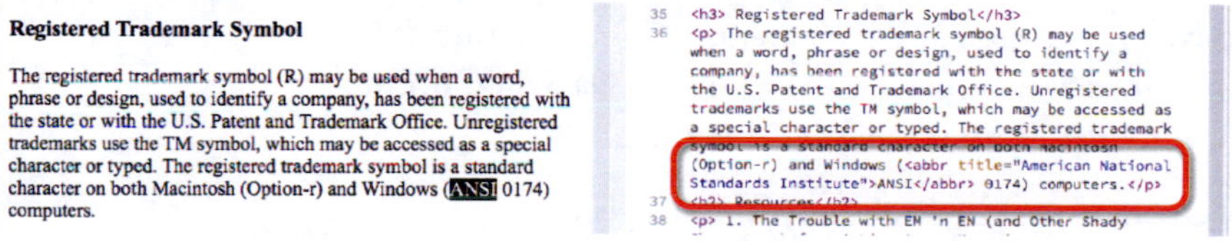

15. **Save the file, then continue to the next exercise.**

Code View Options

Code View options, which can be toggled on or off in the View menu, determine how code displays.

- **Word Wrap** ensures that code does not extend beyond the width of the window. This option only affects the appearance of code in the Code pane — it does not insert actual line breaks in the code or content.
- **Line Numbers** shows numbers to the left of each line.
- **Hidden Characters** displays characters, such as line-break markers, which would not otherwise display.
- **Syntax Coloring** displays the code in defined colors.
- **Auto Indent** indents every new line of code to the same position as the previous line. A new line is inserted each time you press Return/Enter.
- **Asset Preview** shows a preview of defined images, colors, etc., in a pop-up window when the cursor moves over the relevant code.

The three options at the bottom of the menu affect the font size only in the Code view — they have no effect on the font size in the Design pane.

Code Format Preferences

Code Format preferences allow you to specify rules that determine how the code is structured. The sole purpose of these rules is to make it easier for you to read code.

- **Indent With** indents the text within each tag, so you can easily identify each block of code.
- **Tab Size** specifies the number of spaces that each tab character contains. For example, if you type "4" here, four spaces are inserted each time you press the Tab key.
- **Emmet** allows you to use a special type of shorthand when writing code. When checked, pressing the Tab key expands the shorthand into the full HTML or CSS code.
- **Line Break Type** ensures the line breaks inserted by Dreamweaver are compatible with the operating system of the remote server on which your site will be hosted.
- **TD Tag** prevents a line break from being inserted directly after a <td> (table cell) tag, or directly before a </td> tag, which can cause problems in older browsers.
- **Advanced Formatting/Tag Libraries** opens a dialog box where you can define formatting options, such as line breaks and indents, for tags and attributes.
- **Minimum code folding size** determines how many lines must be included in a tag before that tag can be collapsed in the Code pane.

Format with Strong and Em Elements

Two HTML elements can be used to show emphasis — em and strong. The **em** element is used when light emphasis is needed, such as "you should go to your brother's game." For stronger emphasis, use the **strong** element, such as "Don't touch the stove top, it is hot!"

Text marked up with the em element appears by default in italics. Text marked up with the strong element appears in bold. Visually, it is the same as using the **<i>** and **<b>** tags (italic and bold, respectively), but the i and b elements are presentational, not structural, HTML. Screen-reader software changes the tone of voice when it finds em and strong element text, but not when it finds i and b element text.

Note:

Remember that b and i elements are for presentational purposes only, and strong and em elements are for structural purposes.

1. **With typography.html open, open the Preferences dialog box (Dreamweaver menu on Macintosh or Edit menu on Windows) and show the General category.**

2. **In the Editing Options group, make sure the "Use \<strong> and \<em>" option is checked.**

When this option is checked, as it is by default, Dreamweaver inserts strong or em tags when you apply bold or italic (respectively) styling through interface menus or buttons.

3. **Click Close to close the Preferences dialog box.**

4. **In the Design pane, scroll to the paragraph following the En Dash heading and select "not" in the fourth sentence.**

5. **Click the Bold button in the Properties panel.**

There are no special attributes for the strong and em elements, so you can insert these with a single click.

6. **With the text still selected, examine the Tag Selector.**

The selected text is formatted with the **\<strong>** tag, not the **\<b>** tag.

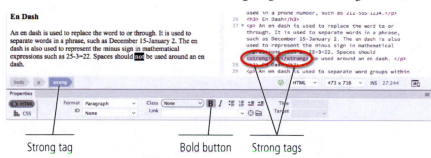

Strong tag   Bold button   Strong tags

7. **In the paragraph after the Em Dash heading, select "more authority" in the third sentence and click the Italic button in the Properties panel.**

The selected text is now formatted with the **\<em>** tag.

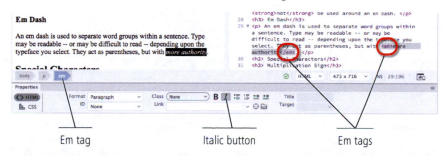

Em tag   Italic button   Em tags

8. **Save your changes and continue to the next stage of the project.**

STAGE 3 / **Working with Special Characters**

HTML character entities are characters not directly available from your keyboard. HTML character entities can be specified in code either by name or by number. Using either method, the code begins with an ampersand (&) and ends with a semicolon (;).

- A named character entity uses a specific name for that character, such as © for the © symbol and ™ for the ™ symbol. Some character names (such as ™) are not supported by all browsers; visitors using these browsers would see ™ in their browser window instead of the ™ symbol.

- Alternatively, you can specify a character using its numeric code, such as ¢ for ¢. When using the numeric code, be sure to insert a "#" between the ampersand and the number. All browsers support the numeric codes.

Insert Special Characters

You don't need to worry about inserting the named or numbered codes for many HTML character entities because you can select some of the most common from a list in the HTML Insert panel; Dreamweaver inserts the code for you.

This HTML Insert panel provides one-click access to many common structural elements — including various levels of headings, as well as headers, sections, and footers.

1. **With typography.html open in Split view, make the Design pane active. Select the hyphen between "December 15" and "January 2" in the paragraph below the En Dash heading.**

En Dash

An en dash is used to replace the word to or through. It is used to separate words in a phrase, such as December 15–January 2. The en dash is also used to represent the minus sign in mathematical expressions such as 25-3=22. Spaces should **not** be used around an en dash.

```
      used in a phone number, such as 212-555-1234.</p>
26    <h3> En Dash</h3>
27  ▼ <p> An en dash is used to replace the word to or
      through. It is used to separate words in a phrase,
      such as December 15–January 2. The en dash is also
      used to represent the minus sign in mathematical
      expressions such as 25-3=22. Spaces should
      <strong>not</strong> be used around an en dash. </p>
28    <h3> Em Dash</h3>
29    <p> An em dash is used to separate word groups within
```

Selected text

2. **With the Insert panel in HTML mode, click the arrow button to the right of the Character button icon.**

   Your button icon might appear different than the one shown in our screen capture because it reflects the last character inserted from this list. Simply clicking the button (label or icon) — not the arrow — inserts the character that appears on the button.

3. **Choose En Dash from the pop-up menu.**

Use the menu to show HTML options in the Insert panel.

Click the arrow to open the Character menu.

Choose the appropriate character from the Character pop-up menu.

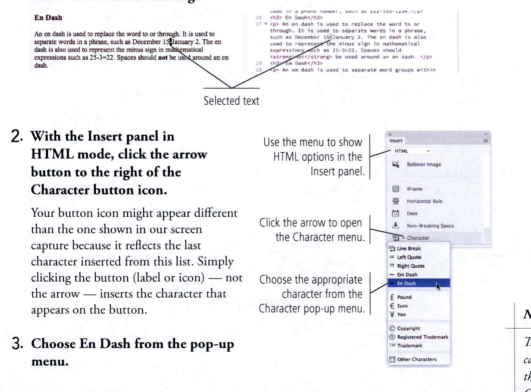

Note:

These same characters can be inserted using the Insert>HTML> Character menu.

4. **Select the hyphen between "25" and "3" in the same paragraph.**

   En dashes are as wide as half an em dash. As you might have read in the text of this project page, en dashes are used to replace the words "to" or "through" or in mathematical expressions of subtraction.

5. **In the HTML Insert panel, click the Character:En Dash button.**

   Because the button defaults to the last-used character, you can simply click the button to apply another en dash.

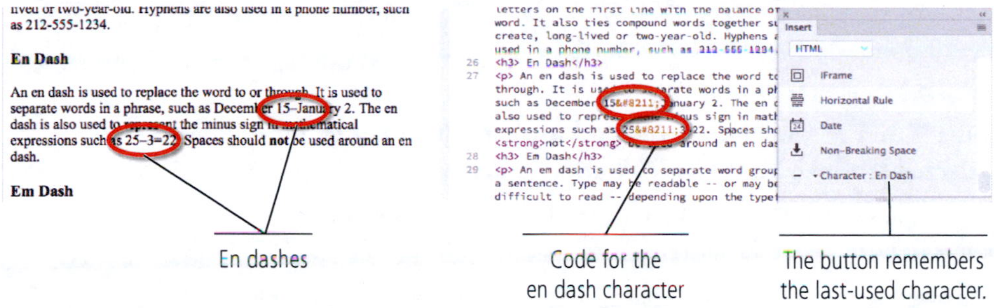

En dashes

Code for the
en dash character

The button remembers
the last-used character.

6. **Use the same techniques from Steps 2–5 to replace both sets of double hyphens with em dashes in the paragraph after the Em Dash heading.**

   The em dash is as wide as the defined type size. This dash can be used to separate part of a sentence — an aside — from the rest of a sentence. Many authors do not know how to insert an em dash. Instead, they use a regular hyphen or a pair of hyphens. As there are strict grammatical rules about when to use a hyphen, an en dash, and an em dash, you should consult a professional copy editor for the proper application of these characters.

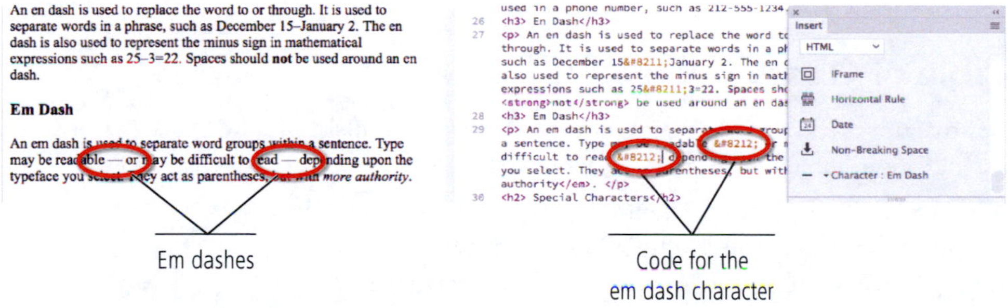

Em dashes

Code for the
em dash character

7. **Select the capital C in the first line after the Copyright Symbol heading. Use the Character menu in the HTML Insert panel to replace the letter with the Copyright character.**

Code for the copyright character

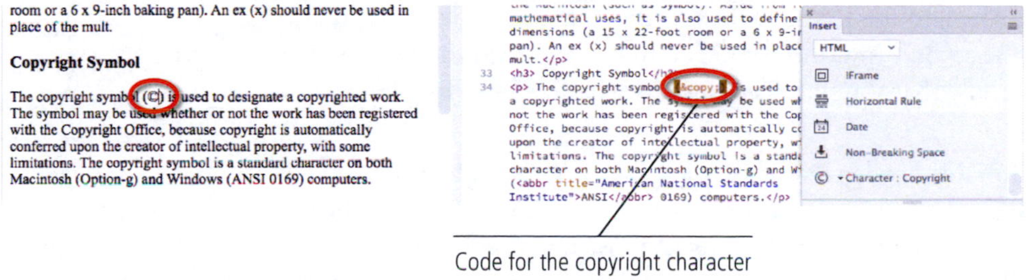

8. **Select the capital R in the first line after the Registered Trademark Symbol heading. Use the Character menu to replace the selected letter with the Registered Trademark character.**

Code for the registered trademark character

9. **Select the capital TM in the same paragraph and use the Character menu to replace the selected letters with the Trademark character.**

In the Code pane, you can see that Dreamweaver creates this character using the numeric code because some browsers do not support the name for this character.

Code for the trademark character

10. **Save the changes to typography.html and continue to the next exercise.**

Create a Table of Quote Characters

Common HTML tables that are used to present data or text information consist of only three components: a caption, table header cells, and table data cells.

A caption can be used to briefly describe the contents or purpose of a table. It generally appears at the top of the table. (You can use CSS to move the caption to another position, but many browsers offer poor support for these properties.)

Table data cells make up the majority of the cells in a table. The **<td>** tag is used to mark up the table data cells.

Table header cells, using the **<th>** tag, appear at the top or left (or both) of the table, and label the contents in the regular table cells. Think about a table of the days of the week across the top, and the hours of the day down the left side. If the cell at the intersection of the second row and second column contained the text "Staff Meeting," you would know that the staff meeting was scheduled for Tuesday at 10:00 a.m.

The information in table header cells is very important for people using screen-reader software. For example, when they reach the Staff Meeting cell, they can prompt the software to read the headers associated with the cell. The screen-reader would report, "Tuesday" and, "10:00 a.m." Without proper cell markup, the software would not be able to report the day and time of the meeting.

Note:

When tables are used for layout components of a web page, they can become very complicated in structure, with tables within table cells (nested tables), and cells that have been merged with others. Tables should only be used to present tabular data.

1. With **typography.html** open in Split view, click in the Design pane to place the insertion point at the end of the first regular paragraph after the "Quotes and Related Characters" heading.

2. Click the Table button in the HTML Insert panel.

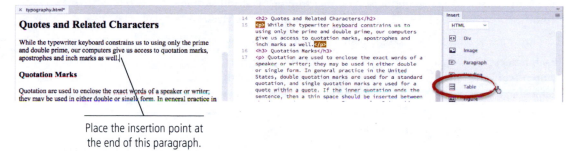

Place the insertion point at the end of this paragraph.

3. In the Table dialog box:

   - Set both the number of rows and number of columns to **2**.

   - Delete any values in the Table Width, Border Thickness, Cell Padding, and Cell Spacing fields.

   - Choose the Top Header option.

   - Type **Quotation Characters** in the Caption field.

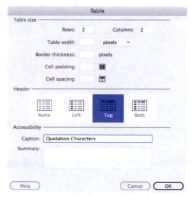

   Many Dreamweaver dialog boxes remember the last-used settings. If you or someone else used the Table dialog box before now, some of these fields might default to other values.

4. Click OK to create the table.

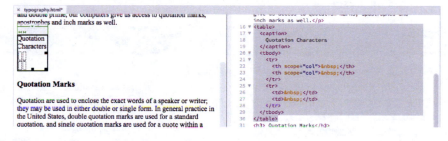

5. Click in the top-left table cell to place the insertion point, and then type **Character Description**.

6. Press Tab to move the insertion point into the top-right cell, and then type **Character**.

7. **In the Code pane, review the code for the table you just created.**

- All content that makes up the table is enclosed in opening and closing **<table>** tags.

- The caption that you defined when you created the table is enclosed in opening and closing **<caption>** tags.

- The body content of a table is grouped together with opening and closing **<tbody>** tags. The <tbody> element must contain one or more <tr> tags.

- Each row in the table is enclosed in opening and closing **<tr>** tags.

- Each header cell is identified with opening and closing **<th>** tags. The **scope="col"** attribute identifies that column as information with the heading defined in the related cell.

- Each regular cell in the table is enclosed in opening and closing **<td>** tags. As you can see, each table row includes two <td> tags — one for each column in the row.

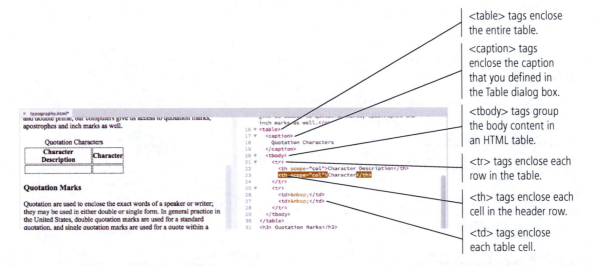

<table> tags enclose the entire table.

<caption> tags enclose the caption that you defined in the Table dialog box.

<tbody> tags group the body content in an HTML table.

<tr> tags enclose each row in the table.

<th> tags enclose each cell in the header row.

<td> tags enclose each table cell.

8. **Save the file and continue to the next exercise.**

More about Working with HTML Tables

When you work with HTML tables, you have a number of options in the Properties panel, depending on whether the entire table or only specific cells are selected. Keep in mind that nearly all table properties are better defined using CSS, which is why we are not explaining all of these options here.

If a table or column has a defined width, the number appears to the left of the column or table menu.

Use these menus to access column-specific options.

Use this menu to access table-specific options.

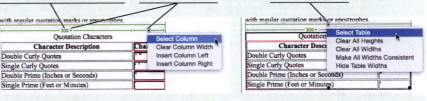

When specific cells are selected, you can change properties of selected cells:

When the table is selected, you can change properties of the overall table:

Use the Insert Other Character Dialog Box

Although a few special characters are available directly in the Characters menu of the HTML Insert panel, there are many more available than those in the list. A number of common special characters are available in the Insert Other Character dialog box, which is accessed at the bottom of the Characters menu. Still others (many, in fact) are only available by typing the necessary code in the Code pane.

1. With **typography.html** open, click in the lower-left empty cell of the table that you created in the previous exercise. Type **Double Curly Quotes.**

2. **Press Tab to move to the right cell, and then choose Left Quote from the Character menu in the HTML Insert panel.**

3. **Press Space, and then choose Right Quote from the HTML Insert panel Character menu.**

   You might have to click after the left curly quote character to re-establish the insertion point before pressing the Space bar. This is a minor bug in the application.

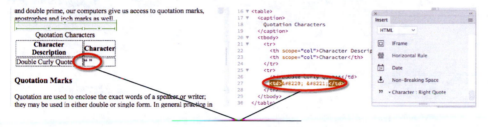

Numeric codes for the special characters are automatically added in the Code pane.

4. **Press Tab to insert a new table row.**

   Again, you might have to click after the right curly quote character to re-establish the insertion point before pressing the Tab key.

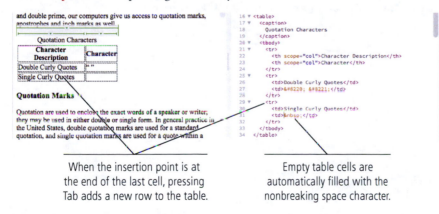

When the insertion point is at the end of the last cell, pressing Tab adds a new row to the table.

Empty table cells are automatically filled with the nonbreaking space character.

5. **In the left cell, type Single Curly Quotes, and then press Tab to move the insertion point into the right cell.**

6. **Using the HTML Insert panel, open the Character menu and choose Other Characters from the bottom of the list.**

   You can use the Other Characters option to find special characters that aren't included in the default list. This option opens the Insert Other Character dialog box, where you can select a specific character, or type the appropriate code in the field at the top of the dialog box.

7. **In the resulting dialog box, click the Single Left Curly Quote character and then click OK to insert it into the active table cell.**

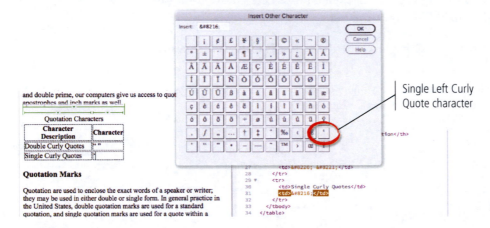

Single Left Curly Quote character

Note:

As you add content into the table, the column width changes to accommodate it. The specific appearance of the table will be determined by cascading style sheets when you attach an external CSS file later in this project.

8. **With the insertion point after the quote, press Space, and then click the Character:Other Characters button to reopen the dialog box.**

   In this case, the button remembers the last-used option (opening the dialog box), but not the last-used character. Clicking the button opens the Insert Other Character dialog box.

9. **Click the Single Right Curly Quote character and then click OK to insert it into the table cell.**

Single Left Curly Quote character

10. **Press Tab to insert another table row. Type Double Prime (Inches or Seconds) in the left cell of the new row.**

11. **Move the insertion point to the right cell of the new row, and then click the Code pane to make it active.**

12. **In the Code pane, delete the code for nonbreaking space. Type ″ (with a capital P), and then refresh the Design view.**

   Remember: After typing in the Code pane, the Properties panel shows a Refresh button. You can click that button, press F5, or click in the Design pane to bring it into focus.

and double prime, our computers give us access to quotation marks, apostrophes and inch marks as well.

Quotation Characters

Character Description	Character
Double Curly Quotes	" "
Single Curly Quotes	' '
Double Prime (Inches or Seconds)	″

Quotation Marks

Quotation are used to enclose the exact words of a speaker or writer; they may be used in either double or single form. In general practice in the United States, double quotation marks are used for a standard quotation, and single quotation marks are used for a quote within a quote. If the inner quotation ends the sentence, then a thin space should be inserted between the inner and outer quotes. For example, Erin said,

```
16 ▼ <table>
17 ▼   <caption>
18       Quotation Characters
19     </caption>
20 ▼   <tbody>
21 ▼     <tr>
22         <th scope="col">Character Description</th>
23         <th scope="col">Character</th>
24       </tr>
25 ▼     <tr>
26         <td>Double Curly Quotes</td>
27         <td>&#8220; &#8221;</td>
28       </tr>
29 ▼     <tr>
30         <td>Single Curly Quotes</td>
31         <td>&#8216; &#8217;</td>
32       </tr>
33 ▼     <tr>
34         <td>Double Prime (Inches or Seconds)</td>
35         <td>&Prime;</td>
36       </tr>
37     </tbody>
38   </table>
```

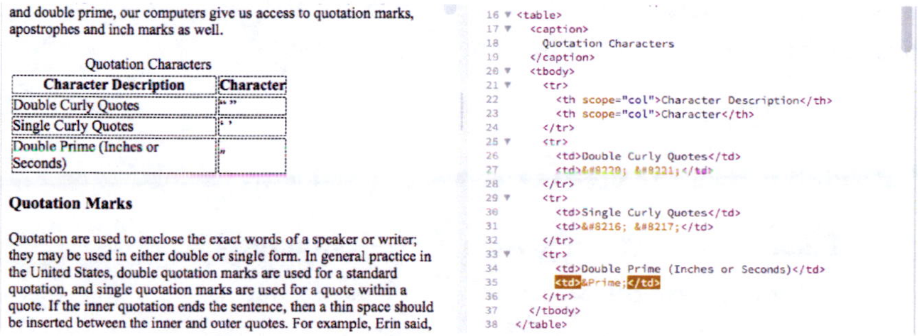

13. **Click in the Design pane to bring it into focus. Place the insertion point after the prime character, and then press Tab to insert another table row.**

14. **Type Single Prime (Feet or Minutes) in the left column, and then move the insertion point to the right cell.**

15. **Click the Code pane to make it active. Replace the nonbreaking-space code with ′ (with a lowercase p) and then refresh the Design view.**

   The single- and double-prime codes are almost the same — capitalization is the difference between the two characters.

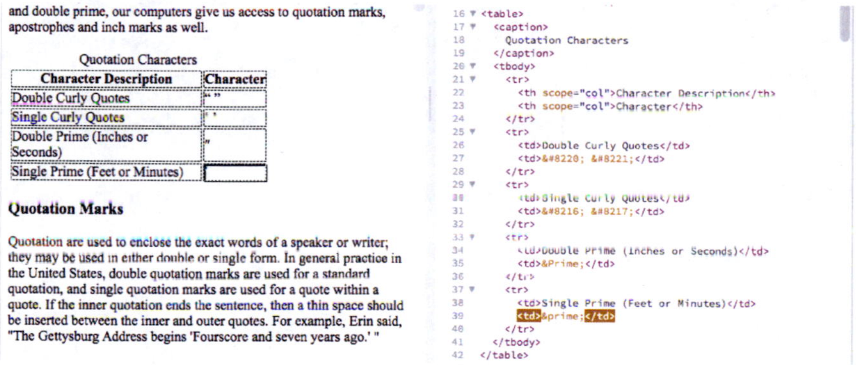

Note:

To find the necessary code for special characters, look for online sources, such as http://www.w3schools.com/html/html_entities.asp.

and double prime, our computers give us access to quotation marks, apostrophes and inch marks as well.

Quotation Characters

Character Description	Character
Double Curly Quotes	" "
Single Curly Quotes	' '
Double Prime (Inches or Seconds)	″
Single Prime (Feet or Minutes)	

Quotation Marks

Quotation are used to enclose the exact words of a speaker or writer; they may be used in either double or single form. In general practice in the United States, double quotation marks are used for a standard quotation, and single quotation marks are used for a quote within a quote. If the inner quotation ends the sentence, then a thin space should be inserted between the inner and outer quotes. For example, Erin said, "The Gettysburg Address begins 'Fourscore and seven years ago.' "

```
16 ▼ <table>
17 ▼   <caption>
18       Quotation Characters
19     </caption>
20 ▼   <tbody>
21 ▼     <tr>
22         <th scope="col">Character Description</th>
23         <th scope="col">Character</th>
24       </tr>
25 ▼     <tr>
26         <td>Double Curly Quotes</td>
27         <td>&#8220; &#8221;</td>
28       </tr>
29 ▼     <tr>
30         <td>Single Curly Quotes</td>
31         <td>&#8216; &#8217;</td>
32       </tr>
33 ▼     <tr>
34         <td>Double Prime (Inches or Seconds)</td>
35         <td>&Prime;</td>
36       </tr>
37 ▼     <tr>
38         <td>Single Prime (Feet or Minutes)</td>
39         <td>&prime;</td>
40       </tr>
41     </tbody>
42   </table>
```

16. **Save the file and continue to the next exercise.**

Insert Special Characters in Code

The multiplication sign, which you need in this project, doesn't appear in the Insert Other Character dialog box. To insert this character, you can type code directly in the Code pane or use the Insert field in the Insert Other Character dialog box.

There are many lists of HTML character entities on the Internet — simply do a search for "HTML characters." Some web pages have more characters than others. For very unusual characters, you might need to check a few sites until you find the code you need. Also, make note of both the name and the numeric code because some browsers support one, but not the other (test both in your browser).

1. **With typography.html open in Split view, use the Design pane to scroll to the paragraph following the Multiplication Sign heading.**

2. **Select the letter "x" between 15 and 22.**

3. **Click the Code pane to bring it into focus, and then delete the selected letter "x".**

4. **Type &tim and press Return/Enter to choose × from the code hint list.**

   The code hints help you insert named character entities, but not numeric character codes.

5. **Refresh the Design view.**

6. **In the Design pane, compare the appearance of the mult (multiply) character and the letter "x".**

7. **Select the letter "x" between 6 and 9 in the same sentence.**

8. **In the Code pane, replace the selected character with × and then refresh the Design view.**

   This is the numeric code for the mult character. Dreamweaver's code hints for character entities in Code view do not support numeric codes for characters.

9. **Save the file, and then continue to the next stage of the project.**

Note:

The current versions of Firefox, Safari, Opera, and Chrome all support both the named and numeric character codes. Older versions, however, might show the characters "×" instead of the actual mult character.

STAGE 4 / Creating Lists

There are two common types of lists: ordered (numbered) lists and unordered (bulleted) lists. The two types are very similar in structure. In this stage of the project, you will create an ordered list of references and an unordered list that becomes navigation links in the final web page.

Create an Ordered List of Web Resources

Ordered lists are commonly called numbered lists, although they are not always numbered. You can use Roman numerals (i, ii, iii or I, II, III) or letters (a, b, c or A, B, C).

The purpose of ordered lists is to show a sequence of steps or hierarchical order. If these purposes do not apply to the content of a list, you should use an unordered (bulleted) list instead.

1. **With typography.html open, click in the Design pane to place the insertion point in the numbered paragraph at the bottom of the page (under the Resources heading).**

2. **Click the Ordered List button in the Properties panel.**

   The **<ol>** tags surround the entire ordered list, identifying where the list starts and ends. Each list item within the list is surrounded by **<li>** tags.

   In the Design pane, the list as a whole is indented from the left edge of the page, and the space between list items is reduced. These presentation properties clearly identify that the text is part of a list, and not part of a regular paragraph.

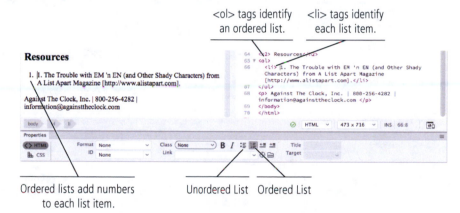

3. **Delete the redundant number from the text at the beginning of the list item.**

   One of the presentation properties of an ordered list is that each list item is automatically numbered. If you receive content from an outside source, the number might already be typed at the beginning of each list item (as is the case in this project). You should remove the original number from the text of each list item.

4. **Click at the end of the text in the numbered list item and press Return/Enter.**

   When you press Return/Enter at the end of a list item in the Design pane, Dreamweaver automatically creates a new numbered list item for you. You have to work in the Design pane to automatically add the new list item. Pressing Return/Enter in the Code pane simply adds white space in the code.

5. Type **HTML entities and other resources at W3schools.com.** as the new list item, but do not press Return/Enter.

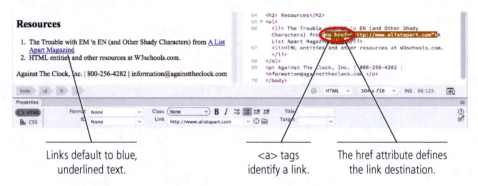

6. In the first list item, select the URL in the square brackets and cut it to the Clipboard (Edit>Cut or Command/Control-X).

7. Delete the two square brackets and the space before them.

8. Select "A List Apart Magazine." Click in the Link field of the Properties panel, paste the copied URL, and then press Return/Enter.

   A link is identified by **<a>** tags. The **href** attribute defines the link destination, or the page that will open when a user clicks the link text.

9. Click to place the insertion point in the link (in the Design pane).

   Placing the insertion point removes the highlighting that was applied to the text in the previous step. You can now see the default presentational properties of the <a> tag — blue, underlined text.

Links default to blue, underlined text.

<a> tags identify a link.

The href attribute defines the link destination.

10. In the second list item, make "W3schools.com" a link to **http://www.w3schools.com.**

11. Save the file and continue to the next exercise.

Create an Unordered List of Navigation Links

A navigation bar is simply a list of links. It is common practice among web design professionals to mark up a navigation bar as a list of links. After CSS has been applied, however, the list takes on a new appearance. In this exercise, you use the unordered list format to create a navigation bar.

1. **With typography.html open, place the insertion point at the end of the last list item in the Resources section in the Design pane.**

2. **Press Return/Enter twice.**

    Pressing Return/Enter once creates the next list item — in this case, #3.

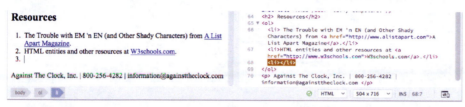

    If you press Return/Enter again (before typing anything else), Dreamweaver recognizes that you want to escape from the ordered list, and it deletes the last empty list item, and moves the insertion point into an empty paragraph below the ordered list.

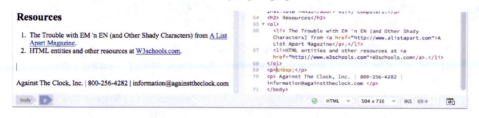

3. **Click the Unordered List button in the Properties panel.**

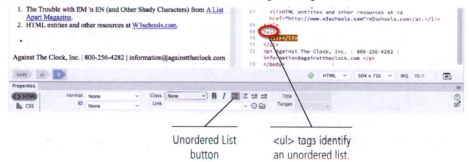

    Unordered List button

    <ul> tags identify an unordered list.

4. **Add four list items: ATC Home, Companion Series, Projects, and Portfolios. Press Return/Enter after each item, but not after the final list item.**

5. **Highlight the words "ATC Home" in the Design pane. In the Properties panel, type # in the Link field, the press Return/Enter to finalize the new link.**

Using the # character in the Link field turns the selected text into a link without defining a specific destination. For the purposes of this project, the important thing is that the text of each list item be tagged as a link.

6. **Repeat Step 5 for each item in the list.**

7. **Save the changes and continue to the next stage of the project.**

STAGE 5 / Attaching an External CSS File

As you might have noticed, we paid particular attention to the tags that were applied to various structural elements throughout this project. Rather than simply accepting the default presentational properties, you can use cascading style sheets (CSS), which contain instructions that tell a browser how to format those elements.

As you complete the rest of the projects in this book, you will work extensively with CSS to format both pages, and specific page content. In this project, you are going to attach the client's existing CSS file to your page, so it matches the rest of the client's website.

Add Tags and Element IDs

Although we will not discuss the finer details of CSS at this point, the following exercises will make more sense if you understand that a CSS file includes **selectors** (rules) that define the appearance of different tags. For the formatting to correctly map to content, you need to apply the appropriate tags to various elements.

In HTML 4, the div element was commonly used to identify different areas, or divisions, of a page. The ID attribute was attached to various div elements to clearly identify different areas, for example: div#header, div#nav, and div#footer. HTML5 includes header, nav, section, and footer elements that allow the same kind of page structure, without the need to define and identify multiple divs on a page.

1. **With typography.html open in Split view, click and drag in the Design pane to select the level 1 heading and the blockquote.**

2. **With the Insert panel in HTML mode, click the Header button.**

HTML5 includes a number of elements that identify common elements of web pages. This button adds the **<header> </header>** tags to identify the header element.

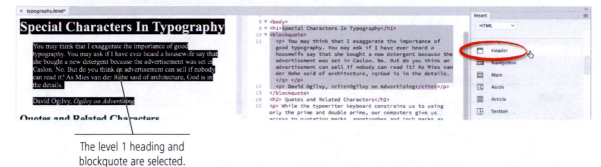

The level 1 heading and blockquote are selected.

3. **In the resulting dialog box, choose Wrap Around Selection in the Insert menu, and then click OK.**

You can use the Insert dialog box (in this case, the Insert *Header* dialog box) to determine where the new element will be placed in relation to the selection. The Insert menu defaults to Wrap Around Selection because content is currently selected in the document. You can also use this dialog box to define a class or ID attribute for the resulting element.

4. **Click once anywhere in the previously selected text to place the insertion point.**

The boundaries of the header element are marked by a thin gray or dotted line in the Design pane. (If you don't see this border, you can turn on CSS Layout Outlines in the View>Visual Aids menu.)

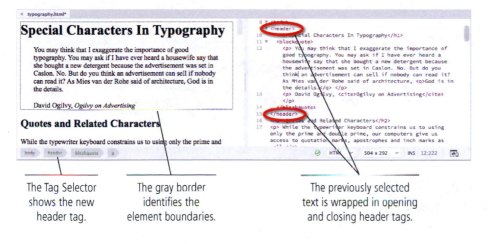

The Tag Selector shows the new header tag.

The gray border identifies the element boundaries.

The previously selected text is wrapped in opening and closing header tags.

5. **Switch to Design view and select all the text from the first level 2 heading (at the top of the page) to the last numbered list item under the "Resources" heading.**

We used the regular Design view simply to make it easier to select the entire body of text. This allows more of the actual document text to be visible in the document window than when working in the Split view.

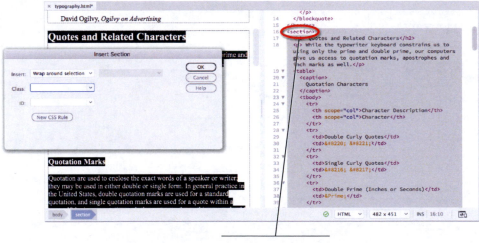

6. **Click the Section button in the HTML Insert panel. In the resulting dialog box, choose Wrap Around Selection in the Insert menu and then click OK.**

The section element identifies (as you might have expected) a section of the page.

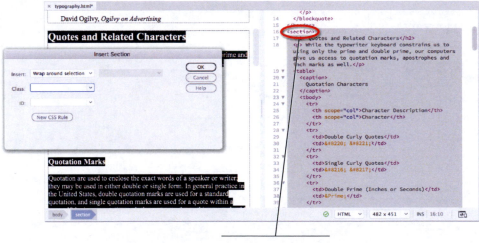

The selection is wrapped in opening and closing section tags.

7. In the Design pane, place the insertion point anywhere in the unordered list near the bottom of the page. Click the <ul> tag in the Tag Selector to select the entire unordered list.

8. Click the Navigation button in the HTML Insert panel. In the resulting dialog box, choose Wrap Around Selection in the Insert menu, and then click OK.

The nav element identifies an area that includes navigation links.

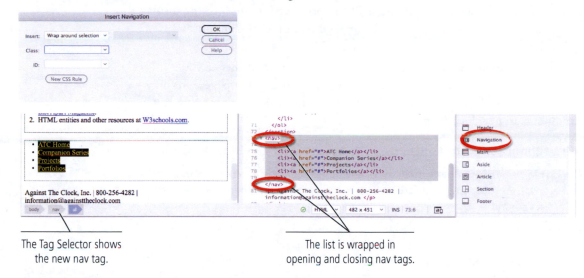

The Tag Selector shows the new nav tag.

The list is wrapped in opening and closing nav tags.

9. In the Design pane, place the insertion point anywhere in the last paragraph. Click the <p> tag in the Tag Selector to select the entire last paragraph.

10. Click the Footer button in the HTML Insert panel. In the resulting dialog box, choose Wrap Around Selection in the Insert menu, and then click OK.

The footer element identifies the footer area of the page.

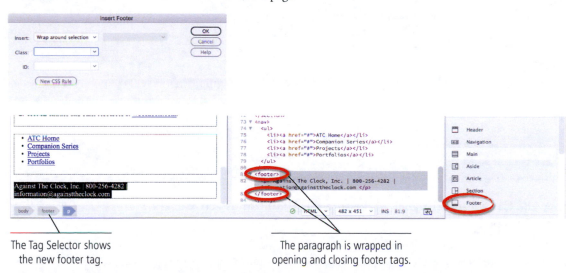

The Tag Selector shows the new footer tag.

The paragraph is wrapped in opening and closing footer tags.

11. Save the file and continue to the next exercise.

Attach the CSS File

To make this page more visually pleasing to ATC site visitors — and to be consistent with the rest of the ATC site — you need to attach the CSS file already used for other pages in the client's site.

The CSS file, which is a set of instructions on how to display the web page, is separate from the HTML document. When a browser downloads an HTML file, it examines the code for external files required to display it, such as images and CSS files. The browser then downloads the external files and merges them into the display of the web page. In the case of a CSS file, the browser reads the instructions, and then applies the styles to the page.

After attaching the style sheet to the page, depending on what the CSS file defines, you might see a dramatic difference in the appearance of the page. Not only will text styling change, but the layout will too — even to the point of moving some page components to new locations.

1. **With typography.html open, turn on the Live view and hide the Code pane.**

    The Live view provides a more accurate view of how the page will render in an actual web browser. At this point, you can see that the file is little more than black text on a white background.

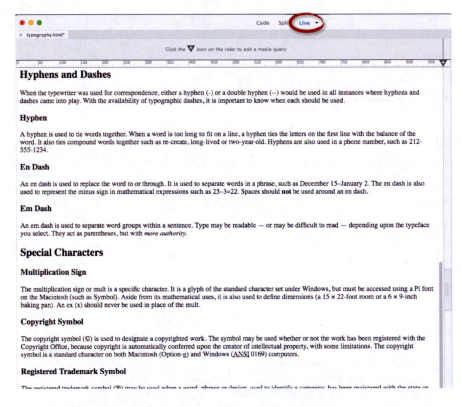

2. **Open the CSS Designer panel. Make sure the All button is active at the top of the panel.**

    Remember, all panels can be opened from the Window menu. If a panel is already available in the dock, you can click the relevant panel tab or button to show that panel.

3. **In the Sources section of the panel, click the Add CSS Source button and choose Attach Existing CSS File from the resulting menu.**

If no CSS file is attached to an HTML file, you can also click the Add a CSS Source button in the Sources section of the panel.

Add CSS Source button

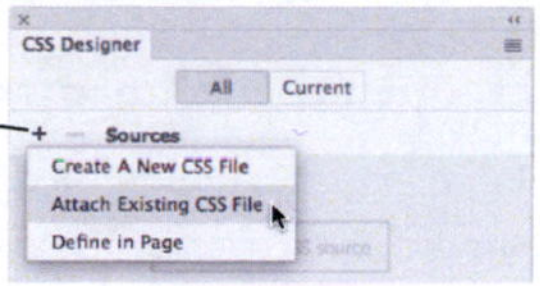

Note:

For now, don't worry about the specifics of how the CSS file formats these elements. You will spend considerable time learning about CSS in the remaining projects of this book.

4. **In the Attach Existing CSS File dialog box, click the Browse button.**

5. **In the resulting Select Style Sheet File dialog box, navigate to styles.css in the root folder of the ATC site (WIP>Chapter). Click Open/OK to return to the Attach Existing CSS File dialog box.**

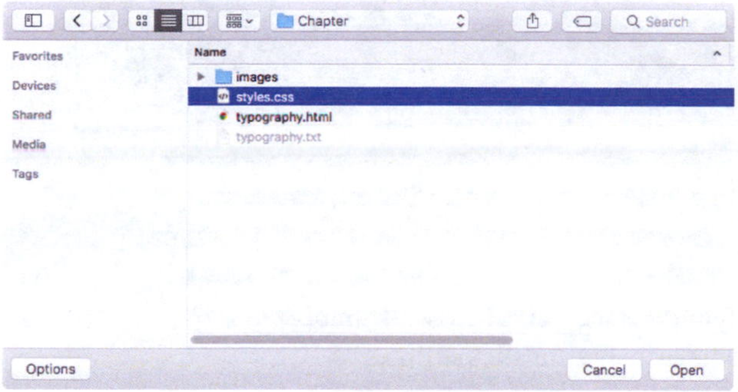

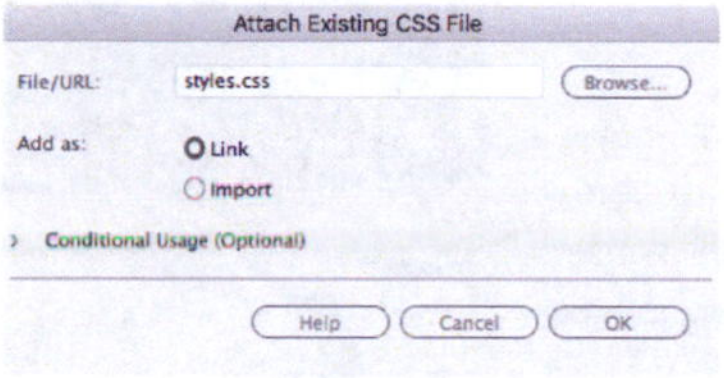

6. **Click OK in the Attach Existing CSS File dialog box to apply the CSS file.**

As you can see in Design view, the main section of the page is clearly not formatted properly. The CSS Designer panel shows a number of selectors beginning with the # character. In the context of CSS, the # character at the beginning of the selector name identifies an ID selector, which can be used to distinguish one element from another on a single page.

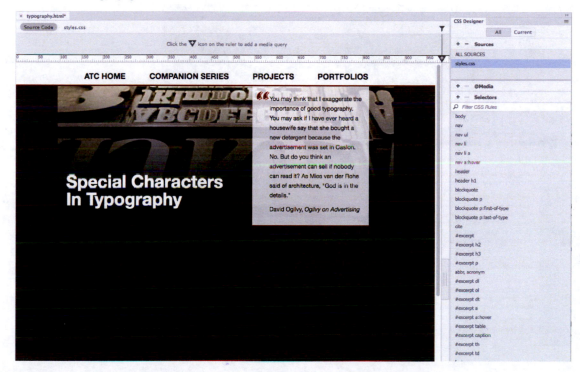

7. **In Design view, click to select the "Quotes and Related Characters" heading.**

8. **Using the Tag Selector, click the <section> tag to select the entire section element.**

9. **In the Properties panel, open the ID menu and choose excerpt.**

   This menu shows all available IDs that are defined in the attached CSS file. This method is an easy way to make sure that the ID you apply already exists in the attached CSS file.

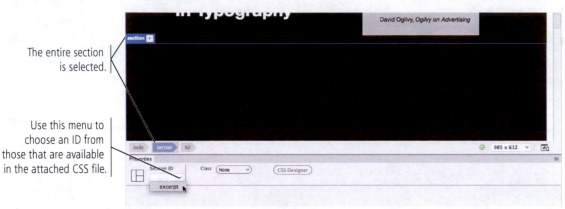

The entire section is selected.

Use this menu to choose an ID from those that are available in the attached CSS file.

By adding an ID attribute, you are uniquely identifying this section. The ID attribute has no effect on the structure of content, but simply identifies it for the purposes of CSS styling. This allows you to define different appearances for the same elements in different sections. For example, **<p>** tags in a section named "content" can have a different appearance than **<p>** tags in a section named "excerpt."

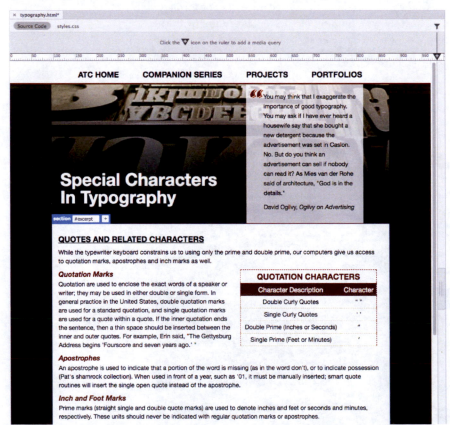

Note:

You will work extensively with CSS in later projects. For now, you should simply understand that the attached CSS file includes an ID selector named "excerpt" that defines the appearance of various elements within the section in which that ID is applied.

10. Save and close typography.html.

11. Choose Manage Sites from the bottom of the Directory menu in the Files panel.

12. In the Manage Sites dialog box, choose the ATC site name, and then click the Export button. Navigate to your WIP>Chapter folder and click Save to create the ATC.ste file.

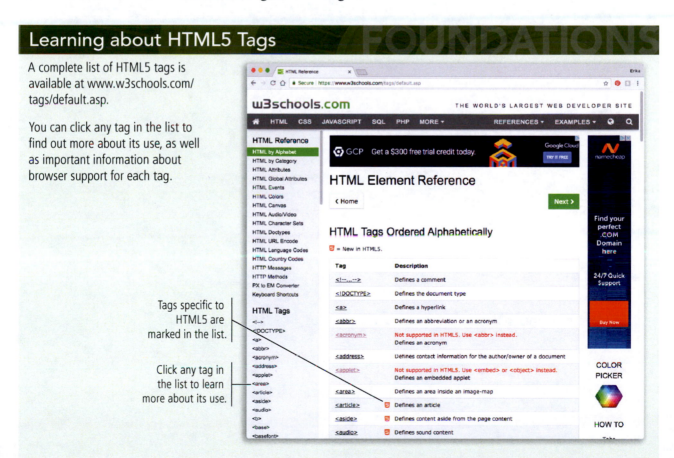

Delete   Export

13. In the Manage Sites dialog box, remove the ATC site from the list, and then click Done to close the Manage Sites dialog box.

Learning about HTML5 Tags

A complete list of HTML5 tags is available at www.w3schools.com/tags/default.asp.

You can click any tag in the list to find out more about its use, as well as important information about browser support for each tag.

Tags specific to HTML5 are marked in the list.

Click any tag in the list to learn more about its use.

PROJECT REVIEW

fill in the blank

1. The _____ tag marks up individual paragraphs in a story.

2. Each HTML page should have only one _____ element.

3. All visible content of a web page is contained within the opening and closing _____ tags.

4. _____ appear when you begin typing in the Code pane, showing a list of tags or elements that can be added at the current insertion point.

5. A(n) _____ tag includes both opening and closing tags, such as <title>text</title>.

6. A(n) _____ adds properties to HTML elements, such as the citation of a quote.

7. The _____ element is used to mark up text that is indented on the right and left, with extra white space above and below the affected text.

8. The _____ element is best used to mark up the short form of a phrase that is spoken as letters, such as HTML.

9. The _____ element identifies an individual item in an ordered or unordered list.

10. The _____ allows you to work temporarily with code, while still working in Design view.

short answer

1. Briefly explain the importance of properly structuring an HTML document.

2. Briefly explain the difference between an ordered list and an unordered list.

3. Briefly explain the importance of structural tags, such as <header>, for formatting an HTML page.

PORTFOLIO BUILDER PROJECT

Use what you have learned in this project to complete the following freeform exercise.
Carefully read the art director and client comments, then create your own design to meet the needs of the project.
Use the space below to sketch ideas. When finished, write a brief explanation of the reasoning behind your final design.

art director comments

The owner of Against The Clock Inc. received a number of positive comments — and new sales — because of the *Typography Companion* sample that you created for her website. She would like to add another page with a sample from the *Color Companion* in the same series.

To complete this project, you should:

❑ Use the ATC site folder that you already created for the new page.

❑ Create a new HTML page and copy the text from **ColorCh3.txt** into the file. (The file is in the **Books_Web20_PB.zip** archive on the Student Files web page.)

❑ Mark up the page text with proper structural tags.

❑ Create header and footer elements, and attach the same CSS file that you used in the type chapter.

client comments

We've had such a positive response from the type chapter that we also want to include a sample from the *Color Companion*. If we get the same increase in sales leads from this chapter, we'll probably go ahead and do online samples for all of our books.

In addition to the text file for the *Color Companion* chapter, we've sent you a PDF file of the printed chapter, so that you can more easily see the different text elements — headings, lists, italics, special characters, and so on. You can just ignore the images and sidebars in the printed chapter; we don't need those in the online sample. There is, however, a table near the end of the file that we would like you to include in the online version.

At the end of the text file, we added in the glossary terms that we think are important for this chapter. There aren't any resources, so you can omit that section.

project justification

No matter how you receive content for a web page, you will likely need to correct the formatting with the appropriate HTML tags. In this project, you learned how to use HTML tags and elements to semantically structure and mark up a document, so all visitors can successfully access and use a web page. You also learned that by applying ID attributes, structural HTML tags such as <header> and <section>, and using CSS, you can turn a plain HTML document into a visually pleasing and highly structured web page.

The web pages that you create for clients will seldom be as text-intensive as this one, but now that you have a solid understanding of how to work with HTML structures from both Design and Code views, you are ready to format any content you receive from a client — regardless of its condition.

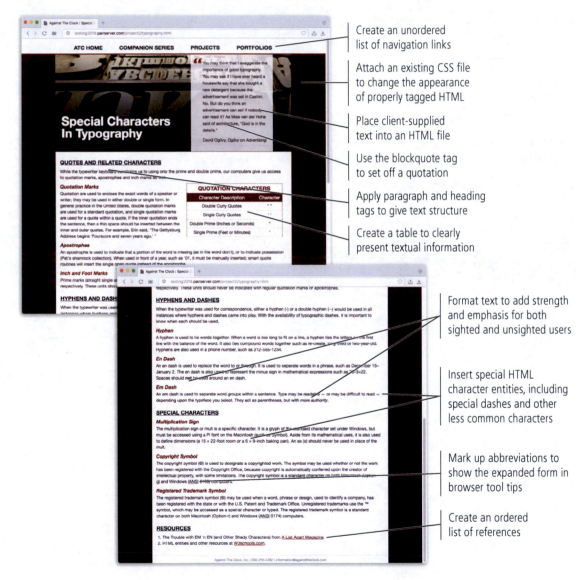

Create an unordered list of navigation links

Attach an existing CSS file to change the appearance of properly tagged HTML

Place client-supplied text into an HTML file

Use the blockquote tag to set off a quotation

Apply paragraph and heading tags to give text structure

Create a table to clearly present textual information

Format text to add strength and emphasis for both sighted and unsighted users

Insert special HTML character entities, including special dashes and other less common characters

Mark up abbreviations to show the expanded form in browser tool tips

Create an ordered list of references

Arts Council Website

The client is the director of a nonprofit guild, sponsored by the city government, with the goal of promoting artistic and cultural activities in the local community. Your job is to implement the client's new website design, based on the approved design that was created in a Photoshop file.

This project incorporates the following skills:

❏ Using various methods to add static images to a web page

❏ Assigning alt tags to images for improved usability

❏ Manipulating images in a web page

❏ Extracting content and styles from a native Photoshop file

❏ Working with CSS to define various element properties

We want our new site to be very basic, highlighting the three main projects of the council — the summer arts festival, kids' workshops, and adult classes.

There will be a lot more information about each of our programs on secondary pages, but we haven't finished writing and gathering the content for those yet.

We have approved the final design comp we saw last week, so we want to get started on the home page as soon as possible. I sent our logo file to the art director, as well as three photos that will be featured on the home page.

We've been working on the design for this project for several weeks, and the client just approved the layout comp that our artist created in Photoshop.

I assigned the HTML structural composition to another web designer, but she has other projects that need to take priority, so your job is to complete the home page. Once you're finished, you'll hand it off to a developer to create the secondary pages and the required interactive elements when the client provides the content.

A few of the images you need have been saved in the project folder, but some of the assets you need are only available in the Photoshop file. Fortunately, you can use Dreamweaver to access what you need to complete the project in a relatively short time.

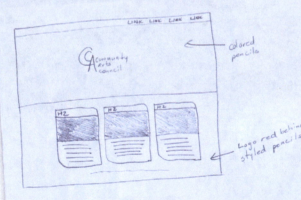

To complete this project, you will:

❏ Use multiple techniques to add images to web pages

❏ Resize images to fit page areas

❏ Resample images to reduce download time

❏ Load a Photoshop file into your Creative Cloud account

❏ Extract text, images, and styles from a supplied Photoshop file

❏ Use CSS to control the appearance of various page elements

STAGE 1 / Placing Static Foreground Images

Important note: This project requires an individual user subscription to the Adobe Creative Cloud service. If your students are working on machines with a device license, they will not have access to the Extract functionality needed to complete the project. An alternate project, which does not require an individual user CC account, is available on the Instructor Downloads page.

As with many tasks, Dreamweaver offers a number of methods for inserting images into an HTML page. The variety of available options means you can choose whichever method best suits your personal working style and space. Before you begin placing objects in a page, however, you should understand the basics of images that will be used for web design.

Image Bit Depth

Bit depth refers to how many bits define the color value of a particular pixel. A **bit** is a unit of information that is either on or off (represented as 1 and 0, respectively).

- 1 bit has 2 states or colors

- 8 bits allow 256 possible colors (2^8, or $2×2×2×2×2×2×2×2=256$)

- 24 bits allow 16,777,216 possible colors (2^{24})

- 32 bits allow 16,777,216 possible colors (2^{24}), plus transparency

Image Formats

Four primary formats are used for images and graphics on the web:

- **GIF** (Graphics Interchange Format) is best used for graphics with areas of solid color, such as logos.

    The GIF format supports 8-bit color, or 256 possible values. To create the illusion of more possible colors, the format supports dithering, in which pixels of varying colors are interspersed in areas in which colors transition from one to another.

    This format supports index transparency, in which specific colors in the image can be defined as transparent areas, as well as simple frame-by-frame animation. It is largely falling out of use in favor of the PNG format for graphics.

GIF

JPEG

PNG-8

PNG-32

- **JPEG** (Joint Photographic Experts Group). This format supports 24-bit color, is used primarily for continuous-tone images with subtle changes in color, such as photographs or other images that are created in Adobe Photoshop. In an RGB photograph, three color channels define how much of each primary color (red, green, and blue) makes up each pixel. Each channel requires 8 bits, resulting in a total of 24 bits for each pixel, called **true color**. The format does not support transparency.

    The JPEG format incorporates **lossy compression**, which means that pixels are thrown away in order to reduce file size. When areas of flat color are highly compressed, speckles of other colors (called artifacts) often appear, which negatively impacts the quality of the design.

- **PNG** (Portable Network Graphics) has two common variants, PNG-8 and PNG-32.

  PNG-8 has 8 bits, which means it can support 256 colors in an image. Although the PNG-8 format incorporates algorithms to better reflect color transitions and colors that are not included in the file's color table, it is still only an 8-bit color format, so it should not be used for true-color images, such as photographs. Like the GIF format, it is more appropriate for logos and other graphics that do not use a large number of colors or smooth tone changes.

  PNG-32 supports 24-bit color, which means the format can be used for photographs and other images with a large range of color. PNG-32 also supports alpha transparency, in which each pixel can have a degree of transparency (the "alpha value") in addition to the three color channel values. In other words, PNG-32 supports smooth transitions from opaque to transparent. (The "32" designation comes from 24 bits for the color definition, plus 8 bits for the transparency information.)

  Both variations of the PNG format use lossless compression, which means no image data is thrown away. This results in better-quality images, but also larger file sizes than can be accomplished using a lossy compression algorithm.

- **SVG (Scalable Vector Graphics)** are made up of mathematically defined lines, called **vectors** (unlike **raster images**, which are made up entirely of pixels). Vector graphics are completely **scalable** without affecting their quality.

Review the Existing Project Status

This project involves working with files that have already been created by another designer. The best way to start this type of job is to evaluate the existing work before you jump in to complete the required tasks.

1. Download `Council_Web20_RF.zip` from the Student Files web page.

2. Expand the ZIP archive in your WIP folder (Macintosh) or copy the archive contents into your WIP folder (Windows).

   This results in a folder named **Council**, which contains the files you need for this project.

3. Create a new site named **Arts-Council**, using the WIP>Council folder as the site root folder.

   The procedure for defining this site is the same as that for the sites you created in previous projects (except for the path, which is unique for every project). If necessary, refer to the first exercises in Project 5: Bistro Site Organization for more detailed instructions.

4. With the Arts-Council site open in the Files panel, double-click `index.html` to open the file.

5. **Review the page contents in the Live view.**

   This is a fairly simple page, with several places marked to add various content. As you complete this project, you will use a number of techniques to place and manage images to add visual interest.

   In the first stage of this project, you will use a variety of techniques to add content that was provided with the basic HTML file. In the second stage of the project you will extract content from a Photoshop file that shows the finished and approved page design.

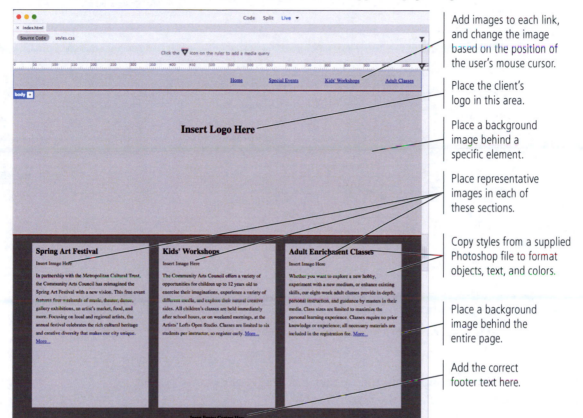

Add images to each link, and change the image based on the position of the user's mouse cursor.

Place the client's logo in this area.

Place a background image behind a specific element.

Place representative images in each of these sections.

Copy styles from a supplied Photoshop file to format objects, text, and colors.

Place a background image behind the entire page.

Add the correct footer text here.

6. **Continue to the next exercise.**

Place an Image in the Regular Design View

Dreamweaver provides many ways to insert images into web pages, one of which is to simply drag an image file from the Files panel to a specific location on the page. (This method only works in the regular Design view. You cannot drag an image from the Files panel when the Live view is active.) In this exercise, you will use this basic technique to place an image in the client's home page.

1. **With index.html open (from the Arts-Council site folder), turn off the Live view to make the regular Design view active.**

2. **Click the Split button in the Document toolbar to show both the Design and Code views.**

   In this project, we use the horizontal split view to maximize the line length that is visible in both panes. Feel free to use whichever method you prefer.

3. **In the Design view, select the words "Insert Image Here" in the left rectangle in the third row of the layout.**

4. **Delete the selected text from the Design view.**

   When you delete the placeholder text, the code for a nonbreaking space (** **) is automatically added as a placeholder inside the **<p>** tags.

The regular Design view is active. Live view is turned off.

The insertion point still flashes in the now-empty paragraph.

The Code pane shows that deleting the text from the Design pane does not delete the <p> tags.

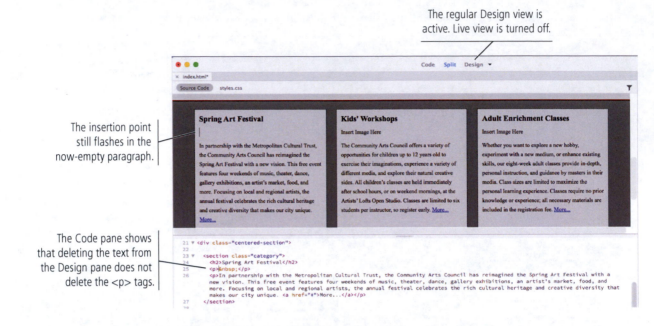

5. **In the Files panel, expand the site images folder and review the contents.**

   These four images have been provided by the client. You will insert them in various places on the client's new home page.

6. **Click the file festival.jpg in the Files panel and drag to the empty paragraph (where you deleted the text in Step 4).**

   When the regular Design view is active, you can drag any image from the Files panel to a specific position in the layout. (This method does not work when the Live view is active.)

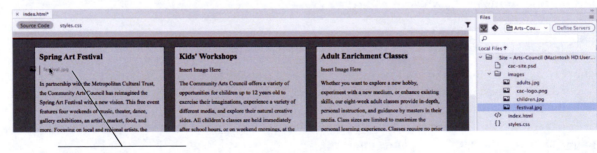

Drag the file from the Files panel to the location where you want to place the image.

7. **With the image selected in the Design view, type Spring Arts Festival link in the Alt field of the Properties panel. Click the image in the Design pane to finalize the change.**

8. **With the placed image selected in the Design pane, examine the Tag Selector and the Code pane.**

The **<img>** (image) tag appears inside the opening and closing **<p>** tags.

Some attributes of the **<img>** tag are automatically populated based on information saved in the image file:

- The **src** attribute defines the file name and location of the image.

- The **width** and **height** attributes are automatically populated based on the file's physical dimensions.

- The **alt** attribute is the alternate text. This is the text that is read by screen-reader software, or appears in place of an image if image display is disabled in a browser. The alt text is also indexed by search engines, which allows them to show your site's images in the search engine image gallery.

  When you place an image, Dreamweaver automatically creates an empty alt attribute in the <img> tag. If you do not add text in the Alt field of the Properties panel (or directly in the Code pane), the attribute remains empty.

Note:

The alt attribute is commonly misnamed the alt tag. It is not an HTML tag, but an attribute of a tag.

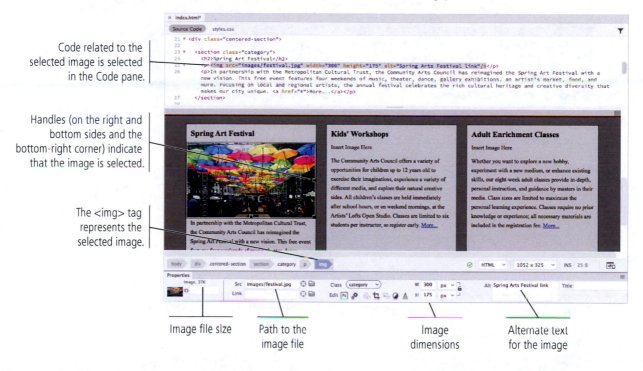

Code related to the selected image is selected in the Code pane.

Handles (on the right and bottom sides and the bottom-right corner) indicate that the image is selected.

The <img> tag represents the selected image.

Image file size

Path to the image file

Image dimensions

Alternate text for the image

9. **Save the file and continue to the next exercise.**

Place an Image with the Insert Panel

In the last few upgrades to the software, the Dreamweaver Live view has been significantly enhanced. You can now access many of the editing features that were previously only available in the regular Design view, so you can immediately see the results in the document window. In this exercise, you will use the buttons in the HTML Insert panel to add a new image element to the page in the Live view.

1. **With `index.html` open, click the Design button in the Document toolbar to close the Code pane, and then make the Live view active.**

2. **Click once to select the "Insert Image Here" paragraph in the middle rectangle in the third row of the layout.**

   When the Live view is active, clicking an object in the document window shows the Element Display. The blue tag shows the specific element, as well as any ID or class attributes that have been defined for that element. In this case, you can see that the selected element is a **p** element — in other words, it is a paragraph.

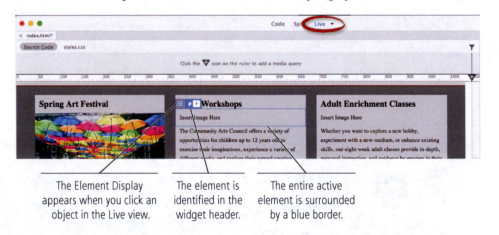

The Element Display appears when you click an object in the Live view.

The element is identified in the widget header.

The entire active element is surrounded by a blue border.

3. **Click the text in the selected paragraph to place the insertion point.**

   Remember, you can place the insertion point and edit text directly in the Live view.

Clicking places the insertion point inside the active element.

The orange border identifies the element in which the insertion point is placed.

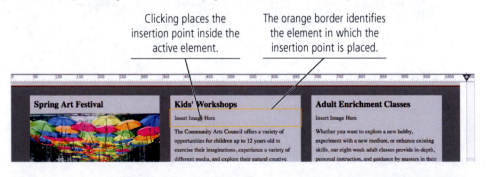

4. **Click and drag to select all the words in the active paragraph element.**

5. **Press the Delete key to remove the selected text from the Design pane.**

6. **Press the ESC key to exit the text-editing mode (unplace the insertion point).**

   You cannot use the Insert panel buttons when the insertion point is placed in the Live view. When you press the ESC key to unplace the insertion point, the actual element — in this case, the p (paragraph) element — becomes the active selection.

7. **Open the Insert panel and, if necessary, switch the panel to the HTML options.**

8. **With the p element selected, click the Image button in the HTML Insert panel.**

   Because an element is selected in the Live view, clicking this button results in the Position Assistant over the selected element, which you can use to determine where the image will be placed relative to the selected element — Before, After, or Nest inside. The Wrap option is not available in this case because you can't wrap an image around another object.

   Note:

   You can also choose Insert>Image.

Use these buttons to place the image relative to the selected element.

9. **Click the Nest button in the Position Assistant.**

   You want to place the image inside the paragraph, so you are using the Nest option.

10. **In the Resulting dialog box, navigate to the file children.jpg (in the site images folder) and click Open/OK.**

11. **With the image selected in the Design pane, click the Edit HTML Attributes button on the left side of the Element Display.**

12. **Type Kids Workshops link in the alt field and press Return/Enter to finalize the new alt attribute.**

    You can use this pop-up window to change various attributes of a placed image without using the Properties panel or Code pane.

Click here to open the HTML
Attributes pop-up window.

13. **Press the ESC key to close the HTML Attributes pop-up window.**

No image handles
are available when
the Live view is active.

14. **Save the file and continue to the next exercise.**

Drag and Drop an Image from the Insert Panel

When the Live view is active, you can drag a button from the HTML Insert panel to place a new element in the page. On-screen guides determine where the element will be placed. In this exercise, you will use this method to place an image in the page.

1. **Make sure index.html is open and the Live view is active.**

2. **Select and delete the words "Insert Image Here" from the right rectangle in the third row of the layout.**

3. **Press the ESC key to unplace the insertion point.**

4. **Click the Image button in the HTML Insert panel and drag to the empty paragraph element.**

When you drag elements within, or into, the Live view, visual indicators identify where the element you drag will be placed when you release the mouse button. A green two-headed arrow indicates that the dragged element will be placed in line with other elements. The line shows exactly where (before or after) the element will be placed. A blue rectangle inside another element indicates that the dragged one will be placed inside of the element to which you drag, referred to as **nesting**.

Drag the Image button to a specific position in the Live view layout.

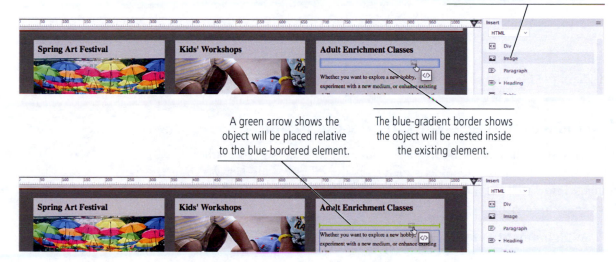

A green arrow shows the object will be placed relative to the blue-bordered element.

The blue-gradient border shows the object will be nested inside the existing element.

5. **When a blue border appears inside the paragraph element, release the mouse button.**

6. **In the resulting Select Image Source dialog box, navigate to `adults.jpg` (in the site `images` folder) and click Open/OK.**

Using the drag-and-drop method, you have to determine which image you want to place when you release the mouse button.

7. Using the pop-up HTML attributes window, define **Adult Classes link** as the alternate text for this image.

8. Save the file, and then continue to the next exercise.

Insert an Image with the Assets Panel

The Assets panel allows you to sort the various assets in a site by type, rather than by their location within the site folder structure. It also offers yet another way to insert an image into a web page. In this exercise, you will use the Assets panel to add the client's logo to the page.

1. With **index.html** open, make sure the Live view is active.

2. Select and delete the words "Insert Logo Here" in the second row in the layout, and then press the ESC key to unplace the insertion point.

    When you unplace the insertion point, the h1 element remains selected.

3. Open the Assets panel (Window>Assets). On the left side of the Assets panel, click the Images button to show all images in the site.

    The Assets panel displays a thumbnail of the selected image at the top of the panel.

4. Click the Refresh Site List button at the bottom of the Assets panel to make sure all images are visible.

Note:

Do not double-click the image in the Assets or Files panels to insert it. Double-clicking an image in either prompts Dreamweaver to open the file in an image-editing application.

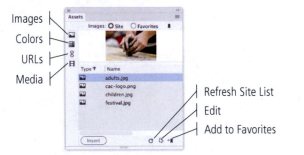

5. Select **cac-logo.png** in the panel.

6. **With the empty header element selected from Step 2, click the Insert button at the bottom of the Assets panel.**

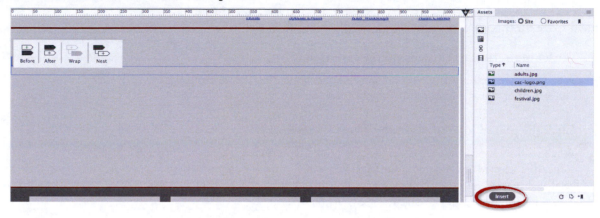

You can also drag an image from the Assets panel to the layout. If the Live view is active, on-screen guides identify where the dragged image will be placed. If the regular Design view is active, simply drag from the panel to a location indicated by the flashing insertion point.

7. **Click the Nest button in the resulting Position Assistant.**

8. **Define Community Arts Council as the alternate text for the placed image.**

9. **Save the file and continue to the next exercise.**

Resize and Resample an Image

As you can see in the Live view, the placed logo is much too large to fit in the defined space. In this exercise, you will adjust the image to fit the space.

1. **With index.html open, turn off the Live view.**

   When the Live view is active, you can only use the Properties panel to change the dimensions of a placed image.

2. **Click the placed logo to select the image (if necessary).**

   When the Live view is not active, the bottom center, right center, and bottom-right corner of a selected image show control handles, which you can drag to resize the height of the placed image. (You might not be able to see the right edge of the image, depending on the size and arrangement of your workspace.)

You can drag the image handles to resize the image in the document window.

You can use the W and H fields to change the image dimensions.

3. **In the Properties panel, make sure the lock icon to the right of the W and H fields is locked. If the icon is unlocked, click it to make it locked.**

   When the icon is locked, changing one dimension applies a proportional change to the other dimension. In other words, changes to the image dimensions maintain the original width-to-height aspect ratio.

Note:

If an image extends outside the edge of the element in which it is placed, you will not be able to use the control handles to resize the image. Instead, you have to use the Properties panel.

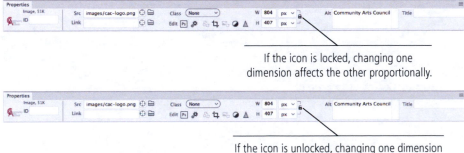

If the icon is locked, changing one dimension affects the other proportionally.

If the icon is unlocked, changing one dimension has no effect on the other dimension.

4. **Highlight the current value in the W field. Type 550, and then press Return/Enter to finalize the change.**

In the Properties panel, the image dimensions appear in bold, indicating that the image has been resized.

Two additional buttons are now available to the right of the W and H fields. Clicking the **Reset to Original Size button** restores the original image dimensions, regardless of how many times you have changed the image size in the page or in the Properties panel.

Clicking the **Commit Image Size button** changes the placed image file to match the current image dimensions on the page.

Note:

You can usually reduce an image without losing quality, but enlarging an image beyond its original size can result in a significant loss of image quality.

Reset to Original Size   Commit Image Size

5. **Click the bottom-right image handle, press Shift, and drag up and left. When the H field shows the height of 250, release the mouse button.**

You can drag any of the handles to resize the image in only one direction (by dragging the side handles) or in both directions at once (by dragging the corner handle).

Keep in mind that manually resizing the image using these handles does not honor the Lock icon in the Properties panel. If you drag either of the side handles, or the corner handle without pressing Shift, the lock icon in the Properties panel is automatically unlocked. By pressing Shift while dragging the corner handle, you constrain the resizing process and maintain the image's original aspect ratio.

Note:

Pressing Shift while dragging a side handle does not maintain the image's aspect ratio. You have to Shift-drag the corner handle to resize the image proportionally.

Drag a side handle to change only one dimension.

Drag the corner handle to change both dimensions at one time.

The Properties panel shows the adjusted size when you drag the handles.

6. **In the Files panel, expand the `images` folder if necessary.**

7. **Control/right-click the `cac-logo.png` file, and choose Edit>Duplicate from the contextual menu.**

   It's a common mistake to insert a large image into a web page, and then simply resize it to take up less space on the page. The problem with resizing is that, while the image *appears* smaller, the file size ("weight") remains the same. Users might need to wait a considerable length of time to download the large image file.

   Instead of simply resizing, you should also resample any resized images to include only the necessary data. **Resampling** discards pixels (while downsizing), so the specified dimensions of the image are its actual dimensions. This reduces the weight of the image, which reduces the download time for your visitors.

   In the next few steps, you are going to resample the image that you placed into the index.html page. However, you should understand that resampling in Dreamweaver permanently changes the image file. Before you make this type of change permanent, it is a good idea to create a copy of the file, so you can still access the original if necessary.

8. **In the Files panel, click the original `cac-logo.png` file once to select it, then click the file name again to highlight it.**

   Make sure you don't rename the one that has "Copy" in the file name, as that is the original-size logo. You want to rename the image file that you placed into the header and decreased to a smaller physical size.

9. **At the end of the current file name, type `-small`, then press Return/Enter to finalize the new file name.**

10. **In the resulting dialog box, click Update to update the link in index.html to the new file name.**

11. With the image selected on the page, click the Commit Image Size button to the right of the W and H fields.

Note:

You could also click the Resample button to accomplish the same effect.

Resample   Commit Image Size

12. Click OK to acknowledge the warning.

As we explained earlier, resampling in Dreamweaver permanently changes the image file — the resized dimensions become its (new) actual size. After resampling, the Reset to Original Size button is no longer visible, and the Resample button is not available.

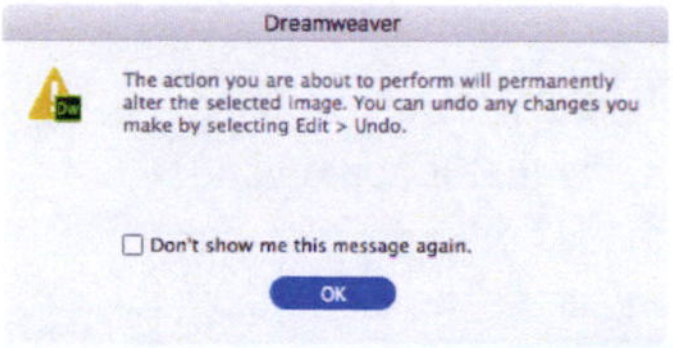

Note:

If another user clicked the "Don't show me this message again" option, you won't see this warning.

After resampling, the Reset
Size button no longer appears.

13. Save the file and continue to the next stage of the project.

The Image Properties Panel in Depth

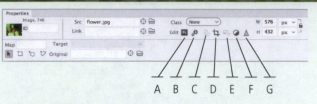

When an image is selected in the document window, the Properties panel not only displays properties (attributes) of the image, but also provides access to a number of image-related functions.

A. **Edit** opens the image file in its native application. GIF, JPG, and PNG files open in Photoshop.

B. **Edit Image Settings** opens a dialog box where you can change a variety of options for the selected file format. You can also use the Format menu to change the format of the selected image. If you change the format, you will be asked where you want to save the new file.

C. **Update From Original** can be used to make sure an inserted Photoshop image in the HTML file is the most recently saved version.

If you insert a native Photoshop (PSD) file into a page, Dreamweaver converts it to a file that is appropriate for web browsers. The Edit Image Settings dialog box automatically appears, so you can define the settings for the generated image.

When you place a native Photoshop file, Dreamweaver stores a link to the original file.

The actual image in the page is converted to a web-friendly format.

The original link to the PSD file is also maintained. If the PSD file is changed, Dreamweaver notifies you that the image must be updated to the most recent version.

An icon appears in the top-left corner of a placed Photoshop file. Moving your mouse over the icon shows whether the image reflects the most recently saved version of the Photoshop file.

Although Dreamweaver is not an image-editing application, you can perform some basic image-editing functions. These tools can't replace Adobe Photoshop, but they are useful for making quick adjustments to an image directly in Dreamweaver.

D. The **Crop tool** can be used to remove unwanted areas of an image. When you click the Crop tool, the lighter area shows what will be included in the cropped image. You can drag the handles around the crop area edge to change the area. Pressing Return/Enter finalizes the crop. Pressing ESC cancels the crop and restores the original image.

Drag the handles to change the area that will become the cropped version.

The lighter area shows what will remain after the crop has been applied.

E. The **Resample tool** changes the number of pixels in an image to match the image's size in the page. This has the same effect as clicking the Commit Image Size button after resizing an image in the Design pane.

F. **Brightness and Contrast** can be used to change those properties in a selected image.

G. The **Sharpen** option can be useful for restoring some detail after resizing/resampling (especially upsizing). Keep in mind, however, that oversharpening can often produce worse results than those you started with.

Remember that all of the Dreamweaver image-editing tools permanently modify the edited file. If you use any of the image-editing buttons, you see a warning that the changes permanently affect the file (unless someone has checked the Don't Show ... option in the dialog box). Always keep a backup image so if you over-edit, you can replace the image and start over.

STAGE 2 / Extracting Photoshop Assets

The "look and feel" of a website is often created in an image-editing application, such as Adobe Photoshop, while the structure and code are created in Dreamweaver. Using the Extract tools that are part of an individual-user subscription to the Adobe Creative Cloud, integrating assets that are defined in Photoshop is now far easier than ever before.

Verify Your Adobe ID in Dreamweaver

In the next exercise you are going to use the Extract tools that are part of your Adobe Creative Cloud subscription services. For that process to work, you must have an active internet connection and be signed in to your Creative Cloud account in Dreamweaver. In this exercise, you will verify that you are signed in to your Creative Cloud account.

Important note: For the Extract functions to work properly, your user ID must be associated with a paid individual-user Creative Cloud subscription account. This service is not available if you have only a free Adobe ID, and is not available if you are using a computer that has a device license instead of an individual-user license.

1. **In Dreamweaver, open the Help menu.**

2. **If you see an option to Sign In, skip to Step 5.**

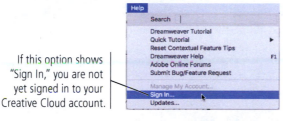

If this option shows "Sign In," you are not yet signed in to your Creative Cloud account.

3. **If you see an option to Sign Out, verify that the listed email is the Adobe ID linked to your Creative Cloud account.**

If this option shows "Sign Out," someone is already signed in to a Creative Cloud account.

This is the email (Adobe ID) that is currently signed in to the Adobe Creative Cloud.

4a. **If the email address listed in the Help menu is yours, continue to the next exercise.**

4b. **If the email in the menu is not yours, choose the Sign Out option. Read the resulting message, and then click Sign Out.**

If you sign out of any Adobe CC application, this message informs you that you are also signing out of *all* Adobe CC applications.

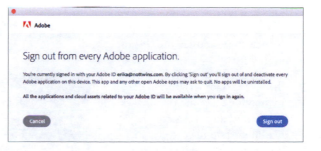

5. **In Dreamweaver, choose Help>Sign In.**

6. **In the resulting dialog box, follow the on-screen instructions to sign in to your Adobe CC account.**

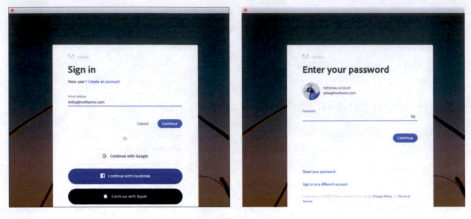

7. **Continue to the next exercise.**

Load a Photoshop File into Your CC Account

The structure of this web page, which you saw as gray rectangles when you first opened index.html, was defined in Dreamweaver using CSS. The overall design, however, was created in an Adobe Photoshop file that was provided with the project's resource files. In this exercise, you will upload the provided Photoshop file to your Creative Cloud account so that you can extract the assets that are defined in that file.

1. **With the Arts-Council site open in the Files panel, open the file index.html if it is not already.**

   A file must be open in Dreamweaver before you can access Extract panel functionality.

2. **Using the Document toolbar, activate the Live view and hide the Code pane (if necessary).**

3. **Choose Window>Extract to open the Extract panel.**

   The first time you (or someone else) uses the Extract panel, you see the introductory version of the panel, shown on the left, with links to a tutorial on the panel's functionality. After using the panel the first time, you see the version on the right.

   The CC Extract service provides a method for accessing the images, text, colors, and styles created in a Photoshop file directly in Dreamweaver — which makes it relatively easy to translate a design into a functioning web page.

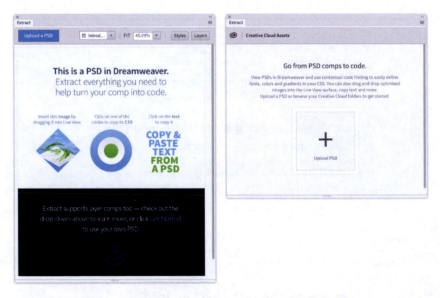

4. **If you see the introductory version of the panel, click the Upload PSD button in the top-left corner to show the standard Extract panel.**

5. **Click the Upload PSD button in the middle of the standard Extract panel.**

6. **In the resulting navigation dialog box, navigate to the `cac-site.psd` file in your WIP>Council folder.**

   This file was created by another designer. It includes the images and text that you need to complete the client's new home page. It also shows the formatting that should be used for various elements, such as the applied font and type sizes, element backgrounds, and colors.

7. **Click Open.**

The new thumbnail shows the progress of the upload.

When the upload is complete, a thumbnail of the file appears.

8. **When the upload process is complete, double-click the cac-site.psd thumbnail in the Extract panel.**

   This opens the file in the Extract panel, which means you can now access the various file assets — images, type styles, etc. — directly in Dreamweaver.

9. **Click the bottom-right corner of the Extract panel and drag to expand the panel as large as possible so you can clearly see the elements in the file, then click the Fit button at the top of the panel.**

Change the view percentage of the preview in the panel.

Drag the corner of the panel to make it larger (if possible).

Note:

Throughout the rest of this project (and this book), we tell you what panels to use at various points. Our screen captures show only the panels most relevant to the immediate discussion. Feel free to arrange the workspace in any way that best suits your working environment.

10. **Continue to the next exercise.**

Extract Text and Images from a Photoshop File

The Photoshop file that you uploaded in the previous exercise defines the appearance and content of the various elements in the HTML page. In this exercise you will extract content that will be required to complete the web page design in Dreamweaver.

1. **With index.html open from the Arts-Council site, make sure the Live view is active.**

2. **With the Photoshop file that you uploaded in the previous exercise open in the Extract panel, move your mouse cursor over different areas of the preview.**

   In the Extract panel, a black border identifies distinct elements (layer content) in the Photoshop file. As you move your mouse cursor over various parts of the preview, you can see which element would be selected if you click.

Move the mouse cursor over different elements to highlight the layer content.

3. **Click the text element in the bottom row of the preview to select it.**

   When you select a specific element in the panel preview, a pop-up window presents options that can be extracted for the selected element.

Click an item to open a window with extract options for the selected layer content.

Note:

Files that you upload are stored in your Creative Cloud account. You can manage those files using the Assets>Files tab of the Adobe Creative Cloud app.

Note:

You can click the Creative Cloud icon in the top-left corner of the panel to return to the list of uploaded files.

4. **Click the Copy Text button in the pop-up window.**

5. **In the document window, select and delete the words "Insert Footer Content Here" from the bottom rectangle in the layout.**

Delete the placeholder text from this area.

6. **With the insertion point in the now-empty paragraph, choose Edit>Paste (or press Command/Control-V).**

Paste the copied text from Step 5 in this area.

7. **Click the Layers button in the top-right corner of the Extract panel.**

These buttons allow you to review all the layers and layer groups that have been saved in the Photoshop file. You can expand layer groups to review the sublayers in those groups, show or hide individual layers, and select specific layers to more easily extract the information they contain.

8. **Click the sketch layer in the list to select it.**

When you select a layer, the available extract options appear in a pop-up window (just as when you selected a specific element in the preview image).

As the preview suggests, this image should be added as the background image for the entire page. Rather than copying the image's dimensions, you are going to extract the image from the Photoshop file into the site's images folder so you can use the image directly in Dreamweaver.

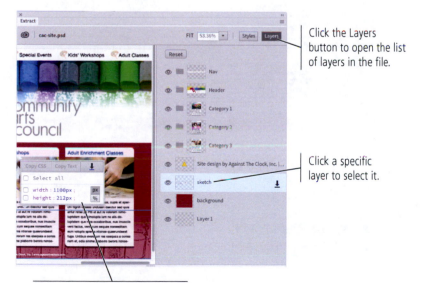

Click the Layers button to open the list of layers in the file.

Click a specific layer to select it.

The pop-up window identifies the selected layer content and presents extract options for that content.

9. **Click the Extract Asset button either on the layer list or on the pop-up window.**

10. **In the resulting pop-up window, click the Browse for Folder button to the right of the Folder field. Navigate to the images folder in your WIP>Council folder, and then click Open/Select Folder.**

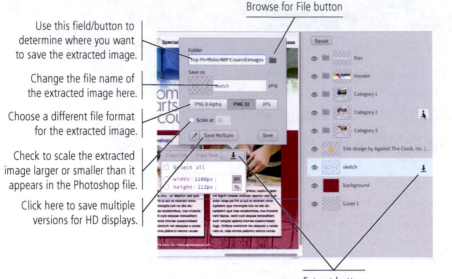

Browse for File button

Use this field/button to determine where you want to save the extracted image.

Change the file name of the extracted image here.

Choose a different file format for the extracted image.

Check to scale the extracted image larger or smaller than it appears in the Photoshop file.

Click here to save multiple versions for HD displays.

Extract button

11. **Make sure the PNG 32 button is active, and then click Save.**

   This layer is semi-transparent, allowing the background layer color to show through the image pixels. To incorporate that transparency into the extracted image, you must use the PNG 32 format (the default format).

   When the Extract process is complete, you see a message that the asset has downloaded successfully.

12. **Click the folder icon to the left of the Nav layer to expand it.**

   The layer group includes a text layer and an image layer for each navigation link. The "fade" icon should be the default image for each navigation link. The "full" icon should appear when the user's mouse moves over that link. For now you need to extract the required images so you can later use CSS to define the link backgrounds, and change the image from "fade" to "full" when the user's mouse cursor moves over a specific link.

Click a folder icon to expand or collapse a layer group and view the sublayers.

13. **Repeat Steps 8–11 to extract the palette-full and palette-fade images as PNG 32 files into the site images folder.**

14. **Click the folder icon to collapse the Nav folder, then click the folder icon to expand the Header folder.**

15. **Click to select the pencils layer, then click the Extract button for that layer.**

16. **In the resulting pop-up window, click the Browse for Folder button to the right of the Folder field. Navigate to the images folder in your WIP>Council folder, and then click Open/Select Folder.**

Note:

You only need to extract one copy of the palette-fade image from the Photoshop file.

17. **Choose the JPG option and set the Optimize slider to 90.**

This image does not require transparency, so you can use the JPG format that allows compression (which can be important for reducing the size of background images). The Optimize slider defines the quality level of the resulting image — higher values result in better quality, but less compression.

18. **Click Save to extract the file.**

19. **In the Files panel, expand the images folder. If you don't see the four extracted files, click the Refresh button at the bottom of the panel.**

The extracted images are:
- palette-fade.png
- palette-full.png
- pencils.jpg
- sketch.png

Note:

You can also drag an image from the Extract panel to the document window. When you release the mouse button, the file is extracted using the default settings, and the image is placed in the location to which you dragged.

20. **Save the HTML file, and then continue to the next exercise.**

Format the Page Body

In the previous exercise you extracted text from a Photoshop file and placed it into your HTML page. You also extracted images from a Photoshop file, one which you will use in this exercise to define the appearance of the overall page background.

1. **With index.html open and the Live view active, click to select the word "Home" link at the top of the document.**

2. **Review the Tag Selector in the bottom-left corner of the document window.**

   The Tag Selector shows the "path of tags," or the nested order of tags to the active selection.

\<body>	identifies the basic page, in which all visible content is contained
\<nav>	identifies the HTML nav element
\<ul>	identifies an unordered list element
\<li>	identifies a list item element
\<a>	identifies the selected link element

   It is important to understand the nested nature of tags — especially how that nested structure relates to CSS. A specific element can be affected by any selector in its path of tags. The **body** element contains all visible elements on the page. The body selector in CSS, then, also affects all visible elements on the page.

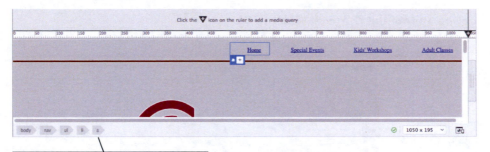

   The Tag Selector shows that this **a** element is nested inside a number of other elements.

3. **Open the CSS Designer panel (Window>CSS Designer).**

   The CSS Designer panel is divided into four sections:

   - **Sources** lists the locations and files containing CSS styles that affect the active site.

   - **@Media** lists media queries, which can be used to define different styles, depending on the size of the device being used to display a site.

   - **Selectors** are the items that define the properties of specific elements. If you have an object selected in the Design pane, only selectors related to that object appear in the list. When a specific selector is active in the panel, the relevant Source and Media options appear bold in those sections of the panel.

   - **Properties** are the rules that define the specific appearance of the selector for which they are defined.

   You can click and drag the lines between sections in the panel to expand a specific section. Clicking a section heading minimizes it, so only the heading is visible in the panel. You can click a minimized section heading to re-expand that section. The + and – buttons on the left side of each section heading are used to add or remove items from the panel — they do not collapse or expand the various section.

4. **If necessary, click the All button at the top of the panel.**

   The CSS Designer panel defaults to Current mode, in which the panel shows only selectors related to the element that is selected in the document window. If you click the All button at the top of the panel, all selectors in the CSS file appear in the Selectors list.

5. **Click the body selector in the Selectors section of the panel.**

   For the sake of readability, we identify selector names in red in the exercise steps.

   Selectors beginning with a # character are **ID selectors**. These apply only to the element that is identified with the matching **ID attribute**. It is important to realize that an ID can only apply to a single element on the page.

   Selectors beginning with a . (period) character are **class selectors**. These apply to any element that has the matching class attribute. A single **class attribute** can be applied to multiple elements on the same page, which means you can define the same properties for various elements at the same time.

   Selectors that do not begin with a # or . character are HTML **tag selectors**. These apply to the specific HTML elements that match the selector name. For example, the section selector applies to all section elements on the page, regardless of any applied ID or class attributes. The section element is enclosed in the opening and closing **<section></section>** tags.

   The body selector applies to the body element (the overall page background), which is enclosed in the opening and closing **<body></body>** tags. All visible elements are contained within the body element.

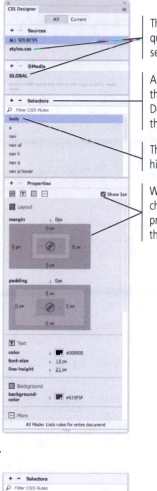

The source and media query of the active selector appear in **bold**.

All selectors related to the active selection in the Design pane are listed in the Selectors section.

The active selector is highlighted in the list.

When Show Set is checked, only defined properties appear in the Properties section.

Note:

If you expand the width of the CSS Designer panel far enough, the Properties section moves to the right, creating a second column within the panel.

6. **In the Properties section of the panel, uncheck the Show Set option.**

   When the Show Set option is checked in the Properties section of the panel, only defined properties appear in the Properties pane. If this option is not checked, all available properties are listed. Properties that appear grayed out are not defined for the active selector.

When Show Set is not checked, the Properties section shows all options that can be defined for the active selector.

7. **With the Photoshop file that you uploaded open in the Extract panel, click the Styles button in the top-right corner of the Extract panel.**

The Styles list shows all fonts, colors, and gradients that are used in the Photoshop file.

As you can see, the file uses only one font (HelveticaNeue), although every font size is listed separately. Rather than defining the font of each separate element in the HTML page, you can define a font for the body element that will apply to every element contained in that body — in other words, everything you can see on the page.

8. **Expand the HelveticaNeue font, if necessary, and then click the 13px option to show where that type size is used in the design.**

When you select a specific font size in the list, you see the font-family and font-weight properties that apply to the selected size.

Click the Styles button to show the fonts, colors, and gradients that are used in the Photoshop file.

Click to expand the font and show the sizes that are used in the design.

Click to select a specific font size.

Arrows in the preview identify the elements that use the selected font size.

9. **With the body selector selected in the CSS Designer panel, click the Text button at the top of the Properties section to show those properties in the panel.**

When Show Set is not checked, the Properties section includes a large number of options that can be defined for the active selector. You can simply scroll through all of the available options, or use the buttons shown in the image at right to quickly jump to specific categories of properties.

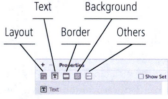

Text Background

Layout Border Others

10. **Click the space to the right of the font-family property to open the menu of available font stacks. Choose the option that includes Helvetica Neue and ends with "sans-serif."**

A **font stack**, also called a **font family**, is a sequence of fonts that can be used to display content. When a browser opens a page, it goes through the various fonts in the list until it finds one that can be used on the active device. If none of the fonts in the list are available on a user's computer, the text will be displayed in the default font that is defined for the style at the end of the list — in this case, whatever the user chose as the default sans-serif font on the computer being used.

11. Review the index.html file in the Live view.

Because every visible element on the page is contained within the HTML **body** element, text in every element now adopts the new font family.

12. In the Extract panel, click the red swatch in the Colors section of the list, and note the color value in the pop-up window.

When you select a specific element in the Styles list, arrows in the preview image identify which elements use the selected color. The color definition appears highlighted in a pop-up window.

Click the Styles button to show the fonts, colors, and gradients that are used in the Photoshop file.

Click a color swatch to show the color definition.

Arrows in the preview identify the elements that use the selected color.

13. With the body selector selected in the CSS Designer panel, click the Background button at the top of the Properties section.

14. **Click the existing background-color value to highlight it, and then type rgb(157, 34, 66) — the value you noted in Step 12 — as the new color. Press Return/Enter to finalize the new background-color value.**

You might be able to copy and paste the color value from the pop-up window in Step 12 to the CSS Designer panel in Step 14. However, there is a bug in the software that prevents users on certain operating systems from using the copy-and-paste method.

Click the Background button to jump to those options.

Click the existing value to highlight it.

Type the value noted from the Extract panel as the new background-color value.

After finalizing the new background color, you can see it in the bottom half of the page. The top half of the page still appears gray because the **nav** and **header** elements — which are nested inside the body element — in this file have defined background colors.

It is important to note that CSS selector rules apply until they are overridden by another value. The CSS Designer panel lists selectors in the order in which they appear in the CSS file. The body selector is first in the list, so it is also first in the CSS file. The nav and header selectors appear after the body selector, so background-color values for those override the background-color value in the body selector.

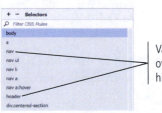

Values in later selectors override those in selectors higher in the list.

15. Look at the top of the document window.

Although you made changes that affect the appearance of the index.html file, the document tab does not show an asterisk — in other words, the HTML document has not been changed. You do not need to save it before continuing.

The index.html file has not been changed in this exercise.

The styles.css file has been changed in this exercise.

All changes in this exercise were made to the CSS file that is linked to the open HTML file. The Related Files bar below the document tab shows an asterisk next to styles.css, indicating that the CSS file has been changed, and so should be saved.

16. Click styles.css in the Related Files bar, and then choose File>Save.

When you click one of the related files in the bar, the document window automatically switches to Split view and the file you clicked is displayed in the Code pane.

Clicking one of the related files opens the Split view and shows relevant code in the Code pane.

17. Click Source Code in the Related Files bar to return to the main HTML file.

Clicking the Source Code button restores the active page's HTML code to the Code pane.

Clicking Source Code reverts the Code pane to the HTML file's code.

18. Click the Live button in the Document toolbar to close the Code pane, and then continue to the next exercise.

Format Element Backgrounds with Extracted Styles

As you can see in the Extract panel, different elements on the page should have different background properties — white background color, an applied drop shadow, and rounding on various corners. In this exercise you will extract settings from the Photoshop file to properly format the backgrounds of various elements in the page.

1. With index.html open and the Live view active, click the Layers button in the Extract panel to show the list of layers in the uploaded file.

The designer of this file provided meaningful names for the various layers in the file, so you can easily see which layer translates to which element in the HTML page. As a general rule, you should use meaningful names when you define elements in a file — whether they are layers in a Photoshop file or elements in an HTML file.

2. **Click the folder icon to expand the Nav folder, and then click to select the nav-bkg layer.**

   When you click the layer in the Extract panel, a pop-up window shows the aspects of this element that you need to apply to the related element in the HTML page. Any properties and styles applied in the Photoshop file that can be translated to CSS are listed in the pop-up window.

   Because Photoshop does not incorporate settings that accurately map to element size and positioning, the width and height properties are not checked, by default.

Properties in the Photoshop file determines the appearance of the layer content.

3. **With the background-color property selected in the list, click the Copy CSS button in the top-left corner of the pop-up window.**

4. **In the CSS Designer panel, Control/right-click nav in the Selector list. Choose Paste Styles in the contextual menu for the header element.**

   Remember, you want to apply these settings to the header element on the page, so you are pasting the copied properties into the header HTML tag selector in the CSS file.

5. **Repeat Step 4 to paste the same copied style into the header selector.**

6. **Click in the document window to select the element containing the words "Spring Art Festival."**

The Tag Selector and Element Display show that this text is an h2 element. The Tag Selector also shows that it is in a section element that has a defined class attribute (.category).

This h2 element is inside a section element
with the class attribute "category".

7. **Click in the document window to select the words "Kids' Workshops" in the middle rectangle of row three.**

Again, the Tag Selector shows that this is an h2 element, which is in a section element that has the same defined class attribute as the first section element in the same row.

Each section element in this row has the same class attribute, which means you can change the background properties of all three sections by changing properties in the related class.

This h2 element is inside a section element
with the class attribute "category".

8. **In the Layers pane of the Extract panel, expand the Category 1 layer group and select the category-bkg sublayer.**

9. **Click the Copy CSS button in the pop-up window for the selected layer.**

10. **Control/right-click the .category selector in the CSS Designer panel and choose Paste Styles in the contextual menu.**

    Because the .category class is applied to all three sections in the row, the pasted properties now apply to all three elements.

11. **Choose File>Save All.**

    This command saves all files that are related to the active site, including the CSS file that you have been editing by defining CSS properties.

12. **Continue to the next exercise.**

Define Background Images

The approved layout includes two separate background images — one for the overall page and one for only the area behind the logo. In this exercise you will use the assets you extracted earlier to create the required background images.

Note:

Every element in an HTML file can have distinct background settings.

1. With **index.html** open and the **Live view** active, click to select the body selector in the CSS Designer panel.

2. Navigate to the Background options, and then click the Browse button to the right of the url option.

   The CSS Designer panel provides available properties whenever possible. In this case, you have to define a file, so you are presented with a text field and a Browse button, which you can use to define the image you want to use as the background.

   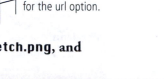

   Click the Browse button for the url option.

3. Navigate to the Arts-Council site images folder, select **sketch.png**, and then click Open/OK.

   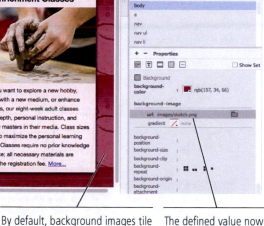

   By default, background images tile both horizontally and vertically.

   The defined value now appears in the panel.

4. Click the no-repeat button for the background-repeat option.

   Unless you specify otherwise, a background image will repeat (tile) across and down, so the background of the element is completely filled with the background image.

   The CSS **background-repeat** property has four options: repeat (the default), repeat-x (horizontally only), repeat-y (vertically only), and no-repeat (the background image appears only once in the top-left corner of the element).

   The background-repeat options are available as buttons.

   Again, the panel provides the available options. The button icons suggest the values that will be defined. If you hover your mouse cursor over a button, a tool tip positively identifies the button.

5. **Move the mouse cursor over the background-position property. Click the "%" option for the first background-position value (X) and choose center from the pop-up menu.**

Because the background-position property does not yet have a value, you have to move your mouse cursor over that property in the panel to reveal the available fields.

In this case, the panel offers a menu with the available values for this property.

The CSS **background-position** property allows two values: X (horizontal) position and Y (vertical) position. The panel lists both on the same line, X then Y.

You can define positions relative to the containing element (left, right, etc.), or use specific measurements, such as "5 pixels," to position a background image.

Click the number and type to define a specific numeric value.

Click the measurement to open a menu to change the active unit of measurement, or to choose a fixed position relative to the document.

Remember, these properties define the horizontal (X) and vertical (Y) positions of the background image *relative to the containing element*.

6. **Click the "%" option for the second background-position value (Y) and choose bottom from the pop-up menu.**

You can now see that the background image is attached to the bottom of the file, and does not repeat.

Depending on your monitor width, however, you might notice that the image is only 1100 px wide. If your document window is large enough, you can see that the background image might not extend the entire width of the page.

7. **With the body selector active in the CSS Designer panel, click the background-size value and choose contain from the pop-up menu.**

The **background-size** property defines the size of background images.

- If you do not define a specific background size, the image will simply display at its actual size. The same result can be achieved using the **auto** value.

- You can define a specific value using a variety of measurement units. You can also use two values to define both the width and height.

      background-size: 400px 600px [width height]

  Instead of specific values, you can use percentages. In this case, the background image appears as a percentage of the container.

      background-size: 80% 100% [width height]

- The **cover** value scales the background image as large as necessary to completely fill the container. If the image has a different aspect ratio than the container, some parts of the background image will be cut off.

- The **contain** value scales the image to the largest possible size so that the entire image fills the container. If the image has a different aspect ratio than the container, some areas of the container will not be filled by the background image unless you tile it.

In this case, the contain value scales the image so that it fills the width of the document window, regardless of the required scaling.

8. **In the document window, click to select the logo in the middle of the page.**

The second background image needs to appear only in the area behind the logo. The Tag Selector shows that this image is placed in the h1 element, which is nested inside the header element.

9. **Using the CSS Designer panel, define `pencils.jpg` as the background image for the header selector, using the following rules:**

> **background-size:**   **cover**
>
> **background-repeat:** **none**

The header element has a fixed height, but it can be narrower or wider, depending on the size of the document window. Using the cover value for the **background-size** property, the image will enlarge or shrink to fill the available window width.

10. **Choose File>Save All, and then continue to the next exercise.**

Format Text with Extracted Styles

The site design is nearly complete, but you still need to adjust a number of text elements based on what you see in the approved Photoshop file. In this exercise you will define properties for the h2 and footer elements to match what you see in the Extract panel.

1. With **index.html** open, make sure the Photoshop file you uploaded is open in the Extract panel.

2. Click the Layers button at the top of the panel to close the list of layers.

3. In the Extract panel, click the "Spring Arts Festival" text to reveal the CSS for that element.

4. In the pop-up window, uncheck the font-family property, and then click the Copy CSS button.

   You already adjusted the body selector to format all text in the page with the HelveticaNeue font family, so you don't need to include this property in the nested elements.

Uncheck the font-family property.

5. Click the "Spring Art Festival" text in the document window to select that element.

6. Click the Current button at the top of the CSS Designer panel.

When Current mode is active, the Selectors list shows only selectors that relate to the active element (what is selected in the document window). This is very useful for finding only and exactly what you need, especially if you are working with a large list of selectors.

The h2 element is selected.

Only selectors related to the active element appear in the list.

7. Control/right-click the .category h2 selector in the CSS Designer panel and choose Paste Styles in the contextual menu.

The styles you copied in Step 3 (color, font-size, and font-weight) are pasted into the .category h2 selector. Because all three of the sections use the .category class, the h2 elements in each section now show the pasted formatting.

8. Repeat the process from Steps 3–7 to change the formatting of the footer p selector to match what you see in the Extract panel.

Again, you do not need to copy the font-family property.

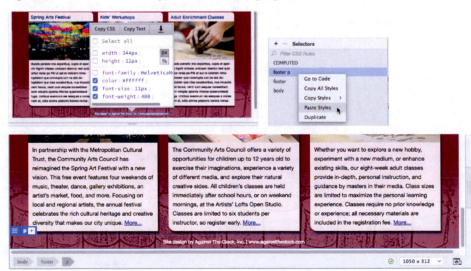

9. Choose File>Save All, and then continue to the next exercise.

Format Links with Descendent Selectors

The final required tasks for this project involve formatting links in various areas of the page. In this exercise you will work with **descendant selectors**, also called **compound selectors**, which allow you to define properties that affect very specific elements.

1. **With index.html open, review the various links on the page.**

   Two different areas include links: navigation links in the nav element and "More..." links in the category sections.

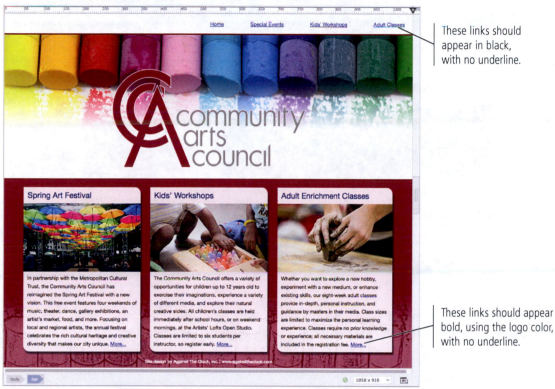

These links should appear in black, with no underline.

These links should appear bold, using the logo color, with no underline.

2. **In the Extract panel, click the "Adult Classes" text to show the CSS for that element. Uncheck the font-family property, then click the Copy CSS button.**

3. **In the Live view, click to select the "Adult Classes" text. In the CSS Designer panel, Control/right-click the a selector and choose Paste Styles.**

The **a** selector affects all links on the page, so they all now show the pasted properties.

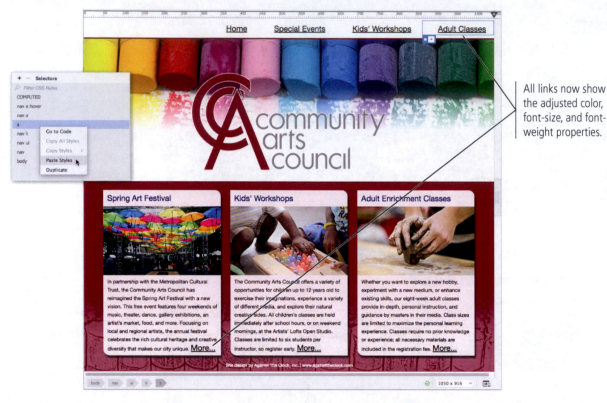

All links now show the adjusted color, font-size, and font-weight properties.

4. **In the Properties section of the panel, uncheck the Show Set option (if necessary), and then click the Text button to scroll to those properties.**

5. Locate the text-decoration property and click the none button.

Because this selector applies to all links in the page, the links in the nav element and the three category sections are no longer underlined.

Tool tips show the meaning of iconized values.

The underline property has been removed from all links on the page.

6. Click to select the word "More" in one of the category sections.

In Current mode, the CSS Designer panel shows two **a** selectors that affect the selected element: the basic **a** selector and the **.category p a** selector.

You already saw that changes to the basic **a** selector affected the links in the category sections — in this case, making the text in these links too large for their context.

The **.category p a** selector is called a **compound selector** or **descendant selector**. It applies only to links (using the <a> tags) which are in paragraph elements (using the <p> tags) in an element that uses the "category" class. Links in other elements are not affected by the properties in this selector, so you can use it to adjust the size and color of only links in these sections.

7. With the **.category p a** selector selected in the CSS Designer panel, navigate to the Text formatting options in the Properties section of the panel.

8. Click the empty space to the right of the font-size property and choose px from the menu. Type **13** in the resulting field, and then press Return/Enter to finalize the change.

9. **Open the font-weight menu and choose bold.**

Defining Color in CSS

Using CSS3, you can define colors in a number of ways:

- Using a **hexadecimal color** code, such as #FF0066. Each couplet in the color value defines the red, green, and blue components of that color, respectively.

  The hexadecimal color code must be preceded by the "#" sign. By convention, the letters should be uppercase, but neither Dreamweaver nor browsers differentiate between #EE04F3, #ee04f3, or #eE04f3.

  When both characters for a particular color value are the same, you can abbreviate to only three characters. For example, the full code for black is #000000, but it can be abbreviated to #000.

- Using a **color name**, such as "aqua" or "green." There are 147 defined color names in the CSS color specification.

- Using specific **RGB** values, in the following format:

  rgb(255, 0, 100)

  Each number in parentheses defines the amount of red, green, and blue, respectively — from 0 (none of a color) to 255 (all of a color) — that makes up the overall color.

- Using **RGBA** values, which adds the alpha property to standard RGB color values, in the following format:

  rgba(255, 0, 100, 0.5)

  The fourth parameter in the parentheses is the alpha value, which defines the color's transparency from 0.0 (fully transparent) to 1.0 (fully opaque).

10. Click the swatch for the color property to open the color picker.

The **background-color** property affects the background of an element. The **color** property affects the color of text in the element.

11. Choose the Eyedropper tool in the bottom-right corner of the color picker.

12. Move the mouse cursor over the red background color (above the background image), then click to sample it as the new color.

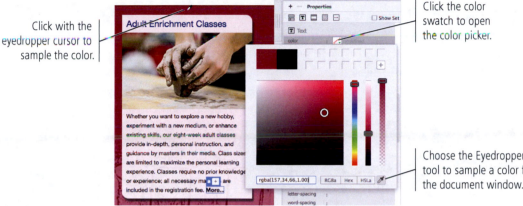

Click with the eyedropper cursor to sample the color.

Click the color swatch to open the color picker.

Choose the Eyedropper tool to sample a color from the document window.

13. Press Return/Enter to finalize the new text color.

Because you edited the compound selector, the changes in Steps 7–12 only affect links in the .category sections — other links on the page are not affected.

14. Choose File>Save All, and then continue to the next exercise.

Define Background Images for Navigation Link States

As you saw in a previous exercise, one advantage of CSS is that you can define different background properties for every identified element. In this exercise, you will use this capability to create a background image for each link in the nav element, and change that background image based on the position of the user's mouse cursor.

1. **In the open index.html file, click to select any of the links in the nav element.**

2. **In the CSS Designer panel, select the nav a compound selector.**

   When you click a selector in the CSS Designer panel, the related elements are highlighted in the Live view. This makes it very easy to see exactly what will be affected by changing the active selector.

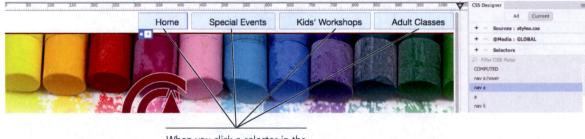

When you click a selector in the panel, all related elements are highlighted in the Live view.

   You can choose View>Live View Options>Hide Live View Displays to turn off this highlighting behavior.

3. **In the Background category of properties, define palette-fade.png (from the main site images folder) as the background image url.**

   As we explained earlier, a background image repeats (tiles) across and down unless you specify otherwise. Each link in the nav element shows the background image tiled down and across, originating in the top-right corner.

Click to jump to the Background options.

4. Choose **no-repeat** for the background-repeat property.

5. Choose **right** in the background-position (X) menu, and choose **center** in the background-position (Y) menu.

   Remember, you have to click the "%" option for the background-position value to open the pop-up menu.

6. Select the **nav a:hover** selector in the CSS Designer panel. In the Text properties, open the Color Picker, and then use the Eyedropper cursor to change the color property to the red background color.

   The **:hover** pseudo-class selector defines the **mouseover state** for a particular link, which determines what happens when the user moves the mouse cursor over the link.

7. In the Background properties, define the following settings:

url:	images/palette-full.png
background-repeat:	no-repeat
X background-position:	right
Y background-position:	center

8. **With the Live view active, move your mouse cursor over the navigation links to test the hover effect.**

The **:hover** pseudo-class is a dynamic effect that Dreamweaver's Design pane cannot display unless the Live view is active.

Some users report a bug that requires selecting each link in the nav before the hover behavior displays properly in the Live view. If your links aren't changing, try clicking each and then again moving the mouse cursor over the links to test the hover behavior.

As you move your mouse cursor over a link, the :hover pseudo-class is activated.

9. **Save all files, and then close index.html.**

10. **Export a site definition named Arts-Council.ste into your WIP>Council folder, and then remove the Arts-Council site from Dreamweaver.**

If necessary, refer back to Project 5: Bistro Site Organization for complete instructions on exporting a site definition or removing a site from Dreamweaver.

PROJECT REVIEW

fill in the blank

1. The _______________ attribute of the <img> tag is required to make images accessible for all web users.

2. The _______________ attribute defines the specific file that will appear in the <img> tag location.

3. The _______________ property of CSS can be used to tile a single background image horizontally, vertically, or both, throughout the entire document window.

4. _______________ is the process of cutting out/off portions of an image.

5. The _______________ format supports continuous-tone color, but not transparency. It is best used for photographs.

6. The _______________ format supports index transparency, but not a large gamut of color. It is best used for graphics and artwork.

7. In CSS, a(n) _______________ selector defines the appearance of specific HTML tags, such as <body> or <header>.

8. In CSS, a(n) _______________ selector begins with a # character, and defines the appearance of the one element on the page that has the matching attribute.

9. In CSS, a(n) _______________ selector begins with a . character, and defines the appearance of all elements on the page that have been identified with the matching attribute.

10. In CSS, a(n) _______________ selector defines the appearance of specific elements within other elements on the page, such as nav a.

short answer

1. Briefly describe three image file formats that might be used on the web, including advantages and disadvantages of each.

2. Briefly explain the importance of resampling relative to resizing images in Dreamweaver.

3. Briefly explain the advantages to using CSS to define background colors and images.

PORTFOLIO BUILDER PROJECT

Use what you learned in this project to complete the following freeform exercise.
Carefully read the art director and client comments, then create your own design to meet the needs of the project.
Use the space below to sketch ideas; when finished, write a brief explanation of your reasoning behind your final design.

You have been hired by the National Aeronautics and Space Administration (NASA) to design a new home page as the entry point to a site that presents general information of interest to the public at large.

To complete this project, you should:

❑ Use the same basic layout structure that you used in this project to create the new NASAview site home page.

❑ Find or create a logo treatment for the new site. Include that logo on every page in the site.

❑ Find or create icons to use as the "hover" treatment for links in the navigation area.

❑ Identify and download images you want to use from the NASA on the Commons web page (https://www.flickr.com/photos/nasacommons).

We want to create a new website called NASAview, which should be a simple, easy-to-navigate site, that includes only the most common things the general public finds of interest.

The main page should eventually include links to secondary pages for each of the three site categories:

• About NASA

• History of U.S. Space Travel

• Upcoming Events and Exhibits

We haven't written the text content yet, so just use placeholder text for the headings and body copy.

NASA images generally are not copyrighted, although we occasionally use copyrighted material by permission. Those images are marked copyright, with the name of the copyright holder; please don't use those images in the new site design.

PROJECT SUMMARY

When you prepare the design for a site, you need to determine which images will carry content (they must be placed in the foreground using the **<img>** tag), and which images will appear in the background. Appropriate alt text — which enables visually impaired visitors, users who have disabled the display of images, and search engines, to use the content of your pages — is required for all foreground images.

Dreamweaver also provides image-editing tools that enable you to crop, resize, resample, and sharpen images. Although these tools do not replace full-featured image-editing applications, such as Photoshop, they enable you to complete simple editing tasks quickly and easily, without requiring another application.

The Extract utility, available to individual-user Creative Cloud subscriptions, provides an easy interface for translating Photoshop page comps into functional HTML and CSS code. By editing various CSS properties, you have virtually unlimited options for controlling the appearance of different sections of a page.

Use CSS to change the appearance of different link states

Use CSS to define background properties for different elements

Extract element styles from a provided Photoshop file

Extract content from a provided Photoshop file

Use a variety of techniques to place foreground images

Resize and resample a placed image

Museum CSS Layout

8

The Getty Foundation hired you to build a new website to provide area visitors with information about the various art collections being displayed at their facilities. The client wants a website that can be quickly and easily updated and modified. In addition, the site should project a consistent look and style across all pages. To fulfill these requirements, you will create and apply a cascading style sheet (CSS) for the website.

This project incorporates the following skills:

- ❑ Creating and linking an external CSS file
- ❑ Understanding the CSS box model
- ❑ Creating a layout with HTML elements
- ❑ Working with templates to improve workflow and maintain consistency
- ❑ Editing CSS rules to adjust the page layout
- ❑ Defining HTML tag selectors, ID selectors, and compound selectors to control the appearance of page content

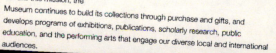

GETTY
FOUNDATION

About the Getty
Traveling Exhibits
Permanent Exhibits

About The Getty Foundation

The J. Paul Getty Museum

The Getty preserves, studies, and interprets the world's artistic legacy for the benefit of present and future generations.

The J. Paul Getty Museum seeks to inspire curiosity about, and enjoyment and understanding of, the visual arts by collecting, conserving, exhibiting and interpreting works of art of outstanding quality and historical importance.

To fulfill this mission, the Museum continues to build its collections through purchase and gifts, and develops programs of exhibitions, publications, scholarly research, public education, and the performing arts that engage our diverse local and international audiences.

Getty Villa Sculpture Garden
Fountain and sculpture in the Peristyle Garden of the Getty Villa Roman gardens. Photo by Bobak Ha'Eri.

Did you know?

Oil baron Jean Paul Getty converted part of his home in Malibu into a museum so that he could share his art treasures with the public.

The Getty Villa was designed as a near replica of the Roman Villa dei Papiri in Herculaneum, Italy, which had been buried in the eruption of Mt. Vesuvius in 79 A.D.

Getty's will left virtually his entire estate to the institution in trust, giving it a greater endowment than any other museum in the world.

PROJECT MEETING

client comments

We want to create a new website to provide a brief description of permanent and traveling exhibits at our museums.

We have a site already, but can't figure out how it was built, so it's extremely difficult to change even a comma. We called the site designer, but he can't work us into his schedule for more than a month, and we don't have the time to wait.

The new site should be very easy to manage and, more importantly, easy to change — whether it's a comma or the entire site layout.

art director comments

When a site is properly designed, the HTML file stores the page content, while the cascading style sheet (CSS) file defines the appearance of page elements. This makes it easier to find and change content, since the HTML code isn't cluttered with formatting instructions.

You're also going to use template files, which are an excellent tool for maintaining consistency across multiple pages of a site. The template defines the overall page structure, including common elements, such as navigation links and editable areas in which content varies from one page to another. If you make changes to common elements in the template file, those changes automatically appear in pages to which the template is applied.

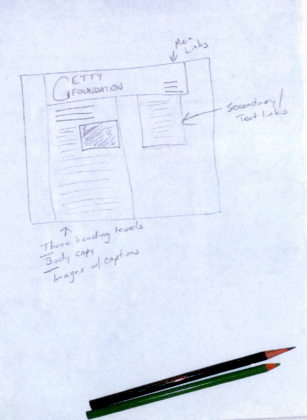

project objectives

To complete this project, you will:

- ❏ Create and link an external CSS file
- ❏ Create ID selectors
- ❏ Create a layout with HTML elements and CSS selectors
- ❏ Use the float property to control nested elements
- ❏ Use margins and padding to affect element placement
- ❏ Define properties for the body tag
- ❏ Create a template file
- ❏ Define named anchors
- ❏ Create figure tags to contain images and captions
- ❏ Define HTML tag selectors
- ❏ Create compound tag selectors
- ❏ Create pseudo-class selectors

STAGE 1 / Creating Layouts with Style Sheets

A **cascading style sheet** (CSS) is a collection of formatting rules that controls the appearance of different elements in a web page. Formatting instructions are stored in **rules**, which consist of two parts: a **selector** (basically, naming the element to be formatted) and **attributes** (such as font, color, width, height, etc.) that will be applied to the selected element.

The following example shows the proper syntax for a CSS rule; **p** is the selector, **font-size** is the attribute, and **14px** is the attribute value:

```
p {
    font-size: 14px;
}
```

There are three types of styles: inline, embedded (or internal), and external. To make the best use of styles, you should have a clear understanding of these different types, including when each is best suited to a specific goal.

An **inline style** applies directly and instantly to an individual element within a tag, affecting only that single element of the HTML page. For example, if you apply a font size and color to a paragraph, the inline style looks like this:

```
<p style="font-size: 10px; color: blue">Paragraph content goes here.</
    p>
```

An **embedded or internal style sheet** is added directly in an HTML page, within style tags. This type of style affects only the particular HTML page in which it is placed. The following code for an embedded style sheet includes a style that defines the formatting of all h1 elements:

```
<style type="text/css"
<!--
h1 {
    font-size: 24px;
}
-->
</style>
```

Note:

The set of <!-- and --> tags prevents a few older browsers from displaying the style rules.

An **external style sheet** is saved as a separate file (with the extension ".css"). HTML files include links to the external CSS files, which are uploaded to the web server, along with the website pages. External CSS files offer several advantages:

- A single CSS file can be attached to multiple HTML pages at once, applying the same rules to elements in different pages. Changes to the styles affect all HTML pages that are linked to that CSS file, which makes it easier to maintain consistency across all pages in a site.

- Different types of styles can control the appearance of general HTML elements — specific individual elements that are identified with a unique ID attribute, all elements that are identified with a specific class attribute, and even elements only within a certain area of a page.

- External styles separate page formatting (CSS) from structure and content (HTML). This helps to reduce file size and server processing time, as well as making it easier for designers and coders to find exactly what they are looking for.

Prepare the Site Files

In this exercise, you will import the client's provided files, then create the HTML and CSS files that you need to complete the project.

1. Download **Museum_Web20_RF.zip** from the Student Files web page.

2. Expand the ZIP archive in your **WIP folder (Macintosh)** or copy the archive contents into your **WIP folder (Windows)**.

   This results in a folder named **Museum**, which contains the files you need for this project.

3. Create a new site named **Museum**, using the WIP>Museum folder as the site root folder.

4. With the Museum site open in the Files panel, choose File>New. Using the New Document dialog box, create a new, blank HTML5 page.

5. Choose File>Save. Save the new page as an HTML file named **design.html** in the root folder of the Museum site.

6. With **design.html** open, open the CSS Designer panel. Make sure the All button is active at the top of the panel.

7. **In the Sources section of the panel, click the Add CSS Source button and choose Create a New CSS File.**

You can also create a new CSS file in the New Document dialog box. Simply choose CSS in the Document Type window and click Create.

Add CSS Source button

8. **In the resulting dialog box, type museum-styles.css in the File/URL field.**

The name you define will be used for the new CSS file that is created. By default, the CSS file is placed in the root folder of the active site. You can click the Browse button if you want to create the file in another location.

9. **With the Link option selected, click OK to create the new CSS file.**

museum-styles.css is now related to design.html.

museum-styles.css is added to the site folder.

10. **Click the Split button in the Document toolbar, and review the page source code.**

Using the Link option, the CSS file is connected to the HTML page, using the **<link>** tag in the HTML page's header information. When a user opens the HTML page, the browser merges the instructions in the linked CSS file with the information in the HTML file to present the final page design.

The <link> tag attaches the museum-styles.css file to the HTML file.

11. **Choose File>Save All, and then continue to the next exercise.**

The Save All command saves any open HTML page, as well as any linked files, such as the CSS file that you created in this exercise.

Define a New Element and Tag Selector

HTML includes a large number of elements that are specifically designed to create common page elements — headers (usually) at the top of the page, footers at the bottom, navigation (nav) areas with lists of links, and so on. In this and the next exercise, you are going to use several of these elements to create the basic page structure for the museum's website.

1. **With design.html open, make sure the Split view is active and the Live view is turned off.**

   You are going to work in the regular Design view in this exercise. In later exercises, you will use other methods in the Live view to add elements to the page.

2. **Click the Header button in the HTML Insert panel.**

3. **In the resulting dialog box, click the New CSS Rule button.**

4. **Choose Tag in the Selector Type menu.**

   In the New CSS Rule dialog box, you can define the type and name of a selector, as well as where to create the rule (in the attached external CSS file or embedded in the active HTML file).

   A tag selector applies to all elements using that tag, such as every paragraph that is structured with <p> tags.

5. **Choose header in the Selector Name menu.**

   When you choose Tag in the Selector Type menu, the Selector Name menu includes a large number of available HTML tags. You can open the menu and choose the tag you want, or simply type the tag name in the field.

   Click here to open the menu of tags...

   ...or type a tag name in this field.

6. **In the Rule Definition menu (at the bottom of the dialog box), choose museum-styles.css.**

If you choose This Document Only, the resulting CSS style will be created in the active HTML file's header information — it will not be available for other files in the site.

Because you want to use these styles in multiple files, it is best to place them in the separate CSS file and link each HTML file to it.

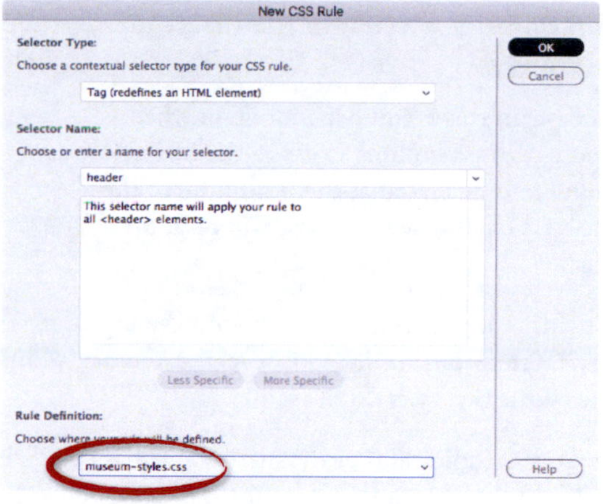

7. **Click OK to open the CSS Rule Definition dialog box.**

This dialog box includes nine categories of options. Many properties that can be saved in a CSS rule are available in the various panes of this dialog box.

8. **Click Background in the Category list. Type #FFF in the Background-color field, or click the related swatch and use the pop-up color picker to define white as the background color.**

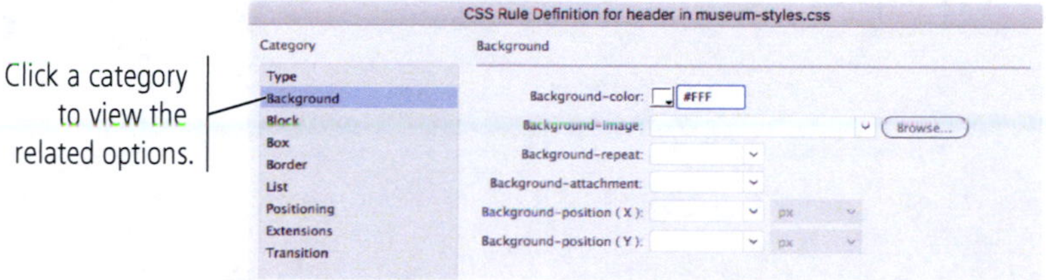

Click a category to view the related options.

9. **Click Box in the Category list. Type 930 in the Width field, and make sure px (pixels) is selected in the related menu.**

If you do not define a specific width or height, elements fill the containing element horizontally; their height expands automatically as content is added.

10. **In the Padding area, leave the Same for All option checked. Type 10 in the Top field, and make sure px is selected in the related menu.**

11. **In the Margin area, uncheck the Same for All check box. Type 0 in the Top and Bottom fields, and make sure px is selected in the related menus.**

12. **Type auto in the Left and Right fields.**

The **auto** value allows the element to be centered within its parent container (in this case, the body element of the HTML page).

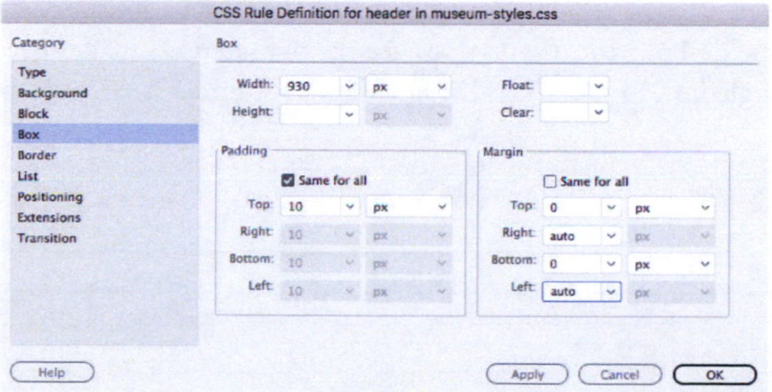

13. Click OK to return to the Insert Header dialog box.

14. Make sure At Insertion Point is selected in the Insert menu, then click OK to return to the HTML page.

Different options are available in this menu depending on what is selected in the document. Because nothing exists in the file yet, the insertion point is assumed to be placed at the beginning of the document body, and that is where the new element will be added.

After clicking OK, the new element is automatically added to the page. Placeholder content is added inside the element. The top edge is slightly indented because Dreamweaver automatically adds several pixels of padding around the content of a new page (some browsers do the same).

In the document tab, an asterisk indicates that the HTML file has been edited. In the Related Files bar, an asterisk indicates that the museum-styles.css file has been edited.

In the CSS Designer panel, the Selectors section shows the new header selector.

15. Review the page code in the Code pane.

Adding elements adds to the page's HTML code. Those elements, however, are very short — they simply identify each element and add some placeholder content. In the page code, there is no mention of background images, borders, or other attributes that make up the page layout. Those attributes are controlled by editing the selectors applied to each element within the CSS file.

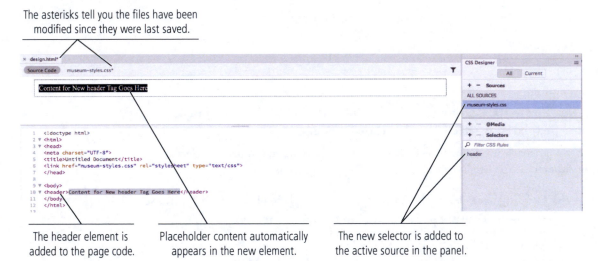

The asterisks tell you the files have been modified since they were last saved.

The header element is added to the page code.

Placeholder content automatically appears in the new element.

The new selector is added to the active source in the panel.

16. In the Design pane, click the edge of the header element to select it.

When an element is selected in the regular Design view, you can see various aspects of the CSS box model in the design pane. If you don't see the margin area, make sure CSS Layout Box Model is toggled on in the View>Design View Options>Visual Aids menu.

Margin   Element edge   Padding   Content area

17. In the Related Files bar, click museum-styles.css to show that file in the Code pane.

Clicking the CSS file name in the Related Files bar automatically switches the document window to Split mode if the Code pane is not already visible. The CSS file code is displayed in the Code pane.

You can now see the code for the new rule you defined. Properties and values for the selector are contained within curly brackets. Each property is separated by a semicolon.

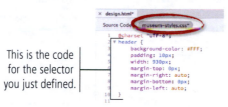

This is the code for the selector you just defined.

18. Choose File>Save All, then continue to the next exercise.

Drag and Drop to Create New Elements

Dreamweaver's Live view enables a drag-and-drop method of adding elements to a page. On-screen prompts allow you to define exactly where you want elements to exist, making it easy to create the proper code, using only visual tools. In this exercise, you use the Live view to add a footer element, and then define the CSS for that element separately.

1. With design.html open, show the page source code in the Code pane and turn on the Live view.

2. Click the footer button in the HTML Insert panel and drag onto the Live view.

3. When a green line appears below the header element, release the mouse button.

When you drag to add elements in the Live view, visual indicators identify where the new elements will be added in relation to the existing ones. A thin blue line highlights the active element, and the green double-headed arrow determines whether the new element will be added above or below the highlighted element.

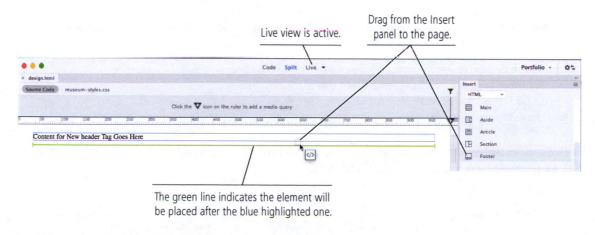

Live view is active.

Drag from the Insert panel to the page.

The green line indicates the element will be placed after the blue highlighted one.

When you release the mouse button, the new footer element appears in the Design pane after the previously selected header element. The box model that you saw in the regular Design view does not appear when the Live view is active — only the element boundary is visible as a thin blue line when the element is selected.

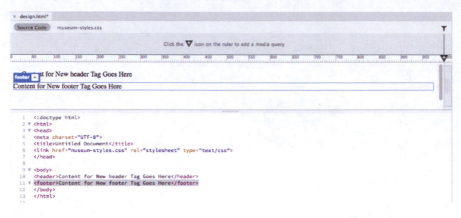

4. **Make sure the CSS Designer panel is displaying the All mode.**

Current mode must be turned off to add new selectors using the panel.

5. **In the CSS Designer panel, click to select museum-styles.css in the Sources section.**

6. **Click the Add Selector button in the Selectors section of the panel.**

Clicking this button automatically creates a descendant selector, with the entire path to the currently selected element. In this case, the new footer element is inside the body element (i.e., the body element is the immediate parent of the footer element), so "body footer" is the default selector name.

Add Selector button

Choose museum-styles.css in the Sources list.

The new selector name includes all parents of the selected element.

This type of descendant selector allows you to define different settings for the same type of element in different areas of the page. Since you will only use one footer element in the client's design, the parent is not necessary in this selector name.

7. **Press the Up Arrow key once to remove the parent ("body") from the selector name, and then press Return/Enter to finalize the new name.**

Depending on the active selection, the selector name might have more than one parent in the path to the active tag. Each time you press the Up Arrow key, the first parent in the list is removed.

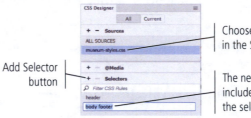

Note:

You can also press the Down Arrow key to add the parents back into the selector name.

8. **In the Properties section of the panel, show the Layout properties and make sure the Show Set option is not checked.**

9. **Double-click the width value to highlight the field. Type 100%, then press Return/Enter to finalize the new value.**

   When you type values for a CSS selector, do not include a space between the value and the unit of measurement.

   If you use percentage as the width measurement, you are defining the element's width as a percentage of the width of its parent container. In this case, the footer element will occupy the same horizontal width as the overall page (the body element).

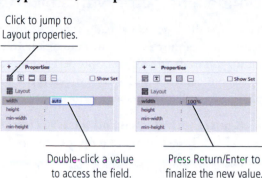

Click to jump to Layout properties.

Double-click a value to access the field.

Press Return/Enter to finalize the new value.

10. **Define 10px top and bottom margins.**

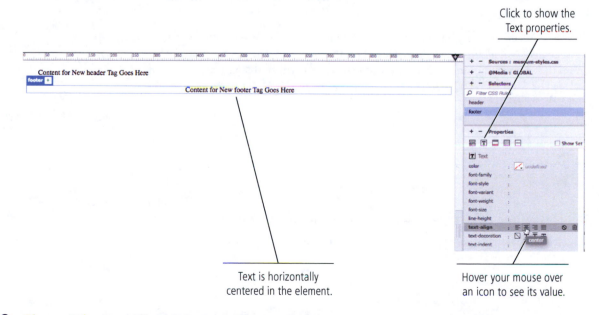

11. **Show the Text properties in the CSS Designer panel. Locate the text-align property and choose the center value.**

Click to show the Text properties.

Text is horizontally centered in the element.

Hover your mouse over an icon to see its value.

12. **Choose File>Save All, and then continue to the next exercise.**

Define a Selector with an ID Attribute

Elements such as the ones you already added are the basic building blocks of an HTML page. You can use ID attributes to differentiate elements of the same type, which allows you to define different properties for different, same-type elements. In this exercise, you define and identify a div element, and then create a CSS selector that applies to only that unique element.

1. **With design.html open and the Live view active, click the div button in the HTML Insert panel and drag onto the Live view.**

   A **<div>** tag is simply a container, identifying a division or area of a page. Although the HTML5 elements, such as header and section, have largely replaced the div element in modern design, you can (and will) still find uses for a nonspecific container. In this case, you are creating a div element simply as a parent container for the two main content areas of the page (which you will create later).

2. **When a green line appears between the two existing elements, release the mouse button.**

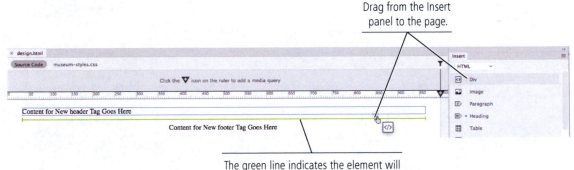

Drag from the Insert panel to the page.

The green line indicates the element will be placed between the existing ones.

3. **With the new div selected in the Design pane, click the + button in the Element Display.**

   The div element is a fairly generic container. If you define CSS for the basic div tag, your changes would affect every div element on the page. Instead, you are going to assign this element a unique ID attribute to better identify it in the page and CSS code.

   Click the + button to open the Class/ID field.

4. **In the resulting field, type #page-content, and then press Return/Enter.**

   ID selectors always begin with a # character — make sure you type it in the field when you assign the new ID attribute.

Note:

Each element on a page can have a different identity (defined using the ID attribute), and each ID can be used only once on a page.

Note:

CSS Selector names are case-sensitive.

5. **Make sure museum-styles.css is selected in the resulting Select a Source menu, and then press Return/Enter.**

   Dreamweaver recognizes that a CSS selector does not yet exist for this ID, so it will create one for you. You are asked to determine where the new selector should be saved.

Type an ID or class attribute in the field.

After pressing Return/Enter, choose where to save the new selector.

6. **In the CSS Designer panel, click to select the new #page-content selector.**

7. **At the top of the Properties section, make sure the Show Set option is *not* checked.**

8. **Click the Layout button to jump to those properties in the panel.**

9. **Double-click the width property value to access the field, then type 950px as the new value.**

10. **In the Margin settings, make sure the Lock icon is not active, then define the following margins:**

Top:	0px
Left:	auto
Bottom:	0px
Right:	auto

    The lock is not active.   The lock is active.

    When the Lock icon is active, all four fields are connected and have the same value. Changing any one of the values applies the same setting to the other three. If you want to define different values for different sides, you have to turn off the lock option.

    Remember, setting the right and left margins to auto centers the element horizontally in its parent container.

    When no setting has been defined for a property that has a numeric value, the fields in the CSS Designer panel appear to show "0" (zero). However, you have to actually highlight the field and press Return/Enter to intentionally define the 0px value for that property. If a "0" value does not show a unit of measurement, it has not been defined for the active selector.

    This field does have a defined value.

    This field does not have a defined value.

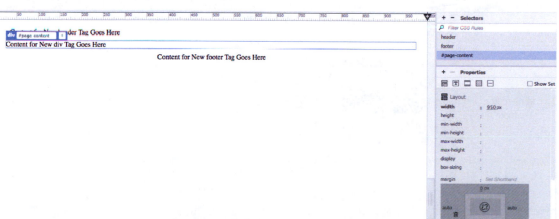

11. **At the top of the Properties section, click the Border button to jump to those properties in the panel.**

12. **Click the Top tab to define border options for only the top edge.**

Click this button to jump to the border options.

Use this tab to define the same Border properties for all four sides.

The tab icons identify which border you can define.

13. **Define the border-top width property as 8 px.**

    The width menu here functions in the same way as the width menu that you used to define the box width: click the value and choose px from the menu, then type the value in the resulting field.

14. **Open the style menu and choose solid.**

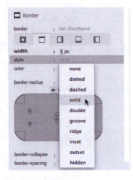

15. **Click the color swatch to open the Color picker. Type #54210F in the hexadecimal value field, then press Return/Enter to finalize the new border color.**

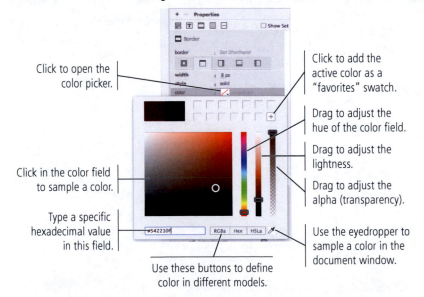

Click to open the color picker.

Click in the color field to sample a color.

Type a specific hexadecimal value in this field.

Click to add the active color as a "favorites" swatch.

Drag to adjust the hue of the color field.

Drag to adjust the lightness.

Drag to adjust the alpha (transparency).

Use the eyedropper to sample a color in the document window.

Use these buttons to define color in different models.

16. **Show the museum-styles.css file in the Code pane.**

    All three defined options for the border-top property (width, style, color) are combined into a single property statement.

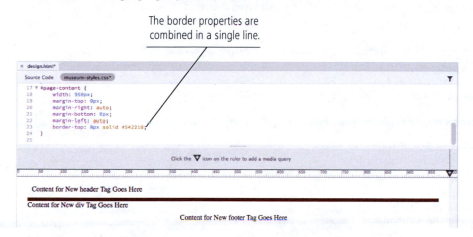

The border properties are combined in a single line.

17. **Choose File>Save All, then continue to the next exercise.**

Understanding CSS Shorthand

In many cases, you will define more than one value for the same CSS property. In the previous exercise, for example, you defined the width, style, and color of the border-top property. In the Code pane, you can see that all three values are combined into a single CSS statement:

    border-top: 8px solid #54210F;

This type of combining properties into a single line is referred to as **shorthand**. Without shorthand, you would require three separate lines in the selector:

    border-top-width: 8px;

    border-top-style: solid;

    border-top-color: #54210F;

Combining the three properties into a single line saves space, and makes the overall CSS code less complex.

The CSS Designer panel includes a number of Set Shorthand fields that allow you to define properties, without interacting with the panel's various menus and fields.

Keep in mind, if you decide to type in the Set Shorthand fields, most CSS property:value pairs have very specific rules. You must use the proper syntax to accurately define those values. For example, do not include a space between a number and unit of measurement.

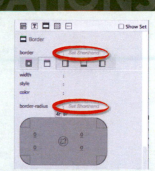

Create New Selectors Using the CSS Designer Panel

The CSS Designer panel offers a lot of flexibility for creating and managing selectors. In this exercise, you will define several new selectors, which will later apply to new elements when you add them to the layout.

Note:

Your changes in the following steps do not affect the HTML files. You are only changing the CSS file that is linked the HTML file.

1. **With** `design.html` **open, click museum-styles.css in the Sources section of the CSS Designer panel.**

2. **In the Selectors area of the panel, click the Add Selector button.**

3. **With the new selector's name highlighted, type** n**.**

   You don't have to accept any part of the default name for a new selector — you can simply type while the name is highlighted to change the selector name.

   When you type a new selector name in the panel, Dreamweaver automatically presents a menu of known selectors that match the characters you type. In this case, a large number of tag names include the "n" character. The tag "nav" is highlighted because it is the first name that begins with the character you typed.

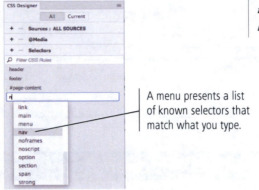

A menu presents a list of known selectors that match what you type.

4. **With nav selected in the menu, press Return/Enter to accept the selected menu item, then press Return/Enter again to finalize the new selector.**

5. **In the Properties section of the panel, define a** 200px **width value and** 10px **padding on all four sides.**

Note:

There are hundreds of available CSS properties. The w3schools website (http://w3schools. com/cssref/css_selectors. asp) is an excellent source of information about each property — including proper names, browser compatibility, and possible values.

6. Click the **Add Selector** button again. Type **#main-copy** as the new selector name, then press Return/Enter to add the new selector.

7. Define the following settings for the new selector:

width:	500px
min-height:	200px
margin-right:	50px
padding (all four sides):	20px

By default, elements collapse to the smallest possible height required to contain their content. By setting the **min-height** property, you prevent an element from collapsing entirely if you delete all of its content.

Elements also expand as high as necessary to display all their content, unless you define a specific height and restrict the overflow content.

Define the min-height property for this selector.

8. Repeat this process to create another new ID selector named **#sidebar**, using the following properties:

width:	350px
min-height:	200px

Note:

Remember that ID selectors always begin with the # character.

9. Show the **museum-styles.css** file in the Code pane.

Because you selected museum-styles.css in the Sources section of the panel, the new selectors are added to that file. You can see the new selectors in the Code pane as long as the museum-styles.css file is showing in that pane.

Nothing has been added to the HTML file, as you can see in the Design pane. The asterisks show that the CSS file has been modified, but the HTML file has not changed.

design.html has not been modified.

museum-styles.css has been modified.

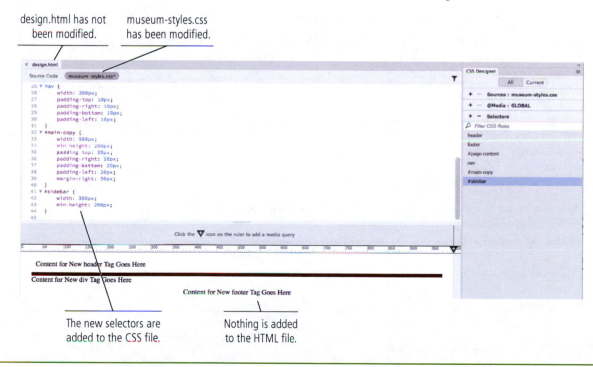

The new selectors are added to the CSS file.

Nothing is added to the HTML file.

10. **Click in the Code pane to make it active, then choose File>Save.**

The Save command (and its shortcut, Command/Control-S) saves the active file wherever the insertion point is placed. By clicking in the Code pane to place the insertion point in the museum-styles.css file, you are saving the CSS file and not the HTML file. (The HTML file did not change in this exercise.)

11. **Continue to the next exercise.**

Create and Manage Nested Elements

The Museum site's basic page structure requires three additional elements, which will be nested inside those you have already created. In this exercise, you use several techniques for creating nested elements.

1. **With `design.html` open, show the page source code in the Code pane.**

2. **In the HTML Insert panel, click the Navigation button and drag into the document window. When a blue border outlines the header element, release the mouse button.**

If you drag an element into an existing one, a heavy blue border identifies the active element. The new element will be nested inside the highlighted one.

Drag onto the existing header element.

3. **Review the page's source code in the Code pane.**

Nested container elements should always appear before other content in the containing element.

As you can see, Dreamweaver properly places the nav element code before the header element's placeholder text.

Because you defined width and padding properties for the nav selector in the previous exercise, those properties automatically apply to the newly placed nav element.

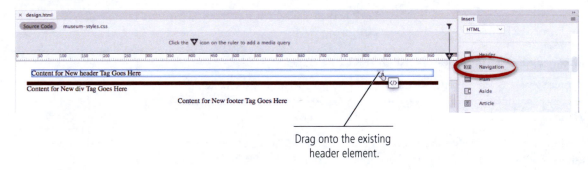

4. **Click the Section button in the HTML Insert panel and drag into the document window. When the mouse cursor is not over any existing element, release the mouse button.**

If you drag an element into an empty area of the page (below other elements), the body element is highlighted. The new element will be added at the top of the page hierarchy.

Drag from the Insert panel to the empty area of the page (away from existing elements).

As you can see in the Design pane, the element is added above the existing header element. The page code shows the position of the new section element, at the beginning of the element hierarchy.

The new section element is added to the page, above the header element.

```
1    <!doctype html>
2  ▼ <html>
3  ▼ <head>
4    <meta charset="UTF-8">
5    <title>Untitled Document</title>
6    <link href="museum-styles.css" rel="stylesheet" type="text/css">
7    </head>
8
9  ▼ <body>
10 ▼ <section>Content for New section Tag Goes Here</section>
11 ▼ <header>
12    <nav>Content for New nav Tag Goes Here</nav>
13    Content for New header Tag Goes Here</header>
14    <div id="page-content">Content for New div Tag Goes Here</div>
15    <footer>Content for New footer Tag Goes Here</footer>
16    </body>
17    </html>
```

5. **Click to select the new section element if necessary, then click the Add Class/ID button (+) in the Element Display. In the resulting field, type #.**

The resulting menu shows all available selectors that match the characters you type. (Remember, ID selectors always begin with the # character.)

You can use the Arrow keys to navigate items in the resulting menu, or double-click an option in this menu to accept it.

The menu presents IDs that match your typing.

6. Click #main-copy in the menu to apply that ID to the active element.

Remember, the #main-copy selector defines a width of 500px and minimum height of 200px, so the section element now shows those dimensions in the document window.

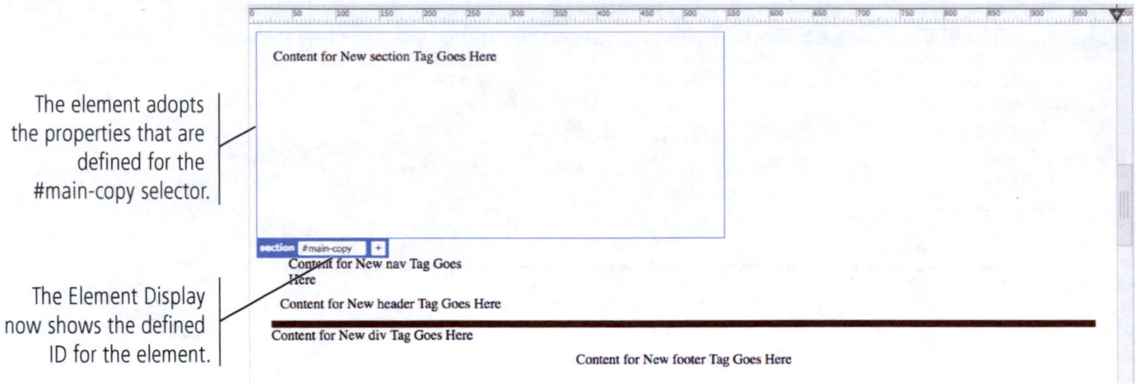

The element adopts the properties that are defined for the #main-copy selector.

The Element Display now shows the defined ID for the element.

7. Open the DOM panel (Window>DOM).

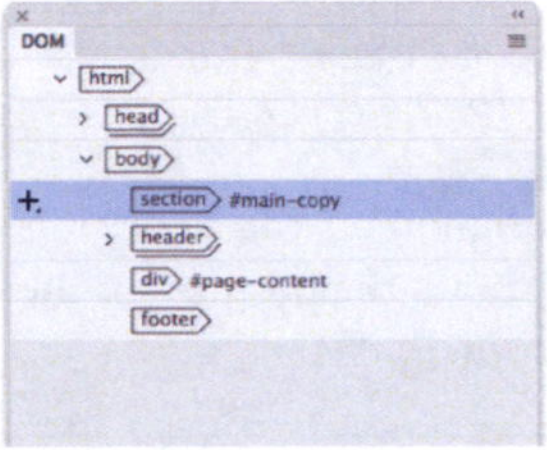

DOM is short for document object model. The DOM panel shows the overall structure of elements in your document. The elements appear in the same order you see in the document window. You can simply review your page content, or drag items in the panel to rearrange the various elements.

8. In the DOM panel, drag the section#main-copy element onto the div#page-content element. When you do *not* see a green line in the panel, release the mouse button.

When you drag elements in the panel, a green line shows where the element you are dragging will be placed in the hierarchy. If you want to nest one element into another, make sure the intended parent is highlighted, but no green line appears.

When you release the mouse button, you can see the section#main-copy element has moved into the div#page-content element.

The section element is now nested inside the div element.

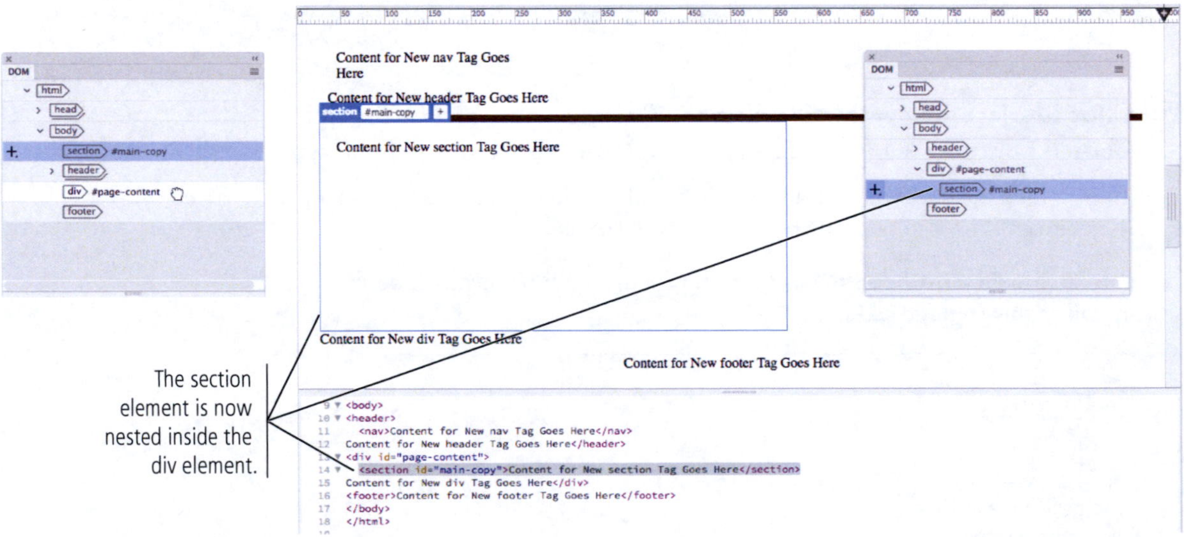

9. Click to select the nested section element in the DOM panel.

10. Click the + button to the left of the section element and choose Insert After in the pop-up menu.

11. With the word "div" highlighted, type **sec**.

The new element defaults to be a div element, but you can type a different element name in the field to change it.

As you type, code hints present a list of options that match the characters you type. As soon as you type the "c," "section" is the only available option in the menu, and it is automatically selected.

12. Press Return/Enter twice to finalize the new element as a section, instead of a div.

The first time your press Return/Enter, you select the highlighted option in the code hint list (section). The second Return/Enter finalizes the new element.

13. Double-click to the right of the section tag in the panel. In the resulting field, type **#**.

The resulting menu shows all available selectors that match the characters you type. You can use each ID only once on any given page. Because the #main-copy ID has already been used on this page, it is no longer available and does not appear in the list. The #sidebar ID is the only option in the list, and it is automatically selected.

14. With #sidebar highlighted in the menu, press Return/Enter to choose that option, and then press Return/Enter to finalize the new section ID.

15. In the Code, select and delete the placeholder content for the page-content div.

This div exists to contain the other two elements, so you don't need the placeholder text.

If you delete the text in the Live view, Dreamweaver leaves a nonbreaking space character in place of the deleted text. By deleting the text in the Code pane, you avoid the unwanted character.

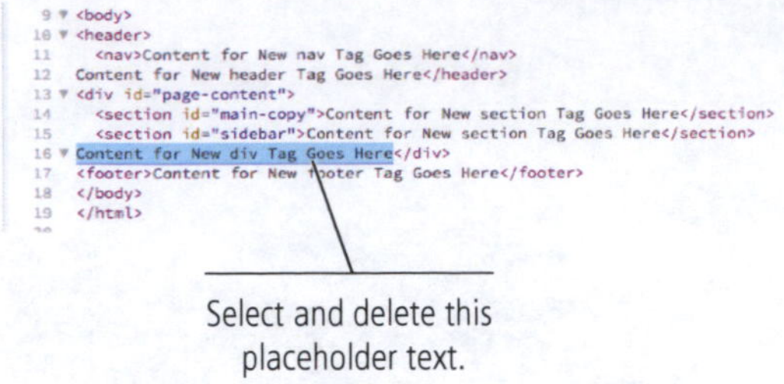

```
9 ▼ <body>
10 ▼   <header>
11        <nav>Content for New nav Tag Goes Here</nav>
12        Content for New header Tag Goes Here</header>
13 ▼   <div id="page-content">
14        <section id="main-copy">Content for New section Tag Goes Here</section>
15        <section id="sidebar">Content for New section Tag Goes Here</section>
16 ▼      Content for New div Tag Goes Here</div>
17        <footer>Content for New footer Tag Goes Here</footer>
18      </body>
19      </html>
```

Select and delete this placeholder text.

16. Choose File>Save All, and then continue to the next exercise.

Control Element Float Position

The nav element should appear on the right side of the header element. Inside the div#page-content element, the main-copy and sidebar sections should appear in the same "row." As you can see in your current layout, several elements do not yet appear in the correct position.

Nested elements automatically align, based on the horizontal alignment properties of the containing element. If no specific alignment is defined, the nested elements align to the left side of the container and each appears in sequential order.

1. With design.html open, show only the Design view and turn off the Live view.

When the Live view is turned off, visual aids make it easier to see the boundaries of various elements on the page.

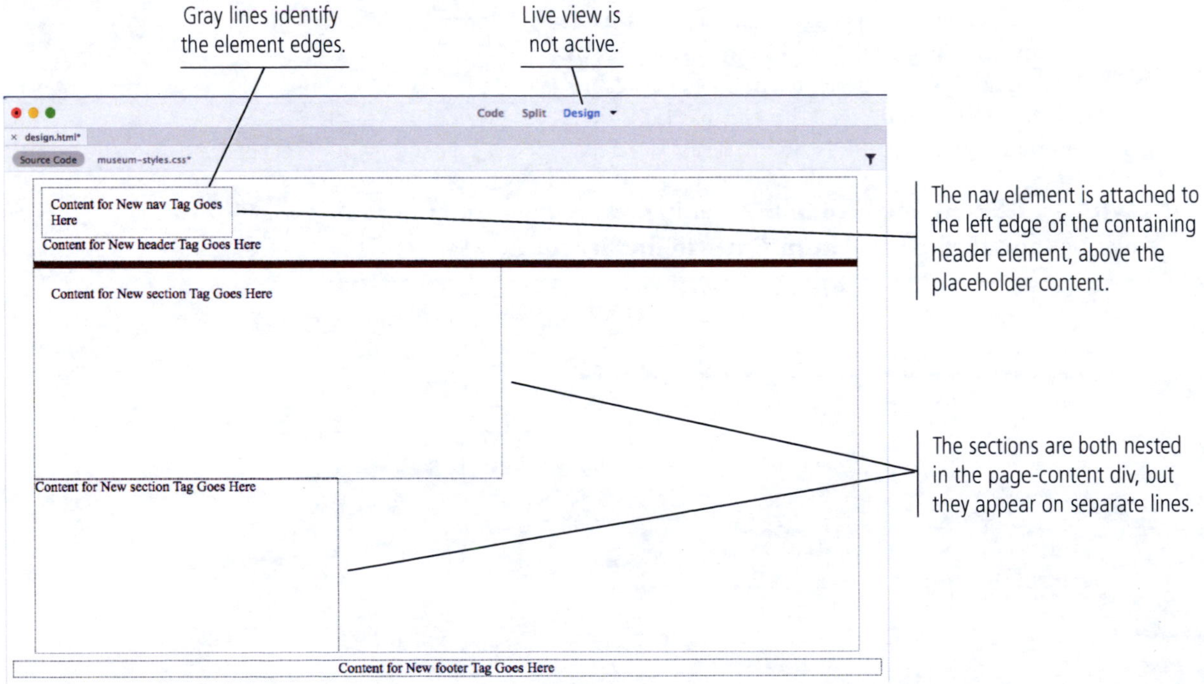

Gray lines identify the element edges.

Live view is not active.

The nav element is attached to the left edge of the containing header element, above the placeholder content.

The sections are both nested in the page-content div, but they appear on separate lines.

2. **Click the Current button at the top of the CSS Designer panel to turn that mode on.**

3. **Click the edge of the nav element in the document window to select it.**

   When Current mode is active, the panel shows only selectors that affect the active selection in the document. In this case, the active element is contained inside the header element, so the selected element can be affected by both the header and nav selectors.

4. **With the nav selector selected in the CSS Designer panel, check the Show Set option in the Properties section.**

When Current mode is active, the panel shows only selectors related to the active selection.

5. **Click in the Add Property field at the bottom of the Properties section and type flo.**

   You can use the "More" section of the panel to add any new property to the active selector. (Many are not available in the other sections of the panel.) Simply type the property name to add the property you want.

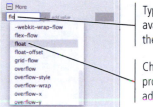

Type in the field to show available properties with the characters you type.

Choose a specific property in this menu to add it to the selector.

   Typing in the field presents a menu of all available properties that contain the characters you type. You can also use the arrow keys to navigate the resulting menu, and press Return/Enter to add the highlighted property.

6. **Click float in the resulting menu to add it as a new property.**

   After you define the property you want to add, the secondary menu presents the possible values for that property.

Choosing a property reveals a secondary menu with possible values.

7. **Click right in the menu of values to select it.**

The CSS **float** property allows you to intentionally attach an element to the left or right edge of the containing element, and other content to sit beside, or wrap around, that element. This gives you greater flexibility when creating complex layouts.

The nav element now properly aligns on the right side of its immediate parent container (the header element).

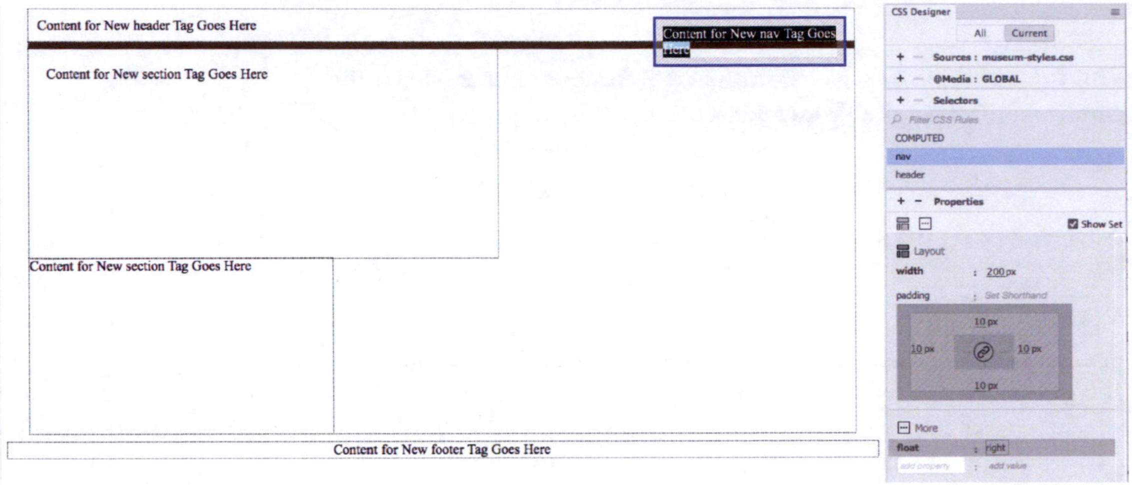

8. **Repeat the process from this exercise to define float values as follows:**

#main-copy	**float:left**
#sidebar	**float:right**

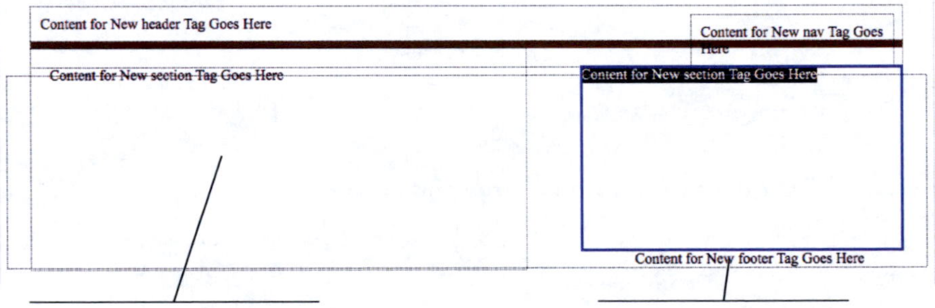

The #main-copy section now appears on the same "row" as the #sidebar section.

The footer element moves into the space immediately below the sidebar.

Note:

You will fix the issue with the nav element height in the next exercise.

9. **Assign the left float value to the footer selector.**

When the footer element had no defined float property, it moved into an unpredicted position to the right of the main-copy section. To solve the problem, you are assigning a specific float property to the footer element to attach it to the left edge of its parent container (the body element).

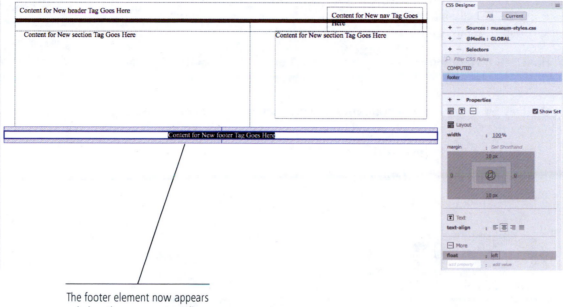

The footer element now appears below the page-content div.

10. **Choose File>Save All, and then continue to the next exercise.**

Work with the CSS Box Model

When you design layouts using CSS, think of any element as a box made up of four parts: margin, border, padding, and content. The object's overall size — the amount of space it occupies on the page — is the sum of the values for these four properties:

- The **margin** is outside the box edges; it is invisible and has no background color. Margin does not affect content within the element.

- The **border** is the edge of the element, based on the specified dimensions.

- The **padding** lies inside the edge of the element, forming a cushion between the box edge and the box content.

- The **content** lies inside the padding. When you define the width and height for an element, you define the content area.

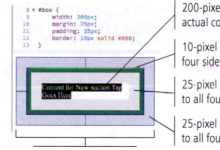

200-pixel width defines the actual content area.

10-pixel border is on all four sides of the box.

25-pixel padding is applied to all four edges.

25-pixel margins are applied to all four edges.

The overall element is 260px wide (200 + 10 + 25 + 25).

1. With design.html open, make sure the Live view is turned off.

2. Drag the file getty-logo.png (from the site images folder) into the header element. Using the Properties panel, define The Getty Foundation as alternate text for the placed image.

    Unless you define otherwise, HTML elements always expand to whatever height necessary to show all content. When you place this image, the header element automatically expands to the height necessary to accommodate the logo.

3. In the Design view, select and delete the placeholder text from the header element.

4. In the Design view, delete the placeholder text from the nav element, and then type the following in the nav element:

    About the Getty [Return/Enter]

    Traveling Exhibits [Return/Enter]

    Permanent Exhibits

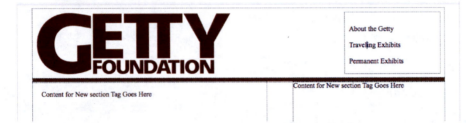

5. Click to select the section#sidebar element in the layout.

6. With the #sidebar selector active in the CSS Designer panel, uncheck the Show Set option and navigate to the Background properties.

7. In the background-image options, define parchment.png (from the site images folder) as the background image, and choose the no-repeat option.

    Some users will see the bottom edge of the parchment in the sidebar (as shown in our screen capture here), while others might see the edge cut off. The next few steps illustrate the problem of relying solely on the regular Design view when working with CSS.

8. Turn on the Live view.

Although the regular Design view makes it easier to see the CSS layout structure (including the element boundaries), it does not always accurately depict CSS. When the Live view is active, you get a better idea of exactly what will appear when a browser renders the CSS.

As you can see, the parchment image is bluntly cut off at the bottom of the section#sidebar element. Background images default to begin at the top-left corner of their containing element.

This section element has a defined min-height property, so it will always be at least 200px high, but it will expand as high as necessary to contain the element content. Since you don't know exactly how high the element will be, you can avoid the cutoff problem by changing the positioning of the background image.

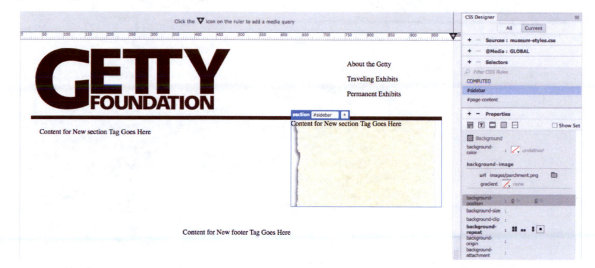

9. With the #sidebar selector active in the CSS Designer panel, choose center in the first background-position menu, and choose bottom in the second.

These settings tell the browser to align the bottom edge of the background image to the center bottom edge of the container. The torn-off edge of the parchment will always appear at the bottom, even when the element expands to contain various content.

You might notice another problem. Placeholder content in the section#sidebar element runs directly into the element edge. In the CSS box model, padding defines a distance at which content exists from the element edge, so you can use this property to fix the problem.

10. **In the Layout properties, define the following padding values for the #sidebar selector:**

padding-top:	10px
padding-right:	30px
padding-bottom:	30px
padding-left:	30px

The background image extends into the padding area because the padding is part of the actual element area. Margin values are added outside the element. Background images do not extend into the margin area.

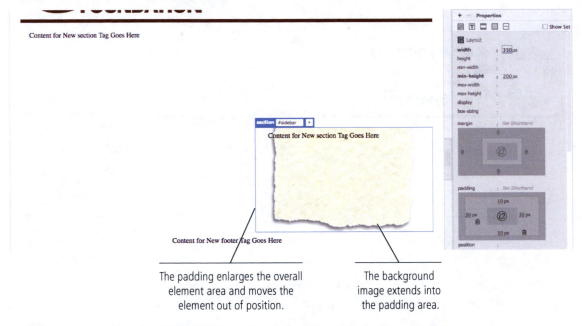

The padding enlarges the overall element area and moves the element out of position.

The background image extends into the padding area.

It is important to realize that both padding and margins affect the overall size of the element. The section#sidebar element is now 410 pixels wide (350 defined width + 30 left padding + 30 right padding). With that width, it no longer fits on the same "row" as the section#main-copy element.

11. **Subtract 60 from the width value of the #sidebar selector.**

To change the existing property values, simply click the value to highlight it, and then type the new value.

When you change margins and/or padding, you often have to make a proportional change to the width and/or height properties if you want the element to occupy the same overall space. After changing the width, the section#sidebar element moves back into place.

12. Click to select the section#main-copy element in the layout.

13. In the CSS Designer panel, make sure **#main-copy** is selected and show the Background properties.

14. Click the background-color swatch to open the color picker, then choose the Eyedropper tool in the bottom-right corner.

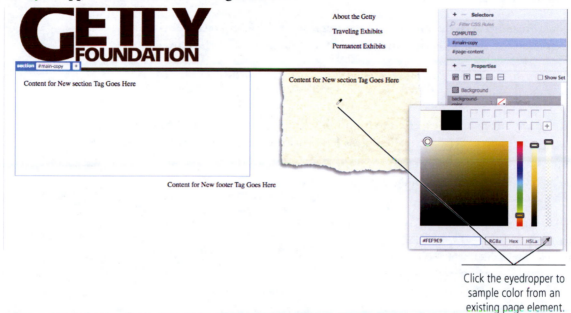

Click the eyedropper to sample color from an existing page element.

15. Move the **cursor** over a medium-yellow shade in the parchment image. Click to select the color, then press Return/Enter to finalize the new background-color property.

16. Choose File>Save All, then continue to the next exercise.

Define Properties for the <body> Tag

The **<body>** tag surrounds all visible content in a web page. Because **<body>** is an HTML tag, you have to create a tag selector to define properties for the body element.

1. With **design.html** open, click All at the top of the CSS Designer panel to turn off the Current mode.

2. Click **museum-styles.css** in the Sources section of the CSS Designer panel, then click the Add Selector button in the Selector section of the panel.

3. Type **body** as the new selector name, then press Return/Enter twice to finalize the selector.

4. In the Layout properties, click to highlight the Set Shorthand field for the margin property. Type **0px**, then press Return/Enter to finalize the new value.

   When you define values for a CSS property, do not include a space between the number and the unit of measurement.

   Important note: The CSS Designer panel uses zeros as placeholders for undefined margin and padding values, which is deceptive. If you don't see the unit of measurement next to the numbers in the panel, those values have not yet been defined.

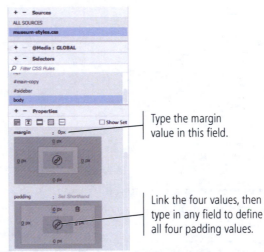

Type the margin value in this field.

Link the four values, then type in any field to define all four padding values.

5. Turn on the Lock icon in the center of the padding proxy to make all four padding values the same. Highlight the top padding field and type **0px** to define a zero-pixel padding.

   Because you linked all four padding fields by clicking the Lock icon, changing one value changes the other three, as well.

6. Review the new selector in the code of the **museum-styles.css** file.

   The margin, which you defined using the Set Shorthand field, only occupies one line. The **margin** property without specific sides defined applies to all edges of the element.

   ```
   57 ▼ body {
   58        margin: 0px;
   59        padding-top: 0px;
   60        padding-right: 0px;
   61        padding-bottom: 0px;
   62        padding-left: 0px;
   63   }
   ```

   The various fields in the Properties panel defined separate properties for each margin: **padding-top**, **padding-right**, **padding-bottom**, and **padding-left**.

7. **With body still selected in the Selectors section of the panel, define the following Background properties for the body selector:**

background-image:	floor.jpg
background-size:	cover
background-attachment:	fixed

The **background-size** property defines the size of background images.

The **background-attachment** property determines whether a background image moves when the page scrolls. By default, background images scroll with the page. When you define the **fixed** value, the background image remains in place, even when the rest of the page scrolls in front of it.

Click here to jump to Background options.

8. **In the Text options, define the following properties for the body selector:**

font-family:	Gotham, Helvetica Neue, Helvetica, Arial, sans-serif
font-size:	14px
font-weight:	300
line-height:	22px

Click the value and choose from the available list of font families.

The **font-family** list defines fonts that will be used to display the text, in order of availability.

The **font-weight** property defines how thick characters should be displayed. Numeric values from 100 to 900 (in hundreds) define this option from thin to thick; 400 is approximately normal.

The **line-height** property defines the distance from one line of text to the next in a paragraph.

9. **Review the results in the Live view.**

Web browsers have default values (which can differ) for many elements, including the body element. By specifying padding and margins of 0, you are standardizing these settings or negating any default values (called "normalizing"), so all browsers will render the body element the same way.

By this point you should begin to understand the concept of nested tags. The **\<body\>** tag is the parent of the tags it contains. Properties of the parent tag are automatically inherited by the child (nested) tags.

In this case, the font family, size, weight, and line height you defined for the **\<body\>** tag are automatically applied to content in the nested elements.

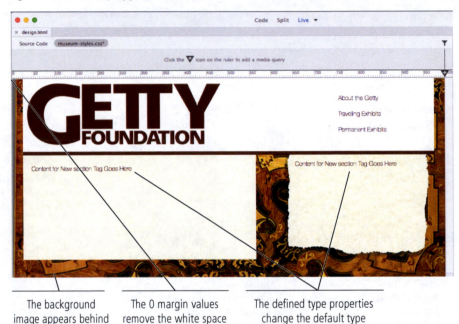

The background image appears behind all placed elements.

The 0 margin values remove the white space around the page.

The defined type properties change the default type appearance for the entire page.

10. **Save all files, and then continue to the next stage of the project.**

STAGE 2 / Working with a Template

Using a template file (with the ".dwt" extension), you can create common page elements only once, rather than recreating them every time you add a new page to a site. If you modify a template, pages based on the template are updated to reflect the same changes.

When you create a Dreamweaver template, you indicate which elements of a page should remain constant (non-editable, or locked) in pages based on that template, and which can be changed.

Create a Template

When all pages in a site will have the same basic layout, you can save the common elements as a template, and then apply the template to all pages. This workflow makes it much faster and easier to maintain consistency, and complete the project.

Following the same logic, keep in mind that the museum-styles.css file in this site is attached to the design.html file, which will become the template. Any pages created from the template file will also be attached to the museum-styles.css file, so changes made in the museum-styles.css file will affect pages created from the template.

1. **With design.html from the Museum site open, turn off the Live view.**

   You can't create a template while the Live view is active.

2. **In the nav element, create links for each paragraph as follows:**

About the Getty	**Link to about.html**
Traveling Exhibits	**Link to traveling-exhibits.html**
Permanent Exhibits	**Link to permanent-exhibits.html**

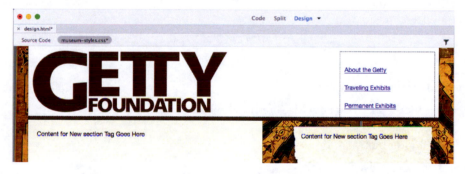

3. **Select and delete the placeholder text in the main-copy and sidebar section elements.**

   Because you defined a minimum height for the #main-copy and #sidebar selectors, the elements do not entirely collapse in the page layout.

4. **In the CSS Designer panel, make the footer selector active. In the Properties section of the panel, show the Text properties and define the text color as white (#FFF).**

   It's important to realize that layout development is an ongoing, evolutionary process. As you continue to work, new issues will pop up. You can always add properties to, or remove them from, specific selectors, edit the values of specific properties, and add new selectors as necessary to meet a project's needs.

5. **Replace the placeholder text in the footer div with the following:**

    Site design by Against The Clock, Inc.

6. **Choose File>Save All.**

    Before creating the template file, you should save the changes you just made to the HTML and CSS files.

7. **Choose File>Save As Template.**

    If this option is grayed out, make sure Source Code is selected in the Related Files bar. The Save As Template option is not available if a linked file, such as museum-styles.css, is active.

8. **In the Save As Template dialog box, make sure Museum is selected in the Site menu.**

9. **In the Description field, type Museum Site Template.**

    The description is only relevant in Dreamweaver; it will not appear in any page based on the template. (You can modify the template description by choosing Modify>Templates>Description.)

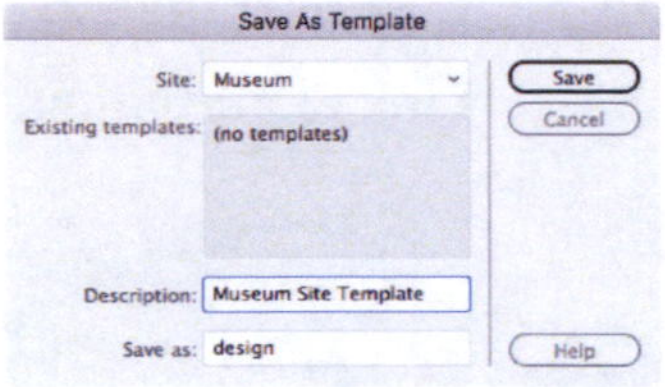

Note:

You can also create a template from the active page by choosing Insert>Template Objects>Make Template.

10. **Click Save to save the active file as a template.**

    The extension ".dwt" is automatically added on both Macintosh and Windows.

11. **Click Yes in the resulting dialog box.**

    The template is saved in a Templates folder, which Dreamweaver automatically creates for you in the local root folder of the Museum site. To ensure that all images and links function properly, you should allow Dreamweaver to update the link information as necessary.

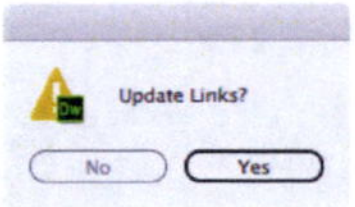

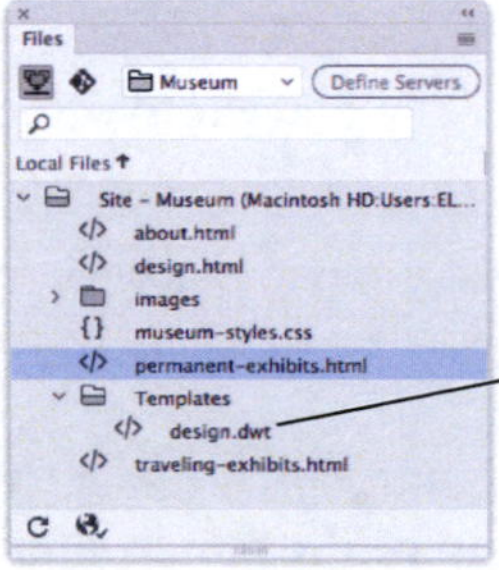

    The template is automatically added to the site in a new Templates folder.

    Your template contains the layout structure you created in the first stage of this project. However, after converting the document into a template, all parts of the page become non-editable. Until you define an editable region, you won't be able to add page-specific content to any pages based on this template.

    Do not move your templates out of the Templates folder or save any non-template files in the Templates folder. Also, do not move the Templates folder out of your local root folder —doing so causes errors in paths in the templates.

12. **Show the page source code in the Code pane.**

13. **Change the Document Title to The Getty Foundation.**

When you define a title in a template file, that title is automatically applied to any page attached to the template. You are adding the basic information in the template, so you can then simply add page-specific information in each attached file.

As you can see in the Code pane, the <title> tag is contained in special tags that define it as an editable region. This means that the title can be edited independently on any page that is attached to the template file.

These tags identify the editable region.

```
x design.dwt*
Source Code    museum-styles.css                                                    ▼
1  <!doctype html>
2 ▼ <html>
3 ▼ <head>
4   <meta charset="UTF-8">
5   <!-- TemplateBeginEditable name="doctitle" -->
6   <title>The Getty Foundation</title>
7   <!-- TemplateEndEditable -->
8   <link href="../museum-styles.css" rel="stylesheet" type="text/css">
9   <!-- TemplateBeginEditable name="head" -->
10  <!-- TemplateEndEditable -->
11  </head>
```

14. **In the Design pane, click to place the insertion point in the main-copy section, then click section#main-copy in the Tag Selector to select the entire element.**

15. **Click the Editable Region button in the Templates Insert panel.**

You can also choose Insert>Template>Editable Region.

Click the section#main-copy tag to select the entire element.

16. **Type Page Content in the resulting dialog box, and then click OK.**

When pages are created from this template, the editable regions will be the only areas that can be modified.

17. In the Design pane, click the blue Page Content tag above the editable region.

In the Design view, editable areas are identified with a blue tag and border. These are for design purposes, and will not be visible in the resulting HTML pages. If you don't see a blue tag with the Page Content region name, open the View>Visual Aids menu and choose Invisible Elements to toggle on that option.

Clicking this tab selects the entire editable template object. This makes it easier for you to see the related code in the Code pane.

Click the tab to select the entire editable region.

The editable region code surrounds only the main-copy section.

The new editable area was added around the selected section element. Because you want the main-copy *and* sidebar sections inside the editable area, you have to edit the page code.

18. In the page code, move the closing code of the editable region (<!-- TemplateEndEditable -->) to be after the closing tag of the section#sidebar element. Refresh the Design view and review the results.

When something is selected in the Code pane, you can click the selected code and drag to move that code to a new position. Alternatively, you can cut (Command/Control-X) the relevant code from its original location, move the insertion point to another position, and then paste (Command/Control-V) the cut code into place.

The editable area now contains the two nested sections, but not the surrounding div#page-content element.

Move the ending code of the editable area after the closing tag of the section#sidebar element.

19. Choose File>Save All, close the template file, and then continue to the next exercise.

Unlike other applications, you do not have to use the Save As command to rewrite a Dreamweaver template. You can simply choose File>Save or press Command/Control-S.

Apply the Template to Existing Pages

Templates can be applied to existing HTML pages, basically wrapping the template around the existing content. You simply map existing page content to editable regions in the template. After the template is applied, you can begin to make whatever changes are necessary based on the actual content in the files.

1. **In the Files panel, double-click the Museum site name in the Directory menu to open the Site Setup dialog box for the active site.**

   Remember, this technique opens the Site Setup dialog box for the selected site and allows you to skip the Manage Sites dialog box.

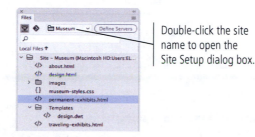

   Double-click the site name to open the Site Setup dialog box.

2. **Expand the Advanced Settings options and click Templates in the category list to show the related options.**

3. **Make sure the Don't Rewrite... option is checked.**

   When you saved the template file, it was placed in a folder named Templates. Links from this template file to images or other pages must first go up from the Templates folder to the root folder (e.g., **../images/getty-logo.png**).

   When this template is attached to a page in the root level of the site, the same link would not be accurate. For example, the path from about.html in the root folder to the same image would simply be **images/getty-logo.png**. If this check box is not active, the links on pages where the template is attached would not work properly.

4. **Click Save to close the Site Setup dialog box.**

5. **Using the Files panel, open about.html from the root folder of the Museum site.**

   Each file in the site contains two areas of content — the primary page copy, and a list of links to help users navigate through the long blocks of text. The two sections are already tagged with ids (#main-copy and #sidebar) that match the ones you used in the template file. This will direct the appropriate elements of the provided pages to appear in the defined areas of the template.

6. **Choose Tools>Templates>Apply Template to Page.**

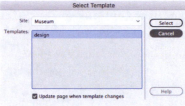

7. **In the Select Template dialog box, make sure Museum is selected in the Site menu.**

   Since this is the active site, the menu should default to the correct choice.

8. **Click design in the Templates list to select it, and make sure the Update Page... option is checked at the bottom of the dialog box.**

9. **Click Select to apply the template to the open page.**

   In the Inconsistent Region Names dialog box that appears, you have to determine where to place the named regions of the open file relative to the editable regions in the template you selected.

10. **In the resulting dialog box, click the Document body (in the Name column) to select it. In the Move Content to New Region menu, choose Page Content.**

    Remember, "Page Content" is the name you assigned to the template's editable region. The page body (named "Document body" by default) will be placed into the "Page Content" editable region when the template is applied to the page.

This refers to content within the <body> section of the HTML page to which you are attaching the template.

This is the name assigned to the editable region in the template file.

Use this menu to map file content to an editable region in the template file.

Note:

You can choose Nowhere in the Move Content... menu to exclude specific content in the newly "templated" page.

11. **Click OK to finalize the process.**

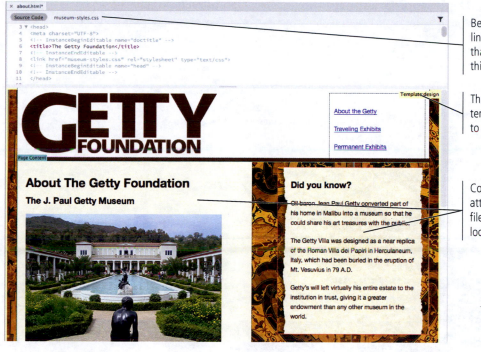

Because the template is linked to museum-styles.css, that file is also attached to this HTML page.

This tag identifies the template that is applied to the HTML file.

Content defined with ID attributes in the original HTML file is moved into the correct location in the template.

Note:

If you move the cursor over areas other than an editable region, an icon indicates that you can't select or modify that area. You can modify only the editable region.

12. **Click the Split button to show the page code (if necessary), and scroll to the top of the code.**

Although you did not specifically define it as an editable area, the <title> tag of each page is always editable, even when attached to a template file.

13. **In the Code pane, add the text | About The Getty (including a preceding space) to the end of the existing document title.**

The title element in the page head is automatically an editable region.

14. **Save the file and close it.**

15. **Repeat this process to attach the design.dwt template to the two remaining pages in the site. Define appropriate page title information to each page.**

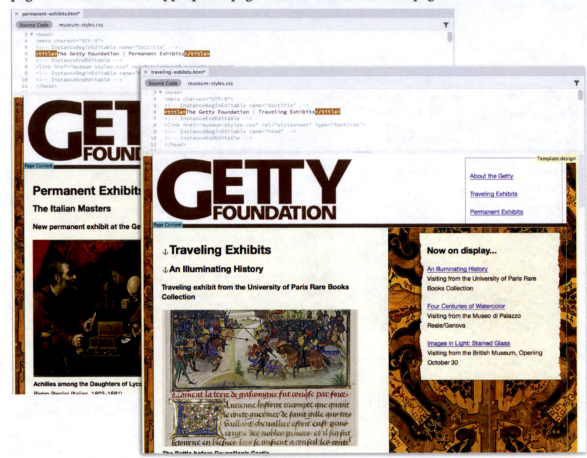

16. **Save and close any open files, and then continue to the next stage of the project.**

More About Working with Dreamweaver Templates

The Insert>Template Menu Options

Template objects consist primarily of different types of regions. These options are available in the Templates Insert panel or the Insert>Template submenu:

- **Make Template** converts an HTML file into a template, automatically prompting you to save the file as a template.

- **Make Nested Template** inserts a template in a page created from an existing template.

- **Editable Region** creates areas of a template that you can modify in pages using the template. You can change the highlight color of editable template regions in the Highlighting pane of the Preferences dialog box.

- **Optional Region** defines a section of the page that will be shown or hidden depending on the content.

- **Repeating Region** creates a section of template content that can easily be duplicated (commonly, tables and lists).

- **Editable Optional Region** combines the Optional Region functionality with the Editable Region functionality. If the Editable Optional Region is shown, the content within the region can be modified.

- **Repeating Table** creates both a table and repeating regions simultaneously. Selecting a repeating table object opens the standard table dialog box for defining rows within a repeating region.

Creating a New Page from a Template

In addition to attaching a template to an existing page, you can also create a new HTML page from an existing template.

You can use the Assets panel (Window>Assets) to show all templates that are available in the current site. Control/right-clicking a specific template file opens a contextual menu, where you can choose New from Template.

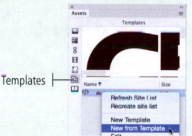

Templates ⊢

This results in a new, untitled HTML file containing all the content that is defined in the template, with the template already attached to the HTML page. Any changes in the template file will apply to files created from it.

Pages can also be created from a template using the New Document dialog box (File>New). Choose Site Templates in the left column of the New Document dialog box, select your site in the middle column, and then choose the template you want to apply in the right column.

The Tools>Templates Menu Options

Commands in the Tools>Templates submenu are useful when you want to make changes to pages based on a template.

- **Apply Template to Page** applies a template to the current HTML page.

- If you don't want a page to be based on a template, **Detach from Template** separates the page from the template. Non-editable regions become editable, but changes in the template no longer reflect in the page.

- **Open Attached Template** opens the template attached to a page.

- The **Check Template Syntax** option enables the software to automatically check code syntax in the template.

- **Update Current Page** updates a page if the template on which it is based is modified.

- You can use the **Update Pages** option to manually update all pages based on the template.

- **Export without Markup** exports an entire site to a different location by detaching all pages from templates on which they are based.

- Use **Remove Template Markup** to convert an editable region to a non-editable region.

- The **Description** is simply a textual explanation of the selected file, which does not appear in the page body.

- **New Entry After** or **Before Selection.** You can use these options to add repeated elements, such as rows of a table, in repeating regions.

- Use **Move Entry Up** or **Down** to move a repeating element up or down.

- Use **Make Attribute Editable** to make a specific HTML tag attribute editable in template-based pages.

Editing a Design Template

When you make changes to a template and save the file, Dreamweaver recognizes the link from the template to pages to which that template is attached. You are asked if you want to update those pages to reflect new template content.

The resulting Update Pages dialog box shows the progress of updating linked files. When you see the "Done" message, you can click Close to dismiss the dialog box.

STAGE 3 / Using CSS to Control Content

The first stage of this project focused on building a layout with properly structured HTML. In the second stage, you created a template file to more easily apply the defined layout to multiple pages. Although defining structure is a significant part of designing pages, it is only half the story — professional web design also requires controlling the content in pages.

In this stage of the project, you will complete a number of tasks required to present the client's information in the best possible way:

- Define CSS to format HTML elements, including headings, paragraphs, and links.

- Create a list of links for users to jump to different parts of a page.

- Define CSS to format the rollover behavior of links throughout the site.

- Define CSS to format specific elements only in certain areas of the page.

- Create and format figures and captions within the copy of each page.

Define HTML Tag Selectors

In addition to the **<body>** tag that encloses the page content, properly structured pages use HTML tags to identify different types of content. As you already know, CSS uses tag selectors to format HTML tags, such as paragraphs (**<p>**), headings (**<h1>**, **<h2>**, etc.), links (**<a>**), and so on.

1. **Open permanent-exhibits.html from the Museum site root folder, and turn on the Live view.**

    When you are editing CSS to define the appearance of page content, it's a good idea to work in the Live view so you can see an accurate representation of the CSS rendering.

2. **In the CSS Designer panel, select museum-styles.css in the Sources list, and then click the Add Selector button in the Selectors section.**

3. **Type h1 as the selector name, then press Return/Enter twice to finalize the new selector name.**

    This tag selector defines properties for any h1 element — in other words, content surrounded by the <h1> </h1> tags. Tag selectors do not require a # character at the beginning of the name, only the actual element name.

4. **In the Properties section of the panel, define the following properties for the h1 tag selector:**

margin:	0px (all four sides)
color:	sample the color of the client's logo
font-size:	30px

Note:

Remember, the CSS color property defines the color of text.

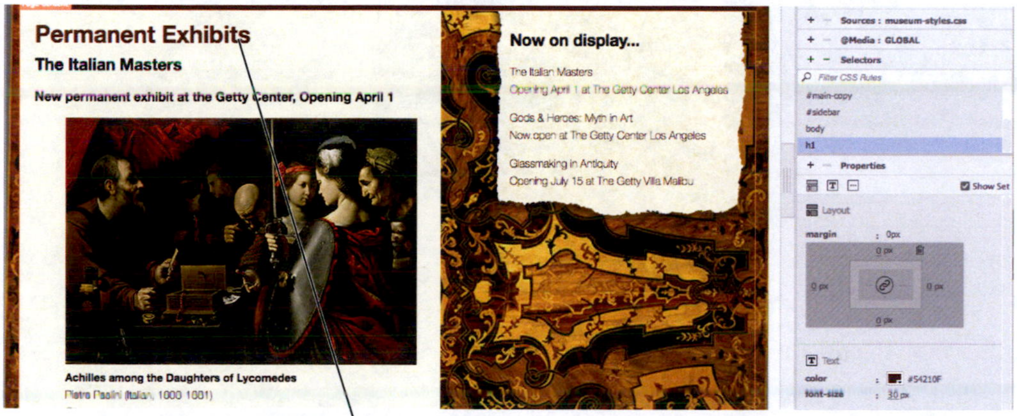

Content block elements, such as headings and paragraphs, have default top and bottom margins equivalent to the current text size. It is common to modify some or all of these margins with CSS. By defining margins of 0 for <h1> tags, any subsequent paragraph or heading's top margin will determine the spacing between the elements.

The first paragraph in the text — which is formatted with the <h1> tag — is affected by the new selector definition.

This is the h1 element.

5. **Create another tag selector for the <h2> tag, using the following settings:**

margin-top:	30px
margin-bottom:	5px
color:	sample the color of the client's logo
font-size:	24px

Note:

We have the Show Set option turned on in our screen captures to reinforce the properties you should define in each step.

The margin settings for h2 elements are not yet apparent because the <h3> margins are still ambiguous.

6. Create another tag selector for the <h3> tag, using the following settings:

margin-top:	0px
margin-bottom:	15px
font-style:	italic
font-weight:	400

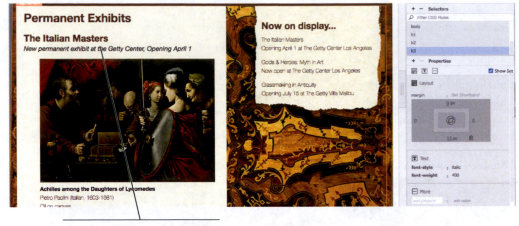

Margin settings for h2 elements are now apparent because the <h3> margins have been clearly defined.

7. Create another tag selector for the <p> tag, using the following settings:

margin-top:	0px
margin-bottom:	10px

Paragraphs in all areas of the page are affected by the p selector.

8. **Add another tag selector for the <a> tag, using the following settings:**

   color: **sample the color of the client's logo**

   font-weight: **bold**

   text-decoration: **none**

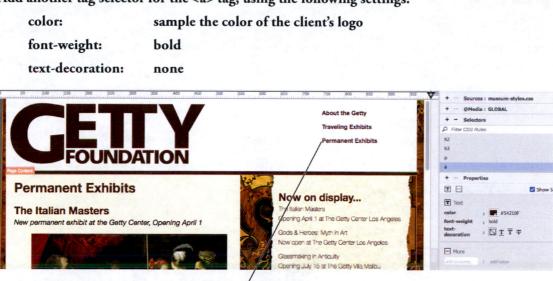

Links no longer have the default
blue underline appearance.

9. **Choose File>Save All, and then continue to the next exercise.**

Create Named Anchors

Documents with large blocks of copy — like those in this site — often benefit
from named anchors. Named anchors mark specific locations on a page that can be
linked from other locations within the same page or other pages. Instead of forcing
the reader to search for the information by scrolling or other means, you can create
a hyperlink that points to the exact location of the information. Clicking the link
moves the linked anchor to the top of the browser window.

1. **With permanent-exhibits.html open, turn off the Live view (if
   necessary) and show the page source in the Code pane.**

   Selecting text and creating links can be a bit easier in the regular Design view.

2. **In the Code pane, click to place the insertion point immediately after the
   opening <h2> tag for the first h2 element.**

Place the insertion
point after the
opening <h2> tag.

3. Type the following code:

```
<a name="masters"></
```

Note:

If the closing tag isn't automatically finished, make sure Close Tags: After Typing "</" is active in the Code Hints pane of the Preferences dialog box.

As soon as you type the "/" character, Dreamweaver automatically closes the last unclosed container tag — in this case, the <a> tag.

```
23    <h1>Permanent Exhibits </h1>
24
25    <h2><a name="masters"></a>The Italian Masters</h2>
26    <h3>New permanent exhibit at the Getty Center, Opening April 1</h3>
```

The tag closes as soon as you type the "/" character.

4. Refresh the Design pane.

When the Live view is not active, a named anchor appears in the page as a small anchor icon. These icons are not visible in the Live view or in the browser.

```
22  ▼ <section id="main-copy">
23      <h1>Permanent Exhibits </h1>
24
25      <h2><a name="masters"></a>The Italian Masters</h2>
26      <h3>New permanent exhibit at the Getty Center, Opening April 1</h3>
27
```

This icon identifies a named anchor.

5. Repeat this process to add named anchors to the other h2 elements on the page. Use gods and glassmaking as the names of the related anchors.

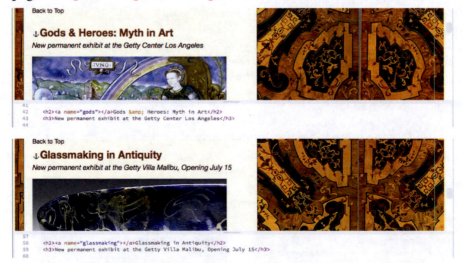

```
41
42      <h2><a name="gods"></a>Gods &amp; Heroes: Myth in Art</h2>
43      <h3>New permanent exhibit at the Getty Center Los Angeles</h3>
44
```

```
57
58      <h2><a name="glassmaking"></a>Glassmaking in Antiquity</h2>
59      <h3>New permanent exhibit at the Getty Villa Malibu, Opening July 15</h3>
60
```

6. In the Design pane, highlight the words "The Italian Masters" in the section#sidebar element.

7. **Click the Hyperlink button in the HTML Insert panel.**

This text is selected.

8. **In the Hyperlink dialog box, open the Link menu and choose #masters.**

This menu includes all named anchors. Each anchor name is preceded by the # character.

9. **Click OK to close the dialog box and create the new anchor link.**

10. **Repeat Steps 6–9 to create links for the other two items in the section#sidebar element:**

Link Text	Link Target
Gods & Heroes: Myth in Art	gods
Glassmaking in Antiquity	glassmaking

11. **In the Code pane, place the insertion point immediately after the opening <h1> tag near the top of the page.**

12. **Define a new named anchor as follows:**

    `<a name="top"></a>`

    To help the reader return to the link list from any section of the page, it is good practice to include a link to the top of the page at the end of each section.

Add the named anchor after the opening <h1> tag.

```
22 ▼ <section id="main-copy">
23      <h1><a name="top"></a>Permanent Exhibits </h1>
24
25      <h2><a name="masters"></a>The Italian Masters </h2>
26      <h3>New permanent exhibit at the Getty Center, Opening April 1</h3>
```

13. **Select the words "Back to Top" above the second <h2> element. Create a link to the #top named anchor.**

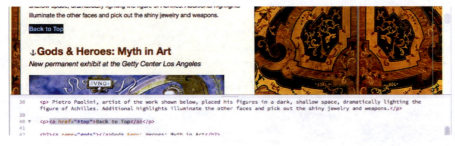

```
38      <p> Pietro Paolini, artist of the work shown below, placed his figures in a dark, shallow space, dramatically lighting the
        figure of Achilles. Additional highlights illuminate the other faces and pick out the shiny jewelry and weapons.</p>
39
40 ▼   <p><a href="#top">Back to Top</a></p>
41
42      <h2><a name="gods"></a>Gods &amp; Heroes: Myth in Art</h2>
```

14. **Repeat Step 13 to link the remaining two "Back to Top" paragraphs to the #top anchor.**

Note:

To reduce the amount of repetitive work required to complete this project, we have already created the named anchors and links in the provided traveling-exhibits.html file.

```
55
56 ▼   <p><a href="#top">Back to Top</a></p>
57
58      <h2><a name="glassmaking"></a>Glassmaking in Antiquity</h2>
59      <h3>New permanent exhibit at the Getty Villa Malibu, Opening July 15</h3>
```

```
72      <p> In about 50 B.C., glassmakers learned to inflate glass into a bubble at the end of a tube. The vessels were decorated
        using a variety of techniques.</p>
73
74 ▼   <p><a href="#top">Back to Top</a></p>
75
76      </section>
```

15. **Save the file and continue to the next exercise.**

Create a Pseudo-Class Selector

A **class selector** is used when the same style needs to be applied to more than one element in a page. Unlike an ID attribute, which is used only once per page, a class attribute can be used to repeat the same style throughout the page.

As you should remember from the previous exercise, controlling the default appearance of link text is accomplished with the <a> tag selector. To affect the rollover behavior, you have to define **pseudo-classes** (or variants) of the <a> selector. Four common pseudo-classes important to the appearance of links are:

- **a:link** refers to a hyperlink that has not yet been visited.
- **a:visited** refers to a hyperlink that has been visited.
- **a:hover** refers to a hyperlink when the mouse pointer is hovering over the link.
- **a:active** refers to an active hyperlink (when the link is clicked before the mouse button is released).

Note:

For them to work correctly in all web browsers, these pseudo-class selectors should appear in the following order in the CSS file:
a:link
a:visited
a:hover
a:active

1. With `permanent-exhibits.html` open, turn on the **Live** view and hide the code pane.

2. Select **museum-styles.css** in the Sources section of the CSS Designer panel, then click the Add Selector button.

3. With the new selector name highlighted, type **a:hover**.

4. Define the following property for the new selector:

   color: **sample a light brown color from the background image**

5. With the Live view active, test the rollover property of the links in various sections of the page.

Note:

You might need to toggle the Live view off and back on to see the results of the a:hover selector.

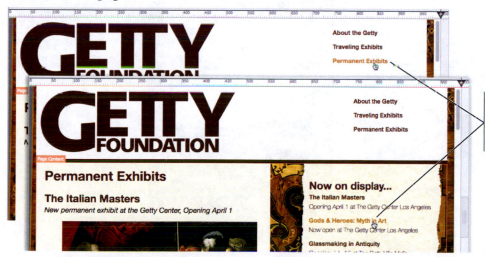

The a:hover selector changes the color of the links in all areas of the page.

6. Choose **File>Save All**, close the HTML file, then continue to the next exercise.

Create a Figure and Figure Caption

The figure element is used to define content, such as illustrations or photos, that are related to the copy. The figure element is a container that can include a nested figcaption element describing the figure, which means the image and caption can be treated together as a single unit.

1. Open **about.html** and make sure the Live view is active.

2. Click to select the image near the top of the section#main-copy element.

3. Click the Figure button in the HTML Insert panel.

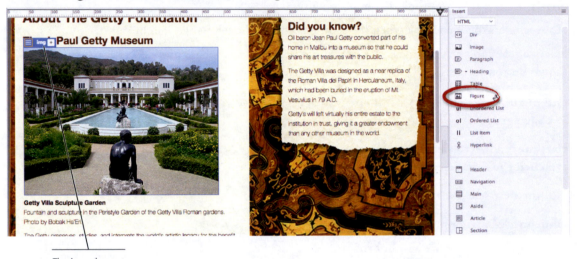

The img element
is selected.

4. **Choose Before in the Position Assistant.**

   For some reason, the Wrap option is not available in this case. You have to use a work-around to move the image into the proper position inside the figure tags.

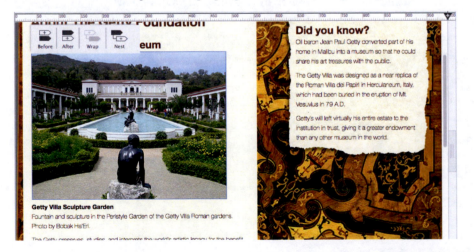

Note:

To minimize repetitive work, we created the figure and figcaption tags for you in the traveling-exhibits.html and permanent-exhibits.html files.

5. With the new figure element selected, open the DOM panel.

The figure element includes placeholder text for the content and the caption.

The DOM panel lists all elements in the page.

6. In the DOM panel, click the arrow to expand the figure element.

7. In the panel, click the img tag and drag onto the figure element. When you don't see a green line, release the mouse button.

This moves the img element into the figure element. The img element becomes nested inside the figure element.

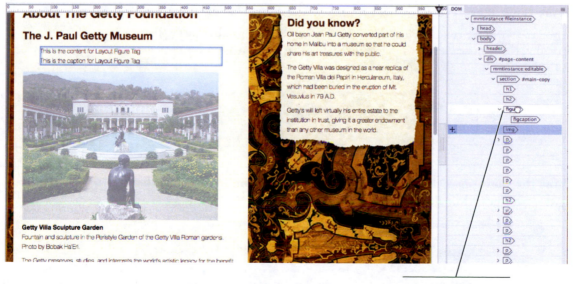

Drag the img element onto the figure element.

8. **In the Design pane, click in the line beginning with "Fountain and..." to select the paragraph immediately below the image.**

If you click the first line of the caption ("Getty Villa..."), the <strong> tag that contains the first line is selected, instead of the entire caption paragraph.

9. **In the DOM panel, drag the selected paragraph onto the figcaption element.**

Click to select this paragraph element.

Drag the selected p element onto the figcaption element.

10. **In the Code pane, review the code related to the figure element.**

As you can see in the code, the img element is nested inside the figure element. The figcaption is also nested inside the figure element, which allows you to treat the image and caption as one unit by editing the figure element.

Placeholder text remains in the code.

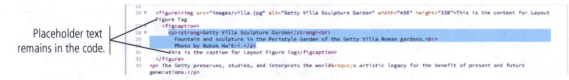

11. **Using the Code pane, delete the placeholder text that was included in the figure and figcaption elements.**

12. **Using the CSS Designer panel, define a new tag selector named figure with the following settings:**

width:	300px
margin-top:	0px
margin-right:	0px
margin-bottom:	10px
margin-left:	10px
float:	right

Because the figcaption is nested inside the figure element, it is also affected by the width and float values you defined here.

13. **Using the CSS Designer panel, define a new tag selector named figcaption with the following settings:**

font-style:	italic
font-size:	12px
line-height:	15px
text-align:	right

14. **Choose File>Save All, and then continue to the next exercise.**

Create Descendant Selectors

Three items remain in the list of known formatting requirements:

- Images in the main-copy section should not extend past the edge of the containing section element.

- The sidebar text should be centered, and a border should appear below the h2 element in that section.

- Navigation links in the header area should be larger and align to the right edge of the nav container.

Each of these items refers to content in a specific area of the page. To meet these requirements without affecting similar tags in other areas, you need to define **descendant selectors** (also called compound selectors) to format certain elements only within a specific area.

1. With **about.html** open, click to select the image in the **section#main-copy** element.

2. Select **museum-styles.css** in the Sources section of the CSS Designer panel, then click the Add Selector button to the left of the Selectors heading.

   When an element is selected in the page layout, the new selector automatically adopts the name of the active insertion point, including all tags in the path to the active insertion point.

   This compound, or descendant, selector specifically identifies where the properties will be applied. In this case, they will be applied to all img elements that exist in a figure element, which is in an element with the #main-copy ID attribute.

3. Define the following properties for the new **#main-copy figure img** selector:

width:	**300px**
height:	**auto**

   If you defined settings for the basic img element, you would affect all images on the page, including the logo at the top of the page. You are using a descendant selector here because you only want to affect images in the main-copy section.

4. **Click the Add Selector button again. With the new name highlighted, type #sidebar p, then press Return/Enter twice to finalize the new name.**

   It is not necessary to first place the insertion point or select an object to create a descendant selector. You can simply type the appropriate selector name.

5. **Define the following settings for the #sidebar p selector:**

text-align:	center

6. **Create another descendant selector named #sidebar h2 using the following settings:**

padding-bottom:	10px
text-align:	center
border-bottom-width:	thin
border-bottom-style:	solid
border-botom-color:	sample the brown color in the client's logo

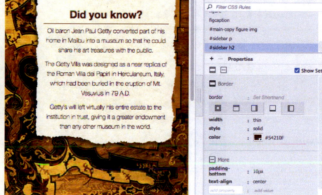

7. Create another descendant selector named **nav p** using the following settings:

   margin-top: 15px

   font-size: 20px

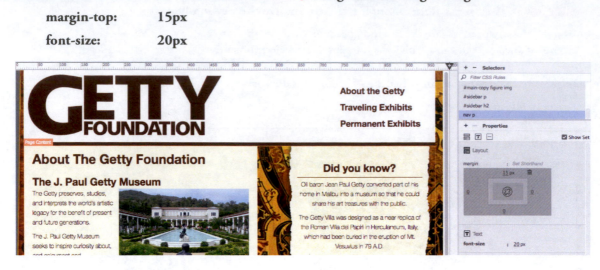

8. Select the **nav** selector in the CSS Designer panel, then add the following properties:

   margin-top: 15px

   text-align: right

When you format various HTML elements, it is not uncommon to find new issues as you progress. Adjusting the nav element's top margin moved the element down, so that the bottom of the third link appears to align with the bottom of the client's logo.

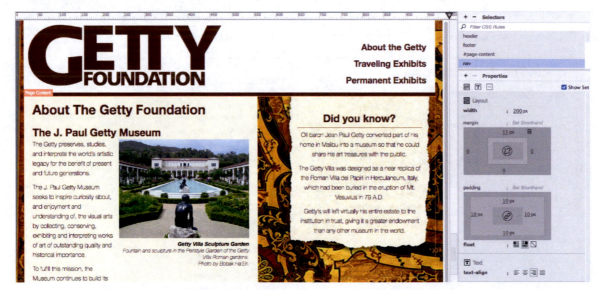

9. Save all files (File>Save All) and close them.

10. Export a site definition named **Museum.ste** into your WIP>Museum folder, and then remove the Museum site from Dreamweaver.

   If necessary, refer back to Project 5: Bistro Site Organization for complete instructions on exporting a site definition, or removing a site from Dreamweaver.

PROJECT REVIEW

fill in the blank

1. The _____ tag is used to attach an external CSS file to an HTML file.

2. A(n) _____ is the formal name of a CSS rule.

3. A(n) _____ style sheet stores CSS rules in a separate file, which can be linked to multiple HTML pages.

4. Click the _____ button in the CSS Designer panel to create a new CSS files, or define an existing external CSS file that should be used for the active page.

5. A(n) _____ selector type is used to control unique div elements.

6. A(n) _____ selector type is used to format specific HTML tags.

7. A(n) _____ selector type can be used to format specific tags only within a certain element.

8. The _____ property can be used to attach an object to the right or left side of the containing object.

9. The _____ property exists inside the container. Background properties of the container extend into this area.

10. The _____ exists around the container. Background properties of the container do not extend into this area.

short answer

1. Briefly explain two reasons why CSS is the preferred method for creating a web page layout.

2. Briefly explain the difference between external, embedded, and inline styles.

3. Briefly explain how padding, margin, and border properties relate to the CSS box model.

Use what you have learned in this project to complete the following freeform exercise. .
Carefully read the art director and client comments, then create your own design to meet the needs of the project.
Use the space below to sketch ideas. When finished, write a brief explanation of the reasoning behind your final design.

art director comments

You have been hired by the local chapter of the Girls & Boys Club of America to design a web page, featuring the programs that are available to the local community. The club director wants the site to be easily navigable, and attractive to both children and their parents.

❏ Download the client-supplied resources in the **Club_Web20_PB.zip** archive on the Student Files web page.

❏ Create a cohesive site design for all pages in the site.

❏ Create individual pages for each category that is defined by the client.

❏ Find one main image that supports the message of each page on the site. Look for public-domain images to minimize costs (try unsplash.com).

client comments

Our group serves thousands of children in the local community, especially during the summer, when school is not in session. We serve children from all demographics, and we encourage kids to build relationships, regardless of social or economic status.

We don't want to present too much information on any one screen, so we'd like each program to be featured on its own page. In addition to the Home page, we want individual pages for:

– Personal Development program

– Summer Tutoring program

– Overnight Adventure program

– VolunTeen Enrichment program

– Career Mentoring program

project justification

PROJECT SUMMARY

Cascading style sheets offer tremendous flexibility when you are designing the look and feel of a website. By linking multiple HTML files to a single external CSS file — with or without an HTML page template — you can experiment with options by altering the CSS selectors and immediately seeing the effect on all linked pages. In addition to this flexibility, CSS is also compliant with current web design standards, which means pages designed with CSS are both search-engine and accessibility-software friendly.

By completing this project, you have worked with different types of selectors to control both the layout of an HTML page and the formatting attributes of different elements in the site. The site structure is entirely controlled by the selectors in the linked CSS file, so you could change the appearance of the entire site, without ever touching the individual HTML pages. The inverse is also true — you can change the content of individual pages without affecting the site structure.

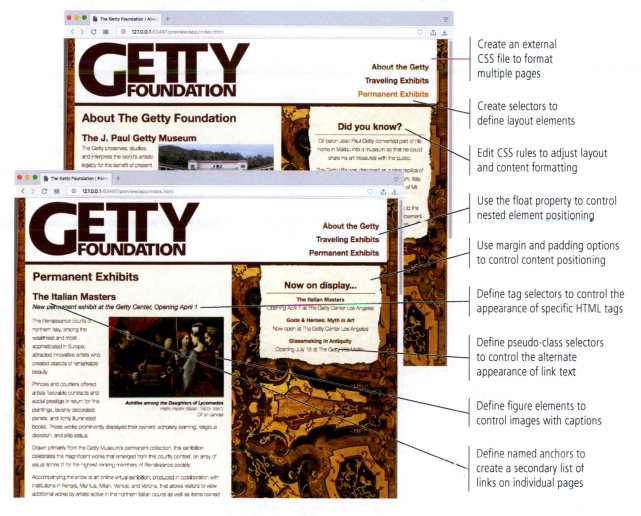

Create an external CSS file to format multiple pages

Create selectors to define layout elements

Edit CSS rules to adjust layout and content formatting

Use the float property to control nested element positioning

Use margin and padding options to control content positioning

Define tag selectors to control the appearance of specific HTML tags

Define pseudo-class selectors to control the alternate appearance of link text

Define figure elements to control images with captions

Define named anchors to create a secondary list of links on individual pages

INDEX

INDEX

INDEX

INDEX

INDEX

INDEX

Q

<q> 330, 332
Quick Mask mode 65–66, 199
quick property inspector 292, 298, 299
Quick Selection tool 79–82
quick tag editor 331, 331–332
quotation marks 332, 334

R

radius 81
raster images 27, 364
rasterize type 199
real time preview 277–278
recent fonts 184
Reconstruct tool 143
Rectangle tool 102, 120, 124
Rectangular Marquee tool 43
reduce noise [resampling] 97
reference point 55
refine edge 68
refresh [Files panel] 287
refresh site list [Assets panel] 372
registered trademark character 340
registration marks 155
Related Files bar 391, 421
relative path 301
remove blockquote 328
remove [site] 312
remove template markup 453
renaming pages 304–305
render 212, 218
repeating regions 453
repeating tables 453
replace actions 228
resample image 230
resampling 30, 95–98, 376, 377, 378
reset actions 228
Reset button 31
reset to original size 375, 377
reset view 20
resize windows to fit 19
resizing 31, 95–98
resizing [images] 376
resolution 28–32, 95, 96
resolution dependence 27
RGB color 67, 138, 404
RGBA color 404
Roll the 3D Camera mode 208
root directory 269, 313
rotate around axis 210
rotate handle 174
rotate transformation 54
Rotate View tool 20

Rounded Rectangle tool 116, 119, 120
rubber band 120
rulers 29, 37
rules 386

S

Safari 346
sample all layers 68, 79
sample size 144
sampling ring 144
Satin style 135
Saturation blending mode 151
save actions 230
save all 394, 417
save as 32, 33, 85
save as template 446
save as to original folder 33
save in background 33
saved workspaces 3, 13–14
scale along axis 210
scale transformation 54, 168
scale UI to font 4
scope attribute 342
Screen blending mode 151
screen modes 4, 23–24
scroll wheel 21
scrubby slider 58, 118
scrubby zoom 19
search engines 304, 328
Secondary View panel 208
<section> 356
section element 352, 387, 431
Select and Mask workspace 80
select color range 69–72
select template 450
Selection Preview mode 69
selections, modifying 65
selectors 250, 350, 386, 415
_self 295
set additional crop options 39
set additional path and shape 104
set shorthand 427, 442
shadow softness 217
shape layers 102, 116–123, 130–131
shape tools 120, 121
sharpen 378
Sharpen Edges filter 98
Sharpen filter 98
Sharpen More filter 98
sharpening 98–99
Shift-drag method 292
shift edge 81
shorthand 427

show cropped area 39
show sampling ring 144
show set [properties] 387, 402
siblings 291
silhouetting 63
site definitions 311–317, 321
site root folder 269, 284, 287
site setup 284, 310, 321, 449
Skin Tones preset 70
skip transform when placing 49
Slice Selection tool 252
Slice tool 252
slice options 252
slices from guides 252
Slide the 3D Camera mode 208
small caps 185, 186
smart filters 139, 175
smart guides 46
smart object layers 49–52, 56, 57, 59,
    63–66, 126, 138, 139, 175, 199, 241
smart radius 81
smooth [edges] 81
smooth [selection] 65
Smooth tool 143
snap 34, 55
Soft Light blending mode 151
sources (CSS) 355, 386
spin blur 178
Split view 273, 391
Spot Healing Brush tool 171
spread 135
spring-loaded keys 12
src attribute 367
stacking order 83, 123
Standard Screen mode 23
STE file 268, 312
stop for errors 234
stop recording 230
straighten 40
stroke color 116, 117
stroke emboss [layer style] 135
stroke [layer style] 135
stroke path 106
stroke type 120
<strong> 298, 328, 336, 337
styles 132–138
Styles panel 130–131
subscript 186
Subtract blending mode 151
subtract from selection 44, 68, 72
subtract front shape 103, 119, 121, 122
subtractive primaries 67
superscript 186
suppress color profile warnings 233

INDEX

Use our portfolio to build yours.

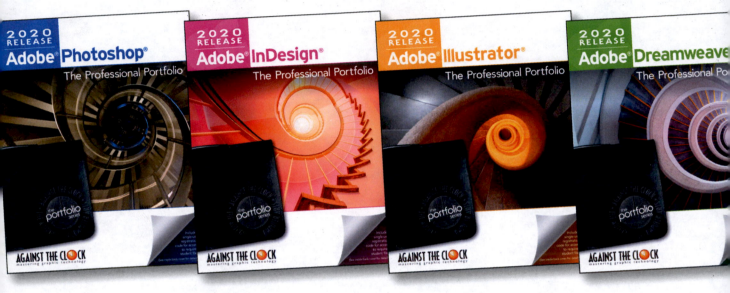

The Against The Clock Professional Portfolio Series walks you step-by-step through the tools and techniques of graphic design professionals.

Order online at www.againsttheclock.com
Use code **2020EDU** for a 10% discount

Go to **www.againsttheclock.com** to enter our monthly drawing for a free book of your choice.